POWER
and
RITUAL
in the
ISRAEL
LABOR
PARTY

*A Study
in Political
Anthropology*

COMPARATIVE
POLITICS
SERIES

POWER
and
RITUAL
in the
ISRAEL
LABOR
PARTY

*A Study
in Political
Anthropology*

Myron J. Aronoff

REVISED & EXPANDED EDITION

M.E. Sharpe • Armonk, New York • London, England

Library of Congress Cataloging-in-Publication Data

Aronoff, Myron Joel.
Power and ritual in the Israel Labor Party:
a study in political anthropology /
by Myron J. Aronoff.—Rev. and expanded ed.
p.   cm.—(Comparative politics)
Includes bibliographical references and index.
ISBN 1-56324-105-6 (cloth)
ISBN 1-56324-106-4 (pbk.)
1. Mifleget ha-' avodah ha-Yiśre 'elit.
2. Israel—Politics and government.
I. Title.
II. Series: Comparative politics (Oxford, England)
JQ1825.P373A76   1992
324.25694′07—dc20
92-13466
CIP

Printed in the United States of America

The paper used in this publication meets the minimum requirements of
American National Standard for Information Sciences—
Permanence of Paper for Printed Library Materials,
ANSI Z39.48–1984.

MV (c)   10   9   8   7   6   5   4   3   2   1
MV (p)   10   9   8   7   6   5   4   3   2   1

For Rebecca C. Aronoff and in memory of Harry J. Aronoff

Contents

Figures and Tables

Foreword

To judge from publishers' announcements and recent political science journals, a "comparative approach" to the study of political science is both widely accepted and widely practiced today. There is, however, a debate over the exact nature of the "comparative" aspect of such an approach, concerning whether this comparative approach is a broad *method* of analysis or rather a general *perspective* on a certain subject matter.

This debate has led to two very different kinds of studies being subsumed under the general category of "comparative politics." The first is explicitly comparative in *method* and is often referred to as "cross-national" analysis. This type of study might focus on, for example, legislatures or interest groups in several settings, and seek to discover and explain similarities and differences across ethnic, regional, or national lines. The second type of study can be referred to as being comparative in *perspective*, sometimes referred to as "case study" analysis. It might focus on political behavior or political institutions in one setting, with the idea that by studying these in some detail the study will draw, either explicitly or implicitly, some lessons for students of political behavior or political institutions in other settings.

Given that the numbers of studies following each approach are quite extensive (indeed, many scholars have utilized *both* approaches, sometimes even in the same study), it would be inappropriate to say that one of these two types of comparative study is better, or preferable, to the other. Rather, we should note that just as the general approaches are different, so too are the kinds of conclusions that we can draw from each type of study. Cross-national analysis may provide us with more opportunity to engage in explicit comparison from one setting to another, but it does not provide the depth and degree of detail provided in the case study analysis.

This volume is an outstanding example of the latter approach. As Myron Aronoff notes in his preface, the first edition of this book was published in 1977, when Israel constituted a different political world from the Israel of today. This book was very favorably received when it first appeared, both because of its approach—the anthropological study of a major national political party was truly groundbreaking—and because of the clarity of the analytical perspective it presented.

Aronoff's approach in his original work was broadly comparative, and the new, expanded edition is explicitly comparative across time, examining the Labor Party from a pre-1977 perspective and again from several different perspectives in the ensuing fifteen years. This volume is an example of an exciting, important, and, indeed, definitive work on the development of a political party in a unique nation-state.

This book is the first publication in M.E. Sharpe's series in Comparative Politics. The series intends to make available studies that focus on a wide range of political institutions and political behaviors, studies that are comparative in the broadest sense of the term. We expect that forthcoming volumes in the series will follow both the cross-national approach to comparative politics and the case study approach. We hope you find this first work and its future companions stimulating and instructive.

Gregory S. Mahler

Preface to the Revised
and Expanded Edition

Plus ça change, plus c'est la même chose.

Just as the first edition of this book was published in 1977, prior to Labor's historic first defeat in that year's national election, this edition goes to press on the eve of its return to power as a result of victory in the 1992 Knesset election. Although the completed manuscript for the first edition was in the publisher's hands by June 1975, the analysis anticipated Labor's defeat by explaining how the party and its leadership had become increasingly unresponsive to the dynamically changing society and had thereby lost their authority. For this expanded edition, four new chapters have been added to the original nine chapters of the first edition.[1] The earlier concluding analysis, Chapter 9 in the original edition, now follows the new chapters as Chapter 13.

The new Chapter 9 examines Labor's very difficult first years of adjustment to the status of the opposition after having dominated the political system for nearly five decades.[2] The transition from a dominant party to a competitive party system was as difficult for the Likud, the leaders of which in certain respects continued to act as if they were still in the opposition, as it was for Labor, whose leaders continued to act as if they were entitled to govern the nation. As Moshe Carmel (former transport minister and a Labor Knesset member for five terms) observed at the time of the Labor Party national convention in November 1991,

> Labor's greatest problem is that it cannot come to terms with being in the opposition. Somehow, subconsciously, it still regards itself as the party to which power naturally belongs. For many years, it was accustomed to running things and determining the fate of the nation, and it can't accept or come to grips with anything different.[3]

Labor's leaders never fully understood nor drew the proper conclusions as to why they had lost the public's trust and confidence. Their symbolic gestures toward reform were too little and too late. The one major area in which significant progress has taken place, albeit belatedly, is in opening up the process through which the party's candidates to the Knesset are selected. This led to the election of more attractive and representative lists of candidates for the 1988 and the 1992 elections. These reforms are analyzed in Chapter 10.[4] One such reform was the major decision to have the Knesset candidates, including the party's top leader, who is its candidate for the premiership, selected in national and regional primary elections by the dues-paying members of the party.

The publication of this new edition as Labor emerges victorious from the 1992 election affords an opportunity to examine important continuities and changes that have taken place in the Labor Party since 1977. To do so comprehensively would require a book at least as long as the original one. However, by selectively highlighting a few key areas central to the original analysis at different time periods between the publication of the original volume and this edition, a perspective from the past decade and a half may add to the insights of the original work.

Obviously, many changes have taken place in Israeli society, culture, and politics during these crucial years. I have dealt with a number of them in *Israeli Visions and Divisions: Cultural Change and Political Conflict* (1989). One of the most significant developments was the impact of the Palestinian uprising, the *Intifada*, which broke out at the end of 1988. Labor's reaction to this important development is explored in Chapter 11.[5] The *Intifada* set off a chain of events that eventually led to the breakup of the national unity government in March 1990 and to the historic preliminary peace conference in Madrid during late October and early November 1991.

In Chapter 12 I consider the dilemmas confronting Labor in the context of this situation as it faces the future.[6] First of all, Labor has yet to settle the problem of succession. At the time of writing (December 1991), Shimon Peres and Yitzchak Rabin were still vying for party leadership as they were when the first edition of this book was published in 1977. Although the national primary elections resulted in reversing their positions on the list, with Rabin emerging in the top spot this time, their influence and their competition with each other continue. This is but one of the several indications of the applicability of the French epigraph that introduces this preface—the more things change, the more they remain the same. A second dilemma Labor confronted was whether to stick to comfortable positions and outdated slogans, try to emulate the Likud in policy and ideology, or produce a new vision more in tune with the rapidly altered domestic, regional, and international contexts. In the earlier draft of Chapter 12 I argued that unless Labor does the latter it has no hope of regaining the public's confidence and its role of leadership of the nation. In the present one I evaluate the outcome of Labor's fifth National Party Conference, the 1992 election, and the extent to which the party has met this challenge.

The retention of the original Concluding Perspectives as the new final chapter recapitulates the theme introduced in Chapter 1, and represents an attempt to evaluate the contributions of the original methodology and conceptual approach employed in this study. To the best of my knowledge, this is not only the first, but remains the only anthropological study of a major national political party. The use of extensive participant observation from the grass-roots branches to the most sensitive and closed inner forums of the national party institutions was without precedent, and regrettably has not (to the best of my knowledge) been emulated. The symbolic analysis of the manipulation of issues and the ritualization of politics in a modern socialist political party was innovative at the time and remains more unconventional than I would have anticipated or hoped it would be a decade and a half after the original publication.

The comparison of my conclusions with those of Peter Medding's excellent traditional political science study, *Mapai in Israel* (1972), focuses on the relationship between methodology, theory, and research findings. My hope is that it will highlight the contribution and insights provided by an anthropological approach to the study of the kind of politics normally the preserve of political scientists. Therefore, I am particularly pleased that the new expanded version of my study of the Israel Labor Party was selected to launch this new series in comparative politics.

In consultation with my editors I have decided that the most useful manner for the reader to be able to evaluate the original work is to reprint it with only minimal editorial revisions. I have resisted the urge to respond to reviewers and to tone down what in retrospect were clearly overly optimistic assessments about the rate and extent of reform that Labor was likely to undertake both at the time I sent the original book to press and at later stages. We believe that the inclusion of the additional chapters provides both continuity of themes and greater historical perspective on the original. Where it was useful to provide context or continuity on the additional chapters I have done so.

My focus is primarily (almost exclusively) on the *internal* organization and dynamics of the party. Labor's relations with the Histadrut, with other political parties, the role of ethnic relations, and the role of religion and the state are analyzed as they impinge upon the dynamics of power, factionalism, leadership selection, the process of debating and suppressing political issues, the ritualization of politics, relations between party center and local branches, and representation on party institutions. These topics are explained and explored through a rather unique conceptual prism explicated in Chapter 1.

The single *external* issue to which I have given somewhat fuller treatment, albeit from the same perspective of the impact on the party, is the Palestinian question. The chapter focusing on the Palestinian uprising, the *Intifada*, deals with the broader implications of the relationship between the state of Israel and the Palestinian people. This is a paramount issue at present, and the resolution of their conflicting claims will determine the futures of both peoples and of the region as a whole. Along with the challenge of successfully integrating the recent mass immigration of Soviet and Ethiopian Jews, the Palestinian question is the most urgent challenge facing the people and the state of Israel.

Labor emerged from the elections on June 23, 1992, victorious and in a position to head a new Israeli government. It will clearly be more forthcoming than the present Israeli government in its willingness to recognize the legitimate political rights of the Palestinians and to make territorial compromises for secure and lasting peace. The likelihood of the success of peace talks has been immeasurably enhanced. This vindicates the greater attention given to this issue in Chapters 11 and 12.

The publication of a second edition of a book, albeit expanded and updated, fifteen years after the publication of the first one, is a risky venture for an author and for his publisher. I have gladly agreed to incur this risk in the hope that the reader will find the contributions of my work as relevant today as they were when the original edition was published. In some respects the retrospective vantage point provided by the passage of time and events may offer a better perspective for evaluating Labor's record than when the book first appeared. In addition, as I have indicated, there is also a timeliness to the publication given the crucial role that Labor will play in leading the next government in the ongoing search for peace between Israel and its neighbors.

Notes

1. I lived in Israel from the summer of 1966 through the summer of 1977. As I indicate in Chapter 1, intensive research for the original edition was carried out from September 1969 through July 1971 and from November 1973 through April 1974. Research continued at a less intense level in the interim period. The final draft of the manuscript was written during the academic year 1974–75, and was handed to the publisher in June 1975. I continued field research on the Labor Party while living in Israel from the summer of 1975 through the summer of 1977. I spent two full years conducting research in Israel in 1982–83 and in 1987–88. The "anthropological present," i.e., the temporal point of reference for the original nine chapters is June 1975. The manuscript of this revised and expanded edition was completed in December 1991 and final revisions were made in June 1992. Three of the four new chapters of this expanded edition have been published previously (see below).

2. An earlier version of this chapter, entitled "The Labor Party in Opposition," was published by Praeger Publishers in 1982 in *Israel in the Begin Era*, edited by Robert O. Freedman. I am grateful to the publisher and editor for permission to reprint portions of this essay and to Drs. Yosef Beilin, Mitchell Cohen, and David Somer for their comments on it. The anthropological present for this chapter is June 1981.

3. Sarah Honig, "Grim, Party-pooping Polls Rain on Labor Parade," *Jerusalem Post International Edition*, November 30, 1991, p. 2. Similarly, Professor Galia Golan (of the Hebrew University), a member of Labor's Central Committee until she resigned in protest against the party's failure to adopt what she felt was a sufficiently dovish platform, said, "The problem is that Labor has never really comprehended that it's in the opposition." Clyde Haberman, "Israel's Labor Party Takes Dovish Line," *New York Times*, November 22, 1991, p. A3.

4. An earlier version appeared as "Better Late Than Never: Democratization in the Labor Party" in *Israel after Begin*, ed. Gregory S. Mahler (Albany: State University of New York Press, 1990). I am grateful for permission to republish a revised version of this chapter. The research was conducted and the original essay was written while I was resident director of the Rutgers Junior Year in Israel Program at Haifa University during 1987–88. I am grateful to Avraham Brichta for his useful comments on an early draft of the essay. I wish to thank Knesset members Uzzi Baram, Mordechai Gur, and Ora Namir, and former Knesset member Yehuda Hashai for granting me interviews. The anthropological present for this chapter is June 1988. Minor revisions were made to update this chapter in June 1992.

5. This chapter first appeared as "The Labor Party and the Intifada" in *The Intifada*, ed. Robert O. Freedman (Miami: Florida International University Press, 1991). I wish to thank Bob Freedman and Walda Metcalf, senior editor and assistant director of FIUP, for permission to republish this essay. The anthropological present for this chapter is December 1989.

6. An early version of this chapter was presented as a paper at the Twenty-Third Annual Conference of the Association for Jewish Studies, which was held in Boston in December 1990. It was revised and updated through December 1991, and again in June 1992.

Acknowledgments

Although such sections of books may appear to some people as being ritualistic (in the commonly used sense of the word, and not in its conceptually more precise meaning, which I employ later in this book), I take the giving of credit to those who made my work possible very seriously. It is even said in the collected wisdom of the Jewish forefathers in the *Pirkei Avot* that by giving credit for what one has learned from one's teachers and by citing one's sources one brings deliverance to the world. Personally, I feel that it would be difficult to exaggerate the importance of the collective contribution of many individuals and institutions to a work such as this, which has been written by a single individual.

This book represents the combined results of two major research projects sponsored by the Social Science Research Council of the United Kingdom, SSRC grant HR779/1, "Socio-Cultural Patterns of Adjustment and Conflict among Israel's Veterans and Immigrants," and the Ford Foundation, grant 8613, "The Internal Dynamics of the Israel Labor Party in the 1973 Elections," which was administered through the Israel Foundation for Research Grants and the Research Authority of Tel Aviv University. I wish to express my gratitude to the sponsoring institutions for their generosity and for the complete freedom they gave me to pursue my research interests. I thank the Wenner-Gren Foundation for Anthropological Research, which made it possible for me to attend the Burg Wartenstein Symposium No. 64, and to the co-organizers, Max Gluckman, Sally Moore, and Victor Turner, for having invited me to participate in it. I am grateful to Tel Aviv University for a sabbatical leave and to the Netherlands Institute for Advanced Study (NIAS) in the Humanities and Social Sciences for inviting me to spend the year 1974–75 as a fellow in residence and for providing me with the most congenial environment imaginable for writing a book. I thank collectively all of the people involved in these institutions who had a share in making my research and the reporting of it in this book possible.

There are several people who have given generously of their time and experience in commenting on various drafts of parts of this manuscript or on the entire manuscript. I have benefited greatly from their comments and criticisms, which have been incorporated into this book. They share much credit for their comments on the contents of the book, although obviously not the blame for the faults that remain. Undoubtedly the greatest single intellectual influence reflected in these pages is that of the late Professor Max Gluckman, my teacher and dear friend who died in April 1975, as the first edition of this book was being prepared for press. Max, as he insisted we call him, was an internationally known and respected scholar, an unusually gifted teacher, and the most loyal friend any person could be privileged to have had. I am one among many who owe him a great personal and intellectual debt (cf. Aronoff, 1976). Not only did Max supervise my training and my earlier research, to the end of his life he continued to mark with red ink the pages of the manuscript of this book in a not always successful attempt to force me to write in clear and simple English and to express my ideas lucidly without resorting to muddled professional jargon. I have tried to follow Gluckman's high standard of scholastic excellence and clarity of thought and style, and where I have failed it is the fault of the student and not of the teacher.

Professors Andre Kobben, Fred Bailey, Peter Medding, and David Rapoport have read and commented on a large part of this book. Professors Joel Migdal, David Nachmias, Yonathan Shapiro, Dennis Beller, and my wife, Rita, commented on a draft of Chapter 2 that was delivered at the 1974 Annual Meeting of the American Political Science Association in Chicago. My colleagues, Asher Arian, Shlomo Deshen, Emanuel Marx, Joel Migdal, Moshe Shokeid, and Moshe Swartz commented on a draft of Chapter 3, which was published in *The Elections in Israel—1973*, edited by Arian (1975) (cf. Aronoff, 1975). I wish to thank Professor Arian and the Jerusalem Academic Press for permission to republish this article and parts of an earlier one (Aronoff, 1972), which are contained in Chapter 7. The aforementioned scholars and Harry Scoble also commented on a monograph presented to the IXth International Congress of Anthropological and Ethnological Sciences in Chicago (cf. Aronoff, 1973a, later published in 1979), an early draft appearing in completely revised form in Chapters 4 and 5. I am especially grateful to Rachel Tokatli and Nissim Shamai for permission to quote form their unpublished work in these chapters.

Chapter 5 is unique in the sense that I consider it to be unusually influenced by the collective intellectual exchange that took place at the Burg Wartenstein Symposium No. 64, "Secular Rituals Considered: Prolegomena toward a Theory of Ritual, Ceremony, and Formality" in Austria in the summer of 1974 (cf. Moore and Myerhoff, 1977). It is at times difficult to differentiate between one's own original ideas and those that have been assimilated from the intensive discussions that characterized this most unusual and stimulating symposium. I therefore give great credit to all of the participants in the symposium, and particularly to Terence Turner and Victor Turner, for a significant influence on my thinking on ritual reported in Chapter 5. In addition professors Abner Cohen,

S.N. Eisenstadt, Don Handelman, and three of my colleagues at NIAS—R.Th.J. Buve, J.M.F. Jaspars, and J.D. Speckman—read and gave valuable comments on this chapter. It was first published in a volume I edited in memory of Max Gluckman (Aronoff, 1976).

My thanks to Yisrael Yossefi, who compiled the tables in Chapter 6. Chapter 7 contains summaries of some of the major findings of my team of research assistants: Benni Agustari, Michael Ashkenazi, Menashe Ben Meir, Sarah Carmi, Meir Charsky, Giora Goldberg, Natur Hazza, Jonathan Korpel, Avraham (Avi) Ofek, and Yochanon Shachamorov. I commend them for having continued to carry out their research assignments to the best of their abilities under impossible circumstances. Most of them were in combat units and were actively involved in the 1973 war—some having suffered wounds—and yet all returned to their research assignments when released, if only temporarily, from the army. I am especially grateful to my colleagues Dina Spechler and Neal Sherman for their valuable editorial comments.

Even with the generous support of research grants from foundations, the dedicated help of assistants, and the helpful comments of colleagues on the reports of one's research, no anthropological research of any worth could be done without the active support of many of the subjects of the research. In the appendix of my previous book (Aronoff, 1974a), I reported the relative ease with which I gained acceptance in the community and the speed with which I gained access to the most sensitive political forums. I can make no such claims with regard to this study, which was much more difficult in these respects. I was initially greeted with great suspicion by most of the people I approached. Even after I was cleared by the party security officer, it took many months of persistent efforts before I began to gain acceptance and access to the party. Therefore I am particularly grateful to the first individuals who actively aided me in my work, and who continued to do so over the course of five years. I can in all honesty say that without their help this book could never have been written in its present form. They are the officials of the Organization Department: Ze'ev Wexler (presently back at his Kibbutz Be'eri), Aharon Tofler (who was the director of the Organization Department at the time this book was first published, and to my sorrow has since passed away), and Yehuda Hashai (director of the Municipalities Department when the book was first published). Of course I had to receive the formal permission of the four men who served as secretary-general during the period of my research, Pinchas Sapir, Arie (Lyova) Eliav, Yisrael Yeshayahu, and Aharon Yadlin, and I sincerely thank them for their cooperation. In addition I received the active support of the men who served as directors of the Organization Department, Chaim Bear and Yisrael Granite, and the rest of the staff of the department. I also had the cooperation of the previous directors of the Municipalities Department, Shriege Netzer and Micha Almog, and the rest of the staff of this department. David Ben-Dov, secretary of the Control Commission, and his staff, and Micha Harish, director of the Foreign Relations Department, and his assistant Yisrael Gat were also most helpful. I also benefited from the technical services of Jacob Eini and Oded Betzer, as well as many of the staff at party headquarters. In addition, there were many other party leaders and activists at the national and local levels who actively aided me in my research, and I express my sincere gratitude to them all. I stress that none of them bears any responsibility whatsoever for what I have written. If my criticisms of the party appear to them to be a bit too sharp, I hope they will understand that they were made in an honest attempt to be as objective as is humanly possible. If I express any normative point of view it is reflected in my concern about the dangers inherent in the erosion of democratic procedures and the indications of a growing lack of responsiveness of the dominant party in Israel to the major problems confronting Israeli society. Within the constraints of these personal values, I have sincerely attempted to make an objective scientific analysis. If my diagnosis of certain ills in the party is correct and convincing, then it is up to them, as leaders of the party, and to the rank and file members, as well as the Israeli public generally, to see that changes are made; they show indications of doing so as I write these words.

I gratefully acknowledge the generosity of Tel Aviv University, through the president's office and the Research Committee of the Faculty of Social Sciences, which provided a grant that facilitated the publication of the first edition of this book.

Finally, since I am not only the product of the professional training I have received, but, like everyone else, have been strongly influenced by the values instilled in me by my parents, I find it fitting to pay tribute to my parents by dedicating this book to them in gratitude for all they have done for me. My father died while the first edition of this book was in press. This edition is dedicated with love to my mother and to my father's memory.

POWER
and
RITUAL
in the
ISRAEL
LABOR
PARTY
A Study
in Political
Anthropology

1

Introduction: An Unconventional Approach Explained and Justified

This is an unconventional study from several points of view. Therefore my first task is to clarify the ways in which this approach to the subject differs from more traditional studies, and my second task is to convince the reader of the usefulness of this different frame of reference. The subtitle of this book, *A Study in Political Anthropology*, summarizes as succinctly as possible the special approach I elaborate in this introduction. The study of political parties has been the traditional domain of political scientists. They have provided us with a rich and diverse literature on the subject, which they have studied from a variety of points of view, ranging from historical analysis of the development of parties and party systems, structural studies of party institutions, to functional analysis of the various tasks performed by parties in the political system—to cite the main general approaches. Although a large variety of methodological techniques have been employed, few, if any, have used the systematic observation of the interaction of party politicians in a wide range of party institutions over a prolonged period of time as the major research methodology. Although various forms of structured and unstructured interviewing with open and closed questionnaires have been employed, and in isolated cases participant observation has been used on a limited scale as a secondary technique, I could not find a single case in the literature where sustained participant observation over a long period was the main research method (although such cases may exist).

This then represents the first major difference between this study and traditional studies of political parties. Research was carried out during two major periods of fieldwork, September 1969–July 1971, and November 1973–April 1974, and since the researcher was in residence in Israel during the interim period, research continued, although at a less intense level. During the first period of fieldwork I traveled extensively and repeatedly, attending meetings of the institutions of the local party branches throughout the country. Several branches were studied intensively as case studies. I also traveled with the regional organizers of departments of the central party headquarters on their visits to the branches, sat in their offices when they received delegations from the branches at party headquarters, and participated in the meetings of the major national institutions with the exception of the top executive body, the Leadership Bureau. Much time was spent observing informal interaction of party officials, particularly at party headquarters as well as at social gatherings.

During the interim period I continued attending meetings of the departments of the party headquarters, meetings of the national institutions, and observed extensive informal interaction among party activists. During the second stage of fieldwork I supervised a team of eight research assistants who were placed in various party branches and departments and in the Histadrut (the General Federation of Labor). I continued participant observation in party headquarters and national institutions, and the assistants participated in the meetings of their branches and departments as well as the national institutions. The analysis in this study, therefore, is based on comprehensive observations of party officials and activists, and party institutions at different levels, for a period of almost five years. The nature of the data gathered from participant observation has direct ramifications for the types of concepts that can be applied in the analysis.

Abner Cohen (1969, 1974) observed that political scientists have been primarily preoccupied with theoretical problems of the relationships of power, and that the central theoretical concern of social anthropology has been with the dialectical relations between symbolic action and power relationships. Whereas various political scientists have also been concerned with political culture, ideology, and even the role of symbols in politics, as represented by the exceptional work of Murray Edleman (1964, 1971), their treatment of these subjects has differed substantially from the anthropological approach. A plea by political scientist David Schwartz for a reorientation in political science addresses itself to this fact (among others). Schwartz (1974:107) argues:

> From anthropology, for instance, we have adopted the concept of "culture" (our term is "political culture") [the author cites the work of Almond and Verba, 1963, and Pye, 1962], but we have not yet gone very far, it seems to me, in applying anthropological work on political myths, rituals, symbols and the like.

After summarizing briefly the contribution of the anthropological literature in these areas, Schwartz states:

> I think that generally we are more or less aware of these things perhaps primarily in a vague or intuitive way, but—from my review of the recent political science literature—we do not seem to be studying these matters very much or very well so as to sharpen our understanding. (Ibid.)

I stress that from my own survey of the literature in political science I find the same gap, and am in complete agreement with Schwartz that it is important that it be filled. It is significant that Schwartz also argues the need for "*in vivo* observation of political events*" (ibid., 111) through "participant-observation" (ibid., 127), among other techniques. Schwartz writes that the traditional methodological techniques employed by political scientists "are highly useful in dealing with articulate introspective respondents *when those individuals are not otherwise engaged in socio-political behavior,*" and points out that the "awesome weakness in these methods" is that "*they do not permit us to make the observations we want to make at the time and place in which we are most interested, namely, when the individual is most actively engaged in the political behavior we are trying to explain*" (ibid., 130, italics in original).

In his critical survey of the literature, Clifford Geertz points out two main approaches to the study of the social determinants of ideology: interest theory and strain theory. Interest theory (which I believe to be most characteristic of political science) views ideology as "a mask and a weapon"; "ideological pronouncements are seen against the background of a universal struggle for advantage" among men who pursue power (Geertz, 1964:52). Strain theory (most characteristic of sociology and social psychology) views ideology as "a symptom [of] and a remedy" for the "chronic effort to correct socio-psychological disequilibrium" in which men flee anxiety (Geertz, 1964:51). Geertz emphasizes that the theories need not necessarily be contradictory, but are both inherently inadequate because of

> the virtual absence . . . of anything more than the most rudimentary conception of the process of symbolic formulation. . . . The link between the causes of ideology and its effect seem adventitious because the connecting element—the autonomous process of symbolic formulation—is passed over in virtual silence. (Ibid., 56)

Geertz argues that ideologies must be studied "as systems of interacting symbols, as patterns of interworking meanings" if we are to understand how "ideologies transform sentiment into significance and so make it socially available . . ." (ibid., 56–57). Geertz asserts that because the "question of how symbols symbolize has simply been bypassed,"

> sociologists [and political scientists—M.A.] lack the symbolic resources out of which to construct a more incisive formulation . . . they evade the problem of constructing the import of ideological assertions by simply failing to recognize it as a problem. (Ibid., 57)

The failure to deal adequately, or even at all, with important problems like symbolic action is a consequence of both the limitations of conceptual frameworks discussed by Geertz, and the restrictions imposed by methodology. I maintain that it is most difficult, if not impossible, to gather data sufficiently rich in the usage of symbols in different social contexts without the researcher's observing and recording the usage of the symbols in the context of ongoing social relationships. Participant observation is therefore a crucial, if not essential, methodology for the study of this key aspect of ideology, as well as various other important aspects of socio-political relationships that I shall discuss.

Recognition of the importance of a focus on the interaction between the institutional structures of power and symbolic universes can be found in the social sciences literature. Peter Berger and Thomas Luckmann (1966:171) assert, "in our view, empirical research in the relation of institutions to legitimating universes will greatly enhance the sociological understanding of contemporary society." However, even those anthropologists who recognize the special contribution that their methodological and conceptual approaches can make to such an understanding have generally refrained from focusing on the national level of party politics. For example, Abner Cohen, almost in response to the previous statement, asserts,

> Political anthropology specializes in unfolding the political implications of symbolic formations and activities—the "mumbo-jumbo" of modern society—which are manifestly non-political, in the informal organization of interest groups. It can thus make an important contribution to the social sciences in the systematic analysis of the dynamic processes involved in the institutionalization and symbolization of power relationships. (Cohen, 1974:17)

While in basic agreement with Cohen, I contend that political anthropologists should not limit themselves to the study of interest groups, and in this study I hope to offer an example of the type of special contribution that political anthropology can make to the understanding of political parties at both the national and local levels.

Significantly, anthropologists are increasingly dissatisfied with and critical of anthropology's limited horizons. They believe that anthropologists should study the politically powerful as well as the weak, the elite as well as the socially subservient in modern society. One example of a cross-section of such points of view is contained in the volume edited by Dell Hymes (1969, 1974; quotations are from the 1974 edition). For instance, Laura Nader (1974) discusses the serious theoretical consequences of not "studying up"—that is, studying the politically powerful—claiming that "if one's pivot point is around those who have responsibility by virtue of being delegated power, then the questions change. From such a perspective, one notices different facets of culture . . ." (ibid., 290). Nader also gives convincing arguments to refute the obstacles and objections that are usually raised to counter the suggestion for such reorientation of anthropology. In the same volume, Eric Wolf argues that "anthropology has reached its present impasse because it has so systematically disregarded the problems of power . . ." (1974:261). The present study, which focuses on the national political elite of the dominant party in Israel, represents just such an unconventional orientation for an anthropological study.

To recapitulate and summarize the unconventional aspects of this study: It applies the anthropological method of participant observation and anthropological conceptual focus on the dialectical relations between symbolic action and power relationships to an analysis of a modern national political party. It is unique in the sense that political scientists who have studied parties have not employed these approaches, and anthropologists who use these methods and concepts have thus far not applied them to the study of political parties at the national level. The exceptional pioneering anthropological study by Leo Despres (1967) of nationalist politics in British Guiana has, to the best of my knowledge, not been emulated. If there have been similar studies, they, like the work of Despres and this study, represent exceptions to the general literature.

Unfortunately, in the early stages of the separate development of political science and anthropology as professional disciplines there was little active inter-disciplinary cooperation. In fact, in one of the first and most influential system-atic comparative anthropological studies of political systems, the editors boldly declared that the study of political philosophy had no scientific value (cf. Fortes and Evans-Pritchard, 1940:5). Ironically, similar charges by the "behavioralist" movement in political science have led to "the nearly complete severance of modern political science from the tradition of discourse which provided it with most of its basic assumptions, concepts, and vocabulary" (Zashin and Chapman, 1974:291). Subsequently, anthropologists who have made valuable contributions to the study of politics have amended their predecessors' statements, acknowl-edging the contribution of contemporary political scientists and the relevance of their approaches to anthropologists, but they tend to continue to disregard the relevance of the classical political theorists (or political philosophers, as they refer to them). Max Gluckman and Fred Eggan (1966:xx–xxi) observed that

> [s]ince Fortes and Evans-Pritchard, with African Political Systems, virtually established "political anthropology," their successors have turned increasingly to political scientists for assistance in their analysis. . . . Political anthropology, at least, is linking up with its cognate discipline: and this clearly is not diffi-cult, since the concepts and analytic framework of political science are not too diverse from those of social anthropology. No new techniques have to be learned to master them.

While in basic agreement with this statement, I would point out that whereas the anthropologist might not have to master new techniques, it would greatly facilitate communication if he would master the (admittedly at times trying) language of his cognate discipline. For example, one otherwise admirable at-tempt by political anthropologists to build conceptual bridges to their colleagues in political science was unfortunately marred by the conceptual confusion caused by their invention of new terms for concepts like "power" and "authority," which were already widely accepted in political science (cf. Swartz, Turner, and Tuden, 1966:114–19). It is therefore particularly important that students of politics who approach their subject from different academic disciplines acquaint themselves with the language and concepts of their colleagues in related disciplines.

Studies of the confrontation between traditional political systems and modern party politics comprise a rich anthropological literature and have led anthropologists to formulate what they consider to be the anthropological contribution to the study of contemporary politics in complex societies. Among these studies, the works of F.G. Bailey (1969), Abner Cohen (1969 and 1974), Marc Swartz, Victor Turner, and Arthur Tuden (1966), and Marc Swartz (1968) are prominent. The organization of special panel sessions at various professional conferences (cf. Claessen and Seaton, 1979) and the appearance of a new journal, *Political Anthropology*, devoted to the subject herald the emergence of a focus of study bridging the traditional disciplines of political science and anthropology. (Although *Political Anthropology* is no longer published, nine volumes of an annual series I edit, now titled *Political and Legal Anthropology*, have been published.) Like the parent disciplines from which it has developed, political anthropology is creating a literature that focuses on problems of common interest and is developing its own concepts for dealing with its unique approach to them. This work is meant to contribute to the development of methods and concepts of political anthropology as an approach to the analysis of contemporary politics in complex as well as traditional and developing societies (cf. Balandier, 1967; Claessen, 1974; R. Cohen; 1965, 1967, 1969, 1970; Colson 1968; Easton, 1959; Kurtz, 1973; M.G. Smith, 1968; Tuden, 1969; and Winkler, 1970).

One of the points of view taken in this book is that the ideal type dichotomous division of societies into traditional and modern, which we have inherited from our intellectual forefathers—e.g., Maine, Morgan, Tonnes, Durkheim, Marx, and Weber—has led to a tendency to reify these concepts on the part of contemporary social scientists. We have tended to view the societies we study as being either traditional or modern, according to the bundle of characteristics defining the theoretical ideal type, rather than, for example, viewing them along a continuum on which they more or less closely approximate the attributes of one and/or the other ideal type (cf. Wolf, 1969 [1974 edition]:260–61, for a similar point of view). One of the contributions that political anthropology can make to its parent and sister disciplines is to illustrate that subcultures and groups within modern society can exhibit characteristics closely resembling those generally considered to exist only in traditional society. For example, I examine in Chapter 5 the conditions under which ritual proceedings take place in a modern political party. I attempt to show that secular political ideologies can take the place of religious and mystical cosmologies in ritual performances. This of course calls for the adaption of concepts derived from the study of traditional religious rituals.

In a similar vein, the passing of traditional society has been assumed to have led to the eclipse of such classical social figures as the court jester:

[W]hen the divinity that hedges a king was broken down the fool lost his freedom, his joke, and his reason for existence. . . . The King, the Priest, and the Fool all belong to the same regime, all belong essentially to a society shaped by belief in the divine order, human inadequacy, efficacious ritual; and there is no real place for any of them in a world increasingly dominated by the notions of the puritan, the scientist, and the captain of industry; for strange as it may seem the fool in cap and bells can only flourish among people who have sacraments, who value symbols as well as tools, and cannot forever survive the decay of faith in divinely imposed authority, the rejection of all taboo and mysterious inspiration. (Welsford, 1935:193)

And yet the same author observes the survival of this ancient role in modern times:

Nevertheless, even in this matter the break between the ancient and modern practice is not complete. In the medieval air of our schools and universities eccentric scholars can still attain to the legendary proportions of the heroes of the jest-books; in the theatre and cabaret the funny man can still exchange badinage with the audience; and at the circus the Clown still plies with undiminished gusto his ancient trade of parody and improvisation. (Ibid., 313)

I maintain that in modern complex society one can find many examples of what Peter Berger (1969:65) calls "signals of transcendence." I illustrate through examples in the Israel Labor Party modern men in a thoroughly contemporary institution who have sacraments, who place a high value on symbols that have a deep meaning for them; it is an institution where taboos are observed, rituals take place, a modern version of a court jester performs his role, and where even mysterious inspiration for the creation of the modern state and its continued existence against formidable odds is believed by significant numbers, if not widely articulated by all who thus believe. I contend that in addition to being influenced by specific historical and cultural aspects of Judaism and modern Israeli society, these are particular forms of more general phenomena. As Berger succinctly states:

In the observable human propensity to order reality there is an intrinsic impulse to give cosmic scope to this order, an impulse that implies not only that human order in some way corresponds to an order that transcends it, but that this transcendent order is of such a character that man can trust himself and his destiny to it. (Ibid., 70)

I suggest that terms such as "court jester," "taboo," and "ritual" have greater value for analysis of contemporary society than merely as metaphors. They can and should be developed and adapted to distinguish between the similarities and differences of the phenomena that occur in ostensibly "traditional" and ostensibly "modern" social contexts. There is a clear danger that if concepts used in the analysis of traditional societies are applied uncritically, stressing only the similarities between the phenomena that occur in different social contexts without adapting them to accommodate important sociological differences, the concepts may become metaphors or analogies, having lost much of their explanatory value. (For an excellent explanation of the differences between metaphor and analogy and their use in political analysis, see Zashin and Chapman, 1974.)

For example, there is a tendency in the work of Edelman (1964 and 1971) and even more so in that of Bocock (1974) to apply the term "ritual" to such a wide range of socio-political phenomena in modern society that by so doing the concept is not sufficiently refined to differentiate between specific types of modern ritual which much more closely approximate those that occur in traditional societies, and other types of activity which are analogues, but differ substantially (cf. Goody, 1977). I will now briefly illustrate more specific examples of the contribution of this unique application of methods and concepts to the study of the Labor Party. This will be expanded upon and amplified throughout the book.

There are many aspects of politics that are of mutual interest to all students of the subject, be they political scientists, political sociologists, or political anthropologists. One phenomenon that has continued to interest students of politics is the faction. Political factions have been studied at local, regional, and national levels, and the growing literature indicates that there is considerable ambiguity on the subject. Having studied factions at both the local and national levels, I am particularly sensitive to the need to examine them within the perspective of institutional hierarchy. In Chapter 2 I propose the adaptation of the characteristics of a model of corporate groups for the comparative study of the structural features of factions. I argue against the tendency to dichotomize concepts into mutually exclusive ideal types like party and faction, and propose the analysis of characteristics—e.g., the degree of corporateness of the units—along a continuum in order to compare the extent to which groups maximize the properties of the idealized polar extremes. I stress that the relationship between structure and the legitimating universe of ideology must be analyzed in specific historic and social contexts, and should not be assumed to be aligned in a particular relationship as a property of structural features, i.e., of party and faction. I trace the impact of social change on the party, particularly in the erosion of ideology—a point taken up again in the analysis of ritual procedures in Chapter 5. Chapter 2 also introduces the background of historical, cultural, and institutional features of the Israeli political system, features essential to an understanding of the analysis of specific problems that follows in the ensuing chapters.

In Chapter 3 I undertake a detailed analysis of the nomination process, which prominent political scientists have considered to be a key to the understanding of power relationships in political parties. Through an examination of a chain of "nomination committees," I trace the mobilization of political support that led to the domination of the main political institutions of the party. I attempt to illustrate that through the systematic observations of the events reported, important insights can be gained as to the nature of relationships of power in the party. For example, through an elaboration of the nature of the dependence of the nominees on the elites who nominate them, the nature of "representation" is given a dimension and perspective very different from that which has been presented in the literature on Israeli politics. The nature of representation is elaborated in Chapter 6.

The concept of "nondecisions" and "nonissues" has precipitated a contentious debate among political scientists and sociologists. Although there appears to be a consensus that the problems raised in this debate might illuminate important aspects of the political process that have thus far been largely neglected, there is major disagreement over the feasibility of identifying and researching the subject. In Chapter 4 I suggest a refinement of the concept, which I argue enables the clear identification and researchability of the important aspect of the suppression of issues. It is shown that an anthropological methodology is essential in identifying the process through which the issue arena is controlled, and the anthropological focus on the interaction between institutional and cultural variables is vital in explaining both the mechanisms of suppression and the consequences and ramifications of the suppression of issues for the party, the political system, and the society.

Whereas the two preceding chapters focus primarily on aspects of power relations, Chapter 4 balances the analysis of power with an emphasis on cultural and ideological features of the party. The following chapter concentrates primarily on the process of symbolic action.

Chapter 5 is devoted to the analysis of ritual proceedings. I use ritual as the key concept in the explanation of important aspects of the behavior of political actors in a specific social context. I argue that one consequence of organizational and ideological changes in the party brought about by rapid socio-economic and political changes in the society was that a particular set of political actors was faced with the need to redefine or assert central values and ideological concepts, and to give new meaning to their roles as a category of party leaders. They did both within the context of a carefully controlled and bracketed ritual setting which allowed them to comment on the party and their roles in it, the party's ideology, and the society at large.

An analysis of the characteristics of the actors in the performance and the audiences or reference groups to which the performance was directed brings out significant differences in the roles of the three main levels of political leadership in the party: the top national elite, the secondary echelon, and the local grassroots leaders. The discussion of ritual form and process reveals how the ritual performance was bracketed and controlled, thereby establishing the formal constraints within which the freer innovative and creative aspect of the ritual process took place.

The heart of Chapter 5 is a discussion of the many levels of the theme of consensus through an analysis of its meaning in different social and symbolic contexts. Ultimately this theme is related to the meaning of democracy within the

the context of a mass pluralistic dominant party in a highly fragmented socially and culturally heterogeneous society which has undergone rapid social, economic, and political change, and which from its birth has been faced with a constant threat to its physical survival. The outcomes of the ritual are related to the various categories of actors and audience in the concluding analysis. The structural and cultural conditions likely to be conducive to such political rituals are outlined in the hope that future cross-cultural research may lead to a refinement of the concepts.

In Chapter 6 I return to the discussion of representation first raised in Chapter 3. The first section discusses continuity and change in representation in the major national party institutions. By examining comparative data on the representation of various ethnic, age, and sex categories in party branches in different regions of the country, major patterns and trends are identified. Particularly important for the discussion is the analysis of patterns of over- and under-representation of specific groups and categories, for this reflects respective dominant and subordinate positions within the party. This discussion is then related to the previous analysis of the nominations process and to the documentation of the significant extent of dependence of members of party institutions on the party and its affiliated organizations for their livelihoods. Previous work on the former Mapai, particularly by Peter Medding (1972), is critically evaluated in assessing the extent to which these institutions can be legitimately and accurately described as *representative* and *decision-making* institutions. It is argued that when one accepts accountability as an important aspect of the concept representative, then the majority of the so-called "representatives" on the Labor Party institutions cannot be considered as representatives in the traditional sense of the term. The bypassing of the constitutional institutional forums for the making of decisions is then related to the increasing centralization of power in the party.

In Chapter 7 I continue the analysis of centralization of power within the party through an examination of the reciprocal relationships between the party center and the local branches. The preceding discussion of representation on national party institutions is related to the analysis of differing degrees of relative dependence upon or autonomy from the national party headquarters that characterized different categories of branches. After discussing the major local centers of power, I compare and contrast the different conditions that prevailed in party headquarters during the 1969 and 1973 elections. The findings of seven studies of branches of the Labor Party are summarized, showing the domination of the branches by local elites who are primarily preoccupied with the perpetuation of their dominant positions. It is demonstrated that national intervention in the nomination of local candidates was harmful to party interests and indicative of the poor communication between the two levels of party leadership and organization. The general lack of responsiveness of national leaders and officials to local situations, and the lack of responsiveness of local elites to their own constituencies, have had wide-ranging consequences which are discussed in Chapter 8.

Chapter 8 summarizes the major events and changes that occurred in the party during the aftermath of the war of October 1973 until May 1975, analyzing them as the consequences of the processes discussed in the previous chapters. It is suggested that these events represent a new threshold in the developing Israeli political system.

Chapter 13 (which was Chapter 9 in the first edition) compares the findings of this study with the work of Peter Medding (1972), the prominent political scientist who studied Mapai in an earlier period, and through this comparison attempts to illustrate the differences between the anthropological approach and the political science approach. It is postulated that there is a direct relationship between the various stages of the mobilization of political power and support, their institutionalization, and the changing role of ideology, i.e., the meaning and importance of ideology for various actors as they perceive it to be effectively related to solving the major problems confronting the party. This case study of the development of the Israel Labor Party is an example of the contributions of the anthropological approach to the study of contemporary society.

2

Fission and Fusion:
The Politics of Factionalism

Introduction: The Conceptual Framework

The Israeli political system has been characterized throughout its brief history by a process of fission and fusion—a splitting apart and remerging of its political parties. I shall analyze this process by focusing on the major labor parties that have dominated the political system since its earliest gestation period before Israeli independence in 1948. I shall explore the historical origins of the factional system in the pre-state Jewish *Yishuv* (the Jewish community in Palestine prior to Independence), and relate the process of fission and fusion to the dynamic socio-economic and political changes that characterized the development of Israeli society. Major characteristics of the political culture and institutional framework are related to their influence on the factional system. The focus of my analysis is on the structural and functional characteristics of the factions in the Israel Labor Party and their impact on the political process, especially the competitive process.

When examining the literature on factions one cannot help but be struck by the ambiguity of the concept of "factions," the lack of consensus on it, and even the contradictory definitions of the term. In addition, one of the most serious problems created by many using the concept is the categorization of entities into dichotomies and mutually exclusive ideal types, contrasting factions with parties and other forms of political groups. I suggest that it would be more fruitful to think in terms of clusters of characteristics along a continuum, which I shall illustrate with three of the clearest defining characteristics that seem to have gained the widest acceptance by those who have written on factions. There appears to be a consensus on the following: (1) factions are sub-units competing within a larger corporate political entity; (2) they are not themselves corporate units; and (3) they pursue particularistic interests generally viewed as selfish or against the common good. Other defining characteristics of factions, such as that they are leader-oriented, temporary, conflict groups, and so forth, can be subsumed within the proposed framework for defining corporate characteristics and will be discussed.

Harold Lasswell's definition of a faction as "any constituent group of a larger unit which works for the advancement of particular persons or policies" seems to have gained general acceptance in the literature (cf. Nicholas, 1965, 1966, and 1969; Benedict, 1957; and Pocock, 1957). Since social anthropologists and political scientists have studied various levels within states, from local-level village factions to factions of national political parties, it is important to define the levels of autonomy within which the faction operates on a continuum of increasing levels (cf. Pettigrew, 1975, for an analysis of factions at all levels in the political system of India). For example, the Israel Labor Party, which is subdivided into three major factions, is joined to another labor party (Mapam) in an electoral Alignment (Maarach), which competes with other parties on a joint electoral list, has joint consultative institutions, and is bound by joint coalition discipline. Within certain contexts, both Labor and Mapam could be viewed, according to the first criterion, as factions within the Alignment. On the other end of the continuum the three factions of the Labor Party can be further broken down for the analysis of political networks (Barnes, 1969; Mitchell, 1969), quasi groups and action sets (Mayer, 1966), and patron–client relationships (Wolf, 1966; Scott, 1972). (These concepts, like factions, are not without their ambiguities and are also in need of refinement.) Depending on the level of analysis, almost all of these units can be viewed as sub-units of a larger whole. By emphasizing a hierarchical continuum it is possible to emphasize important differences between internal party factions and factional aspects of the independent parties within the Alignment in specific contexts. This becomes clearer when we take into consideration the second criterion.

The noncorporate nature of factional structure is generally stressed in the literature. Factions are usually defined as "leader–follower" groups—temporary phenomena, often bridging the transition from traditional to modern party politics, or coping with other forms of transition in social change, such as the adaptation of immigrants to new environments (cf. Shokeid, 1968). For example, in contrasting factions with political parties Ralph Nicholas (1966:57) states,

> The party is a corporate group that continues whether or not a particular follower or a particular leader is present; a faction, by contrast, may disintegrate when the leader dies or ceases to exercise control over the political action of his followers. There is no jural rule of succession to factional leadership positions, though there may be regularities of practice in any area.

There are many examples in the literature of factions with differing degrees of corporateness and longevity ranging from the temporary to those that have persisted for decades. Nicholas (1965:28) has even noted, "That factions are not corporate, that they are basically impermanent, does not mean that they may not persist for a long period of time." Some scholars have analyzed corporate factions (cf. Barth, 1959) and others have found them to have persisted over a considerable period of time (cf. Pettigrew, 1975). We need a framework within which we can systematically order such disparate, if not contradictory, findings.

The first task is to reach an agreed-upon definition of the term "corporate group," which, as Michael G. Smith has pointed out, was defined differently even by classic scholars like Weber, Maine, and Durkheim (cf. Smith, 1966:118). I suggest the acceptance of Smith's definition of corporate groups as having certain properties: presumed perpetuity, boundedness, determinate membership, identity, autonomy, organization, procedure, and common affairs (Smith, 1966:119). Rather than dichotomizing these characteristics into mutually contradictory categories of corporate and noncorporate, I suggest arranging them on a continuum from groups that maximize these features to those that least manifest them. This would enable us to deal with the placement of other characteristics thought to characterize factions: the extent to which they are leader-oriented, the use of diverse principles to recruit factional supporters, their longevity, the extent to which they are exhaustive, exclusive, and functionally undifferentiated, and the extent to which conflict is essential to their existence (Nicholas, 1966).

Taking the last characteristic, for example, it has been widely argued that factions are "conflict groups" (e.g., Nicholas, 1965:27; and Graham, 1969:323). It would seem likely that the less corporate a group, the greater its tendency to perpetuate itself through political strife. Lewis Coser (1956:104) has observed, "Continued conflict being a condition of survival for struggle groups, they must perpetually provoke it." Whereas the institutionalized aspects of corporate groups tend to give them perpetuity even in the relative absence of strife, the noncorporate nature of loosely structured factions make them even more dependent upon strife to maintain their identity and boundaries (cf. Aronoff, 1973b:100–101, 1974a). This is closely related to the third major characteristic of factions: their pursuit of particularistic interests.

Raymond Firth (1957:292) defines factions as, "groups or sections of a society in relations of opposition to one another, interested in promoting their own objectives rather than those of the society as a whole and often turbulent in their operations." David Pocock (1957:296) states, "The behaviour of a faction is such that it attempts to bend the power and potentiality of the whole of which it is a part to its own particular interests and to dominate the other faction or factions which are similarly motivated." Significantly, factions are similarly perceived within the context of the contemporary Labor Party culture. The word faction (*siya*) is generally used to refer to a faction that has split off from the parent party, and is associated with the word split (*pilug*). Other words used in association with *siya* have a definite negative connotation: quarrelsome, provocative, pugnacious (*kantran*), and traitor, renegade, disloyal (*bogade*). When politicians refer to factions that have merged with, and exist within, the party, they refer to:

group, section, block (*chativa*), a much more neutral term. They also refer to the factions by naming them as "the previous Mapai" or the "past Rafi."

Although more neutral terms are used when referring to present factions, they all express the sentiment that factionalism is a negative phenomenon working against the unity and the general interests of the party as a whole. There is constant ritualistic expression of the desire for the rapid demise of the factions, particularly when a party split appears imminent, even by those who work hardest to maintain the factions and who have the most to gain through their perpetuation. While it is important to analyze the significance of conceptual systems in their specific political contexts (cf. Bailey, 1972), we must be careful to differentiate between the actors' values and conceptions and our own analytic framework. This is particularly important with regards to the so-called "selfish" behavior of factions.

I suggest that all political groups, including parties as well as factions, are by definition self-interested in the sense that they are competing for political power. All political groups must also articulate a conception of general societal good, which is expressed through the biased frame of reference of the group's values and interests, because the political actors must legitimate their actions in the eyes of the public to which they appeal for support (and generally in their own eyes as well). Logically, if factions are competing within larger units, the larger unit implies a broader interest—at least in terms of the unity of the whole. Their competition as sub-units means that, by definition, factions express more particularistic interests. Frequently (but not always), the self-interest of factions appears more obvious because their internal competition within the party or larger unit does not have to appeal to an outside public and therefore is usually a more blatant struggle for power, which, by nature, is more difficult to clothe in ideology. I caution against the tendency to make ideal-type distinctions between party and faction in terms of the party pursuing the general good and the faction pursuing selfish goals; rather, I stress the need to focus analysis on the particular historical, cultural, and social contexts in which political groups manifest both types of behavior. I shall attempt to illustrate this in the forthcoming sections.

I first set out the cultural and institutional framework—the arena—in which factional politics takes place in Israel. This entails a brief description of several of the major characteristics of the political system, particularly those that have a bearing on the politics of factionalism. This is followed by a discussion of the major historical splits and mergers among the labor parties without which it would be most difficult, if not impossible, to understand contemporary factionalism in the united Israel Labor Party. The main section deals with factional competition in the Israel Labor Party (1968–74). Here I attempt to illustrate the application of the continuum of factional characteristics. In the concluding analysis I discuss the utility of the conceptual framework in helping to explain the factional process in the Israeli labor parties.

The Arena: The Cultural and Institutional Framework

There is an old saying told by both Jews in the Diaspora and by Israelis about themselves. They say that for every two Jews there are at least three political points of view. The tendency of the Jewish people to divide among themselves into competing political camps is amply illustrated throughout every stage of their history. Even a cursory look at the Bible reveals the difficulties Moses had with rebellious factions, the wars between the Jewish kingdoms of Israel and Judah, and the fighting among Jewish factions within the walls of Jerusalem while the Jews were rebelling against the might of the Roman Empire. Competing interpretations of the Jewish religion have existed since the rival schools of the followers of the famous rabbis Hillel and Shamai, through the competition between the movements of the Haskala and Hasidim in eighteenth-century Eastern and Central Europe (cf. J. Katz, 1961), to the present divisions between Reform, Conservative, and Orthodox Jewry. The cultural tendency for Jews to form factions is represented by the joke about the Jew who was stranded for years on a deserted island and when his rescuers asked him why he had built two synagogues, he replied that one was his *shul* and the other was the one in which he would not be caught dead.

The most important institutional factor influencing the Israel factional system is the electoral system based on proportional representation within a single electoral district. This system, which frequently encourages a multiplicity of parties by the splitting off of sections of parties, has its historic origins in the earliest organizational meetings of the World Zionist Organization (WZO). Since the WZO needed to mobilize the widest possible support among world Jewry, but lacked the resources and sanctions of a state, it sought to attain unity by allowing representation of all the diverse views and interests of world Jewry, which expressed themselves in many organizations, factions, and parties. Since the plurality system of voting leaves some groups unrepresented and involves a certain element of compulsion, and because the WZO's moral authority derived from its claim to represent world Jewry, it adopted proportional representation to ensure the inclusion and support of all groups. Once adopted, this system encouraged continued ideological diversification and the multiplicity of parties and factions. The same compelling need for unity led to the representation of minority parties not only on the Zionist Council and Executive, but in the Zionist organization's bureaucracy as well (cf. Halpern, 1961; Hertzberg, 1966; and Laqueur, 1972).

This framework was carried to Palestine by the pioneering settlers and was adopted for elections to the Histadrut (General Federation of Labor) and to the Elected Assembly in 1920. It was particularly well suited to the voluntary nonsovereign nature of the political institutions of the Jewish Yishuv in Palestine since it protected minority factions. The institutions of the party key assured all participants in coalitions their share of the spoils and resources of office. By 1948 the various parties were so well entrenched, each with its separate ideol-

ogy, bureaucracy, affiliated institutions, patronage, and vested interests to protect, that it was natural that proportional representation was the system adopted
for the elections to the Knesset. The same reasons explain why concerted attempts by no less a figure than David Ben-Gurion have failed to change the
system (cf. Bernstein, 1957; Burstein, 1934; Kraines, 1961; Fein, 1967; and
Safran, 1963).

Observers of Israeli politics have frequently commented on their intense ideological nature, which is obviously related to factionalism. Because the early
Zionist institutions and those of the Jews in Palestine lacked territorial sovereignty and the regular means of coercion available to sovereign governments,
and because they had to appeal to a widely scattered constituency, Zionism and
the voluntary institutions of the Yishuv had to rely heavily on persuasion and
moral pressure. There was a particularly important need for intensive ideological
indoctrination of the pioneering settlers, who had to be motivated to endure great
hardships and sacrifices during the colonization of the Yishuv. The Zionist parties were a product of the late nineteenth and early twentieth centuries, and many
of them arose in Eastern Europe and were influenced by the progressive and
radical ideologies popular at the time.

There are many examples of the high degree to which political passions have
been aroused at various stages of Israeli political history. For instance, debates in
the Elected Assembly between the leaders of the socialist parties and Jabotinsky's
Revisionist Movement led to the outbreak of fist fights between their supporters
in the assembly itself (cf. Burstein, 1934:116–17). When Siya Bet (which included a large section of the Kibbutz HaMeuchad) faction split from Mapai and
later merged with HaShomer HaZair to form Mapam, great ideological arguments, many of which ended in physical fights, raged in many kibbutzim. This
led to the separation of warring factions with barbed wire and the expulsion of
minorities from various kibbutzim. Many explosive issues, such as the German
arms sales and German war reparations, caused volatile public debates and vio-
lent demonstrations between the parties and among the public. Various scandals
such as the Kastner Affair and the Lavon Affair have embroiled top party leaders
and the general public in major confrontations that have had far-ranging political
ramifications.

However, ideology has since come to play an increasingly ritual role among
Israeli party elites, and it has generally appeared to be increasingly less relevant
among the general public. The changing role of ideology is related to major
social, economic, and political changes that have characterized the dynamic
development of Israeli society, in particular the increasing availability of and
reliance on resources of power in the institutions of the state. Whereas ideology
appears to have played an important role in the factional disputes of the earlier
period, competition for power has been the dominant characteristic of more
recent factional strife (cf. Arian, 1968, 1973).

Israeli political parties have been characterized as movements, having provided a wide range of services not normally associated with political parties in the Anglo-American tradition. Political movements provided major services both because they were nonexistent in the pre-state period and because they saw it as their task to cater to the social, cultural, and economic needs of their members. Political party movements founded agricultural movements and their settlements, industry, trade unions, newspapers, publishing houses, schools, youth movements, health clinics and hospitals, banks, insurance companies, housing projects, cultural centers, synagogues, sports clubs, and even paramilitary organizations. The Histadrut (General Federation of Labor) established by the labor parties, and the parallel institutions established by the other movements, embody and symbolize the multiple extrapolitical roles of the parties as movements.

The Israeli political system is characterized by a high degree of centralization of political power. The historical legacy of highly centralized colonial Ottoman Turkish and British rule reinforced the national thrust of Jewish self-government toward the accomplishment of national unity and national goals, resulting in a highly centralized system. The country's small size reinforced the arguments of national leaders that local interests were parochial and detracted from national goals and interests. The fact that the parties of the right had strong local constituencies was an additional incentive for the labor leaders of the national institutions to undermine local authority (cf. Weiss, 1972). The fact that the vast majority of national resources, especially contributions from abroad, were monopolized by the political leadership of the Jewish Agency and later the state enabled the continuation and consolidation of centralized power and control. (See Aronoff, 1974a, for an account of the effects of such centralization on a community that attempted to maintain independent local factions.) Patterns of immigration were also under the control of the central government, and the creation of new towns led to their remote control from the center in their early stages (cf. Aronoff, 1973c; E. Cohen, 1970; Deshen, 1970; and Marx, 1972). The fact that Knesset members do not have local constituencies, but are chosen by and dependent upon national party leaders, also contributes to the consolidation and centralization of power at the center (cf. Brichta, 1972; and Czudnowski, 1970). Although there have been signs of a trend toward greater local autonomy in recent years, the main fact of overwhelming central domination has not changed significantly (cf. Aronoff, 1972).

Since no single party has ever commanded a majority in the Knesset, government has been characterized by coalition bargaining, compromise of ideology and program, and the division of spoils ranging from ministerial portfolios to the rule of various cities. Since no coalition has ever been formed without the main labor party, Mapai (in its various forms), it has traditionally controlled the key ministerial portfolios and has been dominant in the government. Mapai has dominated Israeli politics from its formation in the thirties. Its traditional coalition partner, the National Religious Party (Mafdal), has participated in every government. Mapai (Labor) comes very close to meeting Maurice Duverger's (1963:308) classic definition of a dominant party in a dominant party system: "A party is dominant when it is identified with an epoch; when its doctrines, ideas, methods, its style, so to speak, coincide with those of the epoch. . . ." (See also Arian, 1972; Birnbaum, 1970; and Nachmias, 1973, 1975.)

Israeli society has been characterized by rapid development and growth, the absorption of waves of immigrants from diverse cultural backgrounds (cf. Deshen, 1970; Shokeid, 1974; Eisenstadt, 1967; and Eisenstadt, Bar-Yosef, and Adler, 1970), rapid expansion of the economic sector, and the successful defense of the country in several bloody wars. Throughout this era of dynamic changes and development the political system has remained remarkably stable, and the conservative Israeli electorate has opted for continuity in the rule of the dominant party. Stability notwithstanding, there have been several major ramifications of the socio-economic changes in the political system. Most striking have been the decline in the ideological intensity of politics and the decline in the emphasis on the ideals of voluntarism and egalitarianism, both of which have been influenced by general societal changes such as mass immigration and rapid industrialization. The institutionalization by government ministries of functions formerly performed by party movements and their institutions—e.g., national defense, education, employment, housing—has lessened the dependence of the citizens on the parties and has been accompanied by a general decline in public involvement in political activities, particularly noticeable among the youth. The parties have not recruited significant numbers of young leaders into important national positions and have consequently had to turn to retiring high-ranking military officers in many cases to fill such positions. The dominant position of the Labor Party has gradually been eroded since the 1965 election and having become more noticeable in the 1973 election that led to a precarious coalition with the narrowest margin in the history of the Knesset.

Fission and Fusion: The Historic Splits and Mergers

One of the main responses of the political system to societal changes has been the fission and fusion of parties and factions. Figure 1 illustrates the splits and mergers of Israel's political labor movement. I shall briefly outline this process among the major labor parties to provide the necessary background for understanding the dynamics of factionalism in the newly united Israel Labor Party. The two main labor parties of the Yishuv were founded in 1906. HaPoel HaZair was a purely Palestinian non-Marxist labor party influenced by A.D. Gordan's philosophy of the religion of labor and by the Russian Social Revolutionary Party. Poelei Zion was founded as the Palestinian branch of the European party and was an orthodox Marxist party that stressed a platform uniting socialism and Zionism. These two parties both published journals and established institutions aimed at satisfying the economic and cultural needs of their members. Together they founded the Agricultural Workers Union in 1912. In 1919 most of Poelei

Figure 1. **Splits and Mergers in the Israel Labor Parties***

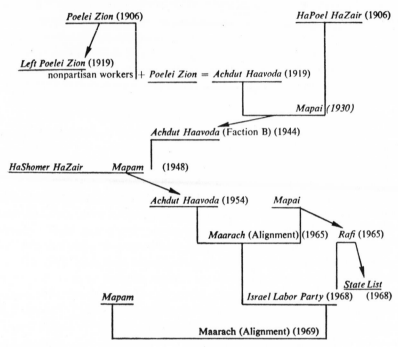

*Straight connecting lines indicate mergers and arrows indicate splits.

Zion, with the exception of its extreme left wing, united with nonpartisan workers to form Achdut Haavoda; together with HaPoel HaZair they founded the
General Federation of Jewish Labor (Histadrut) in 1920, which assumed all of
the economic and part of the cultural work of the two parties. Through the wide
scope of their voluntary activities at the critical stage of the development of these
main political and economic institutions of the Yishuv, the Kibbutz HaMeuchad
movement (founded 1927) gained access to positions of immense importance
and power in these institutions. In 1930 HaPoel HaZair and Achdut Haavoda
merged to form Mapai, which dominated all of the major political institutions of
the Yishuv and has remained the dominant political force in Israeli politics to the
present (cf. Y. Shapiro, 1976).

In the late 1930s and early 1940s a dissident faction within Mapai known as
Siya Bet (Faction B) formed around a group of members who constituted a
majority of the Kibbutz HaMeuchad movement. Aside from their interests within
the kibbutz movement, this faction was ideologically more favorably inclined to
Marxism than was the majority of the party. They also opposed the majority
position on the partition of Palestine. At the Party Conference in 1942 the major-

ity supported Ben-Gurion's proposal to ban all internal factional activity. Although this act was meant to avert a party split, it had the opposite effect. Siya Bet split from Mapai in 1944 and reconstituted itself as Achdut Haavoda, taking with it the majority of the Kibbutz HaMeuchad Federation (which later officially split off, whereby Mapai established Ichud HaKvutzot V'HaKibbutzim as its major settlement organization). In 1948 Achdut Haavoda united with HaShomer HaZair to form the Marxist Mapam Party, which provided Mapai with its major left-wing opposition in the elections to the first Knesset. However, the former Achdut Haavoda faction became increasingly disenchanted with Mapam's pro-Soviet orientation and split off in 1954, reconstituting itself as Achdut Haavoda.

During the early 1950s a group of leading members of Mapai's Young Guard (Zeirim) began making critical public statements about the lack of internal party democracy in decision making. When they held a nationwide conference calling for a Movement for Party Regeneration, the party leadership, with the memory of the bitter split of Siya Bet fresh in their minds, began to fear the possibility of the new faction's following suit. The Zeirim were challenged by the Tel Aviv–based national party machine, known as the Gush (bloc). The tension between these two protagonists broke out during the Eighth Mapai Conference in 1956. The Zeirim succeeded in mobilizing majority support for a constitutional amendment whereby the party Central Committee would be composed of 123 members, two-thirds of whom would be elected from the branches. This marked the only time in the history of Mapai (or of the Labor Party later) that a majority recommendation of the Standing Committee was defeated on the floor of the Conference. This victory was short-lived since the Gush succeeded in getting the Central Committee expanded later to 196 with the addition of their extra central appointments, thereby guaranteeing the continued domination of the party machine (cf. Medding, 1972). I shall demonstrate the historical continuity of the techniques of domination when I analyze the institutions and activities of the Labor Party.

Although there were several important social and ideological features that differentiated the older generation of the Gush from the Zeirim, their struggle became primarily a contest for control of the party and succession to the top leadership. The men of the Gush, as a whole, had no marketable skills other than their political experience, which was vast. They had worked their way up from the bottom of the party and Histadrut hierarchy and were dependent upon their party jobs for their livelihoods. The Zeirim had better formal educations and were not willing to work their way up from the bottom. Since they had not served long political apprenticeships, as had their Gush opponents, they were unable to build strongly entrenched power bases in the party administration to rival those of the Gush. The Zeirim were known as *bitzuistim*, those who get things done efficiently (technocrats), and they had no patience for the abstract ideological hair-splitting of the older generation. They sharply criticized the old-style pioneering symbolized by the Histadrut for its inefficiency and argued that the state should be the vanguard of pioneering. They emphasized scientific development, technological expertise, and efficiency, thereby arousing the wrath and opposition of the leaders of the Histadrut and the kibbutz movement who called for a return to the pioneering values of old. The state had incorporated into its jurisdiction the Defense Forces in 1948, the school systems in 1953, the employment bureau in 1958, and the call of leading Zeirim for nationalization of the Histadrut's health services precipitated a major conflict within the party over the boundaries of Histadrut and state jurisdiction.

The dominant factor was the major struggle for succession to the top leadership of the party and the nation. The catalyst for the major confrontation was the entry of Moshe Dayan into active politics upon his retirement as chief of staff of the Israel Defense Forces (IDF). Ben-Gurion was grooming a young cadre of protégés for Cabinet posts. They were Dayan; Shimon Peres, director-general of the ministry of defense, who was to become Ben-Gurion's deputy minister of defense (and who at the time of writing is the minister of defense); Abba Eban, Israel's ambassador to the United States and to the United Nations; and Dr. Giora Josephthal, the secretary-general of Mapai. This aroused the strong opposition of the Gush, leaders of the party and Histadrut bureaucracies, and particularly the secretary-general of the Histadrut, Pinchas Lavon, who as minister of defense had become embroiled in a bitter conflict with Dayan and Peres later known as the Lavon Affair (cf. Medding, 1972; Perlmutter, 1969). This major power struggle involved deep personal antagonisms, intergenerational conflict—which manifested itself in conflicting organizational interests (i.e., state and Histadrut)—and represented differences in style, values, and ideological positions.

The resignation of Ben-Gurion in 1963 brought in Levi Eshkol as prime minister, but raised the central question of who would succeed Eshkol. For the first time in Mapai history a collective leadership emerged with Eshkol, Golda Meir, Pinchas Sapir, and Zalman Aranne at the head. They in turn gathered around them a top group of Mapai leaders, which excluded the leaders of the Zeirim. The crisis was precipitated by the opening of serious negotiations aimed at an electoral alignment between Mapai and Achdut Haavoda. Mapai sought to increase its declining electoral strength and also hoped to obtain an absolute majority in the Knesset to avoid its great dependence on its coalition partners. However, one of the main reasons Mapai sought a merger with Achdut Haavoda was to bring in a leadership group that would neutralize the influence of Dayan and the other young protégés of Ben-Gurion whom the veteran leadership viewed as a threat to their continued dominant positions. The leaders of Achdut Haavoda—Yisrael Galili, Yigal Allon, and Yitzchak Ben-Aharon, all of whom had served as ministers in the past—constituted a generation between the veteran Mapai leadership and the younger Ben-Gurion protégés. Ideologically the Achdut Haavoda leaders were much closer to the old pioneering values than were the younger proponents of statism. The Zeirim correctly perceived the merger negotiations as a direct threat to their succession to highest political office.

Ben-Gurion openly opposed the terms of the Alignment with Achdut Haavoda, especially Mapai's agreement to drop proposals for electoral reform. He became involved in a bitter personal dispute with Eshkol over the latter's handling of the last stages of the Lavon Affair. The final showdown between the two leaders of Mapai was fought out in the tenth Party Conference in February 1965. On both major issues of the conference, the proposed Alignment with Achdut Haavoda and the attempt by Ben-Gurion to reopen the Lavon Affair, Eshkol defeated Ben-Gurion by a majority of approximately 60 percent against 40 percent. When Eshkol was nominated as Mapai's candidate for prime minister in the forthcoming election, Ben-Gurion announced he would head an opposition list called Rafi and was joined by many of his loyal supporters, including Dayan and Peres. The results of the election proved to be a decisive victory for Mapai under Eshkol's leadership. The Maarach (Alignment of Mapai and Achdut Haavoda) gained 36.7 percent of the vote to Rafi's 7.9 percent.

Unquestionably the most significant of several factors explaining the election results was that when the former Prime Minister David Ben-Gurion led his ardent supporters out of Mapai and into Rafi, they left control of the vast party apparatus in the hands of Prime Minister Levi Eshkol, Golda Meir, and Pinchas Sapir. In addition, many of Ben-Gurion's sympathizers did not leave Mapai to join him in Rafi. Many were dependent upon the party or its related institutions for their livelihoods, others feared jeopardizing their political careers on what they viewed as a gamble. As Medding succinctly summarized the elections, "Organization triumphed over charisma and institutional power over prophetic morality" (1972:279).

I draw the readers' attention to the contrasting histories of the constituent factions of the Labor Party. Poelei Zion existed for twenty-four years; it became Achdut Haavoda when it merged with nonpartisan workers in 1919, prior to its merger with HaPoel HaZair, which also had a twenty-four-year history. Achdut Haavoda was independent during thirteen of the twenty-one years between its original split from Mapai and its realignment with it in 1965. The main body of Mapai continued to function as an independent party throughout the same period. Both maintained their independent institutions during the period of their alignment in the Maarach. Rafi existed a brief two and a half years as an independent party. The separate histories of these groups are an important factor in explaining the nature of their relationships within the Labor Party.

Fusion: The Israel Labor Party, 1968–74

Less than three years after Rafi split from Mapai, and Mapai and Achdut Haavoda joined together in the Alignment (Maarach), all three parties merged to form the Israel Labor Party. In addition to the history of their previous relationships, the nature of their relationships during these last three years had a particularly strong impact on the factional system in the newly merged party. Mapai and

Achdut Haavoda had become very close to one another. Their alignment meant that they submitted a combined list of candidates to the Knesset under the name Maarach. They were therefore automatically partners in the coalition government, and very close working relationships developed among the top leaders of the parties in the Cabinet. Although each party maintained its separate institutions and kibbutz movements, they formed joint bodies of consultation which developed marked cooperation and convergence of views. A complete union of the two parties did not take place, however, because of resistance from within Achdut Haavoda's Kibbutz HaMeuchad movement and from within Mapai, particularly among those who were sympathetic to Rafi.

In contrast, Rafi had become rather isolated. The full impact of Rafi's electoral failure was particularly felt by its leaders, who for the first time in their lives were in the opposition. Having left the vast apparatus of Mapai's bureaucracy and resources, Rafi's leaders were left with little more than their personal popularity and the appeal of their party platform. In addition to its lack of resources, Rafi never really made a serious effort to build a strong central apparatus or an extensive network of local branches. It was also significant for future events that the Rafi leadership spent most of its time in opposition making bitter attacks on the Mapai leadership. However, there were initiatives, particularly from Mapai and Rafi leaders and activists in the kibbutz and moshav movements, to bring Rafi into a union with Mapai and Achdut Haavoda. In spite of the lack of enthusiasm on the part of the top Mapai leaders, events were soon to overtake them and their resistance to unification with Rafi. Among the main factors that led to this situation were the decline in Prime Minister Eshkol's prestige, which was linked to a serious economic recession, large-scale unemployment, a high rate of emigration (particularly among middle-class professionals), and an increasingly serious security situation, which came to a head in the crucial period before the war of June 1967.

During the month of May 1967 tension mounted as the threat of war became almost certain. The government was blamed for indecisiveness, and pressure mounted on Eshkol to relinquish the defense portfolio. Two major partners in the government coalition, the National Religious Party and the Independent Liberals, pressured for the inclusion of Rafi and Gahal (the major opposition party) in the Government of National Unity and received the support of powerful Mapai leaders of the Haifa and Tel Aviv machines and other Rafi sympathizers within Mapai. I shall demonstrate that the top Mapai leaders neither forgot nor forgave the Rafi sympathizers within Mapai and later punished them for what the Mapai leaders considered to be "disloyalty" during this crucial period. Public opinion also played an important role at this juncture, and it was one of the rare occasions in which public opinion has had an important impact on Israeli politics. Led by the press, there was wide public demand for Eshkol to relinquish the defense portfolio to Moshe Dayan. Eshkol could no longer withstand such combined pressure and finally was forced to invite Dayan to accept the defense ministry. Eshkol and his fellow top leaders never forgave the manner in which Dayan entered the Cabinet under the pressure of a national crisis and this was to affect their attitudes and actions toward Rafi when it reunited with them within the same party.

The formation of the Israel Labor Party was preceded by a long period of intensive negotiations led by Finance Minister Pinchas Sapir, who was to play a dominant role in future events as the first secretary-general of the united party. It was decided that the proportion of former party (faction) representation in the new party institutions would be Mapai 57.3 percent and the two remaining partners 21.35 percent each. Whereas the final agreement was unanimously accepted by the governing institutions of Achdut Haavoda, Rafi split over the issue, approximately 60 percent favoring the merger and 40 percent opposed. The majority of Rafi joined the Israel Labor Party, and a minority led by the venerable David Ben-Gurion established an independent State List.

The merger of the three former labor parties—Mapai, Achdut Haavoda, and Rafi—which formed the Israel Labor Party on January 21, 1968, took place within the context of a major struggle for succession to the control and leadership of the new party. The positions of the main protagonists were clear. Minister of Defense Moshe Dayan urged his colleagues in Rafi to join the Labor Party in order to fight to ensure that the prime minister would not be Levi Eshkol and that the finance minister would not be Pinchas Sapir (*Davar*, Dec. 14, 1967, quoted in Medding, 1972:298). Achdut Haavoda was making an equally clear bid for the succession of its leading contender at the time, Deputy Prime Minister and Minister of Education and Culture Yigal Allon. The key to the resolution of this contest became Finance Minister Pinchas Sapir, who had chaired the tripartite negotiating committee that formulated the terms under which the three parties were united. Sapir temporarily resigned as finance minister to become the first secretary-general of the newly united party. As if in response to Dayan's challenge, Sapir dominated the organization of a party census, internal party elections of delegates to the first National Party Conference, and through control of a series of extremely important nominating committees succeeded in gaining a dominant position in the Standing Committee, the new Central Committee, and among the new members of the Knesset. Sapir successfully dominated these party institutions through his absolute control of the party apparatus and its enormous resources, through expert use of traditional Mapai techniques of political manipulation, and by building a force based primarily on former Mapai loyalists. I shall examine this process as it relates to the main theme: the dynamics of factionalism in the Israel Labor Party.

Sapir began his massive organizational effort to mobilize political support during the party membership drive and census, which claimed to have enrolled approximately 300,000 party members. The drive was accomplished under the very close personal supervision of Sapir, who maintained daily contact with his central organization and the major branches even when he was temporarily out of the country. Sapir personally organized and supervised the party's election campaign in 1969, as he had done in 1965. As one high-ranking party official summarized the campaign, "Sapir ran the show" (Aronoff, 1972). Sapir consolidated his alliances with important national and local leaders throughout the country. For example, he used all of his considerable personal influence to gain the renomination of his close friend and political ally, Mayor Rabinowitz of Tel Aviv, thereby guaranteeing the continued loyal support of the Tel Aviv–based Gush. The intervention of Sapir on behalf of many local leaders who were his clients was general and effective. In this way, he guaranteed their continued support through the delegates these branches sent to the National Party Conference and the Central Committee. In several cases Sapir used his influence to prevent the nomination of candidates (for mayor, for example) who were known to be loyal to Rafi or Dayan. As one top party official explained, "Sapir was very interested in having his people as candidates rather than Dayan's boys or someone else's. Sapir talked to people and backed those he could trust" (cf. Aronoff, 1972).

Although Sapir returned to his post as minister of finance after the 1969 election and was replaced as secretary-general of the party by Arie (Lyova) Eliav, he continued informally to dominate the party apparatus. This is seen most clearly in the contradictory goals of Sapir and his successor. Eliav, who had been among those who pressed for the inclusion of Rafi in the Labor Party, worked conscientiously toward the unification of the party through close cooperation with his deputies from the former Rafi and Achdut Haavoda. Meanwhile, in his campaign to build a strong machine based on the former Mapai, Sapir worked to undermine the former Rafi, particularly the members of Mapai who were suspected sympathizers of Rafi or supporters of Moshe Dayan.

The single most important variable to influence the outcome of the internal party elections to the Party Conference was that the organizational apparatus which directed the election was controlled by the top Mapai leadership. In spite of the secretary-general's sincere efforts to reconcile the previous party factions and to achieve genuine cooperation between them, the main efforts of the party apparatus, of which he was not in control, were directed at the mobilization of the branches in solid support of the top Mapai leadership led by Sapir. In addition to the 2,206 delegates to the Conference elected from the branches, an additional 735 were appointed by a central Nominations Committee and represented an overwhelming majority of Sapir loyalists, particularly from the Tel Aviv Gush. In short, the national Mapai leadership went into the Party Conference with a significant majority of Conference delegates on whom they could rely for support.

But the Mapai leadership did not rely solely on its majority support in the Conference. There is an extremely important institution that in a very real sense controls the Conference. This institution is known as the Standing Committee. This committee was in fact the real Conference. Representing all of the major interest groups and factions of which the party is composed, it drew up a new party constitution, debated, compromised, and formulated policy on a wide range of issues; it struck from the agenda those controversial issues that the top party leadership wished to suppress and prevent from being debated in the Conference, and most importantly, it approved the new Central Committee, 45 percent of which had been appointed by a small subcommittee of the Standing Committee.

I shall return to a more detailed discussion of this important committee in forthcoming chapters. For purposes of the present analysis, it is sufficient to point out that the Standing Committee decided that the new Central Committee would be composed of 501 members, two-thirds of which would be elected by the branch caucuses of delegates to the Party Conference, and one-third of which would be selected by a central Nominations Committee. However, after the branch caucuses elected their representatives to the new Central Committee, the central Nominations Committee demanded and received permission to appoint an extra 100 places on an expanded Central Committee. This obviously increased the influence of the top party leaders of the three factions who met separately to appoint their portions of the 267 seats from the central list, which were: Mapai 165; Rafi 50; and Achdut Haavoda 52. The results of the elections of the branch caucuses in the Conference proved the effectiveness of Sapir's organizational campaign whereby Mapai increased its majority from its previous 57.3 percent to roughly two-thirds, largely at the expense of Rafi. The results were: Mapai 233; Rafi 38; and Achdut Haavoda 63. The total factional representation on the new Central Committee of 601 (which was later expanded with the addition of Arab and Druze representatives) was: Mapai 398 (66 percent); Rafi 88 (15 percent); and Achdut Haavoda 115 (19 percent). The composition of the new party executive structure as compared to the 1968 forumla thus represented both a strengthening of the position of top party leaders of all three factions relative to regular party activists, and a strengthening of the Mapai faction relative both to Achdut Haavoda and especially to Rafi.

Decline of the Faction System in the Mid-1970s

The traumatic Yom Kippur War of October 1973 precipitated major changes in Israel's party system and in the Labor Party's faction system. The war went particularly badly for Israel in its early stages, and the leadership of the Labor Party bore the brunt of widespread and severe criticism for what were perceived as near-fatal errors in the preparation for and handling of the war. Criticism and demonstrations eventually brought down the government and led to a turnover in Labor Party leadership. Ultimately, the aftermath of the war resulted in a major restructuring of the factional composition of the entire Labor Party. I will mention briefly some of the more important developments relating to factionalism. These developments are analyzed in greater depth in Chapter 8.

Following the conclusion of the war, as public criticism grew, internal party criticism grew as well. Party conflicts centered on leadership—especially the leadership in the government—and on policy. Many wanted Moshe Dayan's resignation as defense minister; some wanted the resignation of Prime Minister Golda Meir as well. In policy matters, party strongman Sapir sought a change in party policy on several fronts. At a private meeting of top party leaders before the first party Central Committee meeting after the war, Sapir won agreement on his own platform in a compromise, which entailed his continued support for Meir's heading the government, and agreement not to reopen the party lists for candidates in the upcoming elections to the Knesset (which had been postponed due to the outbreak of war).

The Central Committee's meeting in November 1973 was a stormy, day-and-night-long affair. There were attacks on and defenses of individual leaders, particularly Dayan. There was a confrontation over Sapir's platform, particularly with regard to its taking precedence over the party's previous policy, the Galili Statement (so named for its drafter, Yisrael Galili, a leader of the Achdut Haavoda faction). Factional competition played an important role in both personality and policy issues. Yigal Allon, the second-ranking leader of Achdut Haavoda and his faction's leading contender for the premiership, not only attacked Dayan but repudiated the Galili Statement. Dayan and Golda Meir supported the view that the Galili Statement remained in force as party policy; however, Meir did not defend Dayan against attacks on his mishandling of the war. In the end, the meeting avoided a showdown by contriving a ruling that each party member could follow his own interpretation of the status of the previous policy.

In the selection of the party's candidates for the 1973 Knesset elections, the top leaders of all three factions agreed to retain the same numerical positions on the list that each faction had on the party's list in the 1969 election, and they also agreed that each faction would decide on its own candidates. This was in direct contradiction to the decision taken four years previously, which said that the Labor Party candidates for the Knesset would be chosen in a secret election on a nonfactional basis. When one of the rebellious members of the Central Committee challenged the legitimacy of the *en bloc* list submitted by the Mapai faction's nominating committee, basing her charges on the previous decision to have secret open elections, she was rebuffed by the secretary-general who claimed that the unification of the party had not progressed sufficiently to enable it to implement the prior decision. He claimed that "under the circumstances democracy can only work within the previous party factions." The nature of the internal faction democracy was exemplified by the Leadership Bureau's appointment of Pinchas Sapir as chairman of the Nominations Committee, whose members he then proceeded to choose. Authorization of this Nominations Committee was retroactively given by the members of the Central Committee when the Nominations Committee presented its list of candidates to the Knesset for their approval.

Thus, leaders of all three factions were in agreement not to open the party's nominations for intraparty election but to keep candidate choice in the hands of the respective faction leaders. Galili of Achdut Haavoda, Meir of Mapai, and Dayan of Rafi were strongly in support of renewed party approval of the Galili Statement, while Sapir of Mapai and Allon of Achdut Haavoda supported the exclusive applicability of the Sapir platform. Dayan was defended by leaders of Rafi against the attacks of many leaders of Mapai and Achdut Haavoda, although some spokesmen of both groups, including Prime Minister Meir, attempted to remain neutral. These confrontations indicated a renewal of ideologically oriented policy goals, which became a part of the factional competition for power but also led to alignments cutting across old factional divisions at the highest levels of party leadership.

In the Knesset elections, held in December 1973, the Labor Party lost substantial voter support. Although still by far the largest party, its parliamentary plurality diminished by enough seats that the coalition formula of the previous government would now not quite produce a majority. Golda Meir was given the presidential mandate to form a government; but this had now become an increasingly difficult charge, and the country was in a government crisis for some nine weeks, from January to March 1974. The Labor Party itself moved perilously near to breakup in those weeks. Dayan and Shimon Peres, the first and second leaders of Rafi, refused to join Meir's proposed minority government. They complained bitterly about the extreme criticisms of Dayan, which intensified in the early weeks of 1974 in both the mass media and internal party forums such as the party newspaper *Ot*. In February 1974 it was Meir who became the most outspoken voice of growing fears that the party was headed for a split. Eventually she announced her "final decision"—that she was giving up her quest for the formation of a new government—and the crisis became a crisis of the country's dominant party as well.

In early March the Labor Central Committee held a fateful meeting in which factional strife brought the party to the brink of open rupture. Golda Meir succeeded in establishing a minority government which both Dayan and Peres eventually joined. However, the combination of pressures from newly emergent protest groups and internal critics eventually led to the resignation of Golda Meir in the spring of 1974.

Meir's resignation resulted in the party's first open competitive elections in the Central Committee for her successor as the party's choice for the premiership. Pinchas Sapir's backing of Yitzchak Rabin gave him the edge in a close competition with Shimon Peres. Since he had never been formally affiliated with a faction, Rabin became the first prime minister of Israel who was not a member of Mapai. Although the Mapai faction was clearly represented in the government formed by Rabin, it had lost several key ministerial posts.

Rabin moved the Labor Party away from the factional structure that was built into it in 1968 and had almost brought the party to a breakup by 1973. He built a new coalition based on the support of the major big-city machines, and was successful in working around and diminishing the significance of the once-established factions. The effort to abolish the old factions gained considerable support in the branches that asserted their own bids to gain greater influence. The decline of the Labor Party's old system of factionalism weakened the traditionally strong party discipline in voting in the Knesset and contributed to the emergence of new, ideologically oriented factional groups among the party's Knesset members. A group of about twenty members of the Alignment (Maarach) of Labor and Mapam in the Knesset formed a leftist, dovish caucus, called the Free Platform, which met regularly and demonstratively abstained on motions sponsored by the government. An activist wing of Labor Party Knesset members reacted by organizing their own caucus—named after the late Yitzchak Tabenkin, a former leader of Achdut Haavoda who was outspoken in his views that territories occupied after the 1967 war belonged to the historic Eretz Yisrael (Land of Israel).

A more extreme manifestation of such developments was the exodus from the party of a few dissident members who formed a new political party of their own. Former Mapai Labor Knesset member Shulamit Aloni first established a Civil Rights List in the 1973 election and succeeded in winning three Knesset mandates. Former secretary-general of the Labor Party, Knesset member Arie (Lyova) Eliav, also left the party for a newly formed one. These defections were precursors of larger defections from Labor that accompanied the formation of the Democratic Movement for Change in 1977—a significant factor in bringing about Labor's first historic electoral defeat.

Conclusions

The factional system in Israel is related to the country's historical and cultural background: an institutional framework of proportional representation and a multi-party system, which suited the nonsovereign and ideologically plural character of the World Zionist Organization and the pre-state Jewish Yishuv in Palestine. The consolidation of a multiplicity of parties and factions with considerable resources and vested interests, gained largely through the institutionalization of the division of patronage, led to the continuation of the proportional representation system in the post-Independence period. Israel had two major Labor parties since the beginning of the century; the two merged to form Mapai in 1930. They did so in order to consolidate their control of the quasi-governmental institutions of the Histadrut (which they had created) and the representative institutions of the Yishuv. Mapai then gained a dominant position in the major institutions of the Jewish Agency, which monopolized the allocation of the major resources available to the society-in-the-making.

In this concluding analysis of the role of factionalism, I return to M.G. Smith's characteristics of corporateness: boundedness, determinate membership, identity, organization, procedure, common affairs, autonomy, and presumed perpetuity.

Siya Bet was not originally a corporate group, being based to a large extent on a generational difference within Mapai. It expressed a comprehensive ideological orientation of its own in the form of a more Marxist interpretation of socialism, and it had specific national policies, such as opposition to the partition of Palestine. Its major source of strength was the institutional framework of the Kibbutz HaMeuchad movement in Mapai. As its struggle with the Mapai leadership intensified, the Siya Bet progressively acquired greater structural corporateness, chiefly by consolidating its organizational strength around the kibbutz movement, which provided it with sufficient autonomy eventually to leave Mapai altogether.

The 1948–54 Mapam Party existed entirely as a bifactional union, each faction retaining a distinctly corporate character and an independent resource base, especially in the form of its separate kibbutz federation. While ideological agreement on interpretations of socialism was a factor in the merger of these factions, and differing ideological positions toward Moscow were a factor in their split, it was not coincidental that both the merger and the split immediately preceded major national election campaigns. Electoral strategy thus played an important, if not dominant, role in both decisions. The Mapam Party of 1948–54 was a political marriage of convenience between two ideologically compatible partners and it lasted as long as it was deemed politically worthwhile for both. Electoral strategy played an important role in subsequent splits and mergers.

The decreasing importance of ideology reflected significant societal changes that took place at this historical juncture. The mass absorption of immigrants, first from the displaced persons camps of Europe and then from the Islamic states; the gradual taking over by the state of the multiple functions previously performed by the political movements; the developing economy, and so forth, all had an impact on the political system. The monopolization of resources and power in the institutions of the state, and their domination by Mapai—with its unique system of internal nominations and competition and its reliance on coalition partners to rule—all had an impact on the developing factional system.

The Zeirim, or Young Guard, which coalesced as a faction around David Ben-Gurion, was on the whole not a corporate group. Like Siya Bet, the Zeirim consisted largely of younger intraparty rivals of the established Mapai leadership. Although generational differences were expressed in different styles, such as technocratic youth versus machine-type veteran professionals, and although they became involved in ideological debates over their differing interpretations of the proper roles of the Histadrut and the state, the dominant conflict was the competition for succession to the leadership of the party and the nation.

The pattern of factional strife within Mapai had a distinctly noncorporate character in that it was based on the competition between a strong charismatic leader, Ben-Gurion, and the group led by Eshkol, which controlled the party machinery, and their respective followers. The confrontation and the ultimate split of Ben-Gurion and many, although not all, of his followers, highlighted the absence of formal constitutional methods of leadership selection in Mapai. These same aspects of the nominations process were to play a crucial role in shaping factional competition in the Israel Labor Party. The nominations process is the focus of Chapter 3.

The structural features of the three main constituent factions of the Labor Party differ significantly in corporate characteristics, as well as in the effects of these structural differences on the factional competition. Table 2.1 summarizes the comparison of the corporate structural characteristics of the three constituent factions of the Labor Party from 1968 to 1974. After discussing them, I evaluate the major ramifications of factional competition for the party and for the political system as a whole.

Rafi was the least corporate of the three. The boundedness and the degree to which membership could be clearly identified were least clear in the Rafi faction. Not all of those who sympathized with Rafi's cause left Mapai when Rafi was formed as a splinter party; Rafi policy after its remerger with the Labor Party was deliberately to perpetuate this lack of clarity as to the boundedness and identity of its membership. Thus during the party census organized immediately after the merger, the Rafi leadership instructed its members and sympathizers not to answer the question that asked for former party affiliation. Their explanation was that they wished to avoid possible sanctions or discrimination against their members and sympathizers. Given the policies of the Sapir-dominated Mapai faction, this was not an unrealistic fear. For this reason it was clearly to the advantage of the Rafi sympathizers who had remained within Mapai to refrain from identifying themselves. It is also likely that the Rafi leaders wished to avoid the embarrassment of having had it proved that their membership was considerably smaller than they had claimed. For it should be kept in mind that the charismatic leader around whom Rafi had originally formed, Ben-Gurion, opposed the merger within the Labor Party, and a significant minority of the former Rafi party members remained with Ben-Gurion in the opposition and did not join the Labor Party.

Rafi was also organizationally the weakest of the three factions in the Labor Party. Rafi never really organized a sound party apparatus during its brief two-and-a-half-year independent existence. It lacked the time, the resources, and the inclination to organize a national bureaucracy and a coordinated network of local branches. In some cases, local branches of Rafi had been legal fictions, created by local factions or groups to compete in the national election campaign of 1965 (cf. Aronoff, 1974a). Even after the merger, Rafi's leaders, particularly Dayan, showed no inclination to meet the challenge of engaging in practical political organization at either the national or local level. During the factional competition of the census and membership drive, the internal party elections to the Conference, and the selection of the new party institutions, the procedures, tactics, and style of Rafi were the least well organized and the most ad hoc, that is, the least corporate of the three factions. Rafi ignored organization and, for its continued existence as a group, relied almost exclusively on the appeal of the personalities

Table 2.1

Comparative Corporate Characteristics of the Factions

Corporate Features	Faction		
	Rafi	Mapai	Achdut Haavoda
Boundedness Determinate Membership Identity	Least Clear	Clear	Clearest
Organization	Weakest	Strong	Strongest
Procedure	Ad Hoc	Informal	Formal
Comprehensiveness of Common Affairs	Least	Intermediary	Most
Autonomy Achieved Through	Threat of Split	Dominance	Independent Institutions
Presumed Perpetuity	Least Likely	Likely	Most Likely

of its leaders and its platforms. Rafi's procedures were mainly confined to informal meetings among small groups of leaders and irregular meetings of leaders with followers. Eventually, after realizing that there was an organized campaign against them, they began meeting in more formal and larger caucuses.

Rafi members primarily shared loyalty to their charismatic former leader, David Ben-Gurion, and to their more recent leader, Moshe Dayan, who many perceived as charismatic. They shared similar policy views on topics ranging from the need for electoral reform to more conservative policies on social and economic matters, and more militant security and foreign policies. They also shared ties in an elaborate network of patron–client relationships, which joined local to national leaders. Rafi had the least independent resources of all factions. It had neither a kibbutz federation nor a newspaper of its own, nor did it have any of the other institutional resources of the other two factions. The only patronage that Rafi leaders could provide their followers was their modest quota of membership on party institutions, offices, and jobs, and the status and rewards linked to them. One of the key features of these patron–client ties is that they provide the most important, if not almost exclusive, paths to upward political mobility.

The autonomy of Rafi was conditional in that its existence was dependent on the actions of the other two factions, particularly Mapai. Rafi was successful in protecting its position and in gaining concessions by exploiting the ultimate threat of splitting off from the party. In addition to ideological and practical considerations in favor of maintaining the unity of the party, the potential threat that the previously highly popular Rafi leadership might join forces with the opposition at a time when the margin between Labor's lead over the opposition was closing, and when for reasons resulting from factional competition within the National Religious Party the support of Labor's traditional coalition partner was becoming increasingly less secure, was a strong inducement to keep Rafi within the party fold.

Finally, Rafi is the least corporate with regard to presumed perpetuity. Most of its leadership indicated they desire integration within the Israel Labor Party. If the policies of Rabin's new coalition succeed, and they appear to be supported by a substantial majority of the party, then it would seem likely that this integration will take place, and Rafi as it existed in the past will be no more. However, it is likely that certain personal ties and relationships between former Rafi members would continue to have an influence even in a more truly united Labor Party. If the new coalition does not succeed in unifying the party to a much greater extent than in the past, and particularly if the attempts to reconstitute the Mapai faction succeed and if the Mapai faction leaders follow their former policy of undermining Rafi, then it is likely that a substantial section of the Rafi faction would again split off from the party and either set up an independent party or join their former colleagues in the State List, which has joined the opposition Likud Alignment. In either case the continued existence of Rafi as an active faction within the Labor Party is most unlikely.

The second junior partner of the Labor Party, Achdut Haavoda, appears to be clearly the most corporate of the three. The long history of independent existence of Achdut Haavoda produced a membership that is clearly bounded and whose identity can be easily determined. It has a well-organized institutional framework, both in the form of its Kibbutz HaMeuchad movement, which has maintained its autonomy within the framework of the Labor Party, and in its local urban branches. Although the formerly autonomous urban branches of Achdut Haavoda were integrated into the branches of the Labor Party, they continued generally to maintain a sense of their separate identity and interests and met regularly as a factional caucus to determine common policy.

Achdut Haavoda's shared common affairs include the most well articulated ideology among the three factions. This ideology is both more doctrinaire socialist and more militant in security and foreign policy than that of the more pragmatic Mapai. Achdut Haavoda had its own autonomous newspaper, which only fairly recently merged with that of the Histadrut. It has also benefited from special representation in the Conference and in other party institutions, which is guaranteed to the members of kibbutzim in the Labor Party. These independently organized institutions and resources have given Achdut Haavoda the greatest degree of autonomy among the three factions in the Labor Party.

Given the fact that it manifests the most corporate structure and has the most independent institutions and resources, Achdut Haavoda is the most likely to perpetuate itself in the future in its present form. Although there is some support among its leadership for a genuine integration within the Labor Party, there is also resistance to this trend. Such resistance might slow down or even prevent the complete assimilation of the faction; nevertheless, there is no significant movement in the faction to split from the Labor Party, and it is generally thought that such a move would be contrary to the interests of Achdut Haavoda as well as Labor as a whole. Since Achdut Haavoda has increased the strength of its position recently—by having gained the foreign ministry for Allon and by having a prime minister, Rabin, who is considered by the faction to be sympathetic and close to the faction—it is highly unlikely that it will split from the Labor Party in the foreseeable future.

The Mapai faction fits into an intermediate position between its two junior partners on the corporate scale. The identity of its membership is generally clearly bounded, but the exact identity of those former Mapai members who remained sympathetic toward Rafi is not always easy to determine. The core of the faction was a strong, well-organized, but informal party machine consolidated by Sapir and dominated by him, at least until the party crisis in 1974. The common affairs were primarily the elaborate network of patron–client relationships, which successfully gained control of the majority of positions on party institutions, and those of the Histadrut and other affiliated or party-dominated institutions, which gained control of the majority of offices and patronage derived from the resources controlled by the party as a whole. Mapai did not have autonomous institutions other than those of the Labor Party since it successfully dominated the apparatus and institutions of the Labor Party as a whole through the successful efforts of its informal machine. The current struggle for power and control of the Labor Party will determine whether, if Prime Minister Rabin and his coalition succeed, Mapai as a distinct unit will cease to exist in a united Labor Party, or, if Abba Eban and others are successful, Mapai will be formally reconstituted as a faction that will continue to dominate the Labor Party and thereby perpetuate the politics of factionalism in its traditional form.

Finally, it remains for us to consider some of the major functional and political consequences of factional competition for the development of the party and for the political system in general. I have stressed the primary function of the factions in the mobilization of support for the competitive struggle for control of the party's national institutions. It is significant that while factional affiliation played a dominant role in the competition for representation in these institutions, it played a relatively minor role in determining the stands of the participants in the debates in these institutions. This contrasts sharply with both the earlier historical period, when ideological issues played a more important role in factional relationships, and the most recent period, when the old factional divisions based on former party affiliation appear to be breaking down and new ideologically oriented factions are developing in the Knesset's party caucus.

The major function of the factions in the Labor Party from its formation in 1968 to its crisis in 1974 (when the new coalition of internal party forces began to alter significantly the balance of power and factional relationships) was processing competition for representation in party institutions and for acquisition and distribution of power and resources, and providing the main channel of upward mobility in the networks of intrafactional patron–client relationships. The factional base, together with the system of nominations, enabled the top factional leaders to renominate themselves, their protégés, and their clients to all important institutions. The retention of control of the party was the raison d'être for the continuation of factional politics in the Labor Party from 1968 to 1974, and retention of positions is the primary reason for the resistance to the complete integration of the party. These points are amplified in forthcoming chapters.

Historically, such convenient techniques of domination and control have generally benefited the nation as well as its leadership because they contributed stability and continuity to a regime faced with enormous problems of national integration and development, such as the absorption of culturally diverse mass immigration and staggering problems of defense. The factional system performed an additional function for the highly pluralistic mass party—that of providing an additional institutional tie of loyalty that cut across other ethnic, geographic, and interest group ties. Factions thereby helped to prevent a possible polarization along any of these lines and contributed to overall party cohesion (cf. Simmel, 1908; Coser, 1956; and Gluckman, 1955, 1965, for theoretical elaborations of this theme).

Factionalism has not had an altogether beneficial impact on the character of the party and operation of the political system as a whole. Factional splits in Mapai highlighted the absence of formal constitutional methods of leadership selection. The use of nominations committees in the absence of direct and open intraparty elections called into question the legitimacy of the party institutions and left minority factions without any avenue of legitimate appeal to the party membership, or to the electorate, within the party framework. As Medding (1972:279) observed,

> While organizational strength was an advantage for Mapai, tight control by a small group neither directly chosen by nor responsible to the rank and file was a serious disadvantage because it intensified internal opposition that might have been muted by the existence of party bodies enjoying the unquestioned support of rank and file electoral choice and support.

The continuation of these same procedures after the formation of the Israel Labor Party was one of the primary factors that contributed to the perpetuation of factional competition within the party.

Moreover, to the extent that factional politics concentrated on competition for representation in party institutions, it largely detracted from recruitment on the basis of merit. Factional competition leads to bargaining for offices. Each faction attempts to maximize its power and status at the expense of the others; they neglect to find the most qualified party persons to fill the jobs for which they are best suited. This has been abundantly illustrated in squabbling over ministerial portfolios, and is indeed characteristic of most local branch politics. Through the use of nominations committees, national and local patrons perpetuate themselves, their clients, and their allies in power without direct open election. New or opposition groups have no avenue of direct appeal to the party membership or to the electorate; internal opposition tends to become at first intensified, and then alienated, and/or co-opted. This situation has led to almost universal feelings of political inefficacy among branch activists; the same phenomenon is also widespread among members of the major national institutions and among party functionaries, some of the consequences of which are explored in forthcoming chapters.

The fact that the top leadership had lost touch with the rank and file and the general public was vividly demonstrated in the developments that followed the traumatic events of the October 1973 war. When the nation most needed dynamic leadership with fresh approaches to critical problems, the Labor Party became embroiled in an internal factional squabble over the distribution of Cabinet posts. Several high-ranking party officials expressed to me their feelings that through such behavior the party was committing suicide, and if drastic measures were not taken to alter the situation, not only would the government soon fall, but the public would surely vote the party out of power for the first time in the history of Israeli politics.

Factional strife directly contributed to the instability of Rabin's government. The demands of the extreme youth faction of Mafdal (National Religious Party) prevented that faction's participation in the government for several months and makes its continued participation questionable if and when the government will have to make decisions about the return of occupied territories. The government's shaky majority in the Knesset is under constant harassment by the organized and coordinated efforts of all of the main parties of the opposition, and by the challenge of the new Knesset factions, which threaten to break down party discipline completely. Under such circumstances the government's future on critical votes is constantly threatened. This is a most serious situation for a government that almost daily faces decisions that could mean the difference between war and peace.

This negative impact of factionalism on the political system as a whole is of great significance: Its short-term effects are likely to contribute to greater instability of the present government. Its long-range effects may well contribute to the renewal and formulation of ideological positions in party policy which could bring about a more vigorous commitment of party leaders and members to new policies more realistically aimed at solving some of the major problems facing Israeli society. Factionalism, in the long run, may also contribute to new splits in the party. Both are possible.

There are reciprocal relationships among the stages of mobilization and institutionalization of political support, and the changing role of ideology—its meaning and importance for the various actors in the political process, and its capacity to be effectively related to the major problems confronting the political institutions in question. All aspects of these interrelated variables must be examined if we are to understand factional politics and its impact on the wider socio-political environment.

Factionalism in the labor parties of Israel emerged as a fairly flexible means of routinizing relationships among latent groups with competing ideologies, interests, and styles within the larger institutional framework of the party. At different stages in the development of the political system, ideology has played a greater or lesser role in factional competition. When factional strife became almost exclusively a manifestation of a struggle for power and control of the party, its impact on the party and on the political system became increasingly negative. Whereas the various splits and mergers to a certain extent allowed for adaptation of the parties to general social changes, the failure of the factional competition to produce new policy alternatives in solution of new problems from the late fifties through the early sixties had serious ramifications which were manifest in the aftermath of the war in 1973. In the chapters immediately following, I explore various aspects of party structure, proceedings, and culture. These have led to the significant changes in the most recent period, which are discussed in later chapters.

3

The Power of Nominations

"He who can make nominations is the owner of the party."
—E.E. Schattschneider

Introduction

One of the most important and yet little-known aspects of the Israeli political system is the process by which the parties nominate candidates to their internal institutions and to the Knesset. This is particularly surprising and unfortunate, given the consensus among most students of parties as to the central role of the nominations process. For example, Austin Ranney (1966) has pointed out the general agreement with the famous proposition by E.E. Schattschneider (1942:64) that

> The nominating process . . . has become the crucial process of the party. The nature of the nominating procedure determines the nature of the party; he who can make nominations is the owner of the party. This is therefore one of the best points at which to observe the distribution of power within the party.

Although I concentrate in this chapter on the nominations process in the Labor Party, I stress the similarity of this process in most other Israeli parties. I shall attempt to show that in order to understand the process by which candidates are selected to Israel's parliament, the Knesset, it is necessary to analyze a series of linked nominations beginning with the key committees that controlled the first National Party Conference of the newly united Labor Party (April 1971), the selection of the present Central Committee, and finally the nomination of the party's list of candidates to the Eighth Knesset elections (December 1973).

The traditional method of nominating candidates to internal party institutions and selecting the party's candidates to the Knesset has been through a small committee generally known as the Nominations Committee (*vaadat minuim*). The Nominations Committee is appointed by the top party leadership, who generally choose their most trusted lieutenants from the second echelon of leadership to represent their views and interests on the committee. The Nominations Committee is charged with balancing the demands for representation of the various internal party factions and interest groups, and with assuring that those chosen are loyal to their patrons in the top leadership. The list, once compiled by the Nominations Committee, is submitted *en bloc* to the larger party institution, which has constitutional authority to make the nomination. I stress the ceremonial nature of this legitimating vote, since I could not find a single case in which the list proposed by the Nominations Committee was not accepted.

The constitutional structure of authority in the Labor Party resembles a four-tiered pyramid. The membership (approximately 300,000) elect delegates to the National Party Conference (2,206) through internal party elections in the eighty-four branches, the kibbutz and moshav movements; a proportion (735) were selected by a central nominating committee. Constitutionally, this body is supreme, but since it meets irregularly (once every few years) it delegates its authority to a Central Committee, which it theoretically elects. The increasing demands for representation on the Central Committee have expanded its size to unwieldy proportions (presently over 600 members) necessitating the delegation of authority to a Secretariat elected by the Central Committee. [At the time of publication of this second edition the Central Committee had more than doubled to approximately 1,300.] The Secretariat in turn delegates authority to the Leadership Bureau, which it elects. This body is the smallest official party institution that meets regularly, but many important decisions are taken by even smaller informal constellations of top party leaders.

There is an inverse relationship between constitutional supremacy and real power that is most blatant in the Party Conference, the proceedings and decisions of which are dominated and controlled by an institution known as the Preparation Committee before the Conference, and the Standing Committee during the Conference.

The Preparation/Standing Committee

The Standing Committee began as a 26-man Constitutional Committee which was approved by the Secretariat on April 29, 1970, and charged with submitting a proposal for a new party constitution. A prominent member of the Knesset, among others, objected strongly to the "undemocratic" manner in which the committee had been nominated. The Leadership Bureau had authorized the Team of Secretaries (the party secretary-general and his two deputies) to make the nominations, which were then submitted to the larger party institution for approval *en bloc*. I will show shortly that the new Central Committee was nominated in a similar manner. To the 26 members of the Constitutional Committee were added all 33 members of the Leadership Bureau (the top formal party institution), 25 members who were selected by a nominating committee composed of the Team of Secretaries and Yisrael Yeshayahu (chairman of the Constitutional Committee), and 50 members nominated by the party branches according to a special key. The composition of the Standing Committee was completely decided by its nominating committee, headed by Yeshayahu, in coordination with the Leadership Bureau; only later was it brought to the Central Committee for approval of the list of 134 members as a whole. I stress that an overwhelming majority of the Standing Committee was composed of the secondary level of national leadership who were nominated by the top national leaders. Even among those elected by the branches, the majority were dependent upon the party for their livelihoods and career advancement. This was not an insignificant factor in the molding of a consensus in the committee.

The most striking feature about the composition of the committee was that almost all of its members were secondary-level leaders who were highly dependent upon the party and its top leadership. Indeed, 86 percent were ministers, members of the Knesset, mayors, secretaries of Local Workers' Councils or party branches, and functionaries in the party and Histadrut or affiliated enterprises and institutions. The top party leadership had carefully selected the composition of the Standing Committee, and even among the 37 percent elected from the branches, most were party functionaries, including representatives of the kibbutz and moshav movements. Regardless of their subdivisions into various interest groups and former party factions, the membership of the Standing Committee had been selected for their dependence upon and loyalty to the top leadership and they came from a distinctive socio-political category.

Although the numbers of the "Oriental" Jews from North Africa and the Middle East and Ashkenazim from Europe are roughly equal in the party (39 percent and 38 percent, respectively), the disproportionate representation of these two categories on the Standing Committee (see Table 3.1) largely reflects the fact that the Eastern Europeans are the veterans who came in at the earliest period and who built and continue to dominate the party and its most important institutions. Older age categories are also disproportionately overrepresented on the Standing Committee, as are males (who constitute only 54 percent of the general party membership). (See Chapter 6 for an analysis of representation in national party institutions.) In short, although the membership of the Standing Committee was in many respects not truly representative of the party membership at large, it was truly representative of the top and secondary level of party leadership and functionaries, and formed a cadre that could be relied on to represent the various factional interests, compromise their differences, serve the interests of the top party leadership, and preserve and strengthen the unity of the party. This was the primary task of the Standing Committee.

Determining the Composition of the Central Committee

By far the single most important task of the Standing Committee, in terms of its bearing on relationships of power within the party, was the selection of the new

Table 3.1

Characteristics of Standing Committee Members Expressed in Rounded Percentages

Place of Birth	%	Age	%	Sex	%
North Africa and Middle East	15	73+	4	Male	87
Eastern Europe	52	50–72	59	Female	13
Western Europe and United States	9	36–49	33		
Israel	22	35–	3		
Unknown	2	Unknown	1		
Total	100		100		100

Central Committee. This was without doubt the issue that aroused the greatest interest, participation, and tension during all of its meetings. In his introduction of the various proposals for the election of the new Central Committee, the chairman of the Standing Committee, Y. Yeshayahu (the present Speaker of the Knesset) stressed what was to become the theme of the activities of the committee and the symbol of the style of his leadership of its meetings. He emphasized: "Whatever we do we must decide in this committee. If it [the debate] goes to the Conference, that will kill it. *We must finish it here!*"

The main debate over the manner in which the new Central Committee should be elected revolved around proposals for the different ratios that should be elected by the branches and those that should be appointed through a central Nominations Committee. The smaller and medium-sized branches condemned the traditional domination of the Central Committee by the two or three major branches and the kibbutz movements, all of which are overrepresented on these bodies. The groups and interests that were behind the political maneuvering on this issue were very clear. The two spokesmen who persistently demanded an immediate decision on the issue were Abraham Ofer, the protégé and personal representative of Finance Minister Pinchas Sapir on the Standing Committee, and Mayor Rabinowitz of Tel Aviv, Sapir's close political ally. Chairman Yeshayahu stressed that he wanted all differences to be resolved in the Standing Committee because "We want to come out of this conference a united party!" After a lengthy debate, the members of the committee decided that two-thirds would be elected from the branches and one-third would be appointed from the central list.

A committee composed of the chairman of the Standing Committee, the secretary-general, and his two deputies was authorized to nominate two subcommittees. One subcommittee was to decide how the branches would elect their share. The second subcommittee was to appoint the one-third from the national list to the Central Committee. Both key subcommittees were clearly dominated by loyal representatives of the top Mapai leaders. There was never a vote or even a sense of the meeting being about accepting the nominations to these two key subcommittees. Yeshayahu merely gave the vote fictitious legitimization by announcing the appointment of the subcommittees. The whole episode was a masterpiece of manipulation with far-reaching political ramifications.

The decision as to how the branch vote would be administered was far from merely a technical question. Since it had been decided that the branches would elect 334 representatives (three-fourths) from the new Central Committee, which was supposed to be 501 members strong, there were two likely means of allocation. The first would be to divide 334 into the 2,206 elected delegates to the Party Conference, which would produce a formula dictating that 6.6 Conference delegates would be needed to elect one representative to the Central Committee. The second way, which was accepted by the subcommittee, was to divide 334 into the total 2,941 Conference delegates, including those who had been appointed from the central list as well as those elected from the branches. This meant that 8.8 Conference delegates were needed to elect a single representative to the Central Committee from the branches. The first consequence of this decision was to deprive around eighteen small branches of representation on the new Central Committee. The second consequence was that it secured greater representation for several of the large branches, particularly Tel Aviv and the kibbutz movement. This was an obvious deviation from the principle that representation on the Central Committee should have been determined by the number of party members in the branches.

For example, Tel Aviv had 315 elected delegates and 191 delegates appointed to the Party Conference. According to the first formula of 6.6 it would have received 48 representatives on the Central Committee. The chosen key of 8.8 gave it 57, whereas Haifa, which had 268 elected and 71 appointed Conference delegates, would have received 40 Central Committee representatives according to the first formula and 39 under the one adopted. The following branches received *extra* representatives on the Central Committee through the second formula: Tel Aviv (9), Jerusalem (4), Kibbutz HaMeuchad (2), Ramat Gan (2), Givatayim (2), and Ramat HaSharon (1) (cf. Shamai, 1972).

No less significant than the manipulation and its consequences was the manner in which it was done, and the way it was accepted by the members. When questions were raised about this decision, Yeshayahu skillfully averted criticism and a debate by saying, "I ask that there be no misunderstandings that eat our time and soul. Here we are discussing principles. We decided about two-thirds for the branches. The actual mathematical division should not concern us in the

Standing Committee. We are talking here about principles!" Many other issues of disagreement and potential strife were settled in a similar manner. When an argument arose about the rights and duties of the proposed Secretariat, Yeshayahu suggested that it should be decided by the new Central Committee, and said, "if agreed, then we decided," and moved on to the next item of business before anyone could raise an objection.

Most of the activity took place in the corridors outside where caucuses were forming in attempts to mobilize support for representation on the central list to the Central Committee. One example of such activity was told to me by the secretary of the Jerusalem Students' Association. He said he was called out of the Standing Committee meeting by Abraham Ofer and was asked by him if he "backed Sapir all the way." He was asked to give Ofer a list of student candidates for the Central Committee and told that they would choose from the list those whom they could trust to be representatives on the Central Committee. This was a typical manner of assuring that the representatives of various interest groups and social categories would loyally serve their patrons.

This issue dominated the Standing Committee proceedings and continued throughout the Conference while the speeches and ceremony were taking place. Behind the scenes, literally behind the stage of the auditorium where the Conference took place, the Nominations Committee met and heard petitioners who attempted to get representatives nominated to the Central Committee on the central list. The delegates to the Conference from the various branches caucused to elect their representatives to the Central Committee. Among the smaller branches this usually resulted in the election of the top local leadership, either the mayor, and/or the secretary of the Histadrut Workers' Council, and/or the branch secretary, in that order of preference. Local considerations were based on a variety of factors such as previous party affiliation, personal and factional rivalries, ethnicity, and so forth. Another important factor was the nature of the ties of the local leader with top party leaders, as I emphasized earlier. One very clear trend was that members of the former Rafi, and members of the former Mapai who had sympathized with Rafi or who supported Minister of Defense Moshe Dayan, tended to be excluded from representation on the Central Committee. For example, the Ichud HaKvutzot V'HaKibbutzim movement elected only one Rafi member from among their nineteen representatives on the new Central Committee. This was in contrast to the other two former parties (Mapai and Achdut Haavoda), which were far more successful. The results were Mapai 233, Rafi 38, and Achdut Haavoda 63 Central Committee members elected from the branch caucuses of the Conference delegates. After initially meeting together, the Nominations Subcommittee of the Standing Committee proceeded to break up and meet in three separate groups based on the three former parties. Many of the branches delayed presenting their lists of representatives to the Central Committee in the hope of increasing their bargaining positions and getting the Nominations Committee to name some of their delegates from the central list. Many of the branches had not paid attention to the leadership's plea to include representatives of women, youth, ethnic minorities, and new immigrant categories. One of the jobs of the Nominations Committee(s) was to make up for this imbalance.

Of the original 167 places on the Central Committee from the central list, 82 were guaranteed to Cabinet ministers, important members of the Knesset, members of the Leadership Bureau, members of the Executive Committee of the Jewish Agency, and so forth. These 82 places were divided thus: Mapai 46, Rafi 18, and Achdut Haavoda 18. The remaining 85 seats were allocated thus: Mapai 57, Rafi 12, and Achdut Haavoda 18. The factional division of the 167 central list candidates for the Central Committee was: Mapai 103, Rafi 30, and Achdut Haavoda 34.

Rafi had only 38 of its former members elected from the branches. With its share of the central list it had 68 members on the new Central Committee and this represented a serious loss of power. Rafi's representatives on the Nominations Committee were faced with a particularly acute problem in that they had to try to satisfy the 94 Rafi members of the previous Central Committee, plus Mapai supporters of Rafi who had been punished for their sympathies by not being reelected to the Central Committee, central personalities and local leaders who had not been elected from the branches, and demands from youth, Orientals, and others for representation. They clearly could not approach a solution to these problems with the seats that were theirs to allocate, so they precipitated a near crisis by threatening to have all of their prominent national leaders resign from the Central Committee to make places for local leaders.

The position of the other junior partner within the Labor Party, Achdut Haavoda, was much stronger. Having organized its campaign well, and having had the advantage of a well-organized independent bureaucracy, kibbutz movement, newspaper, and so forth, Achdut Haavoda succeeded in gaining 63 representatives from the branches (including the kibbutz movement, whose members' votes were weighted 50 percent more than those of urban members). Along with its central list share, this gave Achdut Haavoda 97 members on the Central Committee. Since the vast majority of its representatives belonged to the disciplined kibbutz movement, the Achdut Haavoda leadership, under Minister Yisrael Galili, could count on solid support. This was also significant given Galili's close relationship with the prime minister.

Mapai had gained a solid majority of representatives on the Central Committee, both from those elected from the branches (233) and from the central list (103). It is very significant that not all of the former Mapai section of the Nominations Committee were included in the decisive stages of the allocation of Mapai's places from the central list. In fact, of the ex-Mapai men on the committee, only Ofer, Kaldiron, and Shapira were really decisive. Each had his own special interests, and there were internal coalitions and bargaining between the three during the negotiations. As Sapir's direct representative, Ofer followed his patron's policy of preventing the representation of Rafi sympathizers whenever possible and of appointing as many loyal Sapir clients and supporters as possible. In addition, Ofer, a former leader of the old ex-Mapai rebellious youth known as the Zeirim, was interested in getting his old colleagues and supporters on the Central Committee to build up his own personal following. Kaldiron, who as one of the leaders of the old Tel Aviv–based machine known as the Gush had fought Ofer and his Zeirim in a serious battle in the "old days," also had his personal interests. The chairman of the Nominations Committee, Yitzchak Shapira, looked after the interests of the old colonies (*moshavot*). All three were important figures in the new Mapai-based machine that Sapir had built. Their collective actions significantly strengthened the position of this group.

Pressures were applied from all sides: former Rafi demanded compensation for the lack of delegates elected from the branches; so did women, youth, Orientals, academics, and others. There was also the problem of prominent old "veterans of the movement" for whom places had to be found. Rumors began to circulate that the Central Committee was to be expanded to 601 members in order to accommodate all the various interests that were "underrepresented."

True to Mapai tradition, the nomination of the Central Committee was dragged out to the last minute as rumors circulated and tension mounted. While the 3,000 delegates of the Conference waited, the atmosphere was created for the next stage in the process—the enlargement of the Central Committee. One of the first sure indicators of such a move was the announcement by the chairman to the assembled members of the Standing Committee that "The baby has not yet been born!" He added ironically, "The ink on the list will be wet when we have to read the list in the Conference and maybe names will be changed during the reading of the list." This was exactly what happened.

Shapira, the chairman of the Nominations Committee, said the team of secretaries had appealed to them to include women, ethnic groups, youth, and others, which was impossible given the fact that they had only 85 places left after the "guaranteed" 82 places had been awarded. He spoke with uncharacteristic emotion in asking that the Central Committee be expanded to 601 in order to give representation to all groups.

Shapira was supported by a number of speakers, the most prominent being Rabinowitz, the two deputy secretaries-general, and Secretary-General Arie (Lyova) Eliav, who gave a moving speech supporting the expansion of the Central Committee. Eliav's last speech was particularly effective, mainly because it was an admission by the secretary-general that he had failed to control the Standing Committee and the branches, which had not heeded his previous pleas. It was an admission of a fact of which most of the members were aware, and yet such was his popularity that many members were moved to support the measure out of personal sympathy for him. (Eliav resigned his position as secretary-general shortly after the Party Conference.) Of course not everyone agreed, but the proposal passed nearly unanimously. Having gained a partial victory, Yeshayahu moved in to make his victory complete. He said it was necessary to change the decision on the one-third/two-thirds division. There were shouts of protest. Yeshayahu continued, "We must say that it is only for this time . . . I am looking for a formulation." A wag quipped, "We have a written constitution and an oral constitution!" A member shouted to Yeshayahu, "We must first debate how to elect the extra 100 before you start your formulations!" Yeshayahu retorted sharply "I am sorry, what we decide now cannot go to the Conference. There will be no end. We are going from here to the Conference unanimously! We must do it in the democratic fashion!"

Wertman of Haifa led the protest. He argued that the 100 should be allocated in the previously decided manner (one-third/two-thirds). He warned that if this was not accepted he would present a minority proposal to the Conference for debate. Yeshayahu replied that the 100 had already been allocated and called a quick vote that defeated Wertman's proposal. He warned, "There will be no amendments or minority reports! We are not leaving here without having decided on a new Central Committee!"

The Haifa leader replied, "It is always the same trick—at midnight they force on a bunch of people from above to stack the Central Committee. We [Haifa] will not agree to it!" However, after strong initial opposition they did agree, and if an extremely powerful branch like Haifa gave in to pressure, obviously so did the smaller and weaker ones.

The Role of Timing and Style

Timing was also extremely important in creating pressure both on the members of the Standing Committee to accept whomsoever was proposed by the Nominations Committee, and on the delegates of the Conference to authorize what they were handed by the Standing Committee. While the Standing Committee adjourned awaiting the list of the new Central Committee from the Nominations Committee, the Conference was adjourned awaiting the same list after the approval of the Standing Committee. The elderly chairwoman of the Conference rushed from the auditorium to Histadrut headquarters, where the Standing Committee met, to demand action. The prime minister had threatened to disband the Conference without electing the Central Committee if they did not hurry.

In the office of the Organization Department of the Histadrut the extra 20 seats that were Rafi's share of the 100 additional Central Committee seats were distributed, bringing its total representation to 88. In another room, Achdut Haavoda's additional 18 seats were allocated, giving it a total of 119. Meanwhile Ofer, Kaldiron, and Shapira had left the Histadrut headquarters and had gone over to Ofer's office at Shikun Ovdim to distribute the extra 62 Mapai seats, totaling 398 members on the new Central Committee. Shapira and Kaldiron returned much later, and when asked for the list they replied that Ofer had it. A cry went up around Histadrut headquarters and the Conference floor: "Where is Ofer?" While it is not possible to verify his whereabouts in the hour he was "lost," given what I have said about Sapir's role in the mobilization and control of the political grouping that successfully dominated the Standing Committee and Conference, it is not unlikely that Ofer had conferred with Sapir to get his final approval and changes of the list.

Tension reached a peak during the hour in which Ofer was "lost"; people were running around wheeling and dealing, and one could hear such conversation as, "What woman from Haifa can we add from Achdut Haavoda?" There was also a considerable amount of joking going on. There were a number of jocular references to the "good old days" when Netzer was the boss of the machine and what a professional he was at drawing up the list of the Central Committee. People laughed about how he used to sit at the Coffee House Vered and receive the various delegations of interest groups, listing those whom he had agreed to place on the Central Committee on the margins of his *Davar* (the Histadrut newspaper). Then someone said more seriously that when Netzer had agreed a person would be on the Central Committee his word was good and he did not fiddle the list afterward as was now being done. The complaints were good-natured. People seemed most indignant about the lack of style in the fiddling of the list, rather than about the fiddling itself. They mostly objected to what they considered to be a violation of the rules of the game, which had occurred when people had been promised places on the Central Committee and later discovered that they had been dropped. But the good-natured joking indicated a professional appreciation of the expert manner in which they were being manipulated (even if it lacked the style of a previous era), and even more so, that when all was said and done, this was what they had expected all along.

Ofer appeared literally at the twelfth hour, grinning broadly with the list in hand. Yeshayahu called the Standing Committee to order and said with marvelous understatement, "This [the drawing up of the Central Committee] could have been done better!" Shapira claimed that in all his experience (which was vast) he had never met such a lack of cooperation from several parts. The chairman of the Election Committee raised an objection that the Nominations Committee had left out parts of its membership when it met to draw up the final list. Meanwhile, the chairman of the Conference had run in and demanded they hurry, and Golda Meir's threat to end the Conference without electing the Central Committee had been delivered. Granite, the director of the Organization Department, began reading the list. He was then swarmed by people, from ministers in the Cabinet to local politicians, attempting to verify that they or their clients were included on the list. Granite took the list ostensibly to type it according to alphabetical order, yet when he read the list to the Conference later it was still in its old handwritten form. It is not unlikely that some changes in its composition had occurred since the Standing Committee authorized the list.

Yeshayahu asked the Conference delegates for a constitutional amendment to increase the size of the Central Committee, which he claimed had been unanimously approved by the Standing Committee (an inaccurate statement). He said that "because of the needs of the party in this transition stage" it was necessary to do so. Many questions were raised from the floor and the delegates lined up to ask how the extra 100 representatives were chosen, whether the one-third to two-thirds ratio had been followed, if they were from the branches or the central list, who were these extra 100, and so forth. In addition there was criticism of the big city branches who, it was claimed, forced the move through under pressure. One person asked, "What gives you the right to do this?" (By now Mrs. Meir was smiling since it was clear that everything was going smoothly.) Another asked, "Will it be only for this time? Why is it necessary this time?"

The ritual nature of these questions did not escape the very bright and politically astute rabbi for the Histadrut and the moshav movement, Rabbi Menachem HaCohen, who said, "It is just like Pesach—'Why is this night different from all other nights?' " He quoted with irony a passage from the Passover service in which the youngest male asks the head of the house the "four questions" that lead to the ritual telling of the story of the Exodus of the children of Israel from Egypt. This quip highlighted the ritual aspect of the questions being asked in the Conference at the time, and indicated that they too would receive formalized answers and they did. Yeshayahu told the delegates of the need to give representation to women, youth, ethnic groups, new immigrants, and "personalities who for one reason or another were not elected." The proposal passed with approximately 100 votes opposed. This was a fairly large symbolic opposition.

While all this was going on Granite was sitting with the list and going over it with various people, including a prominent leader of Achdut Haavoda. At 2:00 A.M. Granite read the list of 601 representatives of the new Central Committee without differentiating between those who had been elected by the branches and those who had been nominated from the center. By this time approximately two-thirds of the Conference delegates had already gone home, and those who remained were exhausted and could not pay close attention to the names being read. Obviously they accepted the list, thereby authorizing the election of the new Central Committee.

Actually, the story of the election of the Central Committee did not end at this point. A month later the party Leadership Bureau further enlarged the Central Committee to include three extra representatives who "were slipped into the list unnoticed by the delegates exhausted at the end of the night-long convention session last month, and unknown to the Steering Committee, which had laboured for hours on end in drawing up the list." The official version given was that "in the final rush to wind up the convention a number of mistakes occurred" (Segal, 1971). The same report said that the Achdut Haavoda members of the Standing Committee were shocked to learn that Granite had included a client of the deputy prime minister, Yigal Allon, on the Central Committee, though they had twice turned him down for membership on that body. This example of how one top-ranking leader applied pressure for the inclusion of one of his protégés was not unique. It was reported that the Labor Party leaders had first considered asking several members of the Central Committee to resign to save the embarrassment of having to expand it again, but as I have said of the party culture, one does not resign from an office once one has attained it. So they chose the easier course of expanding the body. They then had to do so again when they decided to include ten representatives of the Arab and Druze minorities, and this brought the Central Committee to an unprecedented membership of 615.

The Selection of Knesset Candidates

The process through which the group of former Mapai loyalists led by Sapir gained a dominant position on the Central Committee had particular significance for the selection of the party's candidates for the Knesset. The only provision for the selection of candidates in the Labor Party constitution says that the list of candidates must be approved by the Central Committee at least forty-eight hours before the deadline for submitting the list to the central Knesset Elections Committee (Chapter IV, paragraph 62). Although there had been a decision in 1969 that the candidates for the 1973 elections would be chosen through a secret ballot of the Labor Party Central Committee, there were secret ballots for the former Rafi and Achdut Haavoda candidates only in their separate forums, and the Mapai candidates were nominated by the traditional Nominations Committee.

According to its tradition, Achdut Haavoda balanced its ticket between members representing its Kibbutz HaMeuchad movement and its urban branches. The traditional leaders of both wings were reelected with the addition of Avraham Gevelber, the faction's deputy secretary-general of the Labor Party. The former Rafi faction also returned all of its incumbent members of the Knesset with the exception of Mordechai Surkis, who was dropped to an "unrealistic" position on the list. With Achdut Haavoda and Rafi each returning seven of their eight previous Knesset members, the main interest focused on the former Mapai Nominations Committee.

Several aspects of the Mapai selection process were unique variations on a traditional theme. First, and significantly, Pinchas Sapir headed the Nominations Committee himself rather than entrusting a second-echelon surrogate with the job. Second, the Leadership Bureau gave Sapir a mandate to appoint the members of the Nominations Committee, and only asked the Central Committee for its retroactive authorization of the composition of the committee after it had already completed its task of drawing up the list of Knesset candidates. An additional first was the formal meeting of the members of the Labor Party Central Committee representing the former Mapai to authorize the appointment of the Nominations Committee and to approve its list. Whereas the other two former party factions had met separately on previous occasions, this was the first formal meeting of this Mapai forum since the unification of the Labor Party. Finally, there was an unprecedented turnover in the Mapai slate with fifteen new faces (40 percent) in the first thirty-five so-called "realistic" positions.

During the five formal meetings of the Nominations Committee, and informally through personal approaches to the various committee members—particularly to Sapir—representatives of thirty-five different interest groups pleaded their cases for representation on the Knesset. The strongest among these delegations were the party machines of the three major cities, Tel Aviv, Haifa, and Jerusalem, which are organized into independent organizational districts as are the two kibbutz movements and the moshav movement affiliated with the party. The medium-sized and smaller branches had no such formal district organization at the time, but in several cases got together informally to strengthen their cases for Knesset representation. In addition, the Young Guard of the party, the women's section, and various immigrant and ethnic groups made intensive efforts to gain representation. A wide assortment of groups and interests ranging from Muslim, Christian, and Druze minorities to merchants' associations and a group of former high-ranking army officers also pleaded their causes. The Nominations Committee was forced to move secretly to another location on several occasions in order to avoid the insistent delegations that besieged them. The enterprising Young Guard had spies with an internal communications system who kept them informed of the whereabouts of the Nominations Committee at all times.

The former Mapai members of the Labor Party Central Committee were convened on September 23, 1973, to approve the list of their candidates to the Knesset. Secretary-General Aharon Yadlin announced that the Nominations Committee had been appointed by the Leadership Bureau (Lishka) and asked for and received the unanimous retroactive approval of the Central Committee. One humorous member said, "One time we will vote no and we will be finished with democracy!" Pinchas Sapir reported on the work of the Nominations Committee and emphasized the difficulty of having to reconcile the demands of so many different groups. He dwelled at length in praise of the contributions of the several prominent "retiring" members of the Knesset. Only a leader of Sapir's stature could have succeeded in "retiring" so many veteran Mapai M.K.'s (members of Knesset). Some of them had voluntarily retired at their own initiative, others did so after Sapir's persuasion, and still others refused to accept the unrealistic position Sapir offered them. Another technique adopted to make room for new faces on the list was the decision that most Mapai Cabinet ministers would have only honorary unrealistic positions. These included Ministers Bar-Lev, Sherof, Shapira, and Givati. Prime Minister Golda Meir, Sapir, Eban, and Hillel (under the extreme pressure of Oriental party activists) retained their Knesset seats. This move removed several ranking Cabinet members as potential candidates to succeed Golda Meir as prime minister, since the prime minister is required by law to be a member of the Knesset.

During the lengthy speech in which he revealed his long list of realistic candidates, Sapir controlled his audience with all the finesse of a maestro conducting his orchestra, relieving tension with well-timed ironic humor, and getting the results he wanted through the expert use of political and oratorical techniques. For example, he exaggerated the number of realistic places on the list by claiming there were 35 when at most 32 were likely to be elected. He read the list of 35 in alphabetical order, saying the Nominations Committee would order them later, thereby avoiding identification of the 3 or 4 marginal candidates. This was particularly effective in quelling a potential threat from the party's Young Guard, who had gathered enough signatures to demand a secret ballot on the list of candidates but were sufficiently pacified that their leader appeared on the list of the first 35 that they did not raise the issue of the secret ballot. Although Sapir claimed that "nothing is settled yet" and that ultimately the final list would be determined by "this audience," such gestures of dependence for approval on a supposedly independent body were symbolic only, and hid from none of those present the obvious fact that near unanimous support for Sapir's list was guaranteed.

Secretary-General Yadlin introduced the vote by saying, "We are bringing an en bloc list, but it is the fruit of a democratic process. Not a single candidate does not represent a constituency." He asked the members to relinquish their right to speak and to approve the list of candidates. He refused the request of one member to postpone the meeting of the entire Labor Party Central Committee (those members who were not in the former Mapai were waiting outside the auditorium) so that they could have a proper debate on the list. Yadlin claimed that they must get the approval of the Central Committee for the party's list of candidates to the Knesset and their candidate for prime minister and that this could not be postponed. Several speakers were finally given the floor, most of whom complimented the Nominations Committee on its work. Some speakers suggested the need for a better system of making nominations. For example, Dr. E. Gutmann (a political scientist) said that even though the decisions of the Nominations Committee were made by honorable people, the process was not completely democratic. Minister of Police Hillel, a member of the Nominations Committee, agreed on the need to find a better system and condemned the Tel Aviv district for not naming an Oriental among its candidates. Several other speakers supported candidates who were not given realistic positions. Sapir answered the various charges raised by the speakers and concluded that he thought that they had produced an "aesthetic" list. After this ritual-like debate there was a vote in which the list was nearly unanimously approved with only five opposing votes.

When the members of the Labor Party Central Committee from the former Rafi and Achdut Haavoda factions had filed in, Yadlin again asked for the retroactive approval of the Nominations Committee "for legal purposes" (a party member had gone to court in protest against the illegality of the manner in which the Nominations Committee had been appointed). When this was accomplished Yadlin made a nominating speech for Golda Meir as the party's candidate for prime minister and she was unanimously elected. After Mrs. Meir's acceptance speech the meeting of the Central Committee was recessed to enable the Leadership Bureau and the Nominations Committee to meet and iron out some final questions about the composition of the rest of the list of candidates to the Knesset.

The most controversial speech in the debate that followed the intermission was by a former Knesset member who had been dropped from the last Knesset because of her outspoken criticism of the party leadership. Shulamit Aloni reminded her listeners that four years previously they had decided that the party's candidates to the Knesset would be elected through democratic secret elections. She condemned the fact that under the present system a member could not submit himself as a candidate. She attacked the Young Guard, whom she claimed favored secret elections only as long as their candidate was not on the list. She argued for a system of primary elections of candidates. Mrs. Aloni claimed that many members were afraid to voice their opposition since they were dependent on the party for their jobs. She charged that while the members of the Central Committee might be satisfied with the degree of democracy in the party, the people in the street were not so satisfied. Yadlin warned Aloni to be careful about making unjust charges. He claimed that "compared with other Israeli parties and with other democratic socialist parties we can be proud of our representation and freedom of expression." The secretary-general explained that the unification of the party had not progressed sufficiently to enable them to implement prior decisions about secret elections, and he argued that "under the present conditions democracy could only work within the previous party factions." Sapir sharply retorted to Mrs. Aloni's charges and warned her to "think twice and listen to the comrades." He concluded, "I do not want to make you more popular than you are, so I shall continue to read the list." Upon completing reading the list of candidates it was unanimously accepted by the members of the Central Committee. (Shulamit Aloni eventually headed a hastily established Citizens' Rights list, and she and two of her colleagues were elected to the Knesset. She ultimately became a minister without portfolio as her Citizens' Rights movement temporarily joined the coalition government of Yitzchak Rabin.)

Conclusions

A central question must be raised as to how representative of the general membership were those chosen through this nomination process. Medding (1972:302) has said of the internal election processes, "these same processes were able to produce results that were highly representative in terms of the party's social diversity, even if there was a marked degree of control over the exact identity of personnel making up this representative group, which may not have been a true reflection of membership views." Secretary-General Yadlin proudly claimed that not a single candidate for the Knesset did not represent a constituency. The Nominations Committee for the Central Committee justified the need to expand its share of appointments in order to correct imbalances by giving representation to various interest groups and social categories. An important point must be stressed. Many of the so-called representatives were not chosen by their constituencies, that is, by those in the same sex and ethnic categories. They were chosen by representatives of the top national leadership because of their loyalty and services to these leaders. I think the term "client" is appropriate here, since it shows more specifically the nature of their ties to and their responsibilities to serve their patrons in the top party leadership. I elaborate on the nature of these relationships in more detail and in a wider context in Chapter 6.

The composition of the former Mapai candidates on the Labor Party's list to the Knesset bore the strong personal stamp of Pinchas Sapir. The powerful Tel Aviv–based party machine, Gush, gained more than its share of Knesset members, and its most prominent leaders—Sapir's close ally Rabinowitz, and his protégé, Ofer—were elevated from the Knesset to the Cabinet in key posts. Dedicated young clients of Sapir like Yossi Sarid and Adi Yafe were among the "young blood" infused into the Mapai Knesset ranks. Other top party leaders, such as Golda Meir, succeeded in placing their clients (e.g., Aharon Yariv) in the Knesset, but there was no doubt that the majority of Mapai's Knesset members belonged to Sapir's political network. They could be expected to support him and his political views in party forums and the Knesset. Proof of Sapir's dominant position in the party was demonstrated in several critical showdowns in the aftermath of the October war. These will be discussed in forthcoming chapters.

I have traced the mobilization of political support that led to the domination of the political institutions of the Labor Party through an analysis of a chain of key Nominations Committees. From the appointment of the Constitutional Committee, the self-appointment by the members of the Leadership Bureau to the Standing Committee, and the selection of a Nominations Committee, the composition of the important Standing Committee was guaranteed to control the National Party Conference in the interest of the top party leaders. Control of the two subcommittees of the Standing Committee led to the adoption of the key that guaranteed the overrepresentation of the Tel Aviv–based Gush, and the control of the central nominations by the Central Committee. The manipulations through which key constitutional decisions were changed under duress—e.g., the expansion of the Central Committee from 501 to 615 and the increasing of the proportion of central nominations from 33 percent to 45 percent—were analyzed. It was shown how in fact the Nominations Committee did not function in its entirety, and how it narrowed itself to three Mapai men who formulated the final list, which was then taken by one of them who "got lost" for an hour. The successful domination of the Central Committee was then related to the selection of the Mapai candidates to the Knesset. The Leadership Bureau chose Sapir as chairman of the Nominations Committee, which he selected and which then chose the candidates of the party faction for the Knesset. This Nominations Committee was given retroactive authorization after it had already completed its task. It presented a list of candidates, not even in the final order of preference, to the Central Committee, which, after a brief ritual-like debate, unanimously authorized the list.

I have raised questions about the extent to which many of the members of these institutions are representative of their various constituencies by linking together the phases in the process by which the top party leadership nominated themselves, their protégés, and their clients to these bodies, and how they thereby perpetuate themselves in power. I have stressed that the dependence of the vast majority of the members of party bodies severely restricts their ability to make independent decisions; this obviously facilitates and perpetuates the "ownership" of the party (to use Schattschneider's terminology) by those few top party patrons who have the power to make nominations.

4

The Suppression of Issues

Introduction: The Conceptual Framework

Having thus far dealt with the more overt forms of the mobilization of power, factional competition, and the nominations process, I focus now on the more covert control of the issue arenas in the Standing Committee and the National Party Conference. I first introduce a clarification of the concept of suppressed issues, which, I will attempt to show, helps to explain important aspects of power relationships and political culture, particularly by revealing coercive aspects of what might otherwise be perceived as genuine consensus. This is followed by a discussion of selected aspects of the political culture of the party, which are then related to the suppression from the agenda of the National Party Conference of two highly salient and controversial issues. In the concluding section of this chapter, certain aspects of the control function of the Standing Committee are discussed. This discussion provides the background for the explanation of ritual behavior in the Standing Committee in the following chapter.

Peter Bachrach and Morton Baratz (1962, 1963, 1970, 1975) introduced an important notion in arguing that there is a second, less obvious aspect of power that has largely been ignored in the literature. They assert that power is frequently exercised by confining the scope of decision making to relatively safe issues. They state that "power is also exercised when A devotes his energies to creating or reinforcing social and political values and institutional practices that limit the scope of the political process to public consideration of only those issues which are comparatively innocuous to A" (Bachrach and Baratz, 1962:948). They draw on an earlier formulation by E.E. Schattschneider (1960:71):

> All forms of political organization have a bias in favor of the exploitation of some kinds of conflict and the suppression of others because organization is the mobilization of bias. Some issues are organized into politics while others are organized out.

Bachrach and Baratz (1962:949) pose the question,

[C]an the researcher overlook the chance that some person or association could limit decision making to relatively non-controversial matters, by influencing community values and political procedures and rituals, notwithstanding that there are in the community serious but latent power conflicts?

They reply, "To do so is, in our judgement, to overlook the less apparent, but nonetheless extremely important, face of power."

Whereas I and others (cf. Frey, 1971; Crenson, 1971; Stolzman, 1974; and van der Eijk and Kok, 1975) endorse this position, it has proved to be extremely controversial, having precipitated considerable criticism (cf. Merelman, 1968; Wolfinger, 1971; Debnam, 1975). While ignoring the polemical aspects of the debate (which involve competing schools in American political science and sociology), I shall briefly clarify the most important aspects of the concepts that are relevant to the forthcoming analysis. Two essentially related problems arise from the debate, one conceptual and the other methodological. The contention between Raymond Wolfinger (1971) and Frederick Frey (1971) centers around the concepts of nondecisions and nonissues. The conflict primarily involves their different assessments of the relative difficulty in identifying the two. These differences are largely (although not exclusively) due to conceptual ambiguity. For example, it is significant that Wolfinger speaks only of nondecisions, whereas Frey discusses both nondecisions and nonissues.

I suggest that these are analytically distinct terms that need to be subdivided into much more sophisticated categories. Just as a decision not to decide is analytically different from a decision that is never made, so a suppressed issue is clearly different from one that has never reached any stage of development in the issue arena. Although Frey (1971) constructed a typology of nondecisions, by suggesting the substitution of the term "suppressed issue" for "nonissue," he ignores an important distinction made by Rachel Tokatli (1972). Tokatli suggests that the term "latent issue" be applied to potential issues around which political actors have not organized and which have not been brought into the political arena. The term "suppressed issue" would be reserved for issues which, when they reach the decision-making arena, threaten basic values or interests in a political system or institution. Those in power try to avoid decisions on such potentially explosive issues since they fear an open debate would lead to conflict that could seriously damage the institution in its present form and/or their positions of dominance within it.

In elaborating on Tokatli's distinction between latent and suppressed issues, I suggest that political issues pass through different stages of development, reaching different levels and arenas of discussion and debate, before they reach a peak of confrontation, such as in an election campaign, a debate in a National Party Conference, or an institutional decision-making forum. Conversely, issues can be suppressed along the way before reaching these final stages. The phases in the development of political issues might be conceptualized in a model similar to the one suggested by Turner for the analysis of "political phases development" (cf. Swartz, Turner, and Tuden, 1966; Aronoff, 1974b). When preparing the first edition of this book for press, I read a most suggestive analysis of nondecisions by van der Eijk and Kok (1975) in which they adapt a model based on the work of Bachrach and Baratz (1970) giving particular emphasis to the process of agenda-building, an approach particularly compatible with the frame of analysis I employ in this chapter.

Since even strong critics such as Wolfinger (1971:1079) recognize that "[c]learly, the general issues discussed by Bachrach and Baratz are important to the study of politics," and since reservations have been based primarily on the evaluation that "the criteria they propose require data that are difficult to gather or largely unobtainable," a classification of nonissues that isolates a type on which data can be clearly gathered would break the current impasse in the development and application of the concept. Ideally, this would pave the way for further conceptual refinement and more empirical studies. Wolfinger (1971:1078) outlines two standards that must be met in order to guide the researcher in the study of nonissues:

> 1) They would not rely on ex post facto detection based on an increase in political action subsequent to the period under study. 2) Some threshold for the passage from nondecision to a place on the agenda would have to be established.

I shall demonstrate that the criticisms raised as to the difficulty of identifying and researching nonissues apply only to the first type of latent issues and not to the second type of suppressed issues. I shall illustrate this by applying Wolfinger's standard to a brief summary of a previous study of a suppressed issue as an illustration, before elaborating the second case in the forthcoming analysis. In both cases the importance of participant observation as a research method in the study of suppressed issues will be obvious.

In a study of a new community (Aronoff, 1974a:55–71 and 1974c), I found that the issue of high prices in local shops, which was one of the most common complaints of the population, escalated to a new threshold of public salience when a local women's group organized a trade fair for out-of-town merchants to which local merchants responded by threatening a strike of their shops in protest. Both sides circulated flysheets in which they attacked each other, thereby making grievances known to the town's residents. The threat of violence on the part of the local merchants led the mayor to call an informal meeting of representatives of the opposing sides in which they aired their respective grievances and tacitly agreed to the suppression of the issue from the local election campaign, which followed shortly afterward. In this case, the increase in political action was perceived during the systematic observation of political interaction in the field by the researcher, and did not therefore require any ex post facto means of detection. The development of the issue through several stages was traced, and the crucial stage of suppression from the issue arena could be empirically identified and analyzed.

Evidence from this study supports one of the criticisms of the formulation of Bachrach and Baratz—that the suppression of an issue need not necessarily be the result of the calculated interests of status quo–oriented persons or groups. In this case, the suppression of the issue was largely due to the perception of all sides concerned that the exploitation of the issue might seriously threaten communal cohesion and peace (although the merchants did gain most from the perpetuation of the status quo). In cases such as this, one group can manipulate to its advantage the suppression of a potentially explosive issue that is ostensibly legitimated by claiming to protect the unity and cohesion of the group and the society. An a priori connection between the suppression of an issue and the interests of status quo–oriented groups should not be assumed to provide a necessary or sufficient explanation, but is a matter that should be empirically examined along with other variables in attempting to explain the suppression of issues.

I attempt to illustrate in this chapter that an examination of the structural, procedural, and cultural mechanisms of the suppression of issues provides significant insights into both the nature of the political institution in which it takes place and the political process in general. The analysis begins with an examination called for by Bachrach and Baratz (1962:950) of the "dominant values and the political myths, rituals, and institutions," which are most relevant to explaining the dynamics of the suppression of political issues.

Political Culture: Political Inefficacy and Taboos

The cultural context in which the mobilization of political power takes place, the norms that dictate the rules of the game, the style in which the game is played, and the different meanings of symbols are vital yet frequently neglected aspects of the analysis of modern political parties. The general political culture of Israel and the specific culture of the Labor Party were shaped by many diverse influences. The overwhelming majority of the most influential political leaders whose activities left the strongest stamp on the political culture were products of the shtetl life of Eastern European Jewry (see J. Katz, 1961, for an interesting analysis of shtetl life). They had been influenced by the social radicalism of the late nineteenth and early twentieth centuries, and more particularly by their own Zionist variations of these ideologies. They left clear imprints on the organizational structures and norms of the parties they created. The conditions of the pre-state Jewish Yishuv in Palestine also shaped the actions and values of these leaders and their parties, as was discussed in Chapter 2. For example, the secrecy and suspicion of outsiders that is characteristic of the parties, including the

Labor Party, can partly be traced to the clandestine nature of their activities during the British occupation, and for some it traces back even further to such activities in czarist Russia. The history of bitter splits also contributed to the characteristic suspiciousness. The Middle Eastern environment of which the country is a part, albeit a mutant variation, also influenced certain cultural patterns. For example, the elaborate ceremonials of hospitality in which drinks and refreshments are served can very likely be attributed to this influence. Obviously, the rapid change and dynamism of Israeli society, the integration into the society of masses of immigrants who brought with them a rich and colorful diversity of cultural baggage, has contributed its share to shaping the structures and values of the society and the parties.

Political Inefficacy

I shall focus my discussion on specific aspects of the party culture that are most directly related to the problem under analysis. The first aspect of party culture is the general prevalence of expressed feelings of political inefficacy. In order to examine the importance of this phenomenon in the context of the present analysis of the suppression of issues (which is also germane to the analysis in the forthcoming chapter of ritual behavior), I shall describe attitudes of branch activists toward the party center, attitudes of officials of the party center toward the branch activists, and related attitudes expressed in meetings of national party institutions that I attended.

The widespread discontent among local leaders can be classified in terms of five major deficiencies as they see them: (1) lack of influence, (2) lack of substantive debate before decisions had been made, (3) lack of regular communication with party headquarters and national leadership, (4) lack of just representation in national party institutions and in the Knesset, and (5) lack of sufficient and institutionalized aid from the party and the party's ministers in solving problems of local development.

The expressed feeling of a lack of influence, particularly with regard to decisions on important matters of national party policy, was so commonly expressed to me and in public that I do not hesitate to label it as universal among branch activists. This attitude was aptly articulated in the statement of a branch member who said, "In my chutzpa I want to have influence!" Another member added, "We are not a variable. All decisions come from above!" The feeling of powerlessness is aggravated by the conviction that the lack of real debate on substantive issues results in the nonideological factional strife characteristic of branch and local politics. One branch activist expressed this feeling in the following statement:

> For the past two years we have only argued over percentages of representation of previous party factions on various institutions. How long do we have to continue this business? There are only personal and factional squabbles and no

real substantial issues. We are playing around with democracy. Do not come to have us debate an issue when the same evening it was published in the newspaper that the decision had already been made. This is not democracy!

This activist and many others claimed they understood that the top leadership had to make certain kinds of decisions, particularly in the area of security and defense, without consulting the branches. But they claimed that there were other important domestic issues affecting their lives that they should be allowed to debate, and decisions on which they should be allowed to have influence. They most frequently cited the issue of religion and state as an example. Even more than their lack of influence, they resented what they felt to have been a dishonest charade of having been asked to debate issues when it was well known that decisions had already been made.

A closely related and very common criticism was of the lack of communication between party headquarters and the branches. In a special meeting at which the new secretary-general was introduced to the local leaders, one of the local men said, "Every time there is a new leadership they come and listen to our problems, and then we do not hear from them for three and a half years until they are organizing an election!" Many were bitter about the overrepresentation of the major branches and kibbutz movements on important party institutions, and the underrepresentation of the medium-sized and smaller branches (see Chapter 6). Characteristic statements such as, "The party is only interested in Tel Aviv, Haifa, and Jerusalem because all of the important people are there!" and "Give representation to the branches!" were commonly heard.

Finally, although the local leaders acknowledged the considerable aid they had received from the party, which had intervened with government ministries in facilitating the granting of development funds, they complained that such aid was insufficient and that the party's role of broker should be institutionalized. This attitude was expressed very simply by one branch member who said, "The secretary-general is our father and must help us with our problems of development!" As is common in such situations of dependence, the branches and their leaders resented their dependence on the party center for their town's development and for advancement in their own careers.

The officials of the party headquarters, including those in charge of relationships with the branches, tended to consider the interests of the national party leadership to be far more important than the interests of the branches. This priority of interests was partially determined by the awareness of the officials that their own political careers were in the hands of the top party leadership. The following statement of a former director of the Organization Department, made to me privately, is illustrative of the priorities of the party center:

It is most important to strengthen the top national party leadership since they are really what counts in terms of power and importance. More and more with modern technology of radio and television the top leadership can directly approach the public, and local branches are decreasing in importance.

The branches were viewed by the officials of the party headquarters as having been controlled by small oligarchies of aging local bosses who prevented newer and younger elements from participating in the branches. Most branches were known to have been inactive (in some cases dead) and lacking in ideological content. Typical of this perception of the state of the branches was the report given by Granite to the Organization Department after he had completed touring the branches throughout the country. The new Director said,

> My general impression of the branches is a prevalent lack of activities and seriousness. The majority of the branches are really in bad shape . . . [their activities are] based on factional strife and client relationships. This is far from a system of active branches!

The man he replaced as head of the department stated that Granite had come independently to exactly the same estimation of the state of the branches as he and the others in the department. He complimented Granite and the new secretary-general for "descending" to the branches. This widely used term for visiting the branches is symbolic of the low importance of the branches in the eyes of the officials of the party headquarters. This attitude was succinctly stated by the former head of the Organization Department, who said, "They simply do not need the branches, which are *nudniks* [nuisances], even if justified. But who needs them? . . . We really only need them for elections—between elections it is a game!" These attitudes and relationships are analyzed in Chapter 7.

In moments of candor, the professionals at party headquarters admitted to their own feelings of powerlessness. As one said to me, "I work and nobody knows or even cares what I do!" On another occasion, when the possibility of reorganizing the branches was discussed, one of the regional organizers said to his colleagues, "Who will let us decide anything?" This general feeling of lack of political effectiveness, which I have shown to be characteristic of local leaders and common among functionaries at party headquarters, was frequently expressed privately by leaders of the students and the Young Guard of the party, by older rebellious party critics, and even occasionally by respected elder statesmen of the party. An example of the latter was a rare "public" criticism by the former mayor of Tel Aviv, Mordechai Namir, who asked in a meeting of the national Secretariat, "When will we have a real debate before decisions have been made?"

Taboos against Criticism of Leadership and Open Expression of Conflict

Outspoken criticism of the top national leadership, strong disagreement with the policies of the leadership, and open expression of a wide range of conflicting views, loyalties, and interests were generally forbidden to most of the members of the two largest national institutions in the period preceding the war of October

1973. Strong normative and pragmatic political sanctions assured enforcement of these taboos except in the cases of specific members whose social roles gave them ritual license to break them. For example, one individual had the role of court jester, a "fool" who was allowed to speak the truth because he was not taken seriously. Thus, in a meeting of the Central Committee in June 1972 he made an impassioned speech in which he said the only functioning party institution was the Leadership Bureau. He claimed that even the meetings of the Secretariat, when they all too rarely took place, ended up with twenty members. The jester said that members told him, "Why come to meetings? Do we decide anything?" He pleaded that the party institutions be made meaningful and functioning bodies in which free debates could take place and warned that if this were not done the results would be catastrophic. Because of his erratic and sometimes extreme behavior few people took him seriously, and he was frequently the subject of ridicule. At the time this speech was made I had been sitting next to Lyova Eliav (who had recently resigned as the secretary-general of the party), a most perceptive sociological observer, who turned to me and commented that the court jester was at it again (cf. Welsford, 1935, for an excellent historic account of the role of the fool in society).

Another individual, Shulamit Aloni, had the social role of *enfant terrible*. She was allowed and even expected to act as an internal party critic. However, there were limits on the extent to which even a ritually sanctioned critic could criticize. Aloni evidently exceeded these limits and was punished by not being put in a realistic position on the list for the next election to the Knesset. The removal of this party rebel from the Knesset served as a strong warning of the sanctions that could be applied to those who violated the taboo restricting criticism. The application of such sanctions emphasizes the vulnerability of the vast majority of members of the party's institutions and even the party's representatives in the Knesset. They are professional party functionaries and elected officials whose livelihood and careers are dependent upon the goodwill and support of the top party leadership. The process of nomination to all important political offices by small committees under the control of the top leadership ensures that the members of these institutions be primarily answerable to those who appoint them from above.

The top leadership was not well known for its high tolerance of criticism of its policies. One only has to examine any Israeli newspaper or the minutes of the party institutions during this period to verify this. For example, during a meeting of the national Secretariat in May 1970 there was a major foreign policy debate in which intellectuals, professors, and other critics of the government's policies were criticized very severely. Many speakers stressed what appeared to be a dominant norm—that to criticize government policy or to raise controversial issues when the country faced a critical security situation was tantamount to disloyalty to the country. The security situation was used not only to terminate debate, but also as a justification for the suppression of controversial issues that the leadership preferred not be raised. One such issue was that of religion and the state, which many branch activists used as an example of a vital topic on which they disagreed with the leadership's policy and on which they demanded to be allowed to give their views. In the same meeting of the Secretariat previously mentioned, Mordechai Surkis, chairman of the Interior Committee of the Knesset (at the time), said, "Golda [Meir] is trying to keep the people from fighting over a number of issues, such as 'Who is a Jew,' but in this house they fight and undermine [her efforts]!"

When a student organizer from Jerusalem replied, "We are a democratic society. It is healthy that people are thinking and concerned, and criticize," Golda Meir, who was then the prime minister, looked at him from the audience disbelievingly and shook her head in evident disagreement. The younger speaker was constantly interrupted throughout his speech with jeers and heckling so that the secretary-general had to demand order on many occasions. I shall contrast the normal enforcement of the previously mentioned taboo, and the sanctions that accompanied its violation, with an analysis of a meeting of the Standing Committee, which I argue was a ritually sanctioned occasion when this taboo was lifted.

It is significant that as the meeting of the Standing Committee got under way, and as the Conference approached, there were isolated partial breaches of the taboo in party institutions. In a meeting of the Central Committee, for instance, a proposal by the national Election Committee to allow someone to accompany illiterates into the ballot booth for the internal party elections was hotly debated and vociferously opposed. When it appeared likely that a majority of the members would vote against the proposal, it was referred back to the Election Committee (which was authorized to make the decision) by a narrow margin of eight votes. Such narrow margins were as rare as the opposition to the leadership's policies in the Central Committee of the Labor Party, in this case, to a measure they feared would enable party bosses to manipulate the elections undemocratically. As one member put it, "Comrades, now you see that the constitution can be bent for any purpose. A few people will elect the representatives of thousands. This is undemocratic!" This partial breach of taboo, which took place so close to the ritual removal of sanctions during the proceedings of the Standing Committee (discussed below and in detail in the forthcoming chapter), acted as a bridge between the normal situation of restraint that preceded the breach and the ritual rebellion and expression of open conflict that followed it.

Suppressed Issues

The Labor Party has great demographic, ethnic, and ideological diversity among its constituent interest groups and membership. Successful decision making in its institutions therefore necessitates hard bargaining and compromise. However, the types of issues and the kind of debate vary among the different party institutions. While there is a general sanction enforcing moderation on all fronts so as not to alienate any important segment of the party, there is a special occasion where free debate on all issues is allowed and that is in the Standing Committee. During my observations, two major conditions limited and allowed this freedom: the first provided that restraint was shown in the final formulations, which had to be consensual; and the second provided that those issues likely to cause major conflicts or unpredictable outcomes in the Conference were suppressed. I focus in this chapter on the mechanisms through which two issues were suppressed from debate in the Conference.

In my discussion of the suppression of these two major issues, I draw upon the analysis of Tokatli (1972), which, since it is unpublished, I shall briefly summarize and relate to my own analysis. Tokatli takes Butler and Stokes's (1971:410–30) three necessary conditions for a party to form a clear stand on issues and applies them to the two suppressed issues in the Standing Committee. She finds that on both the issues of religion and the state and the Histadrut (i.e., wage policies and labor relations) the first of the three conditions was present and the second and third were absent.

The first criterion—that the issue should concern a great number of the party functionaries—was obviously indicated by their enthusiastic debates in the Standing Committee. The second and third criteria—that the attitudes toward the issue be balanced in favor of the leadership's stand so that they have control over the outcome of the debate, and that public opinion definitely back the leadership's stand—were absent. Tokatli argues, rightly I think, that the main reason these two issues were suppressed was because the leaders lacked confidence that they could control the outcome of a debate in the Conference. I relate these findings to an analysis of the structural, procedural, and cultural mechanisms of the suppression of these issues, after which I compare and contrast the ramifications of their suppression.

Religion and the State

The question of the proper role of religion in the state is unquestionably one of the issues over which there is major, if not the greatest, disagreement among Jews in Israel (cf. Arian, 1971). An attempt was made to "freeze" the balance of relationships and rights and duties between secular and religious in a status quo agreement prior to Independence. Obviously, in such a dynamic and rapidly changing society as Israel, relationships cannot be preserved exactly as they were more than twenty-five years previously, but the major political actors continue to refer to the need to preserve the status quo and use it as an important standard in an attempt to prevent changes or to adjust imbalances caused by changing conditions (cf. Gutmann, 1972). The fact that the leaders of the Israel Labor Party and those of Mafdal (National Religious Party) have developed close working relationships through their cooperation in every Cabinet since the state of Israel was formed shapes both their political behavior on this issue and the stands their respective parties take (cf. Birnbaum, 1970). Finally, it should be remembered that the vast majority of the top leadership of the Labor Party was born and raised in the shtetls of Eastern Europe. Many of them received a traditional religious education, and although personally not religiously observant, they have a deep respect and appreciation for traditional Judaism—feelings that appear to get even stronger as they get older. All of these factors are related to the suppression of the issue of religion and state in the Party Conference.

The wide diversity of views on this subject all received full expression in the Standing Committee (with the exception of the extreme orthodox stand). Colorful and controversial party critic Shulamit Aloni and venerable ex-mayor of Tel Aviv Mordechai Namir co-sponsored a proposal calling for civil jurisdiction in personal affairs as an alternative to the present religious jurisdiction. Offering similar proposals for the separation of religion and politics, but from an entirely different point of view, was the articulate young rabbi of the Histadrut and moshav movement, Menachem HaCohen. The rabbi argued that the politicization of religion in Israel was undermining the spiritual content of Judaism, which, he argued, could only be saved if the two were completely divorced. Both of these proposals received considerable support from the more liberal individuals on the Committee, particularly from among the Young Guard. The majority of the members appeared to hold more moderate or conservative views, and finally a compromise resolution was worked out calling for religious tolerance and expressing their opposition to tabling any legislation that would coerce either religious or nonreligious practices. There were those individuals who suggested that the issue was too controversial and should not be debated in the Conference, but they were a small minority. Even the chairman, Yeshayahu, felt the issue should be debated in the Conference and expressed his confidence that the majority would support the status quo. A subcommittee was appointed to formulate the compromise resolution, which the Standing Committee adopted, and it was printed along with the other resolutions to be passed on to the delegates of the Conference.

At a special meeting of the Standing Committee at 7:00 A.M. on April 5, 1971, Mordechai Surkis proposed deleting the resolution on religion and the state from the Conference agenda. Yeshayahu, reversing his previous stand, supported Surkis's proposal, saying, "The issue of religion and the state demands a serious debate, and one hour is not serious. If we had three or four hours it would be serious. Therefore I am prepared, if the Committee is willing to accept the proposal of Surkis to send this issue to the new Central Committee; and it should not be debated in the Conference." All but two of the members present voted in favor of the proposal. There was an argument about whether the resolution should state that the Central Committee must debate the issue at its very first meeting, or at one of its first meetings. The resolution finally said "one of the first meetings."

When Aloni found out about the deletion of the religion and state issue (she was among the many Committee members who had not been present at the early morning meeting) she was furious. She confronted Surkis at the Conference and protested the suppression of the issue. He humored her, saying, "We should have debated religion and the state instead of the role of science with all of those professors, and socialism. I don't give a damn for socialism. . . ." Aloni was furious and said, "I wish people would stop telling me I am right—and then raise their hands and always vote for the leadership!" She finally gained the floor at the Conference and angrily denounced the suppression of the issue. The chairperson, Senta Josephthal—an equally strong and determined woman—forcefully silenced her, saying that it had been decided by the Standing Committee not to debate the issue in the Conference. It was obvious that a large cross-section of the audience supported Aloni and demanded in vain that she be allowed to continue. There were many shouts of protest, such as, "Why should it be debated in the new Central Committee and not here?"

Aloni had played her social role as the party's *enfant terrible* by articulating the frustration of masses of Conference delegates, and she was silenced, as was the issue of religion and the state. After Surkis had seen the mayor of Bat Yam talk to Aloni, Surkis said to him, "I hope you are not involved with Shulamit Aloni. We have enough problems, and more important things to discuss, without bringing up religion and the state!"

How and why was the issue of religion and the state suppressed? The answer to the first part of the question is simple. The minister of justice, Shapira, heard of the proposal and informed the prime minister, who called in the leadership of the Standing Committee and instructed them to drop the issue. This explains why Yeshayahu reversed his previous stand of support for holding a debate in the Conference. I have argued that the Standing Committee was a ritually sanctioned arena for free and open debate and criticism with two major restrictions or conditions. The first condition was that ultimately a compromise consensual formulation had to be reached. The members of the Committee clearly abided by this rule when even those who made more "extreme" proposals, like Aloni and Namir, agreed to a compromise formulation that was certainly acceptable to all of the Committee members and presumed to be acceptable to the leadership as well. In this case we see clearly documented the enforcement of the second condition: in cases where the leadership lacked confidence in its ability to control the outcome of a debate in the Conference; and when the leaders felt a debate might have been detrimental to the party, to their coalition relations, or to the people, the issue had to be suppressed.

In the case of religion and the states, all of the factors conducive to the suppression of an issue were seen to be present by the top party leadership. There was, and is, a sharp division of opinion on this issue within the party and within the nation. The reason given by leaders for suppressing the issue was that it would likely lead to a coalition crisis with their Cabinet partners—Mafdal (the National Religious Party). It is also likely that given the prior pressure of their religious coalition partners, they sincerely feared that a free and open debate on this issue, particularly if it would assert strong pressures to alter the status quo, would lead to a "split in the Jewish people," and could encourage a *Kulturkampf*—cultural war between the religious and nonreligious. Top leaders such as the prime minister and the minister of justice at the time made repeated public statements to this effect. Their subsequent handling of the issue when it was forced in two different arenas tends to bear out this interpretation. Even when Mafdal was in the opposition in 1958, there was no change in the status quo (cf. Don-Yehiya, 1975:261).

In addition to these factors, it was fairly clear that the sharp division of opinions on this issue within the party prevented the leadership from feeling they could confidently gain a solid vote of support for their stand. The issue therefore had to be suppressed. In addition, considerable hostility against the religious status quo was aroused in the Israeli public by a number of controversial issues, such as the case of the *mumzarim* (bastards) who were prevented from marrying because of religious laws. It was for this reason as well that the issue had to be suppressed in the opinion of the leadership.

When the issue was subsequently forced on the leadership in two different forums—the Central Committee of the party and the Knesset—they succeeded in postponing debates and decisions after great effort. Whereas the Standing Committee had said that the issue of religion and state should be debated in "one of the first meetings of the Central Committee," it was delayed for approximately a year. After the Young Guard of the party successfully mobilized enough signatures to force a debate in several consecutive meetings of the Central Committee, the leadership managed to have the issue sent to the branches for a prior debate before final decisions were taken and implemented. Three years later it has not been debated by the branches and it promises to be a long time before the resolution is operationalized.

Similarly, when the Independent Liberals, a coalition partner, presented a bill that would have made it possible for Jews who could not be married according to the *Halacha* (Jewish law) to be married in civil ceremonies, the leadership of the Labor Party carefully managed a near coalition crisis, and used its majority in the Knesset to have the bill removed from the agenda and sent to Committee, thereby preventing debate on the issue until after the 1973 general election. By June 1976 the legislation had still not been introduced.

Significantly, a closely related issue involving jurisdiction over conversion to Judaism kept the National Religious Party (Mafdal) out of the coalition government of Yitzchak Rabin for the longest period in the history of the state. During this time, the Labor Party's coalition partners in the government—the Independent Liberals and the Citizens' Rights List led by former Labor Party rebel Shulamit Aloni, both of which had campaigned on a program that promised a voter change in the present religious status quo—were prevented from tabling legislation that would alter the status quo. At the same time, the Labor Party conducted protracted and difficult negotiations to get the National Religious Party back into the government. They eventually succeeded by November 1974 (which led to the immediate withdrawal of the Citizens' Rights List from the government).

The Histadrut

The suppression of the Histadrut issues followed a similar pattern, and I shall therefore only mention the essentials of the case. Among the many divisions of opinion and interest within the Labor Party, one of the most important, which has far-reaching consequences for the structure of the economy, was known as the "Histadrut issues." It referred to related issues such as wage policies, labor relations, and questions of internal structure and representation of workers within the Histadrut. On most of these issues the spokesmen for the conflicting stands were two powerful figures, Finance Minister Sapir and Secretary-General of the Histadrut Ben-Aharon. Sapir played a key role through his dominance of the party machinery. Here I shall only mention his stand as finance minister. As the man directly responsible for the state of the nation's economy, Sapir sponsored a "package deal" aimed at curbing spiralling inflation. This obviously included a curtailing of wage increases. Ben-Aharon, spokesman of the nation's workers, frequently sided with the demands of various sectors of the labor force for increased wages. In addition, he sponsored a number of radical proposals for the complete restructuring of the system of internal party elections of the Histadrut governing institutions. His extremely radical proposals to abolish the nominations committees through which the party had traditionally controlled the membership on Histadrut institutions (as well as party institutions) and to allow the workers to elect their representatives directly from the shop floors presented a major challenged to the huge establishment of functionaries who run the Histadrut and to the top party leadership whom they serve. It also might have set a precedent for demands for similar reforms in the party, which would seriously threaten the leadership.

It is significant for an understanding of later events that many delegates (and professional journalists) felt that Ben-Aharon was by far the most impressive speaker of the opening session of the Party Conference. Not only was his oration eloquent, but he also spoke to the hearts of the rank-and-file members when he condemned the lack of communication and trust between the workers and their representatives. He charged that nothing would change unless the Conference and political institutions were so structured that the people could trust and believe in them. He condemned elections on the basis of previous party factions and the political machine. In his concluding remarks he said, "A fat movement does not understand the thin . . . the problem is the character of the rulers—people who are too attached to their chairs. . . . People in high office follow their own philosophies and no one can call us to account. . . ." Upon the completion of this speech, which violated all of the rules about refraining from such divisive criticism in the Conference, he received a resounding ovation in which even seasoned political reporters, who are not generally easily moved by political orations, applauded enthusiastically.

The various issues related to the Histadrut were first discussed in the subcommittee on socio-economic affairs and later in a special subcommittee on trade union affairs, before being debated in the Standing Committee. When Ben-Aharon demanded that the issues related to the Histadrut be deleted, claiming the need for a special Conference on the Histadrut, and because he had not been consulted by the subcommittees of the Standing Committee, a special subcommittee was appointed to negotiate with him. The negotiating subcommittee offered in conciliation to water down its proposals by merely rephrasing former agreed positions on the issue, but Ben-Aharon refused. When Yeshayahu attempted to force a deletion of the issue in the Standing Committee without debate, he aroused much initial opposition. One person said, "In the Conference they do not let us speak, at least let us speak here!" Another protested, "How is it possible to have a Conference and not mention one of the most important subjects?" It was finally decided, after the opposition had been allowed to express itself, to delete the issue and refer it to a special Conference on the Histadrut to be held in the future. One of the members recited the traditional mourner's prayer for the dead in mock solemnity over the demise of the issue. When Yeshayahu then asked Ben-Aharon to write an appreciation of the Histadrut in honor of its Jubilee Anniversary (to be passed by the Conference), there was much cynical laughter among the members of the Standing Committee.

As in the previous case, a controversial issue concerning basic party ideology—the role of socialism in the Israeli economy on which both the party activists and the general membership were divided and which seriously threatened to destroy the carefully projected image of unity in the Conference—was suppressed. By breaking the rules of the game in his initial speech, Ben-Aharon had won and demonstrated great popularity with the delegates of the Conference, and was a potential threat in that he might have mobilized a populist left-wing critique of government policy in the Conference. Rather than risk this showdown, the leaders removed the controversial issue from the agenda.

Ben-Aharon proved in subsequent showdowns with the party leadership that he was indeed capable of such divisive actions. He later resigned his post as secretary-general of the Histadrut in protest against government intervention in collective bargaining. There were widespread workers' demonstrations demanding that he return to office. He complied. A later call by him for a "war economy" and support for various strikes caused the opposition to demand a special session of the Knesset to condemn what they termed his demagoguery. In this session he was labeled a "socialist Little Red Riding Hood" by one member of the opposition (cf. Ben-Dor, 1972). Because the top leadership saw him as both an embarrassment and, more seriously, a threat, they were not anxious for him to continue in his present post. They made it clear that they would not support the renomination of Ben-Aharon to his office, which led to his final resignation. This might serve as a lesson on what can happen even to powerful politicians who do not play by the rules of the Labor Party game in Israel.

Conclusions

By comparing and contrasting the suppression of two highly important and salient issues, I hoped to highlight important aspects of the party, the society, and the phenomenon of suppression in general. Alan (Asher) Arian (1973:55) has shown significantly that religious observance and affiliation to the Histadrut are the two most important factors to determine voting in Israel. Arian (1971) has also demonstrated that the religious issue is one of the greatest areas of dissent in Israeli society. It seems more than coincidental that debate on these two vital issues was suppressed from the agenda of the National Party Conference of the dominant party in Israel. Although there were great similarities in the techniques through which these two issues were suppressed, the issues themselves, and the implications of their removal from the agenda of the Conference, differ substantially.

The issue of religion and the state is one of historical depth, and involves basic ideological elements related to the very nature of Israeli society and the state. The inherent contradictions within modern Zionism—conflicting value systems that pit modern democratic ideas of individual rights, freedom of conscience, and majority rule against traditional Jewish values like the supremacy of religious law (*Halacha*) and deeply rooted ethnic loyalties—date back to the origins of the World Zionist Organization.

David M. Somer (1976) traces the historical development of the duality of cooperation between the secular and religious parties at the organizational level, and the continuing conflict of their world views on the normative level. He identifies three methods by which this conflict has been limited and kept under control. The first is the shared fear of disintegration, or *negative consensus*. Bensman and Preece (1970:143) have argued that "the agreement necessary for elementary stability in the midst of fundamental conflict needs to be no more than minimal," and that "the minimal agreement is often a product of those conflicts. This minimal consensus we have chosen to call negative consensus because it arises from dissensus." They give numerous examples showing that an agreement to suspend conflict on issues basic to identity of the political unit "creates a moratorium on issues and an allowance of the political system to continue" (ibid., 144). Negative consensus was created by the mutual fear among Israeli political leaders that an attempt to resolve the issue of religion and the state by disrupting the status quo would result in a *Kulturkampf*. This led to their cooperation in avoiding a confrontation of the issue in two ways. Somer documents the "fractionation of conflict,"—the breaking down of a complex, emotion-laden issue into smaller parts on which compromises can be found. For example, compromises were reached on such areas as the observance of dietary laws in public institutions, observance of the sabbath, and so forth.

Finally, perhaps the most effective means of controlling conflict was through the limitation of public discussion of the religion and state issue to elite groups. Somer documents that since the early days of the Zionist movement there has been no general debate on the issue. This case illustrates how the elite limit the scope of and access to the issue by allowing a symbolic debate in a ritual forum, after which it is removed from the agenda of the non-elite Conference.

In assessing the reasons for the suppression of the issue, the benefits derived from its suppression, and its ramifications for the political system, the suppression must be viewed from several perspectives. From the perspective of the top leadership of the Labor Party, it was clearly advantageous to prevent a challenge to their policy that could have undermined their position of authority and might have been detrimental to party unity. From the perspective of the elites of both the Labor Party and the National Religious Party (Mafdal), the suppression of the issue aided their close working relationship, which was (and still is) being challenged by the Young Guard of both parties. Cooperation at the elite level is an essential ingredient of what Arend Lijphart (1967) has called "the politics of accommodation" in Holland, and which I contend is an important aspect of the Israeli political system. The suppression of the issue of religion and state must therefore be seen within the context of its importance for the perpetuation of the coalition of political parties that has been the dominant force in Israeli politics since the nation's birth. However, one cannot ignore the likelihood that the top leadership of the Labor Party was genuinely concerned with what they perceived to be the potentially divisive consequences of the alteration of the status quo; they therefore felt justified in suppressing the issue in order to prevent a threat to societal cohesion. A final perspective on the religion issue was aptly expressed by Jacob Talmon (1965:281–82), who stated:

> It would be difficult to imagine a more complex, more insoluble and indeed more poignant problem than the question of religion and State in present-day Israel. . . . [T]he issues involved touch upon some of those basic dilemmas which go to make up the human condition. Ancient exclusive loyalties rooted in the deepest, one may almost say desperate convictions, are pitted against overwhelming forces of change and sweeping innovation. A battle is fought between the urge for free individual self-expression, and the "grantedness" of a concrete, most sharply contoured historic totality. What are the legitimate limits which the heritage of all the ages may set upon the sovereign right of the generation here and now to fashion its life?

In the forthcoming chapter I show how such complex and virtually insoluble problems are coped with by their symbolic presentation in ritual performance. At this point I wish to stress that the issue of religion and the state comes close to what Sidney Verba (1965:533) has identified as the central problem facing a nation: "What is my nation?" Derek Urwin (1970:340) has pointed out, "The experience of Belgium suggests that other problems may be successfully tackled as long as this central question is not asked: once it is raised, then the party system will fail to function satisfactorily until it is resolved." The suppression of the issue of religion and the state shows that the elite of the Labor Party prevented the asking of a question that goes to the heart of the definition of the nation and to which there are mutually contradictory and, to date, unresolvable answers.

The issues related to the Histadrut were of a significant but slightly less far-reaching nature. They must be viewed from three levels: a struggle for power within the elite of the Labor Party; the conflict of institutional interests dominated by and mediated through the party; and a historically protracted ideological debate over differing interpretations of socialism as expressed in conflicting views over the proper role of the Histadrut and the state in Israeli society. The power struggle was represented by the challenge of a nonconformist member of the elite, Secretary-General of the Histadrut Ben-Aharon, both to the policies of the government, represented by the economic policies of Finance Minister Sapir, and to the methods through which the party elite has traditionally maintained its domination of institutions like the Histadrut. It is highly significant for the suppression of the issue and for the eventual outcome of the political confrontation that Sapir also dominated the institutions of the Labor Party. At this level, the suppression of the issue represented the veto power of Ben-Aharon, who successfully prevented the passage of resolutions in the Sapir-dominated Party Conference, and the postponement of the debate on the resolutions to the forthcoming Histadrut Conference in which Ben-Aharon anticipated having greater support. Ben-Aharon's successful veto, which caused the suppression, was due to his proven popularity among the Conference delegates and his potential to disrupt the Conference by provoking a confrontation through his violation of the taboos against divisive criticism in his major speech at the Conference.

The suppressed issues reflected conflicting institutional interests of the government and the Histadrut, issues that preceded and succeeded the terms of office of the two main protagonists in this contest. The most vivid proof of this is the continuing bitter confrontation over economic policy between the successors of Sapir and Ben-Aharon (both of whom were chosen by the Sapir-dominated party machine). This built-in conflict of interests caused by the party's domination of two powerful institutions (the government, particularly the Ministry of Finance, and the Histadrut) has traditionally been mediated through the institutions of the party (cf. Medding, 1972). One of the ways in which these conflicting interests have been successfully mediated and conciliated is the limitation of decision making to the elite and the suppression of debate from larger institutional forums until compromise policies are reached by the elite.

The Histadrut preceded the state historically and performed many functions that were taken over in stages by the state after Independence. As I pointed out in

Chapter 2, a constant theme in the various party splits and mergers since Independence has been differing interpretations of socialism and pioneering—two key elements in the ideology of the Zionist Labor movement. The social, economic, and political conditions of a developing society produced not only differential changes in the power and authority of the Histadrut and the state, but discrepant ideological interpretations of the priorities of these institutions and the party in coping with changing societal conditions. Given the reluctance of party elites to allow free discussion and debate on these issues in the major party institutions, and given their tendency to suppress highly salient but controversial issues as discussed in this chapter, one alternative was to allow symbolic debates of such issues in a controlled ritual forum. This is the theme of the next chapter.

5

Rituals of Self-Identification, Rebellion, and Assertion

Introduction: The Conceptual Framework

In Chapter 2, I said that the Labor Party is the dominant party in Israel's multi-party system. According to Durverger (1969:309), "Domination is a question of influence rather than strength; it is also linked with belief. A dominant party is that which the public opinion believes to be dominant." Israeli public opinion verified by observers of the Israeli political scene seems to concur that the Labor Party has enjoyed this unique position of dominance, at least up to the last election in 1973 (cf. Arian, 1972:187–200, 1975). It is particularly relevant to the present analysis that whereas Labor's dominant political position was still intact during the proceedings of the Standing Committee, its members seemed to recognize that the party's position of ideological or moral dominance, which had identified it with the state in the initial post-Independence epoch, had been gradually eroded as a consequence of subsequent rapid social, economic, and political change (cf. Arian, 1975:303).

The problems generated by the developing structure of the Israel Labor Party in the context of a rapidly expanding and changing society provoked significant organizational changes and the need for a redefinition of central values and ideological concepts. The secondary echelon of party leaders, the main participants in the ritual, lacked the theoretical perspective to view the erosion of their positions and of central party values as a reasoned response to changes in the social system. They therefore attempted, in a controlled and bracketed ritual setting, to comment upon their roles and social order and to redefine their situation by reformulating and asserting their ideological perception of the social order, in which their own roles were given new meaning. When cumulative change has taken a society away from what ideology says it is, there is either a groping for a new transforming pattern, or the giving of a new interpretation to traditional patterns of symbolic action, or a reassertion of the traditional legitimating universe—in the face of a reality that is no longer meaningfully explained by it. The ritual performers in the Standing Committee created a bridge between affective situational reality (i.e., the erosion of the meaning of their roles and central values of party ideology) by asserting a desired normative structure (e.g., transforming their roles by giving them new meaning and reasserting central values such as the equality of all Jews, the importance of equal representation, democratic procedures, and so forth).

The following is a list of ten of the most important characteristics of contemporary rituals which I shall elaborate and illustrate throughout this chapter.

1. They take place in controlled and bracketed social settings.
2. Because of the controlled nature of the ritual performance, the actions of the actors are to a certain extent prescribed or constrained, but within these limits considerable freedom and innovation can exist. This appears to be particularly characteristic of certain types of modern ritual.
3. The actors are at some level conscious of performing ritual acts (although they might not define them as such).
4. The ritual actions have serious implications for those who perform them.
5. The outcomes of the ritual are determined in advance, at least to the minimal extent that it is known that the social unit will emerge united.
6. The ritual performers converse in symbols, which, although multi-vocal (capable of having multiple interpretations ascribed to them), are understood by and have deep meaning for the ritual performers.
7. The ritual is an important means for dealing with ambiguous social roles, conflicting interests, and ideological world views that threaten the unity of the social unit in which they take place.
8. The ritual is an important means for dealing with cognitive dissonance between ideology and social reality, particularly when the latter has changed to the extent that it is no longer meaningfully explained by the former.
9. The ritual presents reality symbolically in a selective and sometimes disguised manner, thereby allowing discourse on it to take place, which can produce the conciliation, affirmation, or transformation of symbolic universes.
10. Ritual in modern society does not generally take place on a society-wide basis, but in subgroups within society in which the necessary conditions of control and bracketing can be assured.

In clarifying the ritual dimensions of the performance in the Standing Committee, I differentiate between this ritual activity and the other processes discussed previously. One such process, the control function of the Standing Committee vis-à-vis the National Party Conference, discussed in the previous chapter, will be considered from an entirely different theoretical perspective in the forthcoming analysis. Such processes as the control function of the Standing Committee, or the allowing of the open expression of discontent on the part of the ritual performers, might be viewed as latent functions. But I shall attempt to go beyond the examination of latent functions, which I consider at best a limited explanation if not a dubious one (in the sense that it is difficult to verify) by analyzing the creative aspects of the proceedings as a ritual of assertion through which the participants forged a bridge between the affective situational reality of their roles, which had lost their former meaning, and the desired normative structure of a true democracy. I stress that this level of activity was going on at different stages interspersed between, and sometimes simultaneous with, the "real" pragmatic political work of the Committee. However, the ritual behavior revealed that something other than the political business was taking place as well.

One of the commonly observed characteristics of ritual is that it is a performance in which actions are prescribed and in which the actors are conscious of performing, at least at some level of their psyches. I shall deal with the former problem first, and return to the aspect of self-consciousness later in my analysis. There are varying degrees of choice and determinacy for actors in different kinds of rituals. The ritual proceedings of the Standing Committee allowed the actors considerable freedom for expression and creativity. Ritual is particularly important in relationships where the actions have significant implications for the lives (moral and socio-political) of the participants. It appears that certain kinds of activities that strongly resemble ritual—such as games and sport—can afford to be indeterminate when they do not directly affect the lives of the participants and audience to the extent that rituals directly affect social relationships. It is clear that ritual is a serious business for those involved.

My application of the term "ritual" is more circumscribed and restricted than is that of Robert Bocock (1974:65), whose broad classification of "civic rituals" (in contrast to "religious rituals") states that the former "carry few implications for other areas of life," and "neither the principal participants nor the onlookers need cultivate deep understanding of the inner meaning of the ritual actions and symbols involved." I shall clarify in this analysis (1) the serious implications of the ritual for the lives of the participants, (2) the extent to which they were involved, and (3) the degree to which they understood the meanings of the ritual actions and symbols involved (cf. Langer, 1967, and Douglas, 1970, for excellent analyses of the concept "symbols").

The conditions of the ritual forum of the Standing Committee appear to meet a criterion of a social ritual stressed by Max Gluckman: that the end is known in advance—the social unit must end united. There was no question that the final outcome of party unity was known in advance, and in fact one of the major purposes of the ritual proceedings was to attain this goal, which was constantly emphasized. The two major conditional constraints that bracketed the freedom of debate within the Committee were: (1) after the wide range of conflicting views, interests, and loyalties were expressed, all resolutions would reach compromise, consensual formulations, and under no circumstances would minority proposals be submitted to the Conference; and (2) all issues likely to cause major conflicts or unpredictable outcomes in the Conference were suppressed by removing them from the agenda of the Conference. Within the confines of these rigorously applied constraints, which determined the outcomes, the participants had practically unlimited freedom to innovate and express themselves in the ritual debates and proceedings. One additional element of constraint was imposed through the setting of the agenda by the chairman, in consultation with the top leadership of the party, but even in this area the participants could and did extend debate on some issues and cut short debate on others.

Most importantly, in spite of the good-humored joking that characterized much of the proceedings, the participants were involved in serious business which affected their authority, power, status, mobility in careers, livelihoods, and individual and collective self-image as leaders within the party. I will explicate the different degrees of dependence and involvement of the various categories of actors and audience, and then I will assess the outcome of the ritual in terms of different levels of meaning and efficacy for these different categories.

Actors and Audiences

As I shall show, the actual participants in the ritual were a limited and fairly homogeneous group, yet it is impossible fully to understand the meaning of their actions without placing them in the wider context of various levels of audiences or reference groups having a significant influence on the form and style of the ritual performance. It is useful to think of the various categories of audience and actors as constituting a pyramid at the apex of which stand the elite, a small group of top national party leaders who hold the greatest power in the party (and indeed in the nation) and have major influence in the making of key decisions. This group was most conspicuous by its physical absence (which was almost total) from the proceedings of the Standing Committee. I argue that the primary role of the top leadership of the party was one of control and manipulation behind the scenes. Their participation in the Conference itself was minimal, and when they appeared it was primarily in ceremonial capacities. I argue, as has Gluckman in a different context, that, "Prescribed absence from a ritual is thus a form of participation in it: though it is not a protest, it states that there is a conflict present in the social process" (Gluckman, 1955:139). I maintain that the prescribed absence of the elite from the debates of the Standing Committee was essential for the successful removal of taboos against criticism of this leadership, and that it allowed the free and open expression of extreme and conflicting views in the meeting. I suggest that had the top leadership been present, this would have considerably inhibited the secondary leaders, who are so dependent upon them, from freely expressing criticisms and views; this restriction would have defeated one of the most important functions of the performance: here I consider I can justifiably call it a ritual.

The next tier of the pyramid is composed of the major actors in the performance I consider to be ritual. They are the 134 members of the Standing Committee, who constitute the trusted and loyal second echelon of party leadership. Practically 90 percent of them are elected party officials, members of the Knesset, mayors, secretaries of Local Workers' Councils of the Histadrut or local party branches, functionaries of the party and Histadrut bureaucracies, and representatives of the major interest groups. They are very dependent upon the top leadership. While they have much higher status and more influence in national affairs than the third tier of local-level leaders, they lack the support of solid grass-roots constituencies that the latter generally have. This is due primarily to their appointment to office through nominations committees rather than election to office in an open process. In the ritual, they were aware of their limited influence in the making of major decisions, and that they were primarily involved in executing the policies of the top leadership. Nevertheless, they felt that because of their high positions their views and opinions should be listened to attentively by the top leadership of the party. The Standing Committee was a ritually approved forum in which normal restrictions against open criticism of party policy and leaders and open expression of contradictory views were temporarily lifted. Because of their ambivalent position, involving high status but limited power, high dependence on the top leadership, and inability to express in public their opposition to or disagreement with the top leadership, the removal of these restraints in the proceedings of the Committee was vitally important to this group.

The third tier, primarily the local leadership that made up the majority of delegates to the National Conference, acted as a very important reference group for the former two categories, whose actions were governed to a large extent by their estimation of the reactions of this audience. The local leaders, as I argued earlier, have a strong feeling of political weakness because of their inability to influence national policy, but nevertheless generally have the security of strong local bases of support. I have shown elsewhere (Aronoff, 1972) that as new categories of local leadership, particularly ethnic minority leaders in development towns, have consolidated positions based on local rather than exclusively national backing, they have successfully achieved greater local autonomy in internal party affairs. Members of this category were different from the majority of the members of the Standing Committee in a number of important respects. Their relationship with the top leaders of the party was more remote, but they were also less directly dependent on them. They were relatively new to positions of party leadership at the local level, whereas the members of the Standing Committee were party veterans. They generally represented Middle Eastern ethnic groups while the upper two tiers of party leadership were mostly of European descent. They had undergone different processes of political socialization and had not internalized party norms to the same extent as the secondary leaders. From the point of view of the top leadership, they were less reliable than the secondary leaders, but more so than the amorphous general party membership and public.

The increasingly wider circles of audiences whom the performers in the ritual took into account were the 300,000 members of the party, the nation as a whole—particularly the voters—the Jews abroad, Israel's allies, and lastly, Israel's numerous foes. Although the ritual performance was much more immediately influenced by the specific contextual relationships with the elite and perceptions of the interests and behavior of the elite and the local leaders, the wider context of Israeli society and its position in the Middle East and the world had an indirect, but significant, influence on the ritual.

Ritual Form and Process

In this section I briefly describe some of the major techniques through which the performance was bracketed and controlled, thereby setting the formal constraints within which the freer innovative and creative aspect of the ritual process took place. As described in Chapter 3, the membership of the Standing Committee was carefully selected by a series of nominations committees to ensure that the actors would abide by the rules of the game. In addition to the general dependence of the secondary leadership on the top leadership, each member had either direct links to patrons in the top leadership or indirect links through membership in common political networks. Throughout various stages of the meetings of the Standing Committee, and after lengthy debates, final formulations and so-called "technical decisions" were relegated to subcommittees thereby facilitating conciliation between opposing views and interests. The calling of special meetings on short notice and the delaying of decisions until the last minute were used effectively to overcome opposition to, and to gain consent for, unpopular measures.

Control of the issues by the elites from behind the scenes was one of the most important constraints. On the one hand, it assured the outcomes that determined the ritual nature of the debates, but on the other hand, it allowed freedom of expression and innovation in the performance. This control was expressed in the setting of the agenda, that is, which issues would be discussed and when. It also meant control of which issues, once debated by the members of the Standing Committee, would be passed on to the delegates of the National Party Conference for approval—in effect ceremonious—and which issues would be suppressed, as discussed in Chapter 4.

Other issues were not actually suppressed, but were handled delicately because they were sensitive. The stage of the proceedings in which the sensitive issues were discussed was marked by observable changes in both the atmosphere of the performance and the behavior of the performers. One day's session began with the final stages of the suppression of the economic proposals concerning labor relations and the Histadrut. This session was characterized by boisterous debate, sarcastic and joking exchanges, and a lot of hearty laughter.

The tone of the meeting began to change when a proposal was made to honor the families who had lost sons in Israel's wars. The question was raised as to how this could be done in "good taste." The chairman of the Organization Department of the party (who was to lose his own son in the forthcoming war of October 1973) objected to debating such a "sensitive" issue in the Conference, saying that it could not be discussed "on the record." After talking to a number of the members privately, he submitted a proposal for a "blessing of Zahal" (the Israel Defense Forces); this was accepted. This is one of many cases in which multi-vocal symbols were used to make indirect reference to issues that were so sensitive that direct reference to them was considered to be in "bad taste." Zahal not only represents the strength of the nation through its armed forces, but in different contexts represents the rebirth of the Jewish nation, which after 2,000 years is capable of resisting persecution; in this case it symbolized the sons of the nation who fell in defense of the Jewish state and people. (For a discussion of memorialization in Israel see Aronoff, 1991b.)

A somewhat similar solution was found to handle the highly sensitive issue of ethnic relations in the party and in the nation. The issue was in a sense forced onto the agenda by the spontaneous formation of a caucus of North African and Middle Eastern delegates to the Conference, led by the minister of police, without its having received the official sanction of the top party leadership or any formal party institution. This so-called Oriental caucus demanded that its members be guaranteed one-third of the membership of all party institutions, and led the debates in the Conference on poverty and the "socio-economic gap." They made direct appeals—"Why don't you give a chance to the sons of the Eastern community [*edot mizrach*]?"—and more indirect references—"Families blessed with many children [Orientals] contribute more to the country than do the rich!" They also invoked multi-vocal symbols that have an almost sacrosanct aura in Israeli society (such as the previously mentioned Zahal and security), particularly the absorption of immigrants, the ingathering of the exiles, and the merging of the diverse communities into a new Jewish-Israeli people. One such usage was, "If we can absorb new immigrants [primarily Europeans] we can absorb the older immigrants [primarily Middle Easterners]." There were many references to the more militant demonstrations of the Israeli Black Panthers, as one delegate put it, "as a symbol of what had been ignored too long!" It is significant that neither the minister of police nor any of the other Conference delegates who participated in the caucus were members of the Standing Committee, and none of them were invited to participate in the Committee's discussions of the ethnic issue. When a member of the Standing Committee rose to introduce this issue, there was, most uncharacteristically, absolute silence in the room. I point out that this silence was not in deference to the status of the speaker, who was the mayor of a small development town (and had risen to national prominence when he became one of the leaders of the splinter party led by Ben-Gurion and Dayan in 1965), but signaled the recognition by the members of the importance and sensitivity of the potentially explosive issue that demanded their attention.

The speaker stressed that he had consulted ministers of the government. He thereby implied that he had received the official blessing of the top leaders of the party, and claimed that this proposal was better than that of the caucus, i.e., it was less radical. He stated that he was opposed in principle to a specifically guaranteed percentage of representation of ethnic groups on party institutions because "that is not honorable." (The speaker, an Iraqi, was married to a European.) He stressed the increased rate of intermarriage between the two main ethnic communities (16.9 percent), and he asked under which ethnic group his daughter would enter the Central Committee. One of the members interjected humorously that she would gain representation as a Sabra (native Israeli), who were also underrepresented in party institutions. This joking was accompanied by laughter and helped to relieve the tension in the room. The speaker continued that this was an issue about which many members felt strongly, and if they wanted to show that it was not a problem, they must do something about it. The chairman of the Committee suggested that the issue not be debated "at the twelfth hour," but be postponed for a future meeting of the Central Committee or the Leadership Bureau. However, this attempt at outright suppression was rejected by the speaker, who insisted, "I still want this Committee to show that they are concerned." When the secretary-general of the party attempted to support the suppression of the issue by assuring the speaker that the leadership and the Nominations Committee would "consider this [ethnicity] at the top of their list of priorities," the speaker replied angrily, "I am sorry, but this is too much!" He insisted on a formal vote on his proposal that Jews from Middle Eastern backgrounds be given greater representation on party institutions.

I stress that there were few formal votes taken in the Committee. When one of the delegates objected to sending the proposal to the Conference saying, "The problem will end in time," the speaker laughed nervously and angrily and said with bitter sarcasm, "There is no problem at all!" There was an immediate vote in which his proposal was accepted unanimously.

I will now look at this type of interaction and the use of symbols that typified much of the proceedings at two different levels. I focus first on what might be viewed as the latent function of the proceedings as a controlling mechanism. The potential for open strife in the Conference led the top leadership of the party to go to great lengths to control the issues brought to the arena of the Conference. The debates in the Standing Committee were a vital means to achieve this control. Through the careful selection of members who could be trusted because of their high degree of dependence on the elites and their strong internalization of party norms, the top leaders could allow a "free" debate of the issues and could be confident that "consensual" agreement would be reached in the final formulations. The Standing Committee could be relied upon to screen out issues that might have disrupted the Conference or had unpredictable results. Even where the leadership did not succeed in removing the ethnic issue from the agenda, because of high salience and the unrelenting insistence of a trusted member of the secondary leadership, it was dealt with in a manner likely to be the least disruptive to party unity.

The critical importance of such control was manifested on several occasions during the Conference. I cite two brief examples related to the ethnic issue. A dramatic direct appeal was made by a young Oriental on crutches who rose from his seat in the balcony of the Conference and plaintively shouted, "Help me!" before he stumbled and fell. The young man (who was not an official delegate to the Conference) was given first aid, and was then escorted into a room where he talked privately with the secretary-general of the party, who promised him aid. He was then whisked off in a car. The man was promised aid because of genuine concern for his plight, but he was quickly removed from the Conference to prevent his case from becoming a cause célèbre that might have precipitated a more emotional and divisive debate on this issue.

As it was, the debate stirred many of the delegates to emotions that were difficult for the leadership to control. When the speech of one of the Oriental delegates in the Conference was interrupted by the chairperson who told him his time had run out, there was a loud protest from the audience. They clapped their hands and insisted that he be allowed to continue, but the chairperson insisted he stop. When the next speaker, an Ashkenazi or European, had run out of time according to the watches of some of the Oriental delegates who were timing him, the Oriental delegates shouted and clapped their hands demanding that he stop. The chairperson said sternly, "I am handling this meeting and he has another minute!" But the speaker stepped down when there was further protest from the audience. These are just a few examples that highlight the importance of the latent controlling function of the proceedings of the Standing Committee.

I am convinced that to leave the analysis at this level would be insufficient in explaining the meaning of this behavior. For its deeper meaning, we must go to a deeper level, one that encompasses a wider social and symbolic context. When the Iraqi speaker in the Standing Committee refused to allow the ethnic issue to be side-tracked or suppressed, and, by demanding a vote, insisted that his comrades demonstrate "that they are concerned," he invoked symbols that asserted a major tenet of Zionist ideology—the ingathering of exiles, which proclaimed the equality of all Jews and the dream that in their new home the various communities would rapidly merge into a newly reborn and reunited people. This is a value of such importance that it goes to the very heart of the raison d'être that gives meaning to and legitimizes the regathering of the Jewish people in their national homeland. Any form of racial or ethnic prejudice or discrimination is reprehensible in Zionist ideology and Israeli culture (cf. Deshen, 1970). But the historical circumstances of the immigration of different ethnic groups have resulted in a correlation of socio-economic categories and political power with ethnic categories in which a very large proportion of the Oriental immigrants are at the bottom of both the socio-economic ladder and the ladder of political power. The refusal of the speaker to allow the ethnic issue to be suppressed was at once a criticism of the breach of a central, even sacrosanct, norm of the ethnically pluralistic party and nation, and an assertion of the continuing vital importance of this norm in spite of reality. This is why I believe he insisted upon and received the unanimous vote, which symbolized *concern* for and recognition of the legitimacy of his assertion that this norm was a central value in party ideology and an integral part of the ethos of Zionism and Israeli culture.

Consensus: Meaning in Social and Symbolic Contexts

The theme of consensus was at once a prerequisite for the success of the Standing Committee meeting, unquestionably the dominant theme of the meeting, and probably its most important outcome. I shall attempt to unravel the many facets of consensus through an analysis of its meaning at different levels of social and symbolic contexts.

The importance of consensus as a prerequisite for the success of what I consider a ritual performance has already been discussed. The members of the Standing Committee were selected because they represented a category of leaders who could be trusted and relied upon to play by the rules of the game. In addition to the nature of their dependence on the top leaders of the party, which I have already explained, I stress an additional factor that determined their actions. Gluckman (1955:134) has argued that ritual protest is inappropriate once there is a questioning of the social order, since the purpose of ritual is to unite people who do not or cannot query their social roles. While obviously the members of the Standing Committee were capable of questioning their roles, the constraints imposed by the political system are such that the costs of opting for other political roles are perceived by almost all as prohibitive. The Labor Party has so dominated the political system that even attempts by the charismatic founder of the party and of the modern state, David Ben-Gurion, to split from the party led to the political wilderness of the opposition. This precedent is a dramatic warning to ambitious leaders who have reached the second echelon of power in the party: to opt for a different political role is not the most efficient means of achieving mobility. I stress also that we are dealing with career politicians who have spent most of their adult lives in public service on behalf of the party and who have deeply internalized party norms. I shall return to this point later in the analysis.

Through an elaboration of consensus as the dominant theme of the ritual performance, the meaning of consensus in the other context will become clearer. The chairman of the Standing Committee introduced the first session with the following admonition: "Whatever we do, we must decide in this Committee. If the debate goes to the Conference it will kill it. We must finish everything here." Although he rarely used foreign words, throughout the proceedings of the Committee he constantly used the English term "consensus": "We must reach a 'consensus,'" or "I feel we have now reached a 'consensus.'" At times, extreme positions were expressed and compromise appeared difficult; issues were then submitted to a "formulation committee," where, the chairman was certain, a consensual formulation (*nusach consensuali*) would be found. And it always was found.

In practice, there are party members such as Minister-without-Portfolio Yisrael Galili, who are known as experts in this special field and are called upon frequently on critical occasions. Although there is a Hebrew expression for general agreement (*haskama klalit*), the use of the English term "consensus," particularly with the incongruous Yemenite accent of the chairman of the Committee, tended to highlight the central importance of the theme of consensus and at the same time lended itself more readily to wider and more varied meanings as a symbol than the more narrow Hebrew term for general agreement (cf. Bailey, 1972, for framework for the analysis of conceptual systems).

The admonition that everything must be done in the Committee was constantly interwoven with openly expressed fear of the indeterminateness of outcomes in the Conference, and therefore a potential for chaos and uncontrolled strife. These threats were carefully juxtaposed with pleas for unity in the party. The potential threat of renewed factional strife, based on the three former parties that had merged to form the Labor Party, was invoked as a reminder of the need for unity. The size of the Conference (3,000 delegates) was emphasized in justifying the need to decide everything in the Committee and to prevent anything but ceremonial debates and votes in the Conference.

The chairman constantly emphasized his fear of chaos should there be too many debates and votes in the Conference: "Not that I am afraid of democracy, but it could be chaos [*balagan*]. Ceremonial votes are all right, but. . . ." Again he stressed the need to prevent chaos by maintaining order and controlling debates and votes through the Standing Committee. The need for consensus in the Standing Committee in order to curtail the possibility of uncontrolled and open strife in the Conference, the outcome of which was unforeseeable and threatening, was constantly expressed through the invocation of the overriding common value and goal of party unity. This was done with constant attempts to legitimize the violation of the equally strongly held value of democratic procedure. In order to resolve the paradoxes, participants resorted to what I regard as ritual performance.

Whereas the members of the Standing Committee constituted a fairly homogeneous group in terms of party status (i.e., what I have termed the secondary echelon of leadership), they represented a great diversity of group interests, ideological points of view, and loyalties. In Chapter 2 I dealt at length with the factional divisions based on the three former parties that merged to form the Labor Party. In addition, there are many more complicated subdivisions within the two broad cultural categories of Orientals and Europeans, since these contain groups with varied cultural traditions. These divisions are also related to various historical waves of immigration to Israel, which in themselves have significant socio-political ramifications.

The three major age categories—Seniors, who are the founding fathers and veterans, the Continuing Generation, and the Young Guard—were very significant in the party. During the period I am reporting on, the last of the founding generation still ruled, and the so-called young leaders of the Continuing Generation, already in their mid-fifties, were growing increasingly impatient for their turn to take over the reins of power. The Young Guard, which officially includes members up to thirty-five years of age (some of its leaders have long passed this fairly liberal definition of youth), complained bitterly about what they perceived to be their underrepresentation on party institutions and in the higher ranks of party leadership. Gluckman (1963:38) has noted that "the growing of younger men into adulthood in which they found their path to power blocked by their elders" was likely to have influenced the recurrent civil wars in some societies—conflicts he characterized as "rebellions" as opposed to revolutions. It is likely that the periodic and regular splits in Israeli political parties are related to the maturation of young cadres of leadership who have found their paths to power blocked by the entrenched veteran leadership. This was certainly one of several factors leading to the split of Rafi from Mapai in 1965. The potential threat of such rebellions necessitated the pacification and integration of the Young Guard through proceedings like the ritual in the Standing Committee. The knowledge that actual splits have not generally been the most successful means of gaining power was probably an additional incentive for rebelliously inclined Young Guardists to play by the rules of the game, and to remain within the fold of the party.

But the threat offered by such groups as the Young Guard was not restricted to the potential of their rebelling or leading a faction into independence. In charging that democratic principles and procedures were being violated, they were a new generation that posed problems of compliance with the operative rules of the game established by the founding generation. As Berger and Luckmann have stated (1966:59), "it is more likely that one will deviate from programs set up for one by others than from programs one has established oneself." An analogous situation existed with the local leaders of newer immigrant and ethnic groups in the smaller branches of the development towns, whose indoctrination into the institutional order was significantly different from that of the generation of predominantly European members of the secondary echelon of leadership.

Important interests were represented by the party branch organizations. The dominant party machine, based in Tel Aviv, competed with the party machine of Haifa, and to a lesser extent with the Jerusalem branch. Each of them also competed, and formed coalitions, with branches in the rest of the country. As reported in Chapters 3 and 4, many complaints were voiced during the proceedings about the domination of party institutions by the major city machines and by the kibbutzim, which are disproportionately overrepresented at the expense of the smaller branches. In particular, severe criticism was voiced about the undemocratic methods through which powerful groups gained more than their share of representation on bodies of the party. Representatives of the smaller branches expressed views such as the following: "Members in the outlying areas need to be given rights!" Again, demands for fair and equal representation were juxtaposed with the criticism that powerful groups perpetuated their dominance of others through undemocratic methods.

Other divisions, such as between the urban and agricultural sectors, represented not only conflicting economic interests, but also distinctly different ideological orientations. For example, the two kibbutz movements were autonomous institutions of the former Mapai and Achdut Haavoda parties with different ideologies and traditions. In turn, the moshav movement represented another set of economic and ideological interests with which the kibbutzim competed.

In addition, the different institutions dominated by the party represented a fairly wide range of frequently competing interests. As shown in the previous chapter, the marked confrontation between the ministry of finance and the Histadrut over wage policies entailed considerably different interpretations of socialism. In fact, a gamut of ideological conflicts was expressed in debates on almost all issues. In the debate over policy on defense and security, for example, the protagonists ranged from extreme hawks, who were unwilling to consider giving back an inch of "the Greater Land of Israel," to extreme doves, who favored the return of "occupied territories" and the creation of a "Palestinian entity." This is one illustration of the great diversity of conflicting interests and ideologies contained within what some Israelis call the "supermarket" of the mass, pluralistic Israel Labor Party.

In a party characterized by such a diversity of conflicting interests and values, there is a great need for procedures that reconcile these interests and their norms in order to keep their protagonists together. This is particularly enforced because the dominant party is a microcosm of the wider society in which great centrifugal and centripetal forces tend, respectively, to pull the society apart as well as to enforce some unity. The social and political strains of a socially and culturally diverse society of immigrants, a society undergoing rapid social change within the context of a constant challenge to its physical survival, creates tensions that are given symbolic representation through the ritual performance in the Standing Committee. Roberto Da Matta (1977) suggests that the ritual life of a given society can express different ways of seeing, interpreting, and realizing the social structure. In complex societies these different domains compete for power. However, generally only one view is legitimated at a given time, and that view may dominate the society.

The competition among the protagonists of these domains produces grave problems of legitimation, particularly when there is an overriding need for integration. The dominant ideology is constantly threatened by the presence of realities that are meaningless in its terms. Berger and Luckmann (1966:96) note:

> The legitimation of the institutional order is also faced with the ongoing neces-
> sity of keeping chaos at bay. *All* social reality is precarious. *All* societies are
> constructions in the face of chaos. The constant possibility of anomic terror is
> actualized whenever the legitimations that obscure the precariousness are
> threatened or collapse.

The importance of specific procedures for maintaining order is critical when
the symbolic universe is questioned. Although the human construction of society
inevitably exposes its symbolic universes to question, some are more vulnerable
than others—as in an institution where rival definitions of reality compete for
power. Berger and Luckmann (1966:114) state:

> The distinctiveness of ideology is rather that the *same* overall universe is
> interpreted in different ways, depending upon concrete vested interests within
> the society in question.

They point out that the pluralistic aspect of many modern societies means, "that
they have a shared core universe, taken for granted as such, and different partial
universes coexisting in a state of mutual accommodation" (ibid., 115), or—I
add—mutual antagonism. Pluralism is seen as an accelerating factor in social
change

> precisely because it helps to undermine the change resistant efficacy of the
> traditional definitions of reality. Pluralism encourages both skepticism and
> innovation and is thus inherently subversive of the taken-for-granted reality of
> the traditional status quo. (Ibid.)

Under such conditions the core symbolic universe may be very vulnerable. In
societies of this type, where conciliation is an important cultural value, and when
the character of the political regime makes it possible, I argue that arenas can be
created for the exposition of different views. But this expression must take place
within limited and controlled borders, in a highly *ritualized* manner, because
otherwise the taken-for-granted nature of reality would be challenged and even
threatened. The dominant political party is a hierarchical system that both cuts
across and represents this wide range of divisions. Israeli society contains groups
which view it differently, and which nevertheless have to remain together without splitting apart in order to survive. Hence the attempt to conciliate the diverse
interests and views through proceedings which necessarily are ritualistic.

Rituals stress basic principles in society, yet at the same time they mask these
principles. They appear when there is a threat within the social structure, for they
deal with the representation of conflicts, ambiguities, and disorder within society. Through ritual performances, social relationships are represented and af-

fected. Reality itself is presented symbolically, but in a controlled and disguised manner. Much like the "encounters" analyzed by Goffman (1961:77–78):

> a disguise may function not so much as a way of concealing something as a way of revealing as much of it as can be tolerated in an encounter. We fence our encounters with gates; the means by which we hold off a part of reality can be the means by which we can bear introducing it. In this way, rituals create an aura of authenticity by activating and selectively condensing reality in a convincing manner.

I have attempted to show for a segment of Israeli society how a controlled bracketing of a ritual encounter provided a period in which the participants could reflect and discourse on their lives and on the social order. They orchestrated a meta-commentary on, and critique of, the social order. Through their performance they tried to create a new authenticity, which transformed their roles and gave them new meaning in a ritual of assertion. Through their commentary on the mundane world they criticized the erosion of their influence and the meaning of their specific roles, and the erosion of such general norms of the party and the society as democracy, participation, pioneering, and equality.

In a sense, the ritual was a temporary recapturing of the comradeship of an earlier period when mutual ideological commitment and a sense of mission bound the party activists tightly together in a common pioneering endeavor. Dramatic changes in Israeli society led to the bureaucratization of the party and to a marked decline in the role of ideology. The pioneering vanguard became a ruling elite and their dedicated comrades-in-arms became party functionaries. (*Askanim*, the Hebrew term, has a decidedly negative connotation in present-day Israel.) As Victor Turner (1969:147) has stated,

> Any developing structure generates problems of organization and values that provoke redefinition of central concepts. This often seems like temporizing and hypocrisy, or loss of faith, but it is really no more than a reasoned response to an alteration in the scale and complexity of social relations, and with these, a change in the location of the group in the social field it occupies, with concomitant changes in its major goals and means of attaining them.

Terence Turner (1977) has shown how rituals function to bridge a gap and transcend structural incommensurability, which cannot be articulated at the lower level. He poses this as a predicament in which people must come to terms with, and regulate, what they cannot articulate. So, he argues, they resort to paradox and ritual. Abner Cohen (1974:58) formulates a related point somewhat differently, saying,

> When society changes, men tend for some time to continue, indeed to struggle hard to preserve their identity, their selfhood, in the old traditional ways.

> Social change is in a way always a threat to our selfhood, particularly if it involves changes in roles. We tenaciously try to maintain our selfhood by giving new interpretations to our patterns of symbolic action.

Rapid social change in Israeli society had produced a reality significantly different from the one proclaimed in the symbolic universe of the party ideology. The previous meanings of the roles of the secondary leaders and of central values in the party ideology had been eroded, and social reality was more than meaningless in its terms for it contradicted what ideology said it was. This appeared to those involved in the proceedings as temporizing, loss of faith, and hypocrisy. It was beyond the cognitive perception of these actors to understand this as a reflection and consequence of social change. It presented them with conflicting cognitions of a real world that sharply contrasted with what it was supposed to be, according to the legitimating universe. They were pioneers, but people saw them as party hacks. All Jews are equal, but some are more equal than others. The party was democratic, but they were involved in, and the victims of, oligarchic manipulations. Cohen has said that as a result of the disturbance in equilibrium between selfhood and disparate roles caused by these subversive processes of change, "there is an active search for a new equilibrium, for a modified symbolic order to accommodate the self within the new alignments of power" (ibid.).

From the alternatives open to them—creating a new ideology, giving new interpretations to old patterns of symbolic action, and so forth—the ritual performers in the Standing Committee sought to resolve the dissonance between their ideology and reality by affirming and reasserting the legitimacy of their traditional symbolic universe. They attempted to transcend this logical impasse by the assertion of meaning—both for their roles and their ideology—which short-circuited the real world they thereby strove to make fit their normative reality. I shall attempt to explain this particular choice in my concluding remarks.

Outcomes and Conclusions

In considering the outcomes of the ritual of the Standing Committee, I shall first relate them to the explicit purposes or manifest goals of the Committee. I shall then consider some of the latent functions of the outcomes, and conclude with a summary discussion of the more creative aspects of the proceedings in terms of the specific and more general social contexts in which they took place. The explicit pragmatic political work of the Standing Committee included approval of a new party constitution, nomination of a significant proportion of the members of the new Central Committee, and the presentation of the party's ideology through the formulation of the platform of issues presented to the Conference.

The primary implicit purpose of the Standing Committee was to control the Conference and thereby guarantee support for the policies of the top leadership.

This was accomplished through the careful selection of the performers, thereby maximizing the chances for the successful bracketing of the proceedings within the constraints imposed, that is, consensual formulations of policies and the suppression of highly controversial issues. The fear of chaos during the Conference in the form of disordered conflict and indeterminate outcomes was constantly impressed upon the performers in the Standing Committee, as if to highlight the importance of the success of their performance and the dangers to party unity were they to fail. There was a juxtaposition in the Committee of the need for minimal order—abiding by the rules—in the face of disorder and possible chaos in the Conference. On the other hand, within the major constraints, the performers were permitted a wide range of freedom to improvise and express themselves. In contrast, the full Conference was much more formal and restrictive and allowed only a minimum of initiative to the delegates, precisely because the threat of real disorder was greater.

I first discuss the immediate effects of the performance for the two major audiences or reference groups—the top leaders and the Conference delegates (grass-roots leaders)—and then for the performers of the Standing Committee themselves. For the top leaders the most important outcome was that they succeeded in maintaining their control of the party, kept the party intact, and their policies were approved without amendment by the overwhelming majority of the delegates to the Conference. In addition, despite the criticism in the Standing Committee (if not through it), the legitimacy of their dominant roles was reaffirmed and strengthened. I shall show, however, that these effects were *limited in scope and duration*.

The Conference was an important occasion for the local leaders to come together and mingle with one another, and to rub shoulders with and talk to the top leaders of the party, who on such an occasion were socially very accessible to them. The finance minister (the most dominant figure in the party among the top leadership) held "court," receiving and speaking with hundreds of delegates. In addition to the more tangible political benefits they may have received from these consultations, as well as the semblance of participation in the Conference debates, Conference participation gave the delegates tremendous prestige and strengthened their own standings in their respective local constituencies. For example, the ultimate status symbol among Israeli politicians, the "James Bond" briefcase, was temporarily edged out by the red plastic document case of the delegate to the Party Conference. Local leaders could be seen demonstratively flashing them around for months after the Conference. I stress then that the surface appearance of democratic participation felt by many Conference delegates was made possible through the tight structure provided by the successful proceedings of the Standing Committee.

The ritual had several results for the participants. In one sense, it was a performance of self-definition that emphasized the solidarity and uniqueness, as a socio-political category, of the secondary echelon of leadership. The exclusion of the other two categories was therefore not only practical in that it facilitated the successful ritual proceedings, but it gave symbolic representation of the uniqueness and importance of the secondary leaders. The rebelliousness of the criticism raised against the top leadership resembles in some ways the analogous conduct of the Lozi priests in Barotseland (Gluckman, 1954) and the chiefs designated by the king of the Baganda as his messengers (Mair, 1934), as opposed to the case of the Swazi, where the entire people participates in the ritual rebellion (Gluckman, 1962, 1963). Gluckman (1965, Chapters 4–6) argues that rituals of rebellion of the Swazi type cease to occur in states where protoclasses have emerged. I contend that a more limited type of ritual of rebellion can occur where the "king" is conspicuously absent—for example, within a segment of a dominant political party, under certain conditions. These conditions are that the dangers and high costs of opting for alternative social roles severely limit mobility and therefore freedom of choice. Coupled with a high degree of internalization of norms, this allows for a successful rigid bracketing of a performance, which meets the definition of a ritual. Another factor is the multiplicity of social relationships. I differentiate the term "multiple" from "multiplex" (coined by Gluckman), recognizing that while socio-political roles of Labor Party politicians overlap with a whole range of other relationships, they differ significantly from the multiplex relationships in traditional societies.

But the performance was ritual in more than mere self-definition or even rebellion. It was transformative in that it created new meaning for the roles of the performers through the assertion of an idealized normative structure. The strong criticism of the lack of internal party democracy raised in the Standing Committee reaffirmed belief in a valued ideal that had been blatantly breached. In a similar way, symbolic references to the inequality of ethnic groups involved criticism of the breach of one of the most important norms in Israeli society and reaffirmed the central importance of that ideal. Therefore, in addition to resolving the ambiguity of their own roles and mediating between competing groups with opposed interests and ideologies, these criticisms orchestrated a commentary on the major contradictions and paradoxes in Israeli society.

The members of the Standing Committee were grappling with universal human dilemmas within the specific context of their party and society. They were dealing with the meaning of consensus, democracy, equality, socialism, and Judaism. Their very actions symbolized the juxtaposition of the need for structure, order, and control with the threat of uncertainty, chaos, and anarchy. For the party, and even more so for the society, the overriding need for unity was constantly subjected to the demands of conflicting groups, interests, and ideologies to be heard, to assert themselves, and to gain greater representation in the centers of power. The dangerous situation of the society makes the price of sacrificing unity so terrifying that extraordinary measures are required to maintain unity in spite of all the objective difficulties.

It seemed as if, consciously or subconsciously, the performers were aware that the party, while still dominant politically, had gradually lost its moral ideo-logical dominance in Israeli society. It was probably beyond their conscious level of perception to analyze the failure of the party and the political structure to adapt adequately to the forces of social change. Yet, through their ritual perfor-mance they reaffirmed the effectiveness, in the face of reality, of a symbolic relationship (a normative code) which they had internalized and which was meaningful to them. However, this had a conservative, if not reactionary, effect in that it helped to keep the system going. Although they constructed a code that helped them cope with a complex and at times oppressive situation, they did not generate new ideas, forms, or norms designed to cope with the changed situation. They contented themselves with reaffirming the validity of the old norms with-out reinterpreting them in the context of new problems.

Given the structural and cultural constraints and the other choices available, the particular ritual "solution" to the major problem confronting the actors can be better understood. The character of the dominant party structure in the Israeli political system was such that it could allow the controlled expression of dissent and discourse on the social and normative order because the outcome of consen-sual unity was predictable—given the nature of dependence of the performers in the ritual and their internalization of party norms, and the overriding necessity of unity imposed by external threats. The normative imperative dictated the need for a semblance of democratic procedure and participation in the process of making decisions.

The discrepancy between ideology and reality could be resolved through a logically limited number of solutions. Reality could be ignored, denied, or in the long run, changed. Ideology could be reinterpreted, or affirmed, or rejected, with a new ideology more meaningfully related to reality offered in its place. There is evidence that for several years various aspects of changing social reality have been ignored by the decision makers, who successfully prevented a confrontation with the problems created by these changed social realities. The suppression of two crucial and highly important issues from the arena of the Party Conference documents one of the ways in which this has been done. It becomes increasingly more difficult, if not impossible, to ignore, dismiss, or deny a social reality that manifests itself in problems that greatly trouble the public, and indeed the profes-sional politicians themselves. For example, the problem of the increasing gap between the "haves" and the "have-nots," a gap that in Israel is intimately related to the problem of ethnic relationships, was given forceful expression by the demonstrations of the Black Panthers and other protesting groups, and received wide coverage by the mass media. It intrudes in many ways into the life of the party, as shown by the Oriental caucus in the Conference, and is deeply felt even by some of the most loyal and trusted members of the Standing Committee. Thus, it is an issue so troublesome that it can neither be denied nor ignored. Problems of this kind, which emerge from a changing social reality, are so complicated that their solution can only be achieved through long-range programs requiring considerable imagination and resources. Yet these are not always available, particularly given the high priority of heavy expenditures for defense and absorption of immigrants (who present the immediate problems of housing and employment). Other problems, such as the inherent contradictions between the values of religiously orthodox and secularly liberal ideologies about the very nature of the society and the state, are even less amenable to solution, even by any expenditure. If they are to be resolved at all, they will require a great deal of mutual goodwill and an extremely imaginative synthesis of symbolic and legitimating ideas. This leads us from the possibility of coping with reality to the choice of ways of coping with ideology.

The outright rejection of party ideology would have been unthinkable, given the character of the carefully selected actors in the ritual of the Standing Committee. Not only would this have been political suicide, but it would have represented a traumatic challenge to the actors' own perceptions of their roles and very selves. The extremely complicated problems posed by changing social reality rendered them not easily amenable to resolution through a reinterpretation of traditional ideology, particularly in the context of a political forum, the major function of which was to maintain a political status quo in which the actors themselves had considerable vested interests. They were not chosen to produce, nor did they produce, imaginative new solutions to the problems of social reality. They were not expected to make these problems meaningful either through a reinterpretation of their ideology or through its replacement with a new ideology. Lacking both the freedom and the resources, including imagination, to opt for other possible solutions for the problem to the conflict between ideology and reality, they asserted the former in the face of the latter.

The successful ritual performance in the Standing Committee allowed for a successful pageant of unity in the National Party Conference. The 3,000 assembled delegates of the Conference more accurately reflected the composition of the general membership of 300,000 than did any other party institution. The ceremonial gathering of these delegates symbolized the unity and strength of the Israel Labor Party, and affirmed the delegates' support of their leadership and its policies to their fellow members and countrymen. It also symbolized the unity and strength of the Israeli people in full view of friend and foe alike. The necessity of presenting this united front to all the different audiences made particularly crucial the successful ritual of consensual relationships of power in the Standing Committee; and the success of this ritual made possible the ceremonial demonstration of unity and strength of the Conference.

As I indicated previously, there is widespread discontent among party activists who complain that they are not able to influence decisions on policy, particularly on issues viewed by the general public to be the most pressing domestic problems. Significantly, these were the very issues that were most carefully controlled, or even suppressed, in the Conference. I stress that the solutions of consensual formulation within the context of carefully bracketed rituals and the suppression of issues through ritual procedures are temporary. Vital issues—such as the relationships between ethnic groups, problems of poverty tied to the ethnic issue and also to wage policies and labor relations, the question of the proper role of religion in the state, and so forth—pose questions that demand policies aimed at their solution in spite of the inherent difficulties involved.

The general public has increasingly demanded solutions to these problems. The procedures used by the top leaders to postpone such decisions have provided a temporary respite in which they have consolidated their control of the party. They have thus far successfully refrained from proposing controversial policies that might antagonize important sectors within the party and the public. But their successful use of procedures of control was most effective with the supporting group closest to them and most dependent on the elite. The sanctions, both normative and otherwise, enforcing loyalty of the members of the Standing Committee to the top leaders were becoming less effective against the third level of local leadership, the general party membership, and the electorate.

The last general election, which took place in the cataclysmic aftermath of the war of October 1973, appears to represent a new threshold in the development of the Israeli political system. The leadership of the Labor Party bore the brunt of severe criticism for what were perceived as near-fatal errors in the preparation for and handling of the war—particularly in its earliest stages.

Although it lost substantial electoral support, the Labor Party managed to stay in power with a coalition that gave it, for some time, only a narrow single-vote majority in the Knesset. Internal party criticism and mass public criticism, including new protest groups and demonstrations, eventually forced the resignation of the prime minister and minister of defense. The party and the political system are presently in a state of flux and transition, but it would appear that because of these changed conditions it will be increasingly difficult to manage a carefully controlled ritual such as that of the Standing Committee in the future.

In conclusion, I would like to draw from this particular case study some points I believe to have general application. First of all, I would expect this kind of political ritual to be more common in certain structural and cultural environments than in others. I would expect that dominant party systems would be more conducive to the creation of this type of political ritual for several reasons. First, such systems by definition limit the possibilities that the control of major political resources and offices may be altered. They offer various categories of political actors limited options for other socio-political roles by making such choices prohibitively costly. Obviously, different degrees of dependence or autonomy between various categories of leadership—e.g., top leaders, secondary echelon, and grass-roots leaders—would affect the types of performances that are possible. The type of ritual I have described is dependent upon a fairly rigid structure in which control can guarantee eventual outcomes. Therefore, the actors' freedom of choice must be limited.

Another important factor in the rituals characteristic of many societies in which there are dominant party systems is that the dominant party is a mass party encompassing and attempting to conciliate a wide range of conflicting groups and interests. This is particularly true in socially and culturally heterogeneous societies where the dominant party has been the vanguard of a successful revolution and/or led the country in its drive for independence (e.g., the PRI of Mexico, the Congress Party of India, and many of the dominant parties in Africa). In such cases there is usually an attempt to conciliate social and ideological differences within the context of the need for national unity to face the struggle, which is legitimated within values of the revolutionary ideology. There is usually a period after the goal—independence—has been achieved, when the revolutionary or nationalistic fervor cools down, the party becomes institutionalized, and the contrast between the normative goals of the ideology and situational reality become more visible. This tendency has been observed by Zbigniew Brezezinski (1962:115), who states:

> One could almost say that there is a kind of "dialectical" relationship between an ideologically oriented party and reality. The ideological party attempts to change reality and, in this way, is a revolutionary force: the new changed reality for a while corresponds to the ideology even while changing itself; in time the ideology may become a conservative force; a new adjustment is eventually forced, and the ideology may then again become a revolutionary force.

(Compare Seliger, 1970, for a discussion of the inherent asymmetry of ideologies.) Particularly in the cases (for which there are ample examples) in which new ideological adjustment has not been made, or in the interim before this has been accomplished, the dominant elites are generally very anxious to maintain the semblance of democratic participation while still controlling outcomes. This kind of situation is ripe for the ritualization of political activities. But because of the ever-present danger that ritual rebellion and/or assertion may break out into a real political revolt, such rituals are only likely to take place when there is virtual certainty that the ritual performance can be successfully bracketed and controlled.

Given the changes now occurring in the Israeli political system, it would appear that the previous certainty of predictable outcomes is becoming more doubtful. It is not clear whether the political actors themselves perceive the implications and the new possibilities arising from the new situation. Early indications are that they do not yet do so. For example, in the aftermath of the last war and national election there was a widespread feeling, expressed by large numbers of party activists and leaders who in turn reflected an equally widespread public sentiment, that the top leaders—such as the prime minister, minister of defense, and other key ministers—as well as party policy, should be changed. The first meeting of the party's Central Committee after the war, called to discuss these issues, was postponed for several hours while the top leaders met to thrash out a compromise among themselves and thereby to avoid an open confrontation in the Central Committee.

While the top leaders sat one floor below, I sat with a group of the secondary leaders in a room at party headquarters. They seriously discussed the need to change the top party and government leadership and drastically revise party policy. As if the reality of what was taking place below radiated upward to the floor above, the tone of the discussion between the secondary leaders began to change markedly. They gradually began to turn their previously serious discussion into a farcical mocking of what they thought was going on below. They satirically nominated the most unqualified party functionaries for the key cabinet posts. Their conduct reminded me of a scene in the film *M*A*S*H*. in which a team of army doctors joked as they operated in a field hospital on men whom they knew were likely to go back into combat and get killed after they recuperated from their operations. Both the doctors and the functionaries of the Labor Party resorted to satire and paradox to express feelings of helplessness in the absurdity of their situations. The functionaries of the Labor Party expressed symbolically through their behavior a perception of their own dependence on the top leaders and their own inability to change the order of things in spite of their sincerely felt need to do so. This is the stuff of which the type of political ritual I have described is made. It remains to be seen whether the perception of the political actors concerned will be altered by the increasingly changed political reality, or whether this will produce new ritual forms, or lead to the dropping of such ritual. It is also uncertain whether new programs will appear, designed to change social reality in order to bring it into line with ideology, or whether new sets of symbols will be produced that are more meaningfully related to this reality.

6

Continuity and Change in Representation in Party Institutions

Introduction

Although the analysis of aggregate data of group representation in party institutions is an important means of identifying major patterns and trends, caution must be exercised in the interpretation of such data. Given the nature of the nominations process, the selection of a particular individual for membership in an institution is frequently influenced to a large degree by the nature of the nominee's relationship with a member of the Nominations Committee and/or a patron among the national party elite. However, in the formal sense his selection is ostensibly as a representative of a geographical region, ethnic group, previous party faction, age or sex category, or a combination of several of these and/or other criteria. Whenever possible, the Nominations Committee will tag a nominee as a representative of as many categories as possible. For example, a young woman of Middle Eastern background who comes from a development town, has an academic education, and is a new immigrant to Israel could be claimed to represent five sets of interests—in addition to those of her patron, which is likely crucial in the appointment of this hypothetical candidate. Some of these problems will be raised in the forthcoming discussion of the nature of representation in the party. I caution the reader, therefore, that the extrapolation of representation in party institutions can only be an approximation of the much more complex reality.

I compare the major elected national institutions of the party: the Central Committee, the Secretariat, and the Leadership Bureau (listed in order of decreasing size and increasing importance). I also make a comparison between the joint institutions formed by the merger of the previous three parties into the Labor Party in 1968, and those elected following the first united Party Conference in April 1971. (The forthcoming internal party elections had not yet been scheduled at the time of writing—January 1975). In addition, I give data for the Standing Committee of the first National Conference of the Labor Party, which I have discussed extensively in this book. Unfortunately, data on prior Standing Committees of the previous constituent parties were not available, thereby preventing comparison of this institution.

In order to measure the extent to which actual representation in national party institutions varied from an allocation based on ratios determined by the percentages of party members of each group or category, a coefficient of representation was devised using the following equation:

$$C = \frac{\text{percent of representation on party body}}{\text{percent of party membership}}$$

The percentage of the category's members out of the whole national party membership was divided into the percentage of its representation on each institution. Line 1 of Figure 2, labeled "equitable distribution," represents a mathematically ideal distribution based solely on relative size of party membership for each category. If each category were allocated representation in institutions in proportion to the number of party members belonging to the category, they would all appear as parallel straight lines on line 1. The actual distribution of positions above and below line 1 indicate relative over- and underrepresentation respectively, that is, deviation from the mathematically determined equitable distribution. Although this standard is obviously an artificially created mathematical index, it is significant that there is a widely held view in the party that representation in party institutions should be made primarily on this basis—with the exception of guaranteed representation for top national party leaders who are viewed as representatives of the party at a national level. (All data used in these calculations were obtained from the records of the national headquarters of the Israel Labor Party and are derived from the official party census.)

Deviation from "Ideal" Representation

There are three main factors that influence deviation from the previously mentioned model of equitable distribution: (1) the organization of the three main cities—Tel Aviv, Jerusalem, and Haifa, the two kibbutz federations, and the moshav federation—into separate districts; (2) the granting of extra weight to the kibbutz members in internal elections; (3) the appointment of a significant percentage of the members of institutions through central nominations committees, which allows the top party leaders to give additional representation to those groups most closely supportive of them. The resultant deviation is clearly shown in Figure 2.

When compared with representation in previous institutions (cf. Aronoff, 1972:154) there is a striking continuity in the basic pattern of over- and underrepresentation. The Tel Aviv district has continued to have increasingly greater

Figure 2. **Representation by Geographic Districts and Regions**

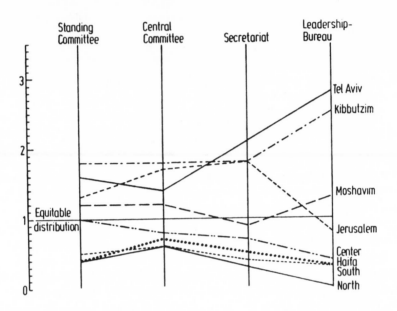

overrepresentation the smaller and more important the institution, reaching approximately three times the number its membership alone would warrant on the top executive Leadership Bureau. The Tel Aviv regional branch has been the real center of power in the Labor Party for many years. Tel Aviv has been the base upon which successive national leaders have built their support in major party institutions from the time that Shriege Netzer built up the political machine known as the Gush (bloc)—which he ran during the better part of Ben-Gurion's rule as prime minister—until the present, when Finance Minister Rabinowitz (the former mayor of Tel Aviv) originally led it in support of Sapir's successful mobilization of a dominant position in the party. In addition, the central party headquarters (the party bureaucracy) and the main offices of the Histadrut and its many institutions and subsidiaries are located in Tel Aviv, thus, individuals representing these bodies in the party institutions are most likely to live in the Tel Aviv region, thereby boosting its number of representatives. The political bosses of Tel Aviv have always managed to get more representatives than their party membership would warrant. This has been accomplished largely through the types of maneuvers analyzed in Chapter 3.

The conspicuous overrepresentation of the kibbutz movements is also due to their favored position in the central Nominations Committees, in addition to other factors. Historically, the consolidation of the kibbutzim and their movements coincided with the development of the major central political and economic institutions of the Yishuv. This allowed them to get in on the ground floor of the institutional building, and to gain strong positions in the two main labor parties, Achdut Haavoda and HaPoel HaZair, and the Histadrut, which was founded in 1920. The scope and intensity of the voluntary activities of the representatives of the kibbutzim within the workers' movement filled a critical gap and constituted an instrument of immense power. The organizational structure of the kibbutz economy allowed the kibbutz and the movement to free members for full-time political activity and to field election staffs during campaigns. This enabled the kibbutz movements to gain disproportionate representation in key party and Histadrut institutions. Also, the kibbutznik was seen as the pioneering elite whose life-style personified the goals of Zionist socialism, legitimizing his key political role within the ideology of the workers' movement. Although the pivotal role of the kibbutz has declined since the state was founded, this change has been slow to be reflected in the institutions of the Labor Party where the kibbutz federations continue to wield power out of all proportion to their numbers. In the past, the vote of the kibbutz member was counted as double that of the urban member in internal party elections. In the last internal party election, the kibbutznik's vote was weighted 50 percent more than that of urban members. This technique automatically guarantees overrepresentation to the kibbutz movements.

A comparison of the overrepresentation of Jerusalem and the underrepresentation of Haifa, the two main cities in Israel after Tel Aviv, reveals other variables that determine power and representation in the party. Jerusalem is the nation's capital and the seat of government. It therefore gains representation through members of the Knesset (legislature) and cabinet members residing there. In addition, the relationship between the Jerusalem branch and the Tel Aviv–based party machine has been more cordial than that between Tel Aviv and the traditionally independent Haifa branch. Haifa is the singular example of a very strong local party machine (built by the late Mayor Abba Choushi) that dared to take a consistently independent stand from the Tel Aviv–based national party organization. Haifa's underrepresentation in national party institutions is partially a result of the sympathy its leaders showed for former Prime Minister David Ben-Gurion, who led a split from Mapai in 1965 when he formed Rafi. (Incidentally, the same reason explains in part the decline of Mr. Netzer and his colleagues from their central role in the Tel Aviv organization.) It would seem that when local autonomy leads to deviation from majority policy on major national issues it causes a weakening of the position in national institutions.

As I explained in preceding chapters, there was a fairly successful purge of members of the former Mapai who had been sympathetic to Rafi. This is also reflected in Haifa's underrepresentation and may partly explain Jerusalem's loss of overrepresentation on the Leadership Bureau.

The branches of the central region achieved equitable representation on the

Figure 3. **Comparison of Representation by Ethnic Category in the Labor Party, National Institutions between 1968 and 1972 Elections**

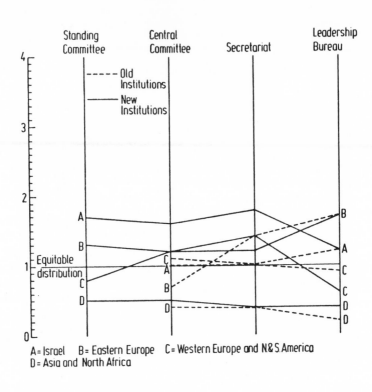

A= Israel   B= Eastern Europe   C= Western Europe and N&S.America
D= Asia and North Africa

Standing Committee but were underrepresented in the other institutions. A similar pattern of decreasing representation in the more important institutions characterized the continuity in underrepresentation of the northern and southern regions, which include almost all of the country's development towns. One striking difference not apparent in Figure 2 is that whereas in the previous Central Committee 40 of the party's 84 branches were not represented at all, in the present Central Committee only 18 branches did not have at least one representative. While this factor was of symbolic significance to the branches concerned, it did not affect the overall patterns of domination and subordination on the major party institutions.

Figure 3 compares representation by country of origin on the previous and present institutions. Again we can observe slight variations or changes within a basically continuous pattern. The increasing overrepresentation of Eastern Euro-

Figure 4. **Representation by Country of Birth According to Region (Percentages)**

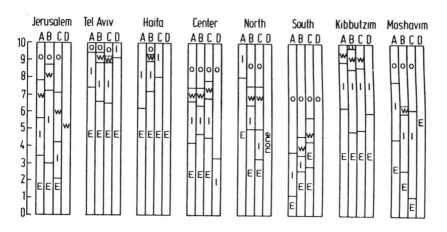

Key

A = Standing Committee
B = Central Committee
C = Secretariat
D = Leadership Bureau

O = Asia and North Africa
W = Western Europe and America
I = Israel
E = Eastern Europe

peans culminates in their domination of the top Leadership Bureau. Most striking is the improved position of native-born Israelis who moved from equitable representation on the previous Central Committee and Secretariat to substantial overrepresentation on these two bodies, and retained the same degree of overrepresentation on the Leadership Bureau. This also obviously related to changes in age distribution (see Figure 5 below) where the aging veteran founders (who are predominantly Eastern European) are gradually being replaced by the Israeli-born Continuing Generation. The (completely artificial) conglomerate category of Western Europeans and North and South Americans increased their overrepresentation on the Central Committee and Secretariat, but are more underrepresented on the Leadership Bureau than previously. The marginal improvement, but blatantly underrepresented position, of party members from Asia and Africa (i.e., the Orientals) is closely related to the underrepresentation of the branches of the development towns in the northern and southern regions where they are a majority of the population (see Figure 3).

Figure 4 gives the breakdown of country of origin by institution for each of the geographic districts and regions. Here we clearly see that the continued domination of Eastern Europeans is strongest in the Tel Aviv and Haifa machines and in the kibbutz movements, which combined have an absolute majority

Figure 5. **Representation of Age Categories, 1968 and 1971**

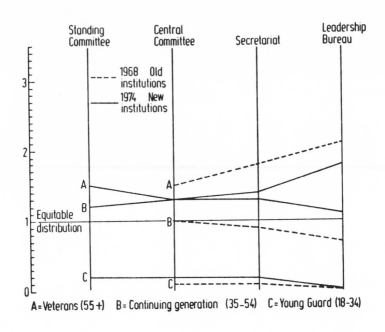

A = Veterans (55 +)   B = Continuing generation   (35–54)   C = Young Guard (18–34)

in all institutions. There is a greater combination of ethnic backgrounds in the Jerusalem district, the central and northern regions, and the moshav movement. The most striking gains for the Orientals have been made in the southern region, and to a lesser extent the central and northern regions, the moshav movement, and the Jerusalem district. I shall discuss some of the major problems arising from this situation in the forthcoming chapter on relationships between the party center and the local branches.

The most striking feature of the comparative pattern of age distribution is that it appears to reflect the long anticipated (and in the opinion of many, long overdue) changing of the guard—the passing of the reigns of power from the veteran (predominantly Eastern European) founding generation to the Continuing Generation (thirty-five to fifty-four years old—mainly Israeli-born). This process has been almost imperceptibly slow and was more than symbolically signified by the competition of two candidates of the Continuing Generation to be the party's candidate for prime minister (following the resignation of Golda Meir), and by Yitzchak Rabin's becoming the youngest and first Israeli-born prime minister of Israel. However significant the changes, the continuing disproportionate representation and dominance of the veteran generation is still striking.

Figure 6. **Representation of Age Categories by Region (Percentages)**

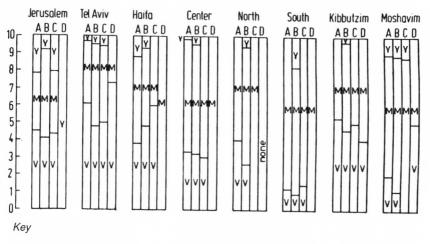

Key

A = Standing Committee
B = Central Committee
C = Secretariat
D = Leadership Bureau

Y = Young Guard (18–34)
M = Continuing Generation (35–54)
V = Veterans (55 and above)

This pattern becomes even clearer in Figure 6 when we see the breakdown of age category by institution with reference to geographic district and region. Here we see the continuation of dominance by the veteran leaders in the most important Tel Aviv, Jerusalem, and Haifa districts, in the kibbutz movements, and to a decreasing extent in the central region, the moshav movement, and the northern and southern regions where members of the Continuing Generation have already gained dominant positions. Whereas the gains of the Young Guard have been marginal, they are most noticeable in Jerusalem (where there is a particularly active students' organization) and in the moshav movement. Minor gains in Tel Aviv and Haifa are linked primarily to patron–client relationships.

It should be noted that in spite of many proclamations and resolutions aimed at redressing the imbalance, men have greatly disproportionate overrepresentation at the expense of women in party institutions.

I have argued consistently throughout this book that one of the major limitations on the freedom of action of party institution members is the large proportion of members who are dependent on the party or party-dominated institutions for their livelihoods. Figure 7 shows the proportion of members by institution broken down into district and region who are employed by (or are full-time functionaries of) municipalities, the Histadrut, and the party, as well as a residual category of government employees, independents, and others. It should be noted that even among civil servants and independents there are those who are dependent upon party patronage either for advancement, contracts, or consultation

Figure 7. **Representation by Employment (Percentage)**

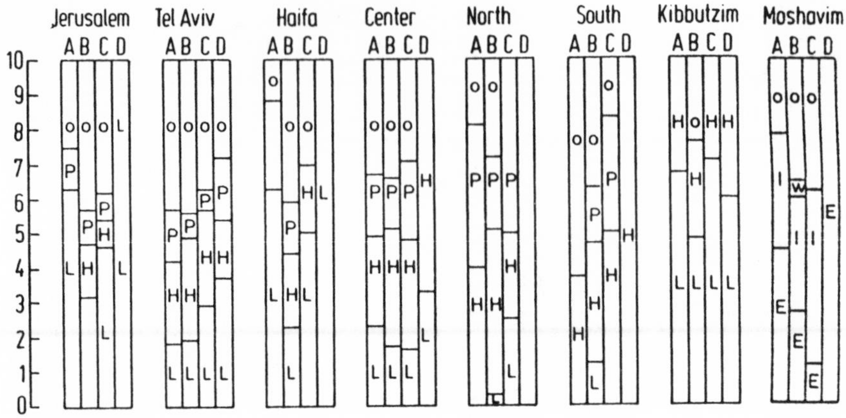

Key

A = Standing Committee   P = Public Sector, Municipalities, etc.
B = Central Committee   H = Histadrut
C = Secretariat   L = Party
D = Leadership Bureau   O = Civil Servants, Independent, others

fees. However, even considering this residual category as independent from party influence, there is still a strikingly large proportion of the members of party institutions who are directly dependent upon the party for their livelihoods. This of course does not take into consideration the additional factor of dependence on the top leadership for career advancement due to the nature of the nominations process.

Even given the inherent limitations mentioned previously, the examination of this aggregate data does present us with some clear patterns and trends largely supporting the participant observations of party activity. They might be summarized by the following statements:

1.   The major national party institutions are characterized by the dominance of certain groups, such as the Tel Aviv Gush and the kibbutz movements, which have increasingly greater overrepresentation on the smaller and more important bodies. In contrast, the other branches, particularly those of the central, southern, and northern regions, are characterized by increasing underrepresentation on these same institutions.

2.   The veteran (Eastern European) generations continue to dominate the most important executive institutions through control of the major urban party machines and the kibbutz movements, which are overrepresented on these institutions.

3.   The Continuing Generation (mainly Israeli-born) has made considerable

gains, particularly on the Central Committee and the Secretariat, primarily through consolidation of dominant positions in the central, northern, and southern regions, and the moshav movement.

4. There is a correlation between the blatant underrepresentation of Oriental members and the underrepresentation of development towns, particularly in the southern region; and the overrepresentation of the powerful Eastern European–dominated Tel Aviv district and kibbutz movements.

5. Men are strongly overrepresented at the expense of women.

6. A significantly large proportion of the members of party institutions are dependent for their livelihoods on party and party-dominated institutions.

The Consequences of Dependence and Control

With reference to this final point it is significant that the financial dependence of members of party institutions on the party is characteristic of the party throughout its history. For example, Medding (1972:158) argues,

> An analysis of the Mapai decision making institutions reveals . . . that they were controlled almost in their entirety by individuals who lived off politics. . . . Few had independent means or professions that would enable them to survive economically with ease outside the party. In other words, they were nearly all totally dependent upon the party for their livelihoods.

Medding's documentation of employment distribution of the Mapai Central Committees in 1954 and 1965 and of 390 leading party activists in 1956 proves this conclusively. He states

> While the effects of the concentration of party officials and men who lived off politics in the party's decision making bodies and amongst its activists may be subject to differing interpretation, the facts of the situation are not. (Ibid.)

Medding and I differ considerably in our interpretations of the effects of this undisputed situation of dependence. Medding recognizes that there are "political realities" that "impinge" on the freedom of the representative or decision maker and tend to make him a "captive." He notes that certain branch machines, most notably those of Tel Aviv and Haifa, voted monolithically, and writes, "what arouses uneasiness is that the majority was nearly always constituted in the same manner, of the same groups . . . it is the solidarity and stability of the majority which raises doubts" (Medding, 1972:108). Medding appears to resolve his own uneasiness by saying:

> But with all this said, in the absence of evidence to the contrary, there is no reason to assume that the majority, however constituted and constructed by the party machine, did not present the views of the majority of the delegates or the

party. . . . In the absence of strong evidence to suggest a "free" vote would have been otherwise, we must either accept the majority decision at Conference as the view of the party majority, or else skeptically argue that we do not know what a "free" majority of party delegates would have decided in a "free vote." (Medding, 1972:108–9)

I think that I have offered strong evidence that the delegates to the Party Conference were not even allowed to debate certain important issues which were suppressed from the agenda of the Conference precisely because the top party leaders feared that they would not receive a majority in support of their positions on these issues. I have also extensively documented the mechanisms employed in the Standing Committee to gain the passage of positions not initially given the support of the majority of the members in the "free" debates that preceded the "consensual" formulations passed on to the delegates of the Conference.

Medding correctly shows that the situation is different when the top party leaders are themselves divided in major struggles for power. The two major power struggles between the top leaders of Mapai in 1942 and in 1965 were eventually resolved in votes of the delegates of the respective National Party Conferences. It is significant that in both instances the dissenters split off to form new parties (see Chapter 2). It is clear that with the exception of these two rare occasions, the Party Conference has an essentially ceremonial function. The same is true to a great extent for the two main representative institutions, the Central Committee and the Secretariat. Medding states that

> the Central Committee usually had before it a recommendation of the Secretariat [or, in the period I am discussing, of the Leadership Bureau] which it almost invariably ratified or approved, so that here too, it demonstrated little evidence of autonomy. This is especially true in the case of nominations to other bodies which were brought to the Central Committee en bloc after being drawn up by an Appointments Committee [what I have termed nominations committees]. Apart from the virtual inability of a large institution to undo the careful work of a small committee in such a delicate area, the *approval of the Central Committee was generally greatly facilitated by the very large bloc vote, if not a majority, enjoyed by the party machine on the Central Committee.* (1972:113; italics added)

However, Medding goes on to argue that the Central Committee was not completely lacking power and importance since certain matters were brought to it on which it did make decisions. He concedes that in many cases, the fact that

> it merely ratified or approved decisions taken in other party bodies does, however, complicate the analysis. We can either assume that it agreed with the decisions made elsewhere, or otherwise would have done something about it, or else that it "really" disagreed but was "captive." As in the case of the Conference, while plausible, there is little evidence to support the latter con-

clusion. A reasonable middle position is that there were many issues which had already been finally decided elsewhere (and sometimes acted upon), and on which the Central Committee was called so that it could be informed, or act as a rubber stamp to legitimize something agreed upon elsewhere. In short, despite its constitutional powers, the reality was such that it was either not expected to decide or in such a position that its disagreement was too late to be effective. This arose from the fact that for reasons of efficiency, policy initiation and the detailed process of policy deliberation usually did not take place within the Central Committee. Issues usually reached it after ample discussions elsewhere, when viewpoints had been crystallised, and some agreement already reached. (1972:113)

Once again I am convinced that Medding underemphasizes, if not ignores, the implications of the crucial fact that the elite control which issues are presented to the Central Committee and when they are presented. Although he offers conclusive documentation of the "captive" nature of dependence of the representatives of these party bodies on the top leaders—such as for selection to these institutions and for their livelihoods—he concludes that there is no evidence that would relate this dependence to the fact that these institutions generally act as rubber stamps in approving the prior decisions of the party elite. Although the event I am about to report occurred after the publication of Medding's book, and he therefore cannot be faulted for ignoring it, it is very likely that similar events occurred during the period he investigated. However, it is possible that the methods he used—the investigation of party archives and intensive interviews—did not lend themselves to the uncovering of such episodes as readily as can be done through use of participant observation.

The first meeting of the Central Committee after the war was scheduled to take place at 9:00 A.M., but was postponed to 6:00 P.M. As I reported in Chapter 5, the top leaders of the party met in a day-long session at party headquarters to work out a compromise position. This delay afforded me the opportunity to participate passively (i.e., through observation) in the discussions among scores of groups of Central Committee members. The climate of the discussion among a group of secondary leaders of the party reported in the previous chapter characterizes almost all of the other discussions. There was a unanimous expression of the opinion that certain key national party leaders, particularly the prime minister and the minister of defense, should be forced to resign and that major aspects of party policy, particularly security matters, should be substantially revised. Whereas different members expressed different opinions as to who should replace the resigning ministers and what the nature of the changes in policy should be, there was definitely a consensus on the former subjects—that is, the need for change—among the scores of members whose views I heard immediately prior to the meeting of the Central Committee. I stress that these views were strongly, frequently passionately, expressed. And yet, when the meeting of the Central Committee was held, these were not the issues discussed.

After paying tribute to the memory of the soldiers who fell in the recent war, the secretary-general announced that he had invited a group of comrades (he specified the names of the top leaders) to consult together. He announced that they had crystallized a platform of party principles for the election, and stressed that the group (of party leaders) was united in accepting full responsibility for the policy, which he then read. He expressed his hope that the Central Committee would accept this platform. The secretary-general went on to justify the post-ponement of the election (which had been scheduled for October 30—before the cease-fire), the decision to hold the election on December 31, and the decision (reached with the agreement of the main opposition party) not to reopen the party lists of candidates for the Knesset. He explained the reasons for these decisions, asked the members of the Central Committee to view these decisions as having been made, and announced that he would allow six speakers (pre-viously determined) to express their views on the election date and the closure of party lists (saying that the debate would continue in a future meeting of the Central Committee).

The debate that followed was about the respective democratic or un-democratic aspects of holding an election at the time and closing the party lists. While I do not deny that these were important subjects, it is striking that a significant proportion of the members of the Central Committee (and the nation) desired a debate on the party leadership's role in handling the war and on major policy issues, and they were given a much more limited and less controversial subject to debate. There were grumbled complaints and murmured expressions of discontent concerning the agenda of the meeting—especially from Committee members who were still in army uniforms. When questioned about their acquies-cence, the answer invariably was that Sapir and the top leaders had laid it on the line and therefore there was no choice but to comply. As for the resolution to hold the election on December 31 without reopening the party lists—in spite of considerable opposition and demands that at least the motion be postponed until all the members of the Central Committee who wished to do so could express their opinion on the subject, Sapir claimed that these were such fateful decisions that the comrades did not need to think them over and "it will be decided and tonight!" And it was decided in the manner that the leadership had determined.

I have documented a series of meetings that ultimately decided the issues under discussion. The first meeting took place at the home of Mayor Rabinowitz and included the inner circle of top party ministers and leaders led by Sapir. They decided not to launch a campaign to replace Golda Meir as prime minister, not to postpone the elections further, not to reopen the party lists of candidates for the Knesset, and to fight for major policy changes in the party platform. The second meeting, also at the home of Rabinowitz, included the top leaders of the Haifa and Jerusalem branches and others who ratified the decisions made in the prior meeting. The third meeting included the representatives of the major agricultural movements and party branches who also concurred with the former decisions. There followed a series of meetings of the members of the Central Committee from the respective branches and organizations at which the line to be followed was presented. There was symbolic opposition only. For example, a member of the Central Committee from Tel Aviv who had lost his son in the war voiced his opposition to Rabinowitz and the secretary of the Tel Aviv district, but was told by the latter that "These are the issues and this is what must be decided!" (This episode was reported and confirmed by participants in the meeting since the author was not personally present).

I stress that in this particular case I was able to document the sharp contrast between the expressed opinions of large numbers of members of the Central Committee and the manner in which they reacted and voted in the Central Committee. By analyzing the series of informal meetings of unofficial groups of party leaders—initiated and decided by the top echelon, which then co-opted and passed on the decisions to increasingly wider levels of leaders—and the manner in which these decisions were then presented as a *line* that was to be followed by the rank-and-file members of the Central Committee, we find the kind of evidence Medding felt was lacking to show the *captive* nature of Central Committee members in the so-called "making of decisions" in the Central Committee. Medding (1972:114) concludes his discussion of the topic with the following statement:

> In conclusion, it seems evident that the large party bodies meeting infrequently did not generally undertake the initiation, detailed discussion and deliberation, and the final decision; nor did they do this even for a small and limited range of important issues. Mostly this was done in smaller executive bodies and at higher levels of the party's leadership. The function of bodies like Conference and the Central Committee was to give recognition to, and legitimate and authoritative registration of, majorities and compromises agreed on elsewhere. But this is not to say that they were entirely powerless, or mere rubber stamps wielded automatically and reflexively. As we took pains to point out above, there were a number of crucial issues, policies and decisions which were made by the Conference and the Central Committee, and which were regarded as the party's authoritative decisions, and we specified those conditions which maximised their power and authority in certain decisions.

I have already stated my concurrence with the unique historical exceptions to the powerlessness of the Conference when the top party leadership was strongly divided, and have documented the normal situation through an analysis of the Party Conference in 1971, when the leaders were united. Throughout the entire period of my fieldwork the strains in the relationships between the top party leaders (which they went to great lengths to prevent) did not result in such an open split, and consequently the large, so-called representative institutions did not have the opportunity to exercise the actual decision-making power that accrues to them in the rare occurrences of a major split at the top. The only other condition that allows these institutions to exercise real decision-making power is when the top party leaders—for whatever reason—decide to let them do so. There was only one occasion of major political significance in which this occurred during the five years I studied the party. When Golda Meir resigned as prime minister, the top leaders of the party made an unprecedented decision to allow a free secret election in the Central Committee between two candidates for the post—Yitzchak Rabin and Shimon Peres. It is fairly certain that had Pinchas Sapir, who was thought by most to be the natural successor to Golda Meir, wished to have the party's nomination for the post there would have been no such competitive election.

There are many possible explanations for Sapir's decision; he was reluctant to serve as a "war-time" prime minister; he was the type of politician that mobilizes support for other leaders (e.g., Eshkol and Meir) but lacks the self-confidence to serve in the top post himself; he calculated that given the climate of opinion in the country after the war it was best that there be a fresh new leader at the helm who was not implicated in the conduct of the war; and/or he simply felt he had served long enough in the government and that it was time to give younger leaders a chance—which was his stated reason. All of these explanations are speculative. However, the fact that Sapir declined to accept the invitation of a delegation of party leaders who asked him to accept the party's nomination meant that there could be an election for the post. This was because there was no other natural successor who had the undisputed backing of the party. In this situation, Sapir's backing of Rabin helped bring him the support of the majority of the Mapai faction in the Central Committee, and because Rabin was felt to be close to the Achdut Haavoda faction they practically unanimously supported him. In addition to the support of the Rafi faction to which he belonged, Peres also received support from a significant minority of Mapai members of the Central Committee. Rabin received 298 votes against 254 for Peres.

Rather than proving the effectiveness of the Central Committee as an institution with the power to make major political decisions, the rare occasions when it is allowed to do so, I would argue, actually highlight the powerlessness that characterizes its normal activities. In contradiction of Medding's interpretation, I would propose that the rare occasions of party splits or instances when the top party leaders allow decisions to be made in wider party forums are grossly insufficient evidence to characterize the Party Conference and the Central Committee as decision-making bodies.

I would concur with Medding that "The questions of representation and responsiveness in relation to the party rank and file are highly complex" (1972:114). I also readily agree with his statement that "Party rank and file organized in local branches had little impact on Conference and Central Committee decisions, either in initiation, in consultation or in the expression of views and opinions" (ibid.). However, I categorically reject his assessment that "these bodies were highly representative" because "Mapai went to great pains to ensure that all diverse social forces were adequately represented on these bodies" (ibid.). He argues that "representativeness, responsiveness, and participation cannot be measured mechanically. The party did not consist only of rank and file members and leaders; and these divisions were cross-cut by important social groupings, forces and interests" (ibid.). Medding concludes this discussion with the argument that "we must recognise that an individualistic, Rousseauian approach to a party like Mapai, which in its patterns of incorporation of diverse social forces was explicitly geared to group, interest, and organizational penetration and control, will produce analysis based upon normative presumptions that distort realities" (p. 115). I do not base my criticism on "an individualistic, Rousseauian approach" (whatever that may be), but attempt to show how Medding's interpretations and conclusions are based upon his own "normative presumptions" of democratic pluralism (which characterizes much of the literature in contemporary American political science) and limited research methodology, which consequently have led him to "distort realities." I elaborate this point in the concluding chapter.

In his excellent analysis of the national Mapai machine known as the Gush, Medding concludes, "Clearly, we can say that Mapai's internal election processes were controlled by a cohesive group"; he continues, "but its effects are hard to assess. For example, the machine strove valiantly to achieve widespread representation of the diverse social forces in the party . . . it centralised internal political power which it put at the disposal of the top party leadership," which he claims promoted efficiency. He continues, "*But the price paid was the exclusion of dissenting groups and views, their under-representation, or their inclusion and cooptation with the agreement of the machine, and the granting of a high degree of autonomy in intra-party affairs to the machine*" (Medding, 1972:160; italics added). While I agree that it is important to make analytic distinctions between these phenomena, it is essential to reintegrate them in analyzing their mutual effects. In my judgment, one of the major weaknesses of Medding's analysis is that he tends to consider these factors in isolation and fails to draw conclusions from the effects of their mutual interaction.

This is most clear in his consideration of the role of what he terms "Appointments Committees" (what I have called Nominations Committees). He states that a number of factors operated to minimize the extent to which Schattschneider's famous dictum, "He who has power to make nominations owns the party," applies to Mapai. He cites from among these factors the fact that these Appointments or Nominations Committees are ad hoc bodies. However, he does not point out that they are almost always composed of the same members who are the chosen representatives of the top leaders and/or the top leaders themselves. Medding (1972:164) also claims, "There is no evidence to suggest that Mapai parliamentarians were dropped because they offended members of Appointments Committees." To cite one example that contradicts this statement: Shulamit Aloni was an outspoken Knesset member who dared to criticize consistently the prime minister and other top leaders including Sapir, and concentrated her criticisms on the undemocratic functioning of the party machine. She was dropped from a realistic to an unrealistic position on the party's list in 1969 and in 1973. After her failure to gain a realistic position on the party's list in 1973, she hastily set up an independent Citizens' Rights List, which she headed. It gained three seats in the Knesset, and she served for a brief period as a minister in the coalition government of Yitzchak Rabin.

There are ample examples of nonconformist members of internal party institutions who failed to gain renomination to them, as Medding himself recognized (e.g., the above quotation referring to the exclusion and underrepresentation of dissenting groups and views). It does not require too many such examples to act as a warning to potentially rebellious members that effective sanctions can be applied. On several occasions—such as in a speech in the Central Committee on September 23, 1973, in which the list of candidates to the Knesset was approved—Shulamit Aloni claimed that many of the members of party institutions are afraid to speak out against the undemocratic nature of proceedings because they are dependent on the party for their livelihoods. Perhaps it is significant that Mrs. Aloni is an independent attorney who is not dependent on the party for her livelihood. In fact, no less a personage than Shriege Netzer, the former boss of the Gush party machine, told me in a personal conversation that he was convinced that the fact that an overwhelming majority of members of party institutions were dependent on the party for their livelihoods prevented these institutions from acting as independent decision-making bodies.

Medding (1972:166) states in reference to the appointments committees that "While in their nature not the most democratic they proved to be adept in balancing conflicting needs." In the conclusion to his formidable study of Mapai, Medding states:

> Its internal operations were flawed by insufficient attention to formal and universalistic criteria, particularly with regard to elections, *which cast doubts upon the legitimacy of its electoral processes*, aroused intense internal dissent and *made it possible for certain groups to impair the participation of others.* On the other hand, these same processes were able to produce results that were *highly representative in terms of the party's social diversity, even if there was a marked degree of control over the exact identity of personnel making up this representative group, which may not have been a true reflection of membership views.* (Medding, 1972:302—italics added)

Conclusions: Representation and Accountability

Clearly, Medding's use of the term "representative" is different from my understanding of the way in which the concept has been traditionally applied. In her study, *The Concept of Representation*, Hanna Pitkin (1967) considers a comprehensive range of the applications of the term in various contexts. One important aspect, which Medding appears to have insufficiently stressed, is that of *accountability*—the holding to account of the representative for his actions. In her summary of Burkean and Liberal theories of representation, Pitkin (1967:209) states, "representing here means acting in the interest of the represented, in a manner responsive to them." In her discussion of representing as a substantive activity she points out:

> A political representative—at least the typical member of an elected legislature—has a constituency rather than a single principle; and this raises problems about whether such an unorganized group can even have an interest for him to pursue, let alone a will to which he could be responsive, or an opinion, before which he could attempt to justify what he has done. These problems are further heightened when we consider what political science teaches about the members of such a constituency, at least in a modern mass democracy—their apathy, their ignorance, their malleability. (Pitkin, 1967:215)

The problem of accountability, or the responsiveness of a representative to his constituency, is extremely important in evaluating the extent to which the term "representative" can be appropriately applied to the members of the Labor Party's institutions or to the Knesset. There are at least two major ideal types of representative–constituency relationships in the Labor Party. There are those representatives who are selected by well-organized and powerful interest groups, like the kibbutz federations, who are then presented to the Nominations Committees as the choice of these groups. In such cases it is reasonable to presume that they are responsive to their respective groups in the sense that they are accountable to them. In the other extreme there are so-called "representatives" whose constituencies are not organized groups, do not have clearly defined memberships, and in many cases are largely fictitious. Representatives of ethnic (e.g., Oriental) and sex (e.g., women) categories are good examples of this type. They are neither chosen by their constituencies nor are they in any sense accountable to them. Students of Israeli politics have labeled them "pseudo" and "symbolic" representatives (cf. Czudnowski, 1970; Brichta, 1972), but (as I argued in Chapter 3) the more accurate term would be "clients," to designate their dependence upon and accountability to the national party leaders who are their patrons. The patrons appoint them to office and can with equal ease refrain from reappointing them when their performance deviates from that which is expected of them.

Most of the members of the institutions of the Labor Party fall within an intermediate type—they ostensibly represent a constituency, but are in no way meaningfully responsive to it, nor are they held accountable by it. For example, almost all representatives of the party branches in the national institutions are local elites and/or the clients of national elites. They neither consult their branches before debates and votes in the national institutions (there are rarely debates in branches prior to debates in national institutions) nor do they usually even report the results of the debates, the positions they took (if any), or the manner in which they voted. (These generalizations are made on the basis of extensive and prolonged observations in party branches throughout the country and extended interviews with the members of the national party institutions.) When asked to identify the constituency represented by a particular member of the Central Committee, party functionaries invariably replied, "his mother!"— that is, none.

I consequently question the applicability of the term "representative" when referring to Labor's national institutions. Even without taking an individualistic approach—and accepting Medding's emphasis on group representation—in showing that by and large the so-called representatives are not responsive to their constituencies, the appropriateness of the term "representative" is brought into question. Pitkin (1967:226) has stated that elected political representatives "are 'true' representatives only if they must eventually account for their actions to those for whom they act." Most members of Labor's national institutions do not have to account for their actions to the constituencies for whom they ostensibly act but instead to the top party leaders who chose them through the Nominations Committees. That the top leaders take into account diverse groups and interests in selecting membership for various institutions—particularly when (as Medding admits) such selection may not have been a true reflection of membership views—is insufficient reason to justify Medding's judgment that these institutions "were highly representative," even with the qualification he used: "in terms of the party's social diversity" (Medding, 1972:302). As I demonstrated in the first part of this chapter, the party institutions are not representative, even in this most general usage of the word, with regard to ethnic, sex, and age composition, geographical distribution, or the division between agricultural and urban sectors.

I have quoted several passages in which Medding has argued that it is reasonable to assume that the majority of institutions—even if constituted through the manipulations of the party machine—agreed with the decisions they were given to ratify simply because they did accept them. Pitkin (1967:231) rejects similar arguments, saying, "it will not do to define representation by the acquiescence of the subjects." She continues,

> It seems to me that we show a government to be representative not by demonstrating its control over its subjects but just the reverse, by demonstrating that its subjects have control over what it does. . . . [I]n a representative government . . . the people really do act through their government, and are not merely passive recipients of its actions. A representative government . . . must also be responsive to the people. (1967:232)

By emphasizing the need for "a constant condition of responsiveness" and for the institutional arrangement through which this is guaranteed, Pitkin (1967:233) highlights a central aspect of representation which, upon investigation, reveals an important institutional weakness in the Labor Party.

The major consequence of the bypassing of constitutional forums for decision making by what were supposed to be representative bodies was the centralization of power in the small executive body, the Leadership Bureau, and even more frequently in even smaller informal groups of top leaders referred to generally as "Golda's kitchen" and "Sapir's new Gush." This practice had already developed in the former Mapai, as Medding (1972:302) clearly showed:

> Similarly, lack of concern with constitutional formality led to centralization of control in the hands of narrower executive bodies, and the inevitable lessening of the influence of the wider representative bodies. (i.e.) . . . the growth of nonconstitutionally recognized top executive bodies wielding effective power. Another was the growth of the party machine which developed to fill the void in the performance of key political functions where formal processes either did not exist or were not so well suited to the task. (And to the extent that the machine stepped in, it later made it more difficult for constitutional procedures to be established.)

In this chapter I have examined the general pattern of continuity in the domination of the national institutions of the Labor Party by showing the over-representation of some groups and the underrepresentation of others. I have pointed to general trends that indicate the evolution of broad changes in representation, such as the increasingly greater representation of the Continuing Generation, who are mainly Israeli-born. I have evaluated the nature of representation in these institutions using traditionally accepted criteria commonly associated with the concept. This I have contrasted with the conclusions of Medding's important study of the former Mapai. In so doing, I have attempted to relate the previous analysis of the nominations process and the nature of the dependence of most of the members of these institutions on the top leadership to show that these members were by and large not responsible to the constituencies they ostensibly were supposed to represent. I continue to illustrate the relationship between the centralization of power in the Labor Party and the increasing lack of responsiveness of its institutions to wider constituencies in the following chapter through an analysis of the reciprocal relationships between the party center and the local branches. In Chapter 8, I show the ramifications of the processes discussed thus far, which culminated in major changes in internal party relationships and wider societal changes in the aftermath of the war of October 1973. In Chapter 13 I integrate the analysis of these processes and evaluate the contribution of the anthropological approach by comparing my conclusions with a more traditional political science approach, as represented by Medding's study.

7

Party Center and Local Branch Relationships

Introduction: The Problem

Politics in Israel is hierarchical, highly centralized, and concentrates great power and resources in the hands of relatively few top national leaders. From the early thirties, when the labor movement captured the key positions in the Zionist executive and other important political positions in the pre-state Yishuv, the top leadership of the labor parties consolidated and entrenched their positions primarily through control of external resources upon which the state-in-the-making was dependent for its survival and development. The authority of this political elite was largely legitimized through the consensual acceptance of their pioneering role in leading the fulfillment of the Zionist dream. With the institutionalization of the political structure and the transfer of many of the major functions to the state in the post-Independence period, the elite further consolidated their positions through control of the expanded position of the state machinery. Again, control over the direction and allocation of resources, capital and human, which flowed into the country from abroad was a major factor in perpetuating the centralization of power. As a result of the consolidation of resources and power at the center, local politics and government in Israel has traditionally played a secondary and dependent role vis-à-vis the central parties and government. This had been particularly true in the case of the thirty new towns established since 1948 and primarily populated by new immigrants from North Africa and the Middle East who were sent to the towns from transit camps or straight from the boats. These were planted communities, created and controlled by agencies of the central government ministries for their development; and, because initially the local inhabitants lacked the necessary skills to communicate their demands to higher authorities, these towns were remote controlled by agents of national agencies, ministries, and political parties.

The new immigrants learned to manipulate as well as be manipulated by the representatives of the national agencies. After mobilizing support, they began taking over various local political offices. The political coming of age of the new immigrants at the local level has led to certain alterations in the relationships between the local branches and their central party headquarters. The development of the local political system is related to the changing role of the party center (specifically) and of the party (generally) in Israeli society.

The Israel Labor Party is, to use Duverger's terms, a strongly articulated, vertically structured, and highly centralized political party. In such a system, one would expect to find all decisions coming from above, and their application controlled by representatives of the center (Duverger, 1963/1965:56). I contend that this generalization, even if it might hold true in many cases, is unsatisfactory for understanding the complexities of internal party organization. Such a generalization tells us nothing about the differential power of various types of branches within the party, nor does it explain the circumstances under which branches may assert greater autonomy from the party center. I argue that even a highly centralized and powerful political party like the Israel Labor Party must allow a certain degree of freedom of action in the branches, particularly once they have reached a certain stage of local political consolidation and development, in order to maintain ultimate control of the central party machinery.

Unfortunately there has been little published research that has specifically focused on this problem. The problem, of course, is an old one that has not escaped the attention of various political thinkers. Burke observed, for example,

> In large bodies the circulation of power must be less vigorous at the extremities. . . . The Sultan gets as much obedience as he can. He governs with a loose rein, that he may govern at all; and the whole of the force and vigour of his authority in his centre is derived from a prudent relaxation in all his borders. (Quoted in Quiller-Couch, 1961:123.)

More recently, Edward Shils (1961, 1968) has developed the concept of center and periphery, which has been applied to the macro-sociological comparison of societies. Shmuel Eisenstadt (1969), among others, has also developed similar general frameworks with reference to the development of political systems. However, such frameworks have generally not been applied to the level of micro-sociological analysis, and when they are applied to a single society they tend to focus on general historical trends and relationships (e.g., Horowitz and Lissak, 1973 and 1978). On the other hand, few studies of political parties and their organizations deal with the problem of relationships between center and periphery in more than a general and descriptive manner. This is generally incorporated into a discussion of the organizational structure of the party.

The literature on political parties in the United Kingdom contains discussions of the role and power of the central offices of parties, of regional and area organization, and of constituency party autonomy and central control. However, there appears to be a decided lack of consensus among observers of British politics as to the nature of these relationships. For example, Robert Mackenzie's (1955/1963:291) claim that "It would be difficult to envisage a more tight-knit system of oligarchical control of the affairs of a political party" has been challenged with persuasive documentation and arguments by Michael Pinto-Duschinsky with regards to the Conservative Party. Pinto-Duschinsky (1972) stresses that the Central Office of the Conservative Party is in a weak position vis-à-vis the local associations since their finances are almost entirely independent. He points out that the Central Office is also handicapped by its lack of patronage, and states, "The financial self-sufficiency of the local associations together with the personal independence of the party workers greatly reduces the ability of Central Office to impose its will" (Pinto-Duschinsky, 1972:9). He also argues that "The weakness of the party headquarters is also apparent in the candidates department. As the constituency leaders, who are finally responsible for the selection of candidates, are almost always independent of the patronage of the central organization, little pressure can be imposed on them to nominate particular Central Office favourites" (ibid.).

In contrast to the aforementioned situation in the British Conservative Party, the dues of the members of the Israel Labor Party are paid directly to the central party and then allocated to the various branches on the basis of branch size. The branches, as opposed to the central party, have no independent sources of income. All party officials, functionaries of the national bureaucracy, and those secretaries of local branches who receive salaries are paid through the national headquarters. There is a wide range of additional patronage which increases the dependence of local officials on national headquarters. Candidate selection at the local level is frequently, although not always, significantly influenced by the intervention of national party headquarters.

In an article devoted to the subject of constituency party autonomy and central control in the British Labor and Conservative parties David Wilson (1973:169) claims that "In both parties the precise nature of the relationship between constituency parties and regional officials has always been rather uncertain." He points out certain differences between the two parties, mainly in the formal powers allocated to Labor Party regional organizers who are allowed to intervene at the constituency level—the National Election Committee (NEC) must be represented at all parliamentary prospective candidate selection meetings. But Wilson shows that constituency autonomy is in fact not stronger in the Conservative Party because of "the idea of loyalty to the centre; in the Conservative Party there is a deep rooted desire not to conflict with the leadership," whereas, "[t]he prevailing atmosphere in the Labor Party, however, demands that the leadership has some authority at the constituency level in matters such as candidate and agency selection" (Wilson, 1973:170). Wilson (1973:174) concludes:

> Regional organizers and area agents lack formal authority at the constituency level. In both parties, however, weak constituencies are heavily dependent upon the services which are provided through the regional and area offices. The services of Labor Party regional organizers are utilized more fully by constituency parties than are those of the Conservative Party's area agents. This is essentially because the Labor Party's constituency organization is relatively unprofessional and therefore requires a greater amount of assistance than their wealthier Conservative counterparts. The role of area and regional officers is to service the local party units, providing advice and assistance when requested. Regional organizers and area agents must persuade local parties to heed their advice. They are in no position to command any constituencies to obey the directives they give.

Derek Urwin has shown that in spite of reforms, the Scottish Conservative Party, although based upon the English model, is "much more decentralized than the English pattern" (Urwin, 1966:149). He notes that the basic feature of the Scottish association is the great emphasis placed on local autonomy and complete freedom of action.

Although considerable research carried out in Britain has concentrated on the national and local levels (such as the works previously cited), it has been noted that "Basic information about the intermediate branch of party organization, the regional and area structures, is lacking" (Wilson, 1972:373; c.f. Blondel, 1963:108, for a similar observation). Although there are significant structural differences in the organization of the Israel Labor Party and the two main British parties, there is a similar gap in research on the nature of relationships and links between the party center and its constituency branches in the periphery. Wilson's (1972:381) research is exceptional in this respect for Britain and indicates that:

> Both parties employ their regional staff to act as field agents for the respective Party leaderships. As field agents, regional and area staff act as the "eyes and ears" of the party leaderships. The major rationale for the development and maintenance of a network of field administration in the Labor and Conservative parties, has, however, been administrative convenience. The degree of control exercised by the respective head offices does not, however, indicate that the two parties are highly centralized. There is no evidence to indicate that the chain of command extends beyond the regional and area organizers to the constituency associations, and local branches are proud of their relative autonomy. Directives from the regional offices are frequently ignored by constituency parties. Consequently it is not possible to speak of two highly centralized political parties in Britain. There is no chain of command from the national party leadership to the constituency and branch levels. The chain of command ends at the regional level.

In the forthcoming analysis I shall try to elaborate the nature of the relationships between the national and local levels of the party thereby revealing specific aspects of the highly centralized structure, and those spheres in which branches have been successfully able to assert their local autonomy within the highly centralized system. The complicated nature of this problem requires the treatment of several topics that may initially appear to the reader to be independent from each other. However, I shall try to show their integration and mutual effect on one another in the concluding analysis. The subjects treated are a reference to representation on national party institutions (treated extensively in the preceding chapter), local leadership, the national bureaucracy, the conditions prevailing during the 1969 election, conditions during the 1973 election, and summaries of case studies. The analysis of the differential representation of various branches (and of other groups) is an important means for differentiating between the various types of branches on the basis of their power and influence. The functionaries of the party bureaucracy and the local leaders are the main actors who embody the institutional relationships between the two levels of the party. Finally, the analysis of the case studies documents the interaction between the two levels and illustrates the impact of the variables discussed in the previous sections.

Representation in National Party Institutions

There is a clear relationship between the extent of a branch's representation in national party institutions and the relative degree of autonomy a branch has in its internal affairs. I have previously argued (Aronoff, 1972:152) that the former determined the latter. Now I would be more cautious in inferring a causal relationship that is most difficult to verify. It is quite clear that both factors reflect the relative power of the branch vis-à-vis the party center. The proposition relating the two variables—the greater the representation of the branch in party institutions, the less likely is the party center to interfere successfully in internal branch affairs—holds true in almost all cases studied. There are two types of exceptions falling in the polar extremes of branches categorized on a basis of power. One extreme is branches so weak and politically insignificant that the party center simply does not consider it worthwhile to interfere in their affairs; as long as they do not become problematic they enjoy relative freedom from outside interference in their internal affairs. At the other polar extreme the powerful Tel Aviv district, as the main seat of the national party machine, the Gush, is of such vital interest to the top national party leaders that they at times exert pressure on the institutions of the district. A classic example of such a situation was the considerable pressure exerted by Pinchas Sapir (who was then finance minister) to obtain the renomination of the incumbent Mayor Rabinowitz of Tel Aviv (a close ally of Sapir's) in both 1969 and in 1973.

In previous research I suggested that economic and social variables affect political strength. I proposed that the stronger and more diverse the economic base of the community, the more likely was the branch to have greater influence. I also suggested that the greater the proportion of veterans to newcomers, the greater the influence of the branch. Physical proximity to the center proved to be a much less significant factor after examination of case studies (Aronoff, 1972). However, the personal relationships between local and national leaders and the internal relationships among the main local leaders proved to have the greatest bearing on center–periphery relationships. I have paid particular attention to these variables, which are most amenable to the anthropological approach, in the intensive study of a much wider range of cases during the 1973 election campaign, which I shall now integrate and compare with the findings based upon my previous research on the 1969 election campaign.

The local leader's personal background and character, country of birth, length of residence in Israel, education, previous army rank or other positions held, and especially former party affiliation, all help to determine his stature and how he will be able to relate to national leaders. The relationships of local leaders with top national leaders, which range from patron–client relationships to relationships of near equality, are of critical importance. The closer the relationship of a local leader to top national leaders, and the more closely this relationship approximates equality, the greater the influence. To the extent that the key local leaders are engaged in competition with one another (to be described shortly), the chances that the central party headquarters will intervene in their internal affairs are increased. The more united the local leaders, the greater their influence.

A strongly united and cooperating team of mayor, party secretary, and secretary of the workers' council makes a formidable impression at party headquarters and can accomplish far more than a team whose members are at each others' throats. The united team is much more likely to bring the party victory at the polls, which is an important ticket to influence in the party center. An analysis of the localities where the Labor Party lost most heavily generally reveals either weak local officials or serious internal rivalries among the local leaders. That is why I propose that the most effective way of analyzing the nature of the relationships among the branches to the party center is to begin with the study of the relationships between the main local leaders—the human links that join the local to the national institutions.

Local Leaders

The major centers of political power, resources, and interests in most Israeli localities are the municipality, the branch of the Histadrut, and the branches of the major political parties. The mayor controls valuable resources of political patronage through the awarding of jobs, public contracts, licenses, and franchises. He generally enjoys the highest status among local leaders and represents the community in dealings with higher national authorities. His position varies according to the size and resources of the community, his competence and control of these resources, his popularity in the community, his control of local political machinery, and his personal connections with national political leaders.

The secretary of the local workers' council of the Histadrut is the second most important local leader with control of major resources. He is the chief local official of the powerful trade union, supervises enterprises and industries affiliated with the Histadrut in his area, and directs the health, social, educational, cultural, athletic, and immigrant absorption activities of the Histadrut. He also has a personal staff, varying in size according to the number of Histadrut members in the community, which frequently is the basis for his political backing in the local branch of the Israel Labor Party.

The secretary of the local branch of the Labor Party must balance the various internal factions that exist as vestiges of the three former parties that merged to form the Labor Party, as well as alignments based on patron–client relationships, personal career ambitions, personal affinities and animosities, ethnic affiliations, and differing institutional interests (especially between municipality, party, and Histadrut). The configuration of the relationships between these three major office holders primarily determines the nature of local politics in Israel.

Finally, the stage of development of the town has a direct relation to the extent of the influence of the branch in central party institutions, and the degree to which local leaders are autonomous in internal branch affairs. A new town is particularly dependent upon the national ministries and agencies for almost all aspects of its financing and development in its initial stages. In this early stage there are almost irresistible pressures that force local political groupings into affiliation with the major national political parties, for this is when local leaders are most dependent upon their central party headquarters (Aronoff, 1974a). As the town develops, as the local leaders mobilize solid support in their constituencies, and as their local constituents gain greater political sophistication, the branches become relatively less dependent upon their central party headquarters in certain areas of internal affairs. The greater the development of the community, the more influence have the branches.

The National Party Bureaucracy: Party Headquarters

The central party headquarters, commonly referred to as the Merkaz (not to be confused with the national Central Committee), is divided into several departments, two of which are primarily responsible for communications with the local leadership. The Organization Department is in charge of the local party branches and is the branch secretaries' main contact with the national party. The budgets of the branches, including the salaries of the branch secretaries, are paid by the party center through the Organization Department, giving it an added dimension of influence over the branches. The Municipalities Department is in charge of municipal problems and deals with the mayors elected on the party ticket. There are other departments in charge of trade unions, the youth wing, women, ethnic groups, finance, and public relations.

The Organization and Municipalities departments have separate functions and staffs, but their activities frequently overlap. They are both involved in the selection and nomination of local candidates for office, in the formation of coalitions in local councils (municipal) and workers' councils (Histadrut), and in the mediation of internal disputes between the mayor, party secretary, secretary of the Histadrut workers' council, and others. The backing of these departments can frequently make or break a local leader on critical decisions and at times of crisis. A leader's relationship with these departments is an important factor in determining his local strength, just as his local strength partly determines his relationships with the departments of the central party headquarters.

A close examination of the functions of the Organization Department shows the dependence of certain categories of local leaders, particularly those from development towns, on the central party headquarters. Although the officially stated task of the Organization Department is to build and maintain strong local branches, this goal must be interpreted within the context of the political interests of the top leadership. It is clearly in their and the party's interests to have an efficient apparatus to mobilize the vote during elections. The Labor Party, unlike many of the smaller parties, has the resources to maintain its local political apparatus during the interim years between elections. It is the Organization Department's job to supervise and maintain this apparatus. However, since it is not in the interest of the top leadership to have a multiplicity of strong and independent bases of local power, relationships are structured as much as possible to maintain the dependence of the local leaders on the central party headquarters (see Chapter 4 for the expressed recognition of this situation by two different directors of the Organization Department).

The nature of a local branch's relationships with the Organization Department is one good test of its power and status with the party. For example, the three major cities, Tel Aviv, Haifa, and Jerusalem, and the kibbutz and moshav federations are organized as separate districts that elect their own district secretary and have nothing to do with the Organization Department. As a former secretary of the Tel Aviv District told me when asked about his relationships with the Organization Department, "We have nothing to do with them! Who needs them?" Another high official of the same district told me that he did not even know what the new head of the Organization Department looked like. He stressed that when the new head took over he should have come to see him at the Tel Aviv District, but since he had not done so, there would be no communication between them. Similarly, the independently organized kibbutz and moshav movements have few if any contacts with this department. The leaders of these key branches and movements have very strong representation in the important party institutions (as mentioned previously) and communicate directly with the secretary-general of the party, government ministers, and other leading national figures through informal personal contacts.

The majority of branches lack such regular opportunities for direct personal contact with top leaders and must communicate with them through various middle-men. The Organization Department appoints and employs regional organizers who are in charge of day-to-day relationships with the branches in the regions for which they are responsible. The regional organizers, like the local branch secre-taries, receive their salaries from the Organization Department. They are fre-quently shifted from one region to another, which prevents them from developing a local constituency or becoming overidentified with any particular region. The status and authority of the organizers depend to a great extent on their personal relationships with the head of the department and other important national leaders. Generally, they exert the greatest influence on the weaker branches, particularly those in development towns. The mayors and party secre-taries of these weak branches are constantly filing into the offices of the organiz-ers for help and advice on a wide range of problems. The same variables discussed earlier, with regard to representation in national institutions, influence the extent to which a branch is dependent upon the department of the central party, or autonomous from it, in its internal affairs.

Conditions during the 1969 Election

During a national election the local branches take on added importance, since the national leaders are dependent upon them to deliver the votes. In the 1959 general election there was a particularly strong head of the Organization Depart-ment who organized the election through his department. But in the elections of 1965, 1969, and 1973, the Organization Department's functions were superseded by a special election staff. Conditions in the party during this period evidently required different handling of the branches during elections than between elec-tions and therefore different types of leaders were required to oversee the two types of relationships.

One of the most important conditions prevailing during the 1969 elections was the merger of Mapai, Rafi, and Achdut Haavoda into the Israel Labor Party. Affiliation to former parties provided a framework within which there formed networks based on personal relationships and support, cliques and factions within the party based on mutual career interests, personal friendship (trust) or hostility (distrust), and shared ideology and policy goals.

The merger of the parties resulted in the division of the various departments of the party headquarters among the factions. Control of the most important departments—Finance, Organization, Municipalities, Foreign Relations, and In-formation—was retained by the dominant former Mapai. The two other partners in the merger were given the directorship of what were considered less important departments, such as the Youth Department. In addition, each party was allotted representation within the various departments. This necessitated a certain amount of reshuffling of party functionaries between departments. For example a Mapai functionary in the Municipalities Department was shifted to the Organization

Department to vacate a place for a member of Achdut Haavoda. When the Mapai head of the Organization Department, David Kaldiron, decided to take up the directorship of a bank, there was an internal dispute within Mapai over his replacement. After consultation with party Secretary-General Golda Meir, Kaldiron asked Chaim Bear, a member of an Achdut Haavoda–affiliated kibbutz, to serve as acting head of the department. However, the formal top directorship of the Organization Department was retained by Kaldiron. Most importantly, he retained control of the budget and financing of the branches. Therefore, when Pinchas Sapir took over from Golda Meir as secretary-general of the party, he could more easily act independently in arranging special election budgets with the various branches, without consulting the acting head of the Organization Department. Bear's authority was severely limited since he was not the formal head of the department, had no control over the budget, and represented a minority faction within the party. He was left with the thankless job of handling internal party rivalries within the branches and carrying out the directives of the secretary-general and national party institutions. Bear was well aware of his limited authority, had no ambitions for a personal political career, and therefore did not attempt to build a power base through the authority he did have over the local branches. During his tenure, which included the 1969 election, the Organization Department lapsed into a period of inactivity.

It is highly significant that secretary-general Pinchas Sapir, who took over prior to the 1969 election, was an extremely dynamic and strong individual. He preferred handling almost all affairs of the party personally, and did not hesitate to bypass those in the party hierarchy who were officially responsible for various areas of party affairs. The combination of a weak head of the Organization Department and an extremely powerful and active secretary-general ensured the shelving of the department during the critical period of the election. Part of Sapir's political power was derived from his former position as minister of finance—a job to which he was to return after the election. He had a domineering personality combined with a capacity to devote long hours to hard, energetic work. He was able almost totally to dominate the party machinery. From this position, he ran the 1969 election very much like a classic political boss, offering manifold resources to those who would comply with his dictates and threatening sanctions against those who would not.

The role of the Municipalities Department during the election was also affected by the dominance of the secretary-general. The head of the Municipalities Department, Shriege Netzer, had very much controlled the party organization until 1965, when former Prime Minister David Ben-Gurion led a split in the party to form Rafi. Netzer's strength in the party declined because of his close association with Ben-Gurion, as well as other reasons, one of which was the rise of Sapir. Although Netzer's power had been curtailed, he continued to maintain strong ties and influence in many branches throughout the country. Although he had formally retired and received no salary, he was at his office every day at

7:30 A.M. His door was always open and he was available even to the least influential mayors from the smallest development towns to listen to their problems and advise them. He had done many favors for many people during his long years of party activity. More than any other prominent national politician in the party, he maintained an intense interest in, and direct involvement with, politicians at the grass-roots level.

During the 1969 elections the Municipalities Department participated in the preparation of the national party platform with regard to municipalities, helped local branches prepare their own local platforms, and coordinated lectures for localities. The department also dealt with the special problems of civil servants. Because candidates are required by law to take a leave of absence from their jobs in order to run for public office, they generally requested that the party subsidize their loss of salary during this period. The decision of whether or not to help a particular candidate was obviously another means through which the party bureaucracy could influence the elections.

The major role that the Municipalities Department has traditionally played at election time stems from its influence in the composition of lists of candidates for the local councils. As always, it acted as an arbitrator of various special interest groups such as women, youth, and ethnic groups. It particularly stressed the importance of including women candidates.

There was also the further complication of negotiating the representation and places on the list of the previous three parties—Mapai, Rafi, and Achdut Haavoda. Although a national party key formula had been worked out, a special Parity Committee composed of representatives of all factions worked practically around the clock settling disputes before the deadline for filling the lists of candidates. Confusion was greatly aggravated by the fact that the Parity Committee held off final decisions on lists of candidates until the final hour in order to prevent fighting between factions of the former parties. Traditionally, the Municipalities Department has taken a particularly great interest in the candidates for mayor and has often influenced or even dictated the choice of this candidate. The official policy during the 1969 election was to give the local branches more independence in their selection of candidates for office than they had in the past. However, some branches had become so accustomed to asking national headquarters that they again requested its intervention. Others were informally made to know which candidates higher party officials preferred.

For example, the branch of a medium-size town in the central part of the country could not find a suitable candidate to head its list for the local council. They asked the Municipalities Department to recommend someone. A committee of the Municipalities Department chose a man who had served in many important capacities in the Ministry of Labor, had been mayor of another town, and had recently completed a tour of duty as ambassador to an African nation. The branch Secretariat of this town voted 60 to 3 in favor of accepting this man as the candidate for mayor. The candidate, therefore, had the official blessing of the

Municipalities Department and of the local party branch. However, on a personal visit to this town, the secretary-general of the party let it be known that the branch could expect difficulties in getting the campaign budget they desired. In this particular case, the candidate recommended by the Municipalities Department was known to have been sympathetic to the former Rafi (he was a supporter of Moshe Dayan) and the secretary-general wanted one of his own people. The local leaders accurately assumed that the secretary-general was not pleased with their choice of candidate for mayor and consequently they reversed their decision and chose another candidate. Incidentally, the Labor Party in this town suffered a serious defeat and Gahal, Labor's major rival, is in local power there. This kind of influence was used in a number of different towns and cities, and generally reflected the nature of the internal competition among the top national party leadership. Since the outcome of this competition determines succession to highest office, these national party interests take priority over local political interests.

In general, the secretary-general did not directly interfere in most coalition negotiations conducted by the Municipalities Department. One major exception was the negotiations with the National Religious Party for a coalition on the Tel Aviv City Council. Not only is Tel Aviv the largest Israeli city and consequently of major importance to the Labor Party, but the party's candidate for mayor (Rabinowitz) was a close political ally of the secretary-general.

The process of coalition building that immediately follows the election is generally one of hard bargaining and horse trading, or, in this case, municipality trading: "you give us the mayorship in X, and we will support your man in Y." Variations on the theme include deals over rotating mayorships when there is a deadlock, deputy mayorships with full or half salaries, chairmanship and/or membership on various municipal committees, and so forth. Even old hands at the game confided that the negotiations after the 1969 election were particularly difficult and hectic. The Alignment of the Israel Labor Party with Mapam had not been a complete success. In a number of municipalities Mapam did not join on the same list of candidates, but presented its own separate list. There were numerous examples after the election in which Mapam even joined in coalitions against the Labor Party.

An additional problem was presented by the Labor Party's long-standing partner in many national and local coalitions, the National Religious Party. When possible, the National Religious Party formed coalitions in which it could gain the mayor's seat. This was considered unfortunate, but legitimate, by the Labor Party men in the central party headquarters. But in those cases where the National Religious Party could not gain control for themselves, they tended to throw their support to Gahal, Labor's arch rival and only serious challenger. This the Labor men considered a serious breach of how the game should be played. The men with whom I talked in the Labor Party headquarters attributed the shift in the National Religious Party's coalition policy to the rising influence of that party's militant youth wing, which favored the right-wing Gahal as their coalition partner rather than Labor. It took the very considerable influence of Secretary-General Sapir himself, as well as a number of major political concessions to the National Religious Party, to prevent it from forming a ruling coalition with Gahal in Tel Aviv in 1969; such efforts failed in 1973. Inevitably in such bargaining situations the interests of some localities are sacrificed for the interests of others, or for what are seen by the national leaders to be in the party's interests.

There is an additional function of the Municipalities Department, and to a lesser extent of the Organization Department, which they view to be of secondary importance, but which a large category of local leaders considers to be of the greatest importance. That function is acting as an intermediary in the relationships between municipalities and government ministries. The vast majority of the budgets for towns comes from government grants and loans. They are highly dependent upon the government ministries for all phases of development—attracting industry, building housing, receiving new immigrants for settlement, and obtaining all sorts of major services. Because of the structure of the highly centralized government bureaucracies, and the fact that top directors of the ministries are the appointees of the major political parties participating in the government coalition, the central party headquarters of these parties have become an important link and channel of communication between many of the localities and the ministries.

There are few mayors in Israel who, like Rabinowitz when he was mayor of Tel Aviv, could pick up the telephone and speak directly to any minister in the government (and generally get results). Many other mayors of less stature have little trouble communicating with lesser personages in the various ministries and rarely, if ever, call upon the party for aid. However, a significant number of mayors, especially those from development towns and/or those who are relatively new to the complexities of Israeli bureaucracy, have trouble even getting their requests met from regional directors of the various ministries. In such cases, the central headquarters can perform the vital function of communicating the needs of these local politicians through higher party channels to the various government ministries. Very often a mere personal call to a friend can remove an obstacle of red tape may have held up a project of major importance. In such a case, the relationship of the local leader with the party functionary can influence his local success or failure.

This particular function, while still important, has become less important in recent years as local leaders learn the ropes and develop their own personal relationships with government bureaucrats. The serious economic restrictions and more detailed planning in recent years have also limited flexibility in this area. However, a telephone call from a top leader like Sapir is still quite sufficient to get the Ministry of Housing to allocate twenty living units in a development town for families with many children living in distressing conditions. (And no one asks to see the person's party card before he moves in.) Very often, a call from a leader of lesser stature can uncover the reason why a particular grant has not been processed faster, or the reason for any one of a hundred problems that local leaders have.

It must be stressed that of the hundreds of incidents that I have seen and documented, none involved any sort of bribery, corruption, or illegal dealings. In almost all cases they involved people with more experience and access to information or personal contacts facilitating something that had been delayed or, at most, getting higher priority for a project. Such aid can be invaluable to the local leader. This process of using influence is known in Israel as *proteksia*, or using vitamin P, and there is no institution in the country with more proteksia than the Labor Party. In fact, it is the main manufacturer and distributor of vitamin P in Israel. This important function of the party is just one of the many strands that bind the branches to the center in a relationship in which the former are by far the more dependent of the partners.

Conditions during the 1973 Election

The Labor Party has undergone an unprecedented turnover at the helm of its bureaucracy. No fewer than five different individuals have served as secretary-general of the party. Pinchas Sapir temporarily resigned his finance portfolio (but remained a member of the Cabinet) while he laid the foundation for the consolidation of his dominant position in the party during his term as secretary-general and completed the consolidation of his position during the terms of his next three successors to the office. When Sapir resigned as secretary-general of the party to return to running the Finance Ministry, he was replaced by Arie (Lyova) Eliav. As I indicated in Chapter 2, Eliav sincerely pursued the official Labor Party policy of integrating the three former party factions, exemplified by his close cooperation with his two deputies representing the minority factions. However, this was in direct contradiction to Sapir's unofficial policy of building a machine based on former Mapai loyalists. In Chapter 3 I showed that Sapir, and not Eliav, was clearly in control of the Standing Committee and the National Party Conference. Eliav even admitted this in his moving speech in the Standing Committee.

Eliav had been very closely identified with former Prime Minister Levi Eshkol. With the death of Eshkol, Eliav failed to identify himself closely with either Eshkol's successor as prime minister, Golda Meir, or the emerging dominant figure in the party, Pinchas Sapir. In a party where patron–client relationships are all-important, and where the greatest avenue to political mobility is devoted loyalty to a top party patron, political independence is a major liability. Eliav paid a high price for his personal integrity and political conscience. He resigned as secretary-general and wrote a book (Eliav, 1973) in which he propounded his nonconformist political philosophy. This included views that at the time appeared to the mainstream party members, and particularly to Prime Minister Golda Meir, as extremely radical: the need to recognize a Palestinian entity, to make major territorial concessions, to take greater political initiatives, and so forth. However, since the October War, these views are much more commonly accepted. This began Eliav's new career as a renegade within the Labor Party, ultimately leading to his resignation from the party in March 1975.

Eliav's successor as secretary-general was Yisrael Yeshayahu, who had served as chairman of the Standing Committee. His tenure was brief, since when the Speaker of the Knesset died, Yeshayahu's loyalty to the party, and particularly to its top leaders, was further rewarded by his election to this prestigious office.

Yeshayahu's successor as secretary-general was Aharon Yadlin. Yadlin's tenure in office was characterized by his lack of independent political initiatives. He dutifully minded the shop and carried out the policies and directives of his superiors. During meetings of national party institutions it was not unusual for Yadlin to receive a steady stream of instructions (in the form of written notes) from Sapir. During a critical meeting of the Central Committee (December 5, 1973) when a major confrontation between Prime Minister Meir and Sapir seemed imminent, Sapir actually mounted the stage, sat next to Yadlin, and instructed him to make rulings that would avoid such an open confrontation (which Sapir sought to avoid at all costs). Yadlin loyally cooperated with the Sapir-dominated election staff during the 1973 election and was duly rewarded by being appointed minister of education and culture in the present Cabinet.

His successor as secretary-general, Meir Zarmi (a relatively unknown kibbutz member), has currently threatened the top party leadership with his resignation if they do not guarantee an immediate flow of funds to the empty party coffers—a situation that prevented the payment of salaries to the functionaries who work in party headquarters (*Ma'ariv*, January 2, 1975:4). This eventually led to a controversial government loan to the political parties.

The successive decline in status and power of those who have served as secretary-general of the party, as well as the frequent turnover of incumbents, signifies an erosion in the importance of this office. This same trend is reflected in lesser positions, such as the heads of various departments of the party headquarters and the functionaries who serve them. I shall briefly discuss the two departments that have the most direct bearing on relationships with the periphery—the Organization and Municipalities departments.

Yisrael Granite, the man brought in to head the Organization Department after the 1969 election, resigned from active service in the Israel Defense Forces (at the rank of Colonel) to take the party position. He had little if any practical political experience and relied heavily on his second in command, Aharon Tofler, to introduce him to the work of the department. In Chapter 4 I cited Granite's view that it was most important to serve the top party leaders, and from my description of his activities, particularly in the Standing Committee, it is clear that he acted in accordance with this view. Granite's involvement in a private business venture kept him from devoting himself full-time to the party job (he was out of the country for a prolonged period). During his periods of absence, Tofler was acting director of the department. Tofler's serious illness during the period of the election campaign detracted from the effectiveness of the department.

During the period of the election campaign it is highly significant that a former head of the Organization Department, David Kaldiron, returned to the department, ostensibly to aid Granite. One of the key members of the former Gush, Kaldiron had been recruited by Sapir as one of his trusted lieutenants. He therefore had a key role in the making of important decisions in the Organization Department during the election campaign. In fact, the tasks delegated to the personnel of the Organization Department during the campaign were primarily of a technical nature, such as organizing the election workers to get out the vote.

The major decisions were made by the special election staff headed by Abraham Ofer, one of Sapir's most prominent protégés. Granite, as director of the Organization Department, served on the special election staff and implemented the decisions made by it, in return for which he hoped to gain a seat in the Knesset. When he was disappointed in this ambition he resigned his position in the Organization Department.

The position of the head of the Municipalities Department, filled by Shriege Netzer, had been in steady decline since 1965—which coincided with the rise of Sapir to a position of dominance. In addition, old age prevented Netzer from taking as active a role in political activity as he had previously done. Netzer's second in command, Micha Almog, was seriously ill for a prolonged period. Almog's work was actually done by Yehuda Hashai, who served at the same time as a regional organizer in the Organization Department. Hashai's personal loyalty to Netzer had prevented him from getting the official appointment to the office he was in fact filling in the Municipalities Department. Given the fact that he was a professional party functionary, he recognized that his advancement was dependent upon his declaration of loyalty to Sapir, which when made resulted in his getting the official promotion to the number two post in the Municipalities Department.

The traditional rivalry between the Organization and Municipalities departments was intensified by the antagonistic personal relationship between the men actually running these departments—Tofler and Hashai. This rivalry was manifest, for example, in the informal sponsoring of competing nominees for the party's candidate for mayor in a number of communities. Some of these communities were included in those studied intensively by our research team, the major findings of which are reported in the forthcoming section.

In addition to the selection of candidates for mayor, the Municipalities Department was primarily occupied with finalizing and approving the list of candidates for membership on the municipal councils and the order in which they would appear. The formal agreement of the electoral Alignment (Maarach), which joined the Labor Party with Mapam, stated that the parties would retain the same positions they had held on the various lists during the 1969 election. However, there were many problems in branches where Mapam had either run independently of the Maarach list locally, or where it had refused to join in a coalition with the Labor Party after the election—in some cases actually joining a coalition in the municipality, thus leaving the Labor Party in the opposition.

There was also an informal agreement to freeze the positions of the previous party factions—Mapai, Rafi, and Achdut Haavoda—keeping the same positions on the lists as they held in 1969. This resulted in many squabbles among the factions in which they jockeyed for better positions, usually justifying such demands by referring to altered relationships of power that were not reflected in the previous positions on the lists of 1969. Not infrequently, arguments for more equitable representation of various ethnic groups were cloaked in references to factional demands. Another new innovation was that the Europeans in several communities demanded either greater representation or higher places on the list, claiming that they were now underrepresented in their municipalities.

These problems were heard by a special Parity Committee of the Municipalities Department. This Committee was composed of national representatives of the three factions of the Labor Party, Mapam, and the Women's Department and the Young Guard. The last two were present to attempt to make sure that the decision to grant greater representation to their respective constituencies was carried out. The typical pattern was for the Committee to hear the conflicting complaints of the various claimants, and after dismissing the locals, attempt to reach a compromise by making reciprocal concessions; for example, Mapam would be granted a higher position on the municipalities list in one town and would be asked to accept a lower one in another town. In the frequent cases where compromise could not be reached, the members of the Committee deferred to their respective superiors among the top leadership. The Committee therefore acted as a screening procedure, settling the great variety of problematic cases among the less important branches, and deferring to the top party leadership for decisions in the important cases.

Structurally, the direction and organization of the 1973 elections followed the pattern established by Sapir in the previous two national election campaigns that he ran. The major difference was that technically the election staff was headed by Abraham Ofer, rather than Sapir, in 1973. There is no doubt, however, that Sapir continued to be the dominant figure in charge of the campaign, although his direct influence was somewhat less apparent than in the previous two campaigns. The fact that the election staff superseded the departments of the party bureaucracy and relegated them to more technical roles of lesser importance had significant political ramifications, which will be discussed shortly.

Obviously, the most important special feature of the 1973 campaign was that it was interrupted by one of the bloodiest and most traumatic wars in the history of the country. The war caught the country completely off guard in the midst of the observance of the awesome Day of Atonement (*Yom Kippur*). The war led to the postponement of the elections and left a significant imprint on the manner in which the campaign was conducted and the results of the election, albeit a much less dramatic impact than many observers had anticipated.

Summaries of the Case Studies

In the previously published analysis of center–periphery relationships in the 1969 elections, two case studies were selected from several studied and reported in some detail. In this analysis of the same theme for the 1973 elections, I shall summarize and integrate the findings of the intensive studies of seven branches of the Labor Party, each of which involved a year of fieldwork based primarily on participant observation. This summary is based on well-documented and detailed studies which I hope to see published in full in the near future. The branches studied included the dominant Tel Aviv district (the unique features of which make any attempt to disguise it futile), four of the major satellite communities in the greater Tel Aviv area, and two of the larger, older, and most established of the development towns. These studies do not constitute a representative sample in the statistical sense. They do represent communities of varying size and ethnic composition; cities where the Labor Party dominated the municipal councils prior to the election and afterward; cities where Labor lost control of the municipality as a result of the election; and cities in which it was in opposition both prior to and after the election. I shall first discuss those general features shared by all of the branches studied, and then compare important areas of difference.

In each case studied, it was found that the institutions of the branch were successfully dominated by a small group of top leaders, most of whom occupied formal political office such as mayor and secretary of the Workers' Council. It was shown that while these dominant leaders represent different institutional (e.g., municipality and Histadrut) and group (e.g., factions or ethnic) interests, they generally reach agreement on major policy issues, and when they do so, they can either successfully suppress issues or gain the ratification of their positions by the respective party institutions. This is because the majority of the members of party institutions are dependent upon the top leadership. This dependence is related to the nominations to these institutions through small committees controlled by the local elite, and to the fact that a significant proportion of members of these institutions (a majority in most cases studied) are professional party functionaries who work for the party, Histadrut, municipality, and other public institutions that place them in positions of dependence upon the local elites in control of these institutions.

For example, in the study by Avraham (Avi) Ofek (1973) of a major city in which Labor has been in the municipal opposition for many years, 40 percent of the members of the most important party institutions are directly subordinate to the secretary of the Workers' Council as employees of this Histadrut institution, and a total of 60 percent are under his general supervision, that is, they work for Histadrut-owned or -affiliated institutions. In the study by Meir Charsky (1973), in which the branch institutions were also found to be dominated by the secretary of the Workers' Council, more than 50 percent of the members of the main branch institutions worked under the secretary's general supervision and/or received their employment through him. Jonathan Korpel (1973) found the same pattern, except in his town the majority of the members of the main party institutions worked in the municipality under the supervision of the mayor, who was the dominant local political figure. A similar pattern was found by Sarah Carmi (1973). This general condition of dominance and dependence is elaborated and enforced through a complex system of personal networks and patron–client relationships that tie the members of local institutions to the top local leaders and tie the local leaders to national leaders.

Representation in local party institutions, as has already been shown for national institutions, is not proportionate to the number of party members in different interests groups and social categories. The smaller and the more important the institution, the greater the overrepresentation of groups favored by and supportive of the local elites, and the greater the underrepresentation of the other groups. I have already mentioned the overrepresentation of workers in the municipality where the mayor is dominant, and employees of the Workers' Council where the secretary of this institution is dominant. The same is true of a specific ethnic group when it is the main base of support for one of the dominant leaders.

The above-mentioned factors have contributed to the fact that debates in local party institutions (as in most national institutions) tend to be more ceremonial, if not ritualistic, than substantive and decisive. The realization by members of these institutions that they have little if any influence in the making of policy has led to their having feelings of political inefficacy. They perceive the party institutions as being unrepresentative and unresponsive to their interests. The lack of substantive debates that are decisive in the formulation of policy has made these local institutions forums for the expression of particularistic factional, group (frequently ethnic), and individual interests. The major goal of most dominant local leaders has become the continuation of their dominance through the perpetuation of the status quo. These conditions have led to the party's becoming less responsive to new problems and issues created by changing social, economic, and political conditions. One of the ramifications has been the increasing breakdown in communication between the national party and its local branches in the periphery—the problem to which I now address myself.

Some of the most striking examples of poor communication between the national and local party levels can be seen in instances where national leaders and officials have imposed candidates for local office, particularly mayor, who have had no backing in the local party branches. In several cases studied these nationally backed candidates for mayor have been perceived by the local elites as threats to their dominant positions. In all instances examined, this was a significant factor contributing to the defeat of Labor in the municipal elections. I shall discuss several such cases.

In two of the communities studied the national headquarters successfully intervened and gained the nomination of former high-ranking army officers who had not been previously involved in local branch politics. Both candidates had gained a certain degree of prominence through their responsible positions in the army. In both towns Labor was in the municipal opposition and the local party branches were dominated by the respective secretaries of the local Workers' Councils of the Histadrut. One of these secretaries enjoyed cordial relationships with the Tel Aviv–based Gush, and the other was on very bad terms with the Tel Aviv machine and the top party leaders supported by it. However, in spite of the differences in their relationships with the national leaders who backed these two outside candidates for mayor, both secretaries of the Workers' Councils perceived the candidates as threats to their dominance of the local branch. Neither local boss cooperated with the party's candidates for mayor, and in fact they informally worked against their candidacies. Although in both instances the Labor candidates competed against popular incumbent mayors, internal branch strife resulting in lack of cooperation and support significantly contributed to their defeat.

In another two branches studied, different national leaders and officials of party headquarters, i.e., the Organization and Municipalities departments, backed competing local contenders for the party's candidate for mayor. In both cases this intensified internal branch strife. In one town it resulted in the nomination of a candidate who had little backing within his own branch; he suffered a major defeat at the hands of the popular incumbent mayor. In the other instance the officials of party headquarters eventually agreed among themselves on one local candidate (the other having been awarded a realistic position on the party's list of candidates to the Knesset) who enjoyed the backing of the branch (including that of his pacified rival), and they regained the mayoralty for Labor, which had been lost in the previous election (cf. Aronoff, 1972:166–71).

In the three communities studied where the local incumbent Labor mayors dominated the local party branches, all incumbents were renominated to head the local party ticket in the 1973 election. In one town, the mayor was firmly in control as the *primus inter pares* among the local elite in a branch that went to elaborate efforts to present a united front, thereby successfully preventing intervention from the party center (Korpel, 1973). There was no opposition to the nomination of the popular incumbent, and he was easily re-elected in the traditionally Labor-oriented community.

In the other city, Tel Aviv, Sapir intervened in support of the renomination of his close political ally, Rabinowitz. In private interviews leading members of the ruling oligarchy of the Tel Aviv district assured me that the main reason the incumbent mayor was renominated was because of the personal intercession of, and pressure from, Sapir (who was at the time the most influential of the top leaders in internal party affairs). They stressed that in spite of the incumbent's lack of popularity among many of the activists of the district, and their assessment of his lack of popularity among the voters, such was the combined effect of his influence and that of Sapir that he gained the renomination.

A great many factors would have to be taken into consideration to account for Labor's defeat in Tel Aviv. Tel Aviv has never been one of the traditional strongholds of Labor. The young Likud challenger created a popular dynamic image of himself which he successfully contrasted to the machine-style party boss image his propaganda projected of the incumbent. Undoubtedly, many voters who wished to register a vote of protest against the Labor government in the aftermath of the war, but could not bring themselves to do so at the national level, expressed their opposition to Labor at the local level. Rabinowitz was a particularly vulnerable target for such displacement because of his known close association and identification with the top leaders of the party in the government. In addition to these and other factors, it would appear significant that numbers of discontented party activists in this district refrained from actively supporting their party's candidate for mayor, some actively campaigned for the party's opponent, and even more claimed to have voted for the opposition.

In the third community in which the incumbent Labor mayor was renominated, studied by Carmi (1973), there was a clear division of authority among four major leaders who dominated all aspects of local branch affairs. In the year preceding the election, the regular branch institutions such as the Council and Secretariat became inoperative, except to approve the lists of candidates to the Municipal Council and the Workers' Council. A special election staff was formed comprising sixty members, but actually it functioned only in the form of an operative staff of thirteen members. In fact, all decisions were made previously in informal meetings by the four leaders, and were automatically approved by the operative staff of which the top leaders were also members. The mayor had the absolute final say in the composition of the list of candidates for the Municipal Council, which he headed. The process through which the candidates were selected was an informal one in which the rank-and-file members did not participate in any way. The branch Council was called to approve the list after it had been passed on to the Nominations Committee by the four leaders. The list was presented *en bloc* to the Council just before the deadline for filing, and they were told to approve it without discussion. The chairman told the Council members, "If we take time for comments and the list is not accepted *en bloc* the whole thing will fall apart. We must bring a complete list, so take it and like it." They did approve it, although objections were voiced after the approval. A similar procedure characterized the choice of the list of candidates for the Workers' Council and its acceptance.

The secretary of the branch had been an official of the national party headquarters for seventeen years and was appointed to his present position by the party center. His main local function was to ensure that party headquarters continued to support the local party elite, such as the mayor, two heads of major municipal departments (one that awards public contracts and licenses for shops and workshops, and the other in charge of the hundreds of municipal employees), and the branch secretary himself (the least influential of the four). In her documentation of his successful performance of this role, Carmi shows how the branch secretary succeeded in gaining the support of the director of the Organization Department of party headquarters in order to frustrate the attempts of an opposition to the dominant leadership from effectively mobilizing support. The mayor was re-elected.

Conclusions

It is clear from the examination of these seven branches (and others examined less intensively) that the direct intervention of the national party headquarters in the nomination of local candidates for mayor was, more often than not, counterproductive. In those instances where the party center backed candidates who lacked local support, the opposition of the local elites directly contributed to the defeat of the party in the municipal elections. In cases where the officials of party headquarters backed competing local candidates, they intensified internal branch strife, which contributed to the defeat of the party locally. Only in the places examined where the national officials reached agreement on local candidates who had local backing, and prevented local opposition by rewarding the other contender for the nomination, or where the national center did not intervene in the nomination of the local candidate, was the party successful in the municipal elections.

There are several good reasons why one could expect national leaders and party officials not to intervene in the nomination of local candidates. In the first place, they are involved with more pressing matters of national importance, which have greater priority. Clearly, their primary political interest is in the election to the Knesset. The local elections of greatest concern to them are those in the major cities that have the most voters and are of greater national importance. With limited time, energy, and resources, and far more important priorities, it would be reasonable to expect that national leaders would not bother much about what amounts to parish pump politics on the periphery. It should be clear that interference from the center, particularly in the nomination of local candidates, can be foolish and costly given the inadequate level of information about local affairs. Control from the center can be inefficient, counter to the party's goal of achieving victory at the polls, and usually breeds resentment at the local level. As a result of social and political changes in the development of Israeli society, local leaders are demanding greater control of their internal affairs and autonomy from central control. It would appear to be clearly in the interests of the party center to accord them a greater degree of autonomy, at least in the nominations to local offices. Yet national leaders tend to do so only when they have reliable people in local office on whom they can rely for support of their personal positions within the party.

In some instances, the concern of certain national leaders (and officials) with supporting local clients, or those whose personal loyalty they could depend upon in their internal party (or departmental) rivalries, took precedence over a consideration of the possible adverse effect this support would have at the polls. It is not clear whether prior calculations of such adverse effects could have been made. If the national leaders and officials acted without realizing the consequences of their actions, at least with regard to the results of the local elections, this seems to indicate a lack of accurate information from the grass roots. It is clear that the party center had limited information about the situation in many branches, particularly about changes that had taken place in several of them. This was most obvious in the backing of local candidates for mayor who not only lacked the support of their local branches, but were in fact opposed by the local party elites.

However, there was not just a lack of accurate communication between the party center and the branches. In all cases studied, the local dominant elites were clearly unresponsive to the rank-and-file members of their party institutions and the membership at large. Medding (1972:86) accurately summarizes the participant ethos of Mapai in his statement that "After 1948 Mapai's local branch organization found it easier to attract members than to give them a sense of participation in party affairs." He continues,

> What the individual member noticed was the sudden formalisation of relations with leaders, the loss of contact, the erection of barriers in what had been direct and informal relationships, his distance from the centres of decision and administration, particularly if the policies were of national significance. Above all, *much of the sense of participation was lost: the participant had become, in the main, an observer.* (1972:87, italics added.)

The same generalization holds true for conditions in the Labor Party, although the qualifying statement "in the main" could be deleted. Medding summarizes the state of the branches in Mapai as follows:

> Dissatisfaction with the role of the individual member in the regular activities of the party branches was constant. Party journals and reports registered continued criticism of apathy, the lack of opportunity for participation, the absence of discussions, ideological clarification, and policy consultation. The feeling was often expressed that except at election times the branches were "dead," that members discovered more from newspapers about party affairs than from the branch institutions, that less than 10 per cent of members participated regularly or actively, that control of party branches was concentrated in the hands of a few activists, and that decisions were made within a small top leadership. (1972:92; reference is made to a Report of Party Control Commission, 1956–60:22.)

Facilitating rank and file participation prior to the decisions of the party's authoritative institutions was made more difficult by the lack of specific procedures or constitutional provisions for bringing issues to the branches and their views back to the Central Committee or Secretariat. Even more detrimental to effective branch discussion was the fact that branch and regional delegates in national party bodies such as the Central Committee, the Secretariat and the Conference, were not obligated to give systematic reports to their branches of the activities of these institutions, and their part in them. *This resulted in feelings of political inefficacy on the part of potential activists who doubted whether views expressed in the branches would carry any influence at the centre,* even if passed on. (1972:92–93, italics added; reference is made to Weitz, Report Eighth Mapai Conference, 1956:339.)

I have quoted at length from Medding's study of Mapai on this point because I emphasize the continuity of the political alienation of party activists and members of party institutions at the local and national levels in the Labor Party. I cited representative views in Chapter 4 which indicate that political alienation and feelings of inefficacy are even greater in the Labor Party than in the former Mapai. Members no longer doubted whether views expressed in the branches or in the Conference or Central Committee would carry any influence: they were convinced that they would not. In fact, branch activists even expressed their convictions that their views carried no weight in their own local branch institutions. Medding (1972:93) points out that despite the constitutional intention that the local party branches control the party's representatives in the municipal and Histadrut bodies, the opposite is true:

> *The party institutions, rather than controlling, were controlled by the party's representatives in the outside institutions.* . . . More usually they provided a rubber stamp for actions of the dominant group, and served as an instrument assisting the dominance of party institutions by a particular group. (Italics in original.)

The pattern of domination of party institutions by small ruling oligarchies at the local level is almost identical to the pattern of domination at the national level. If anything, it is more extreme in most branches. I have focused in this chapter on illustrating characteristic aspects of the reciprocal relationships between the two levels. I have argued that it is the primary objective of the national leaders to maintain loyal and dependent support for themselves at the local level. These national leaders generally act to prevent or suppress independent bases of local power from developing, or else co-opt local leaders who succeed in mobilizing local power bases within the client network of the national leaders. By backing local clients who no longer have the support of the local branch, or by introducing new candidates from outside the local branch, national leaders and officials have contributed to the defeat of the party in several important municipal elections. In the following chapters I shall attempt to analyze some of the long-range ramifications and consequences of this situation.

8

The End of an Epoch and
a New Regime

Introduction

In this chapter I relate the processes analyzed in the body of this book to the
most significant recent major events in the party. The changes in the period
following the traumatic events of October 1973 represent a new threshold in the
developing Israeli political system. I identify this as a major crisis of confidence
in the credibility of the national party leadership and in the Labor Party as a
whole, which led to a "changing of the guard"—a change in the highest level of
party leadership. Closely related to this is the emergence of new internal party
coalitions, which may have a significant effect on the nature of factional politics
and on the future of the party.

The initial public shock at the unexpected outbreak of war began to be articulated from the grass roots to higher echelons of the party even while the fighting
proceeded. For example, Secretary-General Yadlin met with local party leaders
and reported on government policy and developments of the war on October 17,
1973. Many of the local leaders reported "deep shock among the people." They
said that some people were "asking questions which reach the sources of trust."
Some claimed there was developing a "crisis of confidence in the government."
They listed as examples of the kinds of questions that were being asked: "Where
was our intelligence?" "Where were the reserves and why weren't they mobilized sooner?" "What did you tell us about the Bar-Lev Line?" Yadlin, representing the views of the top leadership, replied, "The people will be wise. When the
time comes for them to vote, they will vote correctly."

There were many who disagreed. For example, one local leader demanded,
"A meeting of the Central Committee should be held after the war to allow
members to express their criticisms!" Yadlin claimed at this meeting that one of
the government's dilemmas was "what to explain to the people during the war."

One of the major charges eventually leveled against the government from within and without the party was that they did not resolve this dilemma with sufficient candor and openness, nor did the critics feel that the ministers most directly responsible for failings had sufficiently accepted their responsibility.

Criticism of the government's conduct of the war, particularly in its initial stages, and other closely related aspects of government policy, was widely expressed in forums ranging from letters to the editor and editorials in the daily press to individual sit-down strikes in front of the minister of defense's office demanding his resignation. Criticism was also expressed in the proliferation of various protest movements.

Early Reactions to the 1973 War

One of the earliest internal party reactions took place in a meeting on November 26, 1973, of a group known as "Challenge" (*Etgar*), which was composed primarily of former high-ranking army officers affiliated with the Labor Party. The leader of this group, Joseph Nevo (mayor of Herzlia and a frequent commentator on military affairs in the media), called the meeting to discuss the need to revise party policy on political-military affairs, and whether there was a need to reopen the lists of candidates to the Knesset and postpone the forthcoming elections. Mr. Nevo stressed the moderate views of the group, which had traditionally opposed the more "extreme" policies of both doves and hawks on political-military policies within the Labor Party. He stressed that it was "impossible to separate issues of leadership and policy," and stated that "the Galili Statement [the previous statement of party policy] must be reviewed as a consequence of the war since the basic premise on which it was based—that there would be no more war— was now irrelevant." He asked, "Is it possible to go to elections with the present leadership and policy?" and answered, "if not, the elections must be postponed."

Nevo disagreed with those who claimed that everyone bore responsibility for the failures that became manifest in the war, claiming, "this hides the responsibility of those who are really responsible. Certain ministers have greatest responsibility—in particular the minister of defense. When he sets defense policy no one argues—not even Golda [Meir]. . . . The authority of Moshe Dayan has been seriously damaged as a result of this war and he cannot therefore make the major reforms which are needed in the military establishment." This was a widely held position in the party and among the public.

Nevo also warned his colleagues by saying, "We all know how manipulations are worked out in the party through which the Gush controls the outcome of votes." He went on to predict, "I do not think this will work on Wednesday," which was the scheduled first meeting of the Central Committee after the war. I have already reported in Chapter 6 that the debate on party policy and leadership which the members of the Central Committee had expected to take place in this meeting did not in fact take place, because the top leaders had reached an agreement to limit the debate to two issues of less importance.

There was a wide diversity of views expressed in this meeting of Challenge (*Etgar*), ranging from passionate condemnations of the defense minister to the expression of strong support for the government leaders. The views of one particular member represented those of many. He said, "Until the war I accepted what was said—that borders guaranteed peace. We were wrong and now need to try a new path." Several other members, while agreeing with the need for substantial changes, cautioned their colleagues that they must be realistic. One said that he would like to see three-fourths of the party's list of candidates to the Knesset changed, and asked, "but how do you do it? The Nominations Committee nominates [the candidates]. Explain to me how our party with its rules and procedures will change policy and leadership within a short time—I'll make that person Prime Minister." He cautioned that such radical changes would require considerable time and organization.

Reactions in the Central Committee

If the growing discontent with party policy and leadership failed to gain public expression in the first meeting of the Central Committee after the war on November 28, 1973, it finally did do so in a highly volatile all-day (and night) meeting of the same institution on December 5, 1973. The meeting, which was called for a major policy debate, was characterized by unprecedented public attacks and mutual recriminations between top party leaders and ranking cabinet ministers.

Debate over the Status of the Galili Statement

Yigal Allon (who was then deputy prime minister and minister of education and culture and is presently deputy prime minister and foreign minister) was the first main speaker, and set the tone by calling for "an open and honest debate." He made several indirect attacks on the minister of defense, Moshe Dayan, and direct attacks on the "hawks" within the party. Allon claimed there was "a need to free [the party] from myths, both collective and personal" (an indirect reference to the charisma of Dayan). He stressed that "we are not all responsible in the same manner" for mistakes made in the conduct of the war (implying that the defense minister had greater responsibility than he). While stressing his personal support for Galili (the senior cabinet minister from Allon's Achdut Haavoda faction) he stressed that the new fourteen-point policy (drafted by the leadership) was a "document which limits the supermarket aspect of our policy" and which took precedence over the former policy (the Galili Statement). For the first time publicly, he joined the opponents of the Galili Statement claiming that, "some had supported it for personal profit" and "others, like myself, supported it because of the pressure of those who sat on the fence" (a reference to reputed threats by Dayan that if the Galili Statement did not become official policy, he would not remain in the government). Allon concluded with an ambiguous and controversial statement: "We members of the government should see ourselves as if we had resigned." The following speaker, Uzzi Finerman, asked Allon if he really meant that the government should resign, and saying that he assumed that Allon did not mean this, he claimed that the statement was therefore meaningless.

Many speakers called in vague terms for "a new team," "need for changes in personnel," "new foreign policy," and so forth. In his speech, Moshe Dayan answered those who directly and indirectly called for his resignation by saying, "It is an easy problem to solve." He said the prime minister merely had to accept the letter of resignation he had previously given her. He emphasized that this was a decision for the prime minister to take, and not the mayor of Herzlia or other critics of his policies (he referred to "intellectual circles") who had urged his resignation. He stressed that he had "parliamentary responsibility," that he had not asked to be in the next government, that he had not asked to be deputy prime minister (an indirect criticism of Allon, who had asked to retain this honorary title), and that he stood on clear principles which were his only conditions for remaining in the government. He claimed that he had been among those in the former Rafi who had opposed the original split from Mapai and was happy that they were now reunited in the same party. He said, "I am sorry that I said when I returned that I would fight that Eshkol would not be prime minister and Sapir would not be minister of defense, because that was personal. But I will fight against these matters of principle. . . ." This was the first public apology and gesture of reconciliation toward Sapir on the part of Dayan. Dayan continued by stating his support for the new fourteen-point policy, and stressed that he considered that it did not represent a major change from previous policy.

The different and contradictory interpretations as to whether the new policy statement canceled out or was consistent with the previous policy (the Galili Statement) became the issue on which a major confrontation between the top leaders crystallized, and on which a showdown was narrowly avoided.

One of the regular members of the Central Committee expressed the opinion of many when he said that the present "soul-searching was brought about by the disillusionment with the previous faith that borders ensured peace." The Speaker continued by saying,

> We must go to the Peace Conference [at Geneva] ready to pay the price in territory for real peace. I appreciate Moshe Dayan who said that the parliamentary responsibility was his and who gave Golda [Meir] his letter of resignation . . . I hope he will examine himself and will draw the proper conclusions. I know he has the courage to do this. The people want to see a change of faces. Not that I want to see a revolution, but it is necessary to introduce new personnel [in the government].

The speech by the secretary of the party's Young Guard, Yechiel Leket, precipitated instant reactions in the form of interruptions, including those from Prime Minister Golda Meir and a general uproar from the audience. In calling for a general evaluation of past policies, he singled out Moshe Dayan and the Galili Statement as "the two symbols of this policy" against which the movement of public disenchantment had focused criticism. He claimed that there was "a lack of readiness to admit mistakes and to make changes," which the prime minister protested was not the case. He continued, saying, "We did not hear a full and convincing statement of responsibility." He argued that although the political and parliamentary responsibility was clear, no one had accepted this responsibility. His call for a "positive statement on a Palestinian state" caused a major uproar in the meeting. Leket called for a clarification of the Galili Statement, which would make clear that it was superseded by the new policy statement. Whereas the following speaker, David HaCohen (a veteran party leader who had been "retired" from the Knesset by the present party leadership), supported the government by attacking its internal party critics, even he got into a verbal exchange with Golda Meir, albeit a much more good-natured one than Leket, when he urged the government to negotiate with all Arab leaders including Yasir Arafat.

The debate continued with two conflicting points of view clearly emerging. Top contending party leaders associated with Sapir attacked Dayan and those closely associated with him, like Peres, and claimed that the Galili Statement was inoperative. The supporters of Golda Meir and Dayan attacked those who criticized them and contended that the Galili Statement remained a relevant and active part of party policy. For example, Chaim Tsadok (who was then the chairman of the Knesset Committee on Security and Foreign Affairs and is now minister of justice) attacked Shimon Peres and argued that, "The Yom Kippur War taught us that our political conception was mistaken, and therefore parts of the Galili Statement—particularly those dealing with the settlement of 'occupied territories'—are inoperative. . . ." Abraham Ofer, a close associate of Sapir's, got into sharp verbal exchanges with Golda Meir and Yisrael Galili when he argued that the Galili Statement was no longer relevant, and challenged its supporters saying, "If anyone thinks that a portion [of the Galili Statement] is still relevant let him raise it for the authorization of the Central Committee." Yitzchak Navon (deputy speaker of the Knesset and member of the Rafi faction) indirectly attacked Allon (Achdut Haavoda) and directly attacked Abba Eban (Mapai faction) for failures in foreign policy for which he was the responsible minister.

The confrontation was greatly intensified and nearly brought to a showdown when Yisrael Galili (minister-without-portfolio, leader of the Achdut Haavoda faction, and close personal associate of the prime minister) insisted that no aspect of previous policy contained in the Galili Statement had been canceled, and challenged those who felt otherwise to bring it to a vote. Arie (Lyova) Eliav (former secretary-general of the party and outspoken critic of the government leadership and policy who eventually was to leave the party) asked for a vote on the Galili Statement, saying that he had been reluctant to do so, but the challenge of Galili forced him to do so.

Pinchas Sapir prefaced his speech by saying that he knew nothing about the possible outbreak of war until he was called out of the synagogue on the morning of Yom Kippur. He claimed that he had always had serious reservations about predominant assumptions—that is, he had felt that "the quiet was the lull before the storm"—but had refrained from pushing his ideas because he had been busy with other matters, and "did not want to worsen internal party relations." He stressed that there had been an atmosphere of potential internal party split (from the Rafi faction) prior to the elections. He asserted that the new fourteen-point policy statement was the only "relevant statement for the foreseeable future." Addressing himself personally to Dayan, he specified that there would not be sufficient financial resources for the building of a new (Jewish) port city in the Gaza strip and other settlement projects in the "territories" since security and the absorption of immigrants had greater priority for the limited resources of the state. He stressed, "I ask in a comradely spirit, if this does not cancel the Galili Statement? In my opinion, yes." He argued that "Peace is more important than borders," about which the party must be more "flexible," and stated the often expressed view that there was a "need to re-examine positions." He continued, "the prime minister has a right to build the Cabinet and I do not doubt that she will do it according to the needs of the present and of the future."

In her lengthy speech, Prime Minister Golda Meir stressed the collective responsibility of the entire Cabinet and (according to her understanding of the party constitution) of all party members. She insisted that this claim was not "whitewashing," but that there was general responsibility for government policy. She demanded an additional vote on her candidacy as prime minister. After making a strong defense of her policies, she contradicted Sapir's position on the Galili Statement by clearly stating that she refused to see it as a dead issue. She directly attacked Sapir's stand and called for a vote of the Central Committee on the issue. During this speech (and during others that preceded and followed it), Sapir was sending a constant stream of notes to Secretary-General Yadlin, who was chairing the meeting, and was busily conferring with top leaders of the three factions, including Dayan and Rabinowitz.

The tension caused by the extremely rare direct public exchange of personal criticisms and expressions of opposing views between the two foremost leaders of the party, Sapir and Meir, reached a peak at approximately 2:00 A.M. when Lyova Eliav demanded a vote on his amendment that the new fourteen-point policy statement replace all other previous statements (including the Galili Statement). At Sapir's strong personal request, Eliav withdrew his proposed amendment. Golda Meir demanded that a vote be held on the issue. Sapir had by then gone up onto the stage of the auditorium, had sat next to Yadlin, and with a very worried expression on his face, was giving Yadlin verbal instructions. In response to Golda Meir's repeated demands for a vote, Yadlin declared that a vote was not possible since the proposed amendment had been withdrawn, and after the prime minister again insisted on a vote, Yadlin responded that a vote was not necessary since previous decisions of the Secretariat would not be changed by a vote of the Central Committee. Yadlin then asked Sapir if he had anything to add, and Sapir responded that Yadlin had expressed his views exactly, and addressed the prime minister personally, saying that there would not be sufficient funds in the budget for the projects proposed in the Galili Statement. The prime minister insisted that each project must be individually evaluated. Sapir objected to a public debate on the subject at that time. Galili insisted that if anyone thought that the statement which bore his name was inoperative, there must be a vote on it. The mayor of Beer Sheba demanded to know whether the Galili Statement existed or not. Dayan, ignoring Yadlin's request that he not speak, proposed that acceptance of the new fourteen-point policy statement would neither sanction nor cancel the previous Galili Statement. Golda Meir agreed, if this would not be interpreted as a cancellation of the Galili Statement. Sapir declared that there would be no vote on the Galili Statement and that everyone should remain with his own Torah (in this context meaning that each person should follow his own interpretation of the status of the previous policy statement). Yadlin declared, "There is no need for a vote [on the Galili Statement] and with this we have finished." When asked if Sapir's statement was the official interpretation, Yadlin replied, "Yes," and declared there would not be a secret vote on Golda Meir's candidacy for prime minister. He overruled the objections to his decision and called for a vote by show of hands. The results of the vote were: 291 in favor of Golda Meir as the party's candidate for prime minister, 33 opposed, and 17 abstentions. Most of the remaining 615 members of the Central Committee who had attended the meeting had already gone home by then (it was after 2:00 A.M.).

After the meeting had ended, Golda Meir and Pinchas Sapir engaged in a sharp exchange. The prime minister asked Sapir, "Did you solve anything by this?" Sapir responded, "I did not decide, it was the decision of the Secretary-General." Golda Meir answered, "Really, that does not suit you!" She continued, "After all it was necessary to vote. You did not finish with this." Sapir did not reply.

Golda Meir and Moshe Dayan had been anxious to gain approval of the Galili Statement—especially provisions that sanctioned settlement in the territories occupied by Israel after the 1967 war—in the Central Committee, a forum which, according to the party's constitution, is superior to the smaller Secretariat in which the Galili Statement had been approved before the war of October 1973. Sapir was anxious to prevent this both because of his ideological opposition to the provisions for settlement in the territories, and because he genuinely feared that such a showdown between the prime minister and himself threatened party unity and could possibly lead to a split in the party. As I noted in previous chapters, direct confrontations between the top leaders have led to splits in the party in the past, and especially given the events that followed shortly after this meeting, the danger of a new party split was a real one. Since Sapir controlled the budget necessary to implement projects, he was confident that by preventing a vote on the Galili Statement he could in fact kill those aspects of it which he found most objectionable. This was in accordance with the decision made by Sapir and his supporters in the new party machine, which he had created, to continue to support Golda Meir's leadership while pressing for major policy changes.

Party Unity Threatened

The following meeting of the Central Committee, which took place on February 24, 1974, had two main items on the agenda. The first was a proposal for an amendment to the party constitution for the method of approving membership in the Cabinet, an item that had been previously ignored in the constitution. Before the war of October 1973, the Leadership Bureau (Lishka) had accepted the proposal of the Constitutional Committee, which had recommended that the Central Committee and the executive of the party's faction in the Knesset should be the forums charged with the constitutional authority to approve the prime minister's nominations of the Labor Party's members to the Cabinet. However, after the war the Leadership Bureau changed its previous decision and proposed that the Leadership Bureau itself and the executive of the Party Knesset faction should be the constitutionally authorized forum for this purpose (as one member pointed out this was in fact the traditional informal procedure that had been followed). Despite the opposition of several members and groups (such as the Young Guard), who claimed that the broadest body most widely representative of party interests—the Central Committee—should have this authority, the leadership's proposal passed easily with a wide margin (311 in favor and 23 opposed).

The second main item on the agenda of the meeting was the ratification of the proposal by the party's candidate for Prime Minister Golda Meir, to form a minority government of 58 members of the 120-member Knesset—54 members of the Maarach (Alignment of Labor and Mapam) plus 4 members of the Independent Liberal Party. Labor's traditional coalition partner, the National Religious Party (Mafdal), had, due to internal factional strife (precipitated by the militant and powerful Young Guard of Mafdal and more extreme religious circles), prolonged the coalition negotiations by demanding a government of National Unity that would include the opposition Likud and a change in the status quo agreement on religion and the state; the Labor leadership found this unacceptable (cf. Nachmias, 1975; and Don-Yehiya, 1975).

The real problem was the fear expressed by the secretary-general and Golda Meir (among others) that they would not have the support of all the Labor Party votes in the Knesset since the representatives of the Rafi faction, Moshe Dayan and Shimon Peres, had thus far refused to accept Golda Meir's invitation to join the new Cabinet. Most speakers urged the two Rafi leaders to join the Cabinet and warned against the danger of a new party split. Almost all speakers warned against the real possibility of the destruction of the united Labor Party. One speaker warned against "a sickness in the party," which might prove fatal. There were many calls to cancel once and for all the internal party factions based on the former party groupings. Many referred to the external party critics, the demonstrations against party leaders, the protest groups, and the problems caused by the National Religious Party.

A veteran former leader of the party, David HaCohen, concluded an impassioned speech saying to the troubled leaders, "Your problem is not the religious party. Your problem is us" (internal party disunity), and was given much applause by his comrades. Others warned against the lack of discipline and growing anarchy within the party. Aharon Harel, a member of the secondary echelon of leadership in the Rafi faction, complained about the atmosphere in the meeting and in the party generally. He decried the "drops of poison" that had fallen among them from the press and television, and another member added, "from *Ot*" (the party newspaper, which had led the attack against Dayan). He urged his two comrades (Dayan and Peres) to return to the government, and concluded his speech saying, "We must decide how we will live in this party. Let us remove this bitterness. I am convinced we have not done the maximum [to cooperate]."

In a lengthy speech, Golda Meir expressed her regret that such disputes had taken place. She countered the charges of her internal party critics, many of whom she singled out by name for individual comments. She then addressed herself to internal party affairs saying, "I do not know if there were ever ideal times. Except during party splits (*pilugim*) we looked after each other." She went on to emphasize that not all comrades were suited for the posts they filled, but criticism of them should be made in a "comradely" manner. She claimed that uncomradely criticism made it impossible for other comrades to fulfill the missions (*shlichut*) the party had given them. Addressing herself directly to Dayan and Peres, she said there were times when actions such as theirs (refusing to join the government) were allowable and other times when they were forbidden. She stressed that in the present circumstances they had no alternative but to heed the will of the party. She said, "If we lived in normal times it would not be a disaster that a party so long in power would lose a few mandates and were to be in the opposition. But I do not doubt that if the government would be led by the Likud, it would be a national disaster." She claimed that "The only alternative is a minority government," and said it was critical that they know whether they could depend upon the fifty-four Labor members of the Knesset to fully support this government. She stated,

> I say publicly—I hope Shimon [Peres] and Moshe [Dayan] will not be angry with me—you have no permission to go. I do not know of any comrade who has served in a mission [*shlichut*] who has not suffered hard times. . . . If, G-d

forbid, you stand on this [refusal to join the government] you will bring into question the unity of the party. You will not be able to excuse yourself, Moshe Dayan, if that happens. I have lived through splits in this party, and they did not help anyone. The beautiful periods were those of unity.

She went on to voice her support for the abolition of the party factions, but stressed that it would take a long time. She again urged Dayan and Peres not to put the party in the opposition at a time when the nation needed the leadership of the Labor Party.

Even more significant than what she said was Golda Meir's lack of strong support for her colleague, Moshe Dayan. Dayan had evidently expected strong public support from her, and since this was not forthcoming, and in the light of heightened internal party criticism of him, he refused to join the new government and was supported by his colleague Peres, who also refused to do so. Under these circumstances, Golda Meir threatened to return her mandate to form a new government to the president, who would then, according to the constitution, have to ask another person to attempt to form a government.

Against the background of this very serious threat by Golda Meir, and the atmosphere of impending party split on the part of the Rafi faction, a meeting of the Central Committee was held on March 5, 1974. With the attendance of almost all of the members of the Central Committee, domestic and foreign television crews, and reporters, and with a large demonstration outside the auditorium, an atmosphere of excitement and expectation pervaded this meeting. When the meeting began, the top party leaders were still gathered behind closed doors in a last-minute effort to arrive at some compromise solution. Moshe Baram (who was then the leader of the party's faction in the Knesset and is presently the minister of labor) said in his speech that this was "one of the most fateful meetings in the history of the party—without exaggeration." He called for strengthening the support of Golda Meir and the unity of the party. Danny Rosolio, the dynamic young secretary of the Kibbutz HaMeuchad movement of the Achdut Haavoda faction, warned of the danger signs of the "rule of the street." Others spoke of the "crisis of credibility in the leadership of all of the political parties." Many speakers warned that if the Rafi leaders did not participate in the new government, a new party split would become inevitable, even if this were not their goal.

Pinchas Sapir began his speech by remarking that there was "no better witness to the fatefulness of the hour than the full participation of the entire membership of the Central Committee," which was, indeed, most unusual. He refused to accept the criticism leveled against him that he had been "a factor working against Rafi." He claimed that "When the party was unified we never dreamed that in five years' time the factions would still exist. Everyone here wants unity." Sapir said that all of the leaders were criticized; that sometimes he was the target of criticism and other times Dayan was. He claimed not to understand what had happened recently to cause the leaders of Rafi to refuse to join the government. He said that more than the future of the government was at stake—the futures of both the party and the nation were at stake. Sapir made a strong statement of support for, and praise of, Golda Meir, but made no concessions to the Rafi leaders other than saying that it was not too late for them to change their minds.

Even for a party whose meetings are not normally noted for their decorum, this meeting was characterized by unusual chaos bordering on anarchy as the secretary-general struggled desperately (but not very successfully) to maintain order. After Sapir, the only speakers who received the undivided attention of the audience were Yitzchak Rabin (who, in one of his first speeches in this forum, made an eloquent plea for party unity which drew enthusiastic applause), Shimon Peres, and Moshe Dayan.

Peres assured his colleagues that he had no plans "to cross the floor" (using the English expression), but complained that he was never consulted about important policy when he was in the government. He said, "I was not in the government just to fix telephones. My romantic inclinations go beyond that" (he had served as the minister of communications). He complained bitterly of the organized campaign within the party directed against Dayan, and gave as one example the hostile question in the Knesset from Yossi Sarid (a young client of Sapir's) "when Motti Ashkenazi was demonstrating." (Ashkenazi, a young commander of one of the posts on the Bar-Lev Line of the Suez Canal during the last war, was demonstrating in a demand that Dayan resign.) Peres said with feeling, "These things hurt." He denied that his reluctance to join the new government involved his displeasure with the portfolio offered to him.

In a personal conversation between Aharon Harel (a member of the secondary echelon of Rafi leaders), a colleague from the Mapai faction, and myself, which took place in the corridors outside the auditorium where the meeting was held, Harel claimed that the Rafi leadership had contacted the Gush through its leader Rabinowitz. They had also contacted Golda Meir personally with a proposition that Rafi would join the new government even without Moshe Dayan's participation in it, if Shimon Peres would be given a major portfolio, which they specified as either defense, the foreign office, finance, or education. Harel claimed that they had been turned down. He reported that Mrs. Meir said that these posts had already been promised to others. Harel stated that this created an impossible situation for those in Rafi who were trying to prevent a party split. He asserted that they had great difficulty gaining a majority within Rafi to support participation in the government without Dayan. However, the refusal to give Peres a key portfolio that would guarantee his access to "Golda's kitchen" (the close inner circle of top decision makers in the government who meet frequently at the home of the prime minister) made their position completely untenable. In light of this information and later developments when Peres joined the government of Yitzchak Rabin as minister of defense without the participation of his colleague Dayan, it would appear that in spite of his denials, the importance of the particular portfolio he was to receive was a major factor in his decision. There is little doubt that the exclusion of Peres and Dayan from important informal meetings of top party leaders was an important factor in their reluctance to join the new government at the time when this meeting of the Central Committee took place. In his speech at this meeting, Peres stated, "When I was asked why Rafi met as a faction, I asked why there was a meeting of ministers from Mapai and Achdut Haavoda at a certain house? Why was I not invited? Why do I always have to ask what was decided at this or that [informal] meeting?" He claimed that when a person has the awesome responsibility of sending people to their deaths (reference to Dayan), he could only function in a certain kind of atmosphere. He affirmed that there was a "need for a change in relationships," "greater tolerance" (particularly for Rafi), and the acceptance of greater mutual responsibility. Peres stated that Rafi's members of the Knesset would support the prime minister but would not join her minority government. Although he and Dayan were arguing at the time in favor of a Government of National Unity, which would include the opposition Likud Party, it was clear that the main issues at stake were their opposition to the organized campaign from within the party against Dayan, the undermining of Rafi, and, for Peres, the question of receiving a key ministerial post in the government.

In his speech during this meeting, Yigal Allon (minister from Achdut Haavoda and Dayan's main rival to succeed Golda Meir at the time) made a direct attack on Dayan during which all of the television cameras rushed to photograph Dayan. When Allon mentioned "the former Rafi," Dayan shouted that he wished that the factions were really past, to which Allon said that he agreed with regards to all of the factions. Allon warned that Golda Meir had informed him that she would not establish the new government under the prevailing circumstances, and had only agreed to postpone returning her mandate to the president for two days. He claimed that the Central Committee must convince her to establish the government. He declared that "Shimon [Peres] and Moshe [Dayan] are not unfortunates (*miskanim*)—they know how to take it and how to give it"—"it" being criticism and political infighting. In this lengthy speech he made no overt gestures toward reconciliation with the Rafi leaders. If anything, he further aggravated the already strained relationships.

Dayan's speech was the main event of the meeting. In reference to the previous meeting in which the minority government proposed by Golda Meir had been approved by the Central Committee, he said,

> I voted for the composition of the government even though I opposed it. To say that this was the freest vote—I would not say so . . . I see Golda [Meir] as the most suitable man—eh woman—to be the prime minister . . . I do not challenge the legality of the government.

He went on to make the following comments about Rafi and internal party affairs:

Rafi does not want to exist. It does not have a newspaper, a kibbutz federation.
. . . It only exists because Mapai and Achdut Haavoda make it exist. Rafi
called on Shimon and me to serve in the government. We decided against a
party split unless you throw us out. We will support the government.

Dayan then referred (with considerable sarcasm) to the fact that Secretary-
General Yadlin had asked the Rafi leaders to request President Katzir to urge
Golda Meir to serve as prime minister, and Yadlin called the special meeting of
the Central Committee to persuade her to do so. Dayan said, "This is not to my
taste." He continued in the same vein to castigate his fellow members of the
Central Committee by pointing out that Golda Meir had previously stated that if
the government did not enjoy the support of at least sixty-one members of
Knesset (the barest majority), there would have to be new elections. He claimed,
"If she would come to you today and say the same thing, you would support
her." Dayan said that if they could only have a debate on whether to establish a
broad Government of National Unity, he would attempt to convince his colleagues to vote in favor of such a government. He said he did not make such a
proposal because he knew that Golda Meir was absolutely opposed to the idea,
and he preferred her to be prime minister over his desire to see a wider government. He denied rumors that he had talks with leaders of the Likud (opposition).
Dayan dramatically concluded his speech with the statement, "I am not in favor
of this government," and was immediately swarmed by T.V. cameras and other
members of the news media as he returned to his seat.

Secretary-General Yadlin, as chairman of the meeting, concluded by saying,

> This meeting was the last attempt to establish a government under the leader-
> ship of Golda Meir . . . I do not know to this minute what Golda will decide.
> The Central Committee must urge her to establish the government. The ques-
> tion is do we care if Golda sets up the government or leaves? Everyone must
> express himself on this point. . . . If the prime minister does not reconsider, I
> see black.

Peres insisted that the vote on the call to Golda Meir to establish the government
should be separated from the vote on the authorization of the new Cabinet.
Absolute bedlam broke out as several leading figures in the party expressed their
personal disgust with the proceedings. One remarked, "Without Sapir [who was
absent] they cannot decide a thing." Finally, Galili (the party's expert in such
matters) worked out a compromise formulation in which there was one proposal
that contained two clauses. All but four (who abstained) voted in favor of the
first clause calling on Golda Meir to establish a government; the second clause
approving the proposed Cabinet received the support of 238 members, 7 opposed
it, and 45 (members of the Rafi faction) abstained in the vote.

Yitzchak Rabin expressed the feelings of many participants in the meeting
when he said to a colleague, "I do not understand the guys (*chevrei*). You can go

crazy (*efshar lehishtageia*)!" Many other leading members of the party expressed their anxiety and concern that the deterioration in relationships between factions, groups, and leaders in the party was bordering on anarchy; they feared that if this trend continued the party was headed for a "suicidal course." This exact expression was in fact used by several ranking leaders in private conversations with me.

On March 10 the Knesset voted its approval of the new government headed by Golda Meir, which included the National Religious Party and Dayan and Peres, who eventually joined the government when a particularly serious military alert on the border with Syria justified their so doing in the "national interest." However, the criticism and attacks on both Dayan and Golda Meir from within the party and from increasingly organized public protest groups intensified. The initial interim report (and the later final report) of the Agranat Commission, which was appointed to investigate the conduct of the war in its initial stages, led to the condemnation, and ultimate resignation, of high-ranking military personnel (such as the chief of staff and the head of the Military Intelligence Branch), but refrained from investigating the question of political responsibility of the government.

There would appear to be little doubt that increasing internal party criticism combined with the general mood of public opinion in the country were the main factors that influenced Golda Meir to resign as prime minister on April 11, 1974, which automatically brought down the government she had formed. The agonizing self-criticism, the questioning of basic assumptions that had heretofore been accepted as givens, and the search for alternatives in policy and in leadership that I have reported as they took place in the Labor Party, reflected the same phenomena occurring on a much wider scale at all levels of the society.

The Yom Kippur War as a Catalyst of Change

The trauma of the Yom Kippur War acted as a catalyst, breaking down the immobility in the Labor Party (and in Israeli politics generally) that had evolved over a long period but had become extreme in the period following the Six Day War in 1967. The decline in the role of the old ideologies that characterized the post-Independence period led to factional competition for power among various groups. Fewer policy alternatives were generated, and criticism became more curtailed, leading to greater pressure for conformity with the accepted policies of the leadership. Upward mobility was gained primarily by serving as a loyal client of a powerful patron. As I have gone to great lengths to elaborate, power became consolidated in fewer hands; the control of issues—through their suppression and the predetermination of their outcomes—led to the leadership's becoming increasingly less responsive to the elected party institutions.

The same factors led to widespread feelings of political inefficacy, frustration, and passiveness on the part of the members of party institutions and the middle-

level and the local leadership. The successful ritualization of the political participation of members of party institutions reflected and reinforced their inability to
affect the outcomes of major party policy decisions in a meaningful way.

This same pattern was reflected in the ineffective relationships between the
national and local levels of party leadership. The domination of community-level
institutions by local elites was a microcosm of the national scene: there existed
the exact general lack of responsiveness of local leaders to their constituents and
widespread feelings of political inefficacy on the part of local activists and
members of local party institutions. It is not surprising that such a system would
show signs of breaking down under the severe strains to which it was subjected
in the aftermath of such a traumatic event as the Yom Kippur War. In fact, it is
remarkable that the system held up as well as it did under the circumstances.

The Changing of the Guard

The changes, when they came, took several unexpected forms. For example,
most observers of the Labor Party and Israeli politics had expected Pinchas
Sapir, who had built such a strong and dominant position in the party, either to
become the prime minister himself or to play a dominant role behind the scenes
after playing the role of a kingmaker by selecting the party's candidate for the
highest position of power in the country. As I pointed out earlier, Sapir had long
claimed that he would not become prime minister. He was key in the designation
of Yitzchak Rabin as the successor to Golda Meir by giving his personal support
to Rabin. Sapir refused to accept a Cabinet post and became the chairman of the
Jewish Agency. He refrained from taking a more active behind-the-scenes role in
the government and in the party.

The composition of Yitzchak Rabin's Cabinet reflected other unexpected
changes, as did the fact that he competed in a free and open campaign for the
post with Shimon Peres, who drew the support of many loyal members of the
Mapai faction. Peres emerged from his defeat by Rabin not only as the new
leader of Rafi, but even more importantly as minister of defense, implying a
stature beyond the confines of his old faction. Yigal Allon, who retained his
honorary title of deputy prime minister, gained the important post of foreign
minister, while former foreign minister Abba Eban was not included in the
government. Eban's exclusion was primarily due to his strained relationship with
Rabin. As foreign minister, Eban had been very critical of Rabin, whom he
accused of following his own independent line as ambassador to the United
States. Since Rabin had not been affiliated with the former Mapai (and in fact
was considered by many members of the Mapai faction to be closer to Achdut
Haavoda), this meant that for the first time in the history of the independent state
of Israel neither the prime minister nor the foreign minister were members of
Mapai, and the defense ministry remained in the hands of Rafi. Although the
Mapai faction was represented in the Cabinet—by Sapir's close associate

Rabinowitz, who succeeded Sapir as the minister of finance; by Abraham Ofer, Sapir's protégé who became minister of housing; and by Moshe Baram, the leader of the Jerusalem branch who became the minister of Labor, among others—Mapai had lost the key ministerial posts.

There were concerted attempts led by Abba Eban and (half-heartedly) supported by Sapir to reconstitute the former Mapai as a formal faction in an effort to regain its lost influence. However, Rabin succeeded in building a coalition of support based on the main city branches through the backing of Rabinowitz (who confronted his old ally Sapir on this issue), the dominant leader of the Tel Aviv machine, Baram, who ruled the Jerusalem branch, and the mayor of Haifa, Almogi, leader of the Haifa party machine (who became chairman of the Jewish Agency after Sapir died). This coalition has thus far been successful in thwarting the efforts to reconstitute the old Mapai faction, which would be an obvious threat to Rabin.

It is most significant that both Haifa and Jerusalem have led the movement to abolish the former party factions by resolving to integrate completely the institutions of their district branches. It is still too early to know whether the momentum gained in the drive for Labor Party unity will continue; more importantly, whether or not it will be reflected in the forthcoming internal party elections remains to be seen.

There are other indications of the success of the new internal party coalition. For example, the new leadership was instrumental in gaining the passage of a law authorizing large government loans at low rates of interest to political parties; this was most unpopular among the public, who were at the same time being subjected to new taxes and economic restrictions. One of the most important internal political reasons why the new leaders of the Labor Party wanted this loan was to free themselves from financial dependency upon the powerful Histadrut financial institutions such as Bank HaPoalim, whose director was a strong supporter of Pinchas Sapir.

Labor in Disarray

There have been other significant developments, such as the breakdown in the traditionally strong party discipline in Knesset voting. In an article headlined "Collapse Feared of Labor Knesset Faction," the political correspondent Mark Segal (1975) of the daily *Jerusalem Post* wrote, "Fear of the 'complete disintegration' of the Knesset Labor faction has been raised by one of the party's senior parliamentarians." The report describes the contacts that Knesset Finance Committee Chairman Israel Kargman made with the government whip and the party secretary-general in an effort to stop the rash of subfactional organizations within the Knesset faction. Kargman was particularly upset by the organization of 20 to 22 Labor Alignment members of Knesset in a dovish caucus called "The Free Platform," which met regularly and demonstratively abstained on a motion sponsored by its own party. The more activist wing of the party reacted by organizing its own caucus, named after the late Yitzchak Tabenkin. Kargman, a Mapai veteran, was quoted as saying, "If this carries on then our Knesset faction loses its value and meaning, especially when the others meet in caucus and decide on a common stand . . . I have seen this process start before in such a way when Siya Bet first met just to exchange views, until finally it voted itself out of the party" (forming Achdut Haavoda—see Chapter 2). Kargman was also reported to be concerned about the emergence of an interfactional Oriental lobby formed by Oriental members of Knesset from Labor, the Likud, the Independent Liberal Party, and the National Religious Party.

The main editorial for January 10, 1975, in the *Jerusalem Post*, a paper traditionally supportive of the Labor government, was headlined, "Labour Disarray" and began,

> It has by now become almost a cliché to remark on the disarray inside the Labour Party. And while the other political parties may be in an equally sad state, the inner weaknesses and tensions of the Labour Party are of more interest and importance since they intrude more easily and directly into the arena of government.

Other pertinent parts of the editorial were as follows:

> The machinery of the historic party, with its forums for airing issues of state and giving direction to the party "representatives" in government, have become moribund. The only forum that still exists, though not with adequate purpose or muscle to assure parliamentary discipline, is the caucus of Labour Knesset members. Little wonder then that other unauthorized groupings spring up like the "Open Forum" established recently by the party doves together with Mapam. And little wonder that the party does not fulfill its role of recruiting and attracting new leadership potential . . . a political party cannot for very long draw its own existence from the sterility of its opposition.

The editorial mildly criticized Prime Minister Rabin for having failed to show any sign of interest in resuscitating his "ravaged" party. It attributed this to his natural caution, his absorption in the affairs of state, and to the rapidity of his jump from a career entirely divorced from party organization. The editorial cautioned that this is a course Rabin cannot afford to follow for long, "for the very demands of government leadership cannot be fulfilled without guaranteeing the political base from which this leadership derives."

An example of the unprecedented breakdown in party discipline in the Knesset was the vote for the government loan to the political parties. Some Labor Party members of Knesset refused to attend the Knesset meeting, others demonstratively remained in the cafeteria or left the Knesset before the vote. Many others prefaced their vote "for" with remarks such as: "to my great sorrow," or "under duress," which Knesset reporters claimed they had never witnessed before (cf. Betzur, 1975). Former secretary-general of the Labor Party,

Arie (Lyova) Eliav, violated the stringent party discipline enforced in this vote and voted against the proposal. Shortly afterward he formally left the Labor Party, claiming that the vote on the party debt consolidation loan was the breaking point. His letter of resignation contained a bitter attack on the party leadership, which he said was "bereft of all vision, seeking only half solutions and enveloping the people in a cloud of vagueness" (*Jerusalem Post*, March 25, 1975:4). Eliav also charged that the only thing which bound the party leadership together was a drive for power. (The internal factional strife within the National Religious Party, which was precipitated by this vote, was even greater than that within the Labor Party). The vote succeeded in uniting all of the other parties, from the communists on the left through the orthodox religious Agudat Yisrael on the right, against the two largest parties, which sponsored the bill. The high court subsequently issued orders delaying the state-guaranteed loans to the political parties.

Mood of Reform

In a meeting of the secretaries of the twelve largest branches in the Labor Party, a call was made for "a revolution from below." The participants resolved to abolish the pre-merger divisions that had remained as factions—Mapai, Rafi, and Achdut Haavoda—which would be accomplished through the new internal party elections called for by the end of 1975. (These elections are scheduled for early 1977.) The most radical recommendation is to abolish the traditional quota of one-third of delegates to the Party Conference being appointed by headquarters. The secretaries insisted that all delegates stand for election in the branches. Given the traditional means I have reported used to manipulate the one-third of the delegates appointed by a central Nominations Committee in order to give greater representation to the groups and individuals most supportive of the top leadership, such an innovation, if made, could possibly have far-reaching consequences.

The *Jerusalem Post* editorial, "Mood of Reform," on April 25, 1975, accurately captured the new mood in Israel and in the Labor Party at the time. The editorial stated:

> Slowly but deliberately a new mood is emerging in Israel. It is the mood of reform. Where in the past the desire for change lurked in disparate places in disparate ways, it is now beginning to take hold in the very bastions of rigidity that have been so much and for so long in need of reform. . . . In the political parties too there is a growing sense that party members will no longer docilely accept hoary old conventions. In the Labour Party, for example, the effort to dismantle the component factions, and relieve members, old and new, from these sectional identities in order to create a genuine party, has gained unstoppable momentum.
> Prime Minster Rabin himself gave the new mood an added push, when in

an Independence Day interview he not only criticized Histadrut orthodoxies, but also encouraged the citizenry to take a tougher and more critical stand, reminiscent of Ralph Nader, against private and public power abuses.

As we approach the first anniversary of the tenure of the Rabin Cabinet, it must be said that one of its principal contributions has been in encouraging this mood and creating confidence that finally, the national broom is taking aim at some of our national cobwebs.

Another example of the new mood of reform and change was the merger between several of the leading protest and reform movements that arose in the aftermath of the Yom Kippur War. The Citizens' Rights Movement (CRM) led by former Labor Party rebel and M.K., Shulamit Aloni, the group of Labor Party dissidents led by former Labor Party Secretary-General Arie (Lyova) Eliav, M.K., and a splinter group from *Shinui* (Change), chose the name *Ya'ad* (Goal) for their new party. However, the new party eventually split apart again, thereby demonstrating a continuity in the traditional tendency toward factionalism in Israeli politics, even in a new reform-oriented group.

Conclusions

For many Israelis the initial enthusiasm and hope for reform turned to disappointment, disillusionment, and frustration when expected reforms either failed—as with Ya'ad's inability to unite the various reformist groups—or did not succeed as quickly as had been expected. This has led to increasing skepticism and even cynicism regarding the possibilities of reforming the political system. This attitude strengthens the tendency toward political acquiescence and alienation discussed earlier. It can be found among a wide and diverse sector of the public, representing all political views and orientations.

The movement for internal reform within the Labor Party is far from certain of success. Prime Minister Rabin has been a disappointment for those who had expected him to take an active role in the leadership and reform of the party. Rabin has concentrated all of his efforts on the government and matters of state, to the total exclusion of the party. He has relied on his coalition of the three major metropolitan machines for political support. However, because they too are preoccupied with the pressing demands of their offices, the leaders of these machines—Finance Minister Rabinowitz, Labor Minister Baram, and Chairman of the Jewish Agency Almogi—devote much less of their time to party affairs now than before they attained these offices. At the same time, the secretary-general of the party is particularly weak and has resigned several times in protest against the fact that the Rabin government has not even consulted with party institutions, much less involved them in any stage of decision-making. As a result, the party institutions have practically atrophied from disuse.

The situation became so extremely serious that a special team of top party leaders, the *Tzevet Moveele* (leadership team), was established as a top executive body to coordinate policy of the government and the Histadrut through the party. Golda Meir was brought out of her retirement from active party leadership to take an active role in the desperate attempt to keep the party together, to give it a semblance of unity and leadership, and to reassert the role of the party in the governing of the nation.

With the exception of the top executive team, the only other party forums that have functioned with a semblance of meaningful purpose have been that of the party's members of the Knesset (in spite of previously mentioned ideological divisions), and the recently created regional districts. These districts provide a framework for the coordination of the activities of the smaller branches in different geographic regions, which gives them a combined membership on a par with, and in some cases larger than, the districts of the three main cities and the agricultural movements. Much of the drive for party reform is led by these new branch districts in their attempts to increase their representation in party institutions at the expense of the central lists, which they are trying to abolish, and at the expense of the older districts, which have traditionally enjoyed disproportionate representation and power in the party.

This struggle has now begun and will be fought out in several arenas; one example is the present fight over the composition of the Preparation (Standing) Committee, which will prepare the agenda and control the issues to be presented to the Party Conference, and which will also largely determine the composition of the new Central Committee. As I have demonstrated, this key committee to a large extent determines the allocation of power in the Labor Party. The other main arenas will be the internal party elections to the National Party Conference, perhaps the National Party Conference itself might be a forum, and especially the elections to the new party institutions. The outcome of this struggle will determine: (1) who will lead the party; (2) which group or coalition of groups, if any, will dominate the party; (3) which reforms, if any, will be made in the party; and as a consequence of the resolution of these issues, (4) whether the Labor Party will continue to lead the nation by remaining dominant in the government of Israel.

The position of Yitzchak Rabin as leader of the party is far from secure. Former Minister of Foreign Affairs Abba Eban has made no secret of his plans to challenge Rabin. If the reports that before his death Sapir was considering switching his support to Eban were accurate, then Eban's loss was a considerable one. Unquestionably, the death of Sapir removed from the scene the dominant political actor who, more than any other individual, influenced the development of the party since its formation. Defense Minister Shimon Peres, whose relationship with Rabin is increasingly strained, is another likely contender for the premiership.

Even more important than the question of who will lead the party is the question of whether any one individual or group will succeed in providing the type of leadership that can successfully carry out the reforms necessary to make the party's institutions and its leaders more representative of, and responsive to, those who elect them. This, in addition to the question of whether the other parties will succeed in accomplishing similar reforms, will determine who will rule Israel, and will also strongly influence the character of the political system for the future. It is my evaluation that the Israeli political system is at such a critical juncture in its development that the choices made and the determination of events in the forthcoming year will set the pattern that will strongly influence the shape of the system for many years to come.

_____ **9**

Adjustment to Being in Opposition

Introduction: The Decline and Fall of the Labor Party

In evaluating the performance of the Labor Party in the opposition, it is essential to understand how it came to be there. But first it must be understood how Labor came to dominate Israeli politics for almost fifty years. The formative period during which the most important institutions of the political system were created determined to a significant extent the character and relations of power within the system for decades thereafter. The period from the creation of the Histadrut in 1920, through the creation of Mapai in 1930, to Mapai's capturing of the dominant position in the Executive Committee of the Jewish Agency a few years later witnessed the creation by the Labor Movement of the system's major institutions. Labor came to dominate most of these institutions in the remaining years prior to Independence. Yosef Gorni (1973) attributes the high degree of legitimacy of the Labor Movement's leadership during this period to their successful articulation and implementation of the ideology to which their followers adhered. Yonathan Shapiro (1976) balances the picture by showing the pragmatism of the leaders in building strong and centralized political organizations.

Some of the main characteristics of emergent Labor rule during this period became dominant in later periods and contributed to the decline in the party's responsiveness. They were:

1.   The emergence of a top group of national leaders supported by a secondary echelon of leaders who controlled the party and the Histadrut ensured that political goals dominated economic ones.

_____

This chapter is a revised version of the previously published chapter by Myron Aronoff entitled "The Labor Party in Opposition," in *Israel and the Begin Era*, ed. Robert O. Freedman, Praeger Publishers, 1982. Used with permission of Greenwood Publishing Group.

2. A system of indirect elections to party and Histadrut institutions (and later to the Knesset) through oligarchic appointments committees guaranteed elite domination of these institutions.
3. Dependence on the elite was reinforced by the predominance of functionaries of the party and Histadrut bureaucracies in the aforementioned institutions.
4. Certain categories and groups (particularly those most supportive of the leadership) were overrepresented in these institutions. Recruitment and mobility were primarily through patron–client relationships.
5. Democratic procedures and the party constitution were frequently ignored or put aside for reasons of expediency.
6. Criticism of and/or opposition to the elite was suppressed.
7. There were isolated cases of corruption in the misuse of public funds, which were suppressed. These were minor in their scope and impact compared with the public scandals that rocked the party fifty years later.

With Independence, many of the important functions and services previously carried out by the Histadrut and other voluntary agencies were taken over by the state. These included defense, education, and employment exchanges. Ben-Gurion's articulation of *mamlachtiut* (literally, statism) attempted to give ideological legitimacy to this process. However, it created strains within the Labor Movement. Among other consequences, this process led to a lessening of the citizens' dependence on the political movements. With the mass immigration of Jews from Islamic countries, Mapai relied more and more on material inducements to mobilize their support. Ideology became increasingly irrelevant. Party machines developed in the major cities with smaller versions in the periphery. Support was organized through an elaborate system of patronage, which the leaders of the machine effectively employed to guarantee unquestioned support for the top leaders and their policies.

A number of increasingly serious internal party conflicts, starting with the Lavon Affair and including a complicated dispute between the Young Guard and the leaders of the dominant party machine, culminated in a major leadership struggle that led to the split of the Ben-Gurion–led Rafi from Mapai in 1965. As Medding (1972) aptly summarized the outcome of the 1965 election: "Organization triumphed over charisma and institutional power over prophetic morality." Unlike previous party splits, ideology played a secondary role, as it was overshadowed by the struggle for power. The decline in the role of ideology corresponded to a parallel rise in the importance of the party machine. In the ensuing years internal unity decreased, feelings of political inefficacy increased, and party institutions became increasingly less effective. The net result was a decline in the party's responsiveness to the demands resulting from the dynamic changes taking place in the society.

The period between the 1967 and 1973 wars was one of political immobility.

Ideology was restricted to ritual discourse. Power and the resources of the party-dominated institutions, inertia, the conservatism of the electorate, and the ineffectiveness of the opposition all maintained Labor's rule. Party activists generally felt powerless and ineffectual but were severely constrained from expressing criticism of the top leaders and their policies. Control of the nominations process perpetuated the domination of the party by the elite and their clients. The issue agenda and decision making were effectively controlled by the elite, and controversial issues were suppressed. The ritualization of important aspects of politics contributed significantly to the further erosion of the responsiveness and effectiveness of the party. Although marginal improvements were made, the pattern of unequal representation of various groups in the party continued. However, in response to the demands of various groups for representation in party institutions, the institutions were simply expanded. This made them both easier to control and less effective deliberative bodies. Consequently, decisions were made by informal gatherings of the elite. This expanded the growing gaps between the elite, the party, and the general public. The cumulative effect of this process crystallized in the catalytic "earthquake" of the Yom Kippur War.

The period that followed was characterized by a major crisis of confidence in the credibility of the national party leadership and the Labor Party as a whole. The combination of mass public protests and internal criticism led to the resignation of Golda Meir and to the changing of the guard at the helm of the party and the nation. The succession of Yitzchak Rabin essentially left the party, if not the nation, leaderless. In spite of Rabin's efforts to build a new coalition, desperate attempts to bring back Golda Meir to help revive the party, and other tactics, the party and its major bodies atrophied from lack of use under Rabin's rule. Whereas a number of organizational reforms were undertaken to make the party more democratic and responsive, they were insufficient to convince even those involved in them, much less the wider public, that the party had substantially reformed itself to merit their confidence. These efforts could be simply summarized as having been too little and too late.

Besides these cumulative, long-range factors, there were many more specific and immediate causes for Labor's defeat. The more important factors included the decision to hold the Knesset elections prior to the Histadrut elections and the decision to separate Knesset election day from local election day, two major departures from tradition that cost the party dearly at the polls. Similarly, Rabin's decision to force the National Religious Party (NRP) out of the government was hardly a politically astute one.

The public scandals that rocked the party, including the Asher Yadlin affair, Abraham Ofer's suicide, and Prime Minister Rabin's resignation over his wife's foreign currency account conviction, further undermined public morale and confidence in the Labor Party. President Carter's statements about a Palestinian homeland hardly helped Labor's cause either. Severe economic hardships, spiraling inflation, devaluations, and severe labor strife contributed to the growing social malaise, which was symbolized by the decrease in immigration to, and the increase in emigration from, Israel. As the dominant party, Labor was blamed for all these ills and many more.

With the newly gained respectability and legitimacy of the Likud, and the idealistic appeal of the promising Democratic Movement for Change (DMC), there were for the first time serious alternatives for disenchanted Labor supporters (Levite and Tarrow, 1983; Torgovnik, 1979). Long-range demographic trends relating to age, ethnicity, and class further undermined Labor's traditional base of electoral support (Arian, 1980). In sum, a complex combination of long- and short-range factors contributed to the public's loss of confidence in the Labor Party.

The leaders of the Labor Party temporarily recovered from their respective states of shock, disbelief, dismay, and demoralization to contest desperately the elections to the Histadrut. They were able to prevent the calamity of defeat in this important institution through the infusion of masses of kibbutz volunteer workers sent by the agricultural movements. The kibbutzim were shocked out of their complacency and frightened by the clear and present danger to them of a Likud-dominated government hostile to their interests possibly gaining control of the last bastion of Labor influence. The fact that many voters felt that Labor had been sufficiently punished by the loss of governmental power, the likelihood that some former Labor supporters were having second thoughts as to the wisdom of their Knesset votes or abstentions, and the rationale of others that it would not be a bad idea if the government and the Histadrut were controlled by different parties undoubtedly aided Labor in maintaining its narrow margin of ascendancy in the Histadrut.

Continuity and Change: The Internal Party Dimension

The Labor Party has found it difficult to accommodate the real ideological diversity and conflicting interests of its varied groups. The need for consensus and a semblance of party unity is reinforced by the potential explosiveness of serious policy questions within the party, particularly on such issues as peace, security, and the territories. Clearly, this need is not new. It has been one of the dominant characteristics of the party since it was formed. The real question is, has there been any change in the manner in which consensus is reached? Are alternatives raised and are they seriously considered? What groups are represented in the decision-making processes that set party policy? Are policymakers responsive to the constituencies they represent? In short, how much has the Labor Party really changed? I shall attempt to give at least tentative answers to these related questions.

Histadrut and Kibbutzim

The central role and importance of the Histadrut—both its central office and its labor councils—to the party after Labor's loss of government office and patronage is obvious. As was shown in Chapter 7, in communities where Labor lost control of the municipality, the officials of the local Histadrut labor councils gained political ascendancy in the local party branches. Similarly, the national leaders of the Histadrut (Yorucham Meshel, Yisrael Kessar, Aharon Harel, and Nava Arad, among others), who retain control over the considerable resources of the Histadrut, have grown in relative stature and importance. Consequently, they exercise their power with much less direction from the party than they and their predecessors had done in the past. Because the party was considerably weakened by its defeat in 1977 as well as in the aftermath of this defeat, the relative position of the Histadrut has been strengthened.

The relative importance and power of the kibbutz movements also grew after 1977 and will undoubtedly be enhanced once the recent decision to merge them is fully implemented and consolidated.[1] They provided the personnel and resources that saved the Histadrut for Labor, helped save the party from financial bankruptcy, and replaced with their own volunteers a significant proportion of the functionaries of the party bureaucracy who were laid off after the party's defeat. Therefore, the kibbutz movements pressed for greater influence commensurate with their increased activities.

Dramatic changes have taken place at the central party headquarters at 110 Hayarkon Street in Tel Aviv. The professional party functionaries are now outnumbered by the young volunteers sent by the kibbutz movements to man the party bureaucracy. They partly account for Rabin's place as number four on the Knesset list. Motivated by the anti-kibbutz propaganda of the Likud, the *kibbutznikim* (kibbutz members) moved in to fill the political vacuum created by the disintegration of the old political alignments and machines. Two of the most important departments of the party were taken over by these new men—the Organization Department and the Information Department. Mussah Harif (who died in a traffic accident on January 16, 1982), former secretary of the Ichud Kibbutz movement, and Danny Rosolio, former secretary of the Kibbutz Ha Meuchad movement, were among the group representing this important power base in the party.

Regional Districts

The increasing involvement and power of the kibbutzim was not seen as a universal blessing. Clearly, those whose power was based on the big city machines of Tel Aviv, Jerusalem, and Haifa could not be expected to remain content with the erosion of their bases of power and the growing power of the kibbutzim. There has been an interesting rise in the status of the eight regional councils created during the political vacuum that accompanied the party's changing of the guard in 1974. In order to attempt to retain the influence they gained through the competition between Peres and Rabin (as was reflected in the list to the Knesset), these regional councils are likely to align with a nascent Tel Aviv–

based group (see below). They can potentially provide channels for more responsive representation of groups that the party must attract in order to make a strong
political comeback—groups like the Orientals in the development towns and
poorer areas of the main cities. The competition between those new urban alignments and the kibbutzim in the party has serious socio-political implications.

For example, in order to increase their own political influence, members of
the kibbutz movements are taking part in the establishment of new regional labor
councils of the Histadrut. Designed by Labor to counter the growing power of
the Likud, these councils will unite a number of urban labor councils with
kibbutzim in the area. Unless there are strong regional party branch councils, this
could lead to the domination of the development towns and other smaller urban
communities by the kibbutzim. Since the kibbutzim are predominantly Ashkenazi and the development towns are predominantly Oriental, this could reverse some of the progress made by the Orientals in recent years in gaining
greater political representation and influence in the party. Not only do the kibbutzim represent different economic and political interests than the urban
branches, given the differences in ethnic composition between them and the
development towns, there is a grave danger of the reappearance of a new form of
political paternalism, which characterized the party in earlier years.[2]

Internal Groupings

Dov Ben-Meir, secretary of the powerful Tel Aviv Labor Council, estimates that
approximately 70 of the previous 814-man Central Committee (of which only
around 200 bothered attending meetings) were the bases for tactical coalitions
that swayed party decisions (Goell, 1978). This group's members could be
ranked hierarchically with Peres at the apex of a ruling group that includes
former Foreign Minister Abba Eban and the secretary-general of the party.
Chaim Bar-Lev was designated to become defense minister (before Peres and
Rabin made a last-minute deal prior to the election). Yitzchak Rabin retains
considerable stature and is again showing signs that he may make another bid to
regain the party leadership. The rest of the former Labor ministers, the present
members of the Knesset, and the members of the party executive Leadership
Bureau form the respectively wider circles that constitute the top and secondary
echelons of party leadership. They are tied to one another, and to lower ranking-
party activists, through links of patron–client relations and more ramified social-
political networks.

There is an amorphous middle-aged stratum of party activists who constituted
the reportedly now-defunct Shiluv Circle. Many of them were involved in the
group organized to back Peres in his struggle with Rabin over the party leadership. Most reports indicated the dissolution of the temporary factions that supported the two candidates. Many of the members of this category are linked into
the above-mentioned patron–client ties and more extended socio-political net-

works. There appears to be a potentially powerful alliance emerging between the leadership of Tel Aviv, the moshav movement, Haifa, and the urban sector of the former Achdut Haavoda faction. This nascent alliance could become a new Gush under the leadership of Tel Aviv strongman Eliahu Speiser (Honig, 1981).

During the period under discussion two new informal party groupings emerged. The Beit Berl group (named after the party's ideological institute where they met) included among its more prominent participants Ya'acov Levinson, the party's leading economic expert; the late Mussah Harif, who was at the time the secretary of the Ichud Kibbutz Federation (formerly affiliated with Mapai); Uzzi Baram, who served as secretary of the Jerusalem district; and the official leadership of the Haifa district. The image that emerged of this group was predominantly Ashkenazi, liberal, intellectual, and moderately dovish. Although the group supported Shimon Peres against the challenge of Yitzchak Rabin (who was backed by the Kibbutz HaMeuchad and urban supporters of the former Achdut Haavoda), it clashed with Yahdav, another group that also backed Peres.

The Yahdav group (named after the party club house where they met) was led by the two top Tel Aviv party officials—Eliahu Speiser, secretary of the Tel Aviv district, and Dov Ben-Meir, secretary of the powerful Tel Aviv Workers' Council of the Histadrut. The group included Histadrut and trade union officials like Aharon Harel, leaders of the moshav movement, leaders of the opposition to the official party leadership in Haifa and Jerusalem, and former Police Minister Shlomo Hillel. The image this group projected was less elitist than the Beit Berl group's, more trade union and Histadrut oriented, more Oriental, and more hawkish. Although its leaders claimed his sponsorship, Peres never officially adopted this group. However, the combined support of the Beit Berl and Yahdav groups helped Peres to defeat Rabin's challenge to his leadership.

Before the elections, Peres promised to support Eliahu Speiser's candidacy in the race for party secretary-general, but agreed to postpone the contest until after the national election at the request of Uzzi Baram, the leader of the Beit Berl group who also desired the post. At the time Peres was convinced that Labor would be returned to power and the present party secretary-general, Chaim Bar-Lev, would receive a senior cabinet post. Facing a challenge to his leadership of the party after its failure to regain power in the election, Peres is desperately trying to keep Bar-Lev in his post. Peres fears that if Speiser successfully challenges Bar-Lev, his own standing as party leader will be imperiled. Speiser, an Ashkenazi, has attracted the enthusiastic support of most of the party's Oriental activists in his own constituency, Tel Aviv, as well as in the development towns and the moshavim throughout the country, where it is argued that he is Labor's answer to Begin. Speiser has made overtures to the urban members of Rabin's camp, and if he succeeds in bringing them into his nascent group it might well swing the balance of power in the party.

The category of intellectuals and academics, or as they were traditionally called, "the working intelligentsia," include a group of university professors called Group 77, who demonstratively joined the party in its worst moments after defeat. They have figured most prominently in the efforts to reform both party structure and ideology as a prelude to its return to power. They have attempted to link up with the kibbutz groups, which share this penchant for ideological politics. Although the groups share a propensity for ideology, their views differ on important issues. The professors tend toward the dovish end of the ideological continuum, and the kibbutznikim by and large tend toward the hawkish end— with some notable exceptions like Yitzchak Ben-Aharon. While most observers agree that the party under Peres is far more hospitable to intellectuals than in the past, there are markedly different estimates of the influence of this group.

Closely linked ideologically are the members of the Young Guard (including members up to the age of thirty-five) who in many cases are the students or former students of the aforementioned professors. Traditionally, they play the roles of the *enfants terribles*, proponents of party reform and, most particularly, of the need to democratize the party's representative institutions and decision-making processes, because they have so little influence on these institutions.

Bar-Kedma (1979) quotes party secretary-general Bar-Lev at length and uncritically about the "new momentum" in the party, the commission to investigate the party structure to make recommendations for reforms, the new form of leadership slowly emerging, and the forty new members of the Central Committee and three new members that were added to the Leadership Bureau. The latter were the retiring chief of staff of Zahal, Mordechai Gur, the retiring ambassador to the United Nations, Chaim Hertzog, and the former chairman of Bank HaPoalim, Ya'acov Levinson.

Unfortunately for those who hoped for democratic reform, the three appointees were "parachuted" from above (co-opted) by oligarchic appointment to the top party executive. This is yet another indication of continuity of traditional practices that contributed directly to Labor's decline. Clearly, the Labor Party did not learn all there was to learn from its 1977 defeat. Although there were some promising moves in the right direction, such as the breaking up of the centralized oligarchy, fundamental structural changes and renewal of basic principles did not take place to a meaningful extent.

Evaluations of Continuity and Change

What can be concluded about the nature of continuity and change in the Labor Party during the Begin era? Certain things are obvious: There is no single, strong, and cohesively united elite that dominates the Labor Party. Nor is there a single major party machine, like the Gush when it was led by Netzer, the new machine dominated by Sapir, or even the coalition based on the big city machines on which Rabin had depended for support. At this stage the situation appears to be somewhat in flux. Peres has clearly established a position of preeminence, but not of absolute dominance. He has gathered around him most of his generation of former ministers and high-ranking personnel, with the exclusion of Rabin and his closest supporters. There is the possibility of a split in the group that centered around Rabin. The Kibbutz HaMeuchad has merged with the Ichud in the newly united Kibbutz Federation. Rabin's urban supporters are likely to collaborate with the group led by Speiser.

There have clearly been significant changes in the relative positions of power, not only of individuals, but more importantly of groups within the party. The Histadrut leadership and the kibbutz movement appear to have been the biggest gainers as a result of the reversal of party fortunes at this stage. The major city machines are rebuilding to recoup their losses. Tel Aviv is the most successful, having made strategic alliances with the moshav movement and the branches in the outlying areas, which had only recently made gains through their organization into districts. It is not yet clear how stable these new alignments are, nor what their relative positions of power are within the party.

New groups like the university professors, who have traditionally not been particularly active or influential in the party, have been recruited and might be influential in some policy areas. They, and their allies in the Young Guard, are pressing for major structural reform and ideological rejuvenation. However, their gains in these areas appear to have been limited to symbolic gestures and minor reforms.

In terms of the major party institutions, their membership, methods of nomination, size, and functions, there have been no significant changes. There has been no attempt to curtail the size of the institutions to enhance their efficiency. On the contrary, both the party's new executive and the Central Committee are larger than those that preceded them. This can hardly be seen as a harbinger of the democratic reforms that have been called for by those who view reform as essential to making the party worthy of regaining public confidence.

Given the new openness of the party today, it is most unlikely that there will be the type of ritualized decision making that took place when the party was led by Golda Meir and Pinchas Sapir. On the other hand, if the various proposals of the new task forces are not really taken seriously, then they run the risk of being the new ritual-like formats in which the intellectuals are allowed to play at formulating party policy without having any real influence. There is a real possibility, although not certainty, that this could happen. This problem is aggravated by the sharp differences in policy represented by the new groups, such as the professors and the intellectuals; older groups that have made gains in their positions, such as the kibbutzim; and those groups that are presently aligning around the different urban branches—Speiser's new Tel Aviv–based Gush, for example.

The problems created by the reversals in relative positions of power within the party were manifested in the power struggles over the new party institutions, from the taking of a new party census (which involved the struggle over "real" as opposed to "fictitious" members), the election of delegates to the new Party Conference, and the selection of the membership of the other important party institutions. While these proceedings were more open and democratic than in the past, there was considerable continuity of the old oligarchic practices. For example, Knesset members who had served two terms were required to receive the support of 60 percent of the Central Committee to stand for a third term. Half of the names for the Knesset list were chosen by a nominating committee of five members, which was appointed by the party's Political Bureau. As a democratic concession, the other half were chosen by the party branches. The ordering of the names on the list was done by a special committee, and this determined who had a realistic chance to be elected. The committee consisted of Peres and the leaders of the two kibbutz movements, the moshav movement, and the three major cities—Tel Aviv, Haifa, and Jerusalem. Most of the actual work of the committee was done by Speiser (Tel Aviv) and Baram (Jerusalem). The first twenty names on the list were mainly national leaders, the following ten were mostly the leaders of the districts, and the next ten were a mixture of both. Therefore, while the nomination process through which members of Knesset are chosen and ranked remained an oligarchic one controlled by the party bosses, it gave greater representation to the leaders of the larger regional branches.

Most of the changes that took place in the party after 1977 were the consequences of the calamity of Labor's defeat, rather than having been part of any well-considered or purposeful plan. Although there were those among the party ideologues and intellectuals who understood the long-term and deeply rooted causes for Labor's decline and defeat, most of the leaders—some of whom are intellectually impressive individuals—gave far more superficial explanations.

The weakest explanation of all was that of Yitzchak Rabin, whose memoirs indicated his inability to comprehend or explain his own downfall or the decline of the party (Sinai, 1980). According to Rabin, he was brought down by personal intrigues against him. Abba Eban's explanation was published in his autobiography shortly after the fall of Labor. Although it was obviously added on to an already complete manuscript, this does not excuse the superficiality of the analysis from someone of Eban's intellect. He attributes Labor's defeat to a badly organized election campaign and "a sharp swing toward political militancy and social conservatism in Israel" (Eban, 1977).

Peres' views, which shall be discussed below, while more sophisticated than the above-mentioned accounts, were still an inadequate explanation, failing to take into account the long-range reasons for Labor's decline and defeat. From among the top leaders, Chaim Bar-Lev, who as secretary-general of the party commissioned more scientific analyses of the party's 1977 defeat, offered the most sophisticated explanations (Goell, 1981). But even his analysis lacked a deeper historical and structural perspective.

Since the top leaders of the Labor Party failed fully to comprehend the causes and significance of their party's defeat in 1977, they failed to press for the more fundamental structural reforms that would have been required to democratize the party and make it more responsive to the party membership and the wider public.

They also failed to press for more open discussion of the wide range of policy options and the kind of ideological changes and rejuvenation that such discussions would have required. In order to reverse its defeat of 1977 in 1981, Labor had to convince the Israeli public that it had drawn the proper conclusions from its punishment by the voters and had undergone a fundamental change of attitude and heart. Before the election David Krivine (1981) prophetically ventured the opinion that "The expected change of heart did not take place. Perhaps the Alignment is not chastened enough by its once-only defeat at the polls. Perhaps it is too sure of victory next time. Perhaps it will have a nasty surprise when next time comes around."

Opposition Behavior: The Public Dimension

First Phase

With the partial exception of the Histadrut campaign, the Labor Party was characterized, from its defeat in May 1977 until approximately the middle of February 1978, by a general state of disarray. The defeat was followed by a long series of bitter recriminations as different individuals (and factors) were singled out as scapegoats and blamed for the party's misfortunes. The public was "treated" to the spectacle of a party airing its dirty linens in public, a fact that did little to improve Labor's already besmirched public image. The head of the party's campaign committee, Chaim Bar-Lev, and individuals in charge of various aspects of the propaganda campaign, such as Yossi Sarid, were subjected to particularly severe criticism. Former Premier Yitzchak Rabin published (in *Ha'aretz* and later in his memoirs) a particularly bitter attack on Shimon Peres, whom he blamed for his downfall. Peres reciprocated with a more indirect attack on Rabin, stressing the tremendous difficulties imposed on the party by Rabin's resignation as premier and party leader only six weeks before election day.

In an interview in the *Jerusalem Post* Peres said, "The Likud did not bring us down, it was the Democratic Movement for Change that did it. We fell because of our internal weaknesses and failings in office, not because of the Likud's unassailable appeal. . . . Our way was not proven wrong, it was our conduct that caused our ruin" (International Edition, January 28–February 3, 1979). He claimed that the scandals that engulfed the party leadership (another oblique swipe at Rabin), combined with raging inflation and the rash of strikes, caused Labor's defeat.

During this period, Labor spoke with more than one voice as various leaders, particularly Peres, Rabin, Allon, Eban, Bar-Lev, and others criticized the Likud government and proposed variations of Labor's approaches to a peace settlement. However, during this period a fairly consistent line evolved, and it was most frequently and most forcefully articulated by Shimon Peres. Peres adamantly rejected Menachem Begin's (and later Ezer Weizmann's) proposals that

Labor join in a Government of National Unity. Instead, he stressed the differences in Labor's approach, particularly the need for territorial compromise in the West Bank (which, during Likud rule, was becoming increasingly known by the Biblical names Judea and Samaria) with a close link to Jordan. Peres criticized Begin's plan for West Bank autonomy as being "worse than the Rogers Plan." In the meantime, Rabin and Bar-Lev stressed the strategic importance of the Sinai bases and eventually led the attack on Begin's relinquishment of them.

Organizationally, the Labor Party was visibly in a state of chaotic disarray. Even the traditionally pro-Labor *Jerusalem Post* editorialized about "Labour in Decay" (International Ed., January 18, 1978). The fact that Labor continued to employ its traditional oligarchic nominations process is clear evidence that those in power failed either to recognize or to give sufficient importance to the claim that such undemocratic procedures contributed directly to the lack of responsiveness of the party and its leadership to public demands, which led to its defeat. For example, the fact that the executive forum remained at the inflated number of sixty-one ensured the likelihood of the emergence of a smaller informal elite group to fulfill the executive function in traditional Mapai/Labor style.

Second Phase

The second period of Labor's development in the opposition lasted from approximately mid-February 1978 through September 1978 and began with Shimon Peres' participation in the conference of the Socialist International in Vienna, Austria, where he also held discussions with Egypt's President Sadat. These talks gave Peres the needed image of a leader with international recognition, capable of dealing with Sadat and, as it appeared to many, more likely to come to terms with him than the prime minister at the time.

Labor stepped up its attacks on Begin for contributing to the impasse in the peace talks and pushed with greater force and clarity its own policies, which offered greater willingness to make territorial concessions on the West Bank. In various forums, Labor spokesmen led by Peres and including Rabin, Eban, Professor Shlomo Avineri (former director-general of the Foreign Office), and others launched an increasingly effective campaign.

Begin's political honeymoon was clearly over, and he was losing considerable popularity at home, a development that added to the growing confidence of Labor, whose leaders were moving on to the offense. Infighting within Begin's cabinet was growing and constantly publicized in the media. Increasing wildcat strikes and a runaway inflationary situation made it clear that the government had neglected vexing domestic issues. Many began to perceive that the government's shift toward a free-market economy was not benefiting the average wage earner. At the same time, public euphoria precipitated by Sadat's visit to Jerusalem on November 9, 1977, had been replaced by a pall of depression as the peace talks became bogged down, and many felt that there was some justice in

Labor's charge that Begin bore a share of the blame for the stalemate. This is best exemplified by the spontaneous popular support that arose from the letter to Begin signed by 350 reservists, which led to the Peace Now Movement and its series of successful mass demonstrations and rallies. Dovish Labor M.K. Yossi Sarid is reliably reported to have helped in the drafting of this famous letter, and Mapam's Kibbutz Artzi is known to have given considerable backing in resources and manpower to the Peace Now Movement. Peres met with the movement's leaders and declared they made a favorable impression on him. Many of Labor's more prominent doves gave them more enthusiastic support, although some party hawks opposed the movement.

More importantly, Labor's renewed attack on the Begin government coincided with the independently run Peace Now campaign for greater flexibility in government policy. In April, Peres launched a particularly sharp attack on the Begin government's handling of the peace negotiations, particularly on Begin's interpretation of Resolution 242 in a manner that precluded the return of territory in the West Bank (Judea and Samaria). This campaign apparently struck a responsive chord in Israel as well as abroad. Signs of growing popular discontent with the government, and signs of renewed support for Labor, such as the very successful May Day celebrations sponsored by the Histadrut, convinced Peres that the Likud could not last out its term of office.

The publication of Peres' fourth book, *Ka'et Mahar* (At This Time Tomorrow), in which he outlined Israel's tasks and goals, symbolized the beginning of the forthcoming election campaign. Peres revealed in June 1978 that in his well-publicized "friendly" talks with Sadat, the Egyptian president had agreed to Israel's retaining military strongholds on the West Bank. Peres and Sadat also unofficially agreed to President Carter's "Aswan formula" as guidelines for a statement of principles, something the Begin government had rejected. In addition, Austrian Chancellor Kreisky and Willy Brandt, chairman of the German Social Democrat party (with the behind-the-scenes help of Abba Eban, it was later revealed) introduced a similar draft and recommended its acceptance as the Socialist International's Middle East policy statement. All of this infuriated Begin and his supporters, who contended that Peres was attempting to thrust himself into the political limelight and undercut Begin at a time of delicate diplomatic maneuvering to revive direct contacts with Egypt.

Begin so resented this episode that he vented his displeasure in an uncharacteristic unparliamentary manner, leading certain Labor leaders to question his physical and psychological fitness to remain in office. This precipitated one of the most acrimonious periods of hostility between an Israeli government and the opposition in recent history. The Laborites' charge that Begin was unfit to rule was made in a meeting of the Labor Party's Political Committee, and resulted in a statement from Begin's personal physician denying that the prime minister was in any manner incapacitated. The accusations were called "slanderous" by Begin, who clashed bitterly with Peres in the next meeting of the

Knesset. The ensuing interchanges were accompanied by decisions of the Cabinet to curb meetings between opposition leaders and foreign leaders, and specifically Begin's refusal to permit Peres to meet with Jordan's King Hussein (at Hussein's initiative).

It was clear that by now the government's period of grace was over, and its domestic and foreign policies were increasingly under attack. Serious cabinet infighting became common public knowledge. The combination of growing international and domestic criticism for what was perceived as the government's hard-line stand in negotiating with the Egyptians, the demonstrations of Peace Now, and equally strong internal criticism of the government's economic policy gave Labor plenty of ammunition to fire at the Likud government. The internal frictions within the government only aggravated its plight and tended to give credence to Peres' view that the Likud was helping Labor to return to power.

Third Phase

Given this political climate, President Carter's invitation to Premier Begin to attend the Camp David summit conference with President Sadat was almost a providential way out of an extremely difficult domestic political situation. This was one of several factors that undermined Labor's efforts against the government. The Labor Party changed its tactics during this new phase, which lasted approximately a year, extending from the Camp David summit conference in September 1978 through the signing of the peace treaty between Israel and Egypt on March 26, 1979, and its subsequent ratification by the Knesset.

Labor had already been severely criticized for going too far in its questioning of Begin's fitness to rule; this criticism came from many groups within Israel and abroad, who were not linked in a partisan way to the Likud government. These reactions were warnings that immoderate criticism of the government could be counterproductive, causing groups Labor was eager to attract to support the government. A second factor was the traditional closing of ranks behind the leader when the country is being subjected to pressures that are perceived to threaten the security of the nation.

A third factor was the unexpected flexibility Begin demonstrated at critical stages in the Camp David talks, which took the wind out of the sails of Labor criticism, temporarily at least, on the critical occasions when such spurts of flexibility led to concrete political achievements. The leadership of the Labor Party was clearly far too responsible to oppose the first peace treaty Israel had ever had a chance to reach with any of its Arab neighbors, particularly since it was with the largest and most politically significant and militarily powerful of its Arab neighbors—Egypt. A fourth factor that constrained Labor's campaign against the government was the increasingly divisive nature of the internal struggle within the party between its own doves and hawks.

Labor's questioning of Begin's fitness to govern drew a strong reaction from several U.S. Jewish groups, constituting an almost unprecedented intervention on their part in internal Israeli political conflicts. For example, the Anti-Defamation League of the B'nai B'rith in the United States and the World Council of Synagogues and the United Synagogues of America (the conservative movement) strongly criticized Labor Party leaders for their personal attacks on Prime Minister Begin. They claimed that such attacks crippled the U.S. Jewish community's information efforts and damaged Israel's image. Labor received a clear and unambiguous message to moderate its attacks on the government or risk jeopardizing the goodwill of important nonpartisan groups at home and abroad.

Prime Minister Begin expertly exploited the strong tendency of the Israeli people, including opposition politicians, to rally around the leader at times of crisis. He was thus able to weaken the opposition within his own party and government as well as that of the Labor Party in the Knesset. Furthermore, when his tactics—balanced by what appeared to be considerable flexibility—succeeded in actually producing a peace treaty, Labor could do little else but congratulate the prime minister and give the treaty their political support while claiming that they would have negotiated a better one.

However, the increasingly divisive ideological disputes between Labor Party doves and hawks, which were related to internal power struggles, set additional constraints that limited the effectiveness of the opposition during this period. All of the various Labor spokesmen were most critical of Begin's having sacrificed the strategically important air bases and the major naval base in the Sinai. There were also extremely critical of Begin's autonomy plan, which Peres labeled "a mine-laden course." In addition to the traditional hawks in the Labor Party, the late Yigal Allon, who had generally appeared to have been dovish, strongly opposed the Camp David agreement. New hawkish voices were added to the top executive body of the Labor Party in the forms of the newly retired chief of staff of the army, Mordechai Gur (who announced his eventual aspirations to the premiership), and some of the representatives of the increasingly influential kibbutz movement.

Alarmed by the increasingly hawkish tones of Labor spokesmen, the party doves called a meeting at the end of December 1978, which they were forced to cancel because of the strong opposition of party chief Peres. Obviously, Peres was suspicious of the makeup of the dovish group, which was viewed as too closely paralleling the old Mapai, especially since it was led by his arch rivals, Yitzchak Rabin and Yehoshua Rabinowitz. The power of these individuals and the old Mapai machine they led had been seriously undermined with the ascension of Peres to leadership, the debacle of the 1977 election, and the rise in the influence of the kibbutz movements with their disciplined bloc of ten thousand active members. The concern of many Labor doves was expressed by former party Secretary-General Arie (Lyova) Eliav, who said, "Some voices in the Labor Party are once again becoming louder in trying to outflank Begin on the right" (*Jerusalem Post International Ed.*, Jan. 28–Feb. 3, 1979).

While Labor's political support of the government in the two critical Knesset votes (the first in support of the Camp David accord and the second in support of the Israel–Egypt peace treaty), along with its vocal articulation of serious reservations about both, received the most attention of the foreign media, the less-publicized Labor attack on the government's economic policies was probably, in the long run, of greater internal political significance. In the forefront of this campaign was the Histadrut, led by Secretary-General Yorucham Meshel. Meshel, who worked his way up through the ranks of the trade union movement, has an exceptional knack for teamwork, which has aided him in achieving an unchallenged position of leadership in the Histadrut and in the Labor Party. Clearly, the Likud's weak domestic performance considerably helped to fortify the authority of both the Histadrut and Meshel. The Histadrut's campaign against Finance Minister Ehrlich's economic policies culminated in a half-day general strike at the end of March 1979 in protest against price rises in basic foods and the government's failure to control inflation. A million workers were reported to have participated in the strike, and Ehrlich resigned his post as finance minister shortly thereafter.

Fourth Phase

The fourth phase of opposition behavior was ushered in with the resignation of Moshe Dayan as foreign minister in October 1979, witnessed the resignation of Ezer Weizman as defense minister at the end of May 1980, and culminated with public opinion polls predicting an unprecedented absolute majority of 61 seats in the Knesset for Labor (to the Likud's 29 seats) in October 1980. Never before had an Israeli government suffered the resignation of the three most important ministers after the prime minister, that is, the ministers of defense, treasury, and foreign affairs. Nor had any Israeli political party ever received an absolute majority in a public opinion poll forecasting a Knesset vote, although, to be sure, the unprecedentedly high proportion of undecided voters qualified the implications of this poll's results. Likewise, no Israeli cabinet had ever had three different finance ministers during its tenure of office; but then, Israel had never had triple-digit inflation before either. During this period Israel passed Argentina to lead the world in inflation.

For the first time in its history, the Knesset was asked four times to lift the parliamentary immunities of three of its members—all of whom were associated with the ruling coalition—at the request of the attorney general. Given the grim record of the Begin government, the Labor Party had little to do but get its own house in order to topple the weak and wobbling Likud coalition Cabinet.

Party Chairman Shimon Peres labored diligently, traveling long hours to practically every branch in the country to rebuild the party. In so doing he won the respect, if not the affection, of a broad spectrum and cross-section of the party rank and file and activists. The grass-roots reconstruction of the party appeared to be paying off in terms of a resurgence of labor morale, self-confidence, and even a semblance of long-lost unity. With the apparent debacle of the Begin government and the rising popularity of Labor (even taking into consideration the large proportion of undecided voters), Labor's return to power began to appear to be a foregone conclusion. The main question seemed to be whether a vote of nonconfidence would bring down the government, or whether the government would determine the date for early elections. This was the peak of Labor strength, unity, and popularity in the opposition.

Fifth and Final Phase

The final phase was ushered in with former Prime Minister Yitzchak Rabin's formal announcement that he would challenge Shimon Peres for the party's candidacy for prime minister. Rabin had narrowly defeated challenges by Peres for leadership of the party in 1974 (after Golda Meir resigned) and in 1977, only to have to resign the party leadership to Peres when his wife's illegal foreign currency account was made public. This challenge was the third major confrontation between the two leaders. Originally, Rabin had supported Yigal Allon's candidacy in contesting the party's nomination for the premiership. However, with Allon's death in February 1980, Rabin (who had served as Allon's deputy commander of the Palmach [an elite unit of the Yishuv's defense forces] before it was disbanded in 1948) assumed the leadership of the group centered around the Kibbutz HaMeuchad, which challenged Peres' leadership of the Labor Party.

Rabin (1979) reveals in his memoirs that his bitter conflicts with Shimon Peres and Moshe Dayan began in the early 1950s, a development he claims slowed his rise to the office of chief of staff, which he attained in 1964. Tension between them intensified in the period preceding the outbreak of the war in June 1967 and resurfaced later in Rabin's Cabinet. Although his campaign actually began a year before, Rabin did not formally announce his candidacy for the top party spot until October 1980.

The publication of Rabin's memoirs, in which he made numerous accusations against Peres, set the bitter, personally antagonistic tone of the competition for Labor Party leadership. For example, a few days before the election to the Party Conference, the French weekly *L'Express* published a false charge that Lea Rabin's fine for maintaining an illegal foreign currency account in Washington, D.C., had been paid by a reputed underworld figure. Rabin immediately denied the charges and accused the Peres camp of responsibility. Several months later, *L'Express* retracted the story, claiming that it had been given false information by "persons known as Shimon Peres' friends." Peres, who had condemned the original report, denied having anything to do with it. The obsessive hatred between Rabin and Peres caused organizers to schedule their speeches carefully so as to avoid the possibility of the two candidates meeting. As was the case four years earlier, their competition did little to raise the level of debate over the most outstanding issues, the morale of the party, or its public image.

The intensely bitter personal leadership struggle considerably weakened the party at a time when it desperately needed to maximize its unity and strength. The intemperate public attacks that constituted the Rabin/Peres campaign of mutual recrimination were particularly senseless given the lack of significant ideological or policy differences between them. Ultimately, the Rabin supporters were unable to convince more than a minority of the party members that the difference between Rabin and Peres was sufficient to warrant the terribly divisive campaign.

Also, as a party politician Rabin was no match for Peres. To be sure, Peres had the advantage of being the formal leader of the party apparatus during the contest, and he proved his skill in knowing how to use the position to his advantage. Even his critics grant Peres credit for having devoted tremendous time and effort to rebuilding the party from the local branch level up, although he did so within the frame of reference of the Labor Party in its traditional oligarchic form, albeit with minor changes.

No significant reforms were initiated during this period of the leadership of Peres. He rebuilt the party and his power in it in traditional Mapai/Labor style: the fraudulent national membership drive, the internal party election of candidates to the National Party Conference, the preparation and control of the Conference, and the election of the party's candidate for prime minister were, according to all reports, almost identical to the processes that took place in previous Conferences (related in earlier chapters). The most tangible differences were the absence (mostly due to death) of a few of the old actors and the appearance of a very few new actors to take their places.

Of course, as far as Peres was concerned, the most important difference between the party's second and third National Conferences was the outcome of the election of the party's candidate for prime minister. Whereas Rabin had narrowly defeated Peres in their previous contest, this time around Peres soundly defeated Rabin with slightly more than 70 percent (2,123 votes) of the 3,028 votes cast.

The Conference was very much Shimon Peres' show. It was his reward for three-and-a-half years of arduous and painstaking labor and preparation. He played if for all it was worth. Leading European socialist leaders attended the Conference, which was addressed by François Mitterrand, head of the French Socialist party, vice-chairman of the Socialist International, and subsequently president of France. The Egyptians also sent a high-level delegation. Peres, as party chairman, delivered the main address, which was timed to make the prime-time television news. After the election results were announced (in a different session of the Conference), Rabin made a less than magnanimous concession speech. Peres immediately capitalized on this by prefacing his victory speech with a dramatically demonstrative shaking of Rabin's hand and the announcement, "I want every delegate who voted for Yitzchak Rabin to know that I feel as if I have just shaken each of your hands as well" (Twersky, 1981). This is reported to have brought the house down.

The second most important event after the nomination of the party's candidate for the premiership—the election of the new Central Committee—did not take place at the Conference as had been planned. Sharp rivalries between the different groups fighting for representation on the Central Committee, particularly a last-ditch effort by Rabin's supporters to ensure representation proportionate to their strength, necessitated the postponement of this decision to the convention's second session in February 1981. Indeed, the party had been thrown into turmoil the day before the Conference opened when the Tel Aviv District Court accepted the Rabin camp's challenge to the party election results in Rehovot and disqualified that city's thirty-nine Conference delegates.

A controversial resolution sponsored by a group of hawkish kibbutz members that would have amended the party platform to support the annexation of the Golan Heights was hotly opposed by party doves who threatened to break up the meeting over the issue. The traditional technique of postponing a decision on a proposal by referring it to the new Central Committee succeeded in temporarily defusing the issue. Similarly, the perennially controversial plank of the party platform on religion and the state ended up after a hot debate as a carefully worded compromise on the coexistence of the Orthodox, Conservative, and Reform trends in Judaism.

Peres delivered another severe blow to the demoralized and disintegrating Rabin camp by excluding Rabin from his shadow Cabinet. However, he was careful to assure the leadership of the Kibbutz HaMeuchad group—Yisrael Galili, Ya'acov Tzur, M.K. Danny Rosolio, and Mulla Cohen (who had originally supported Allon and, subsequently, Rabin)—that their interests would be represented and taken into consideration. In fact, the jockeying for position in the shadow Cabinet occupied a good deal of the time and attention of the top leadership of the party in the ensuing several months after the Party Conference.

One of the most serious of several errors made by Shimon Peres after his resounding defeat of Rabin was his handling of the drafting of a shadow finance minister. It was widely publicized that Ya'acov Levinson, who was then chairman of the board of directors of the Histadrut's Bank HaPoalim, was Peres' first choice for the job. The consensus of Conference delegates appeared to be that Levinson was the star of the second session of the Conference as Peres had been at the first session. Levinson presented the main economic platform for the renewal of the Israeli economy. When Peres refused to guarantee Levinson considerable power on economic matters, which he demanded as a condition for accepting the post offered to him, Levinson declined the offer. (Levinson later committed suicide after depression over accusations of financial misdealings in Bank HaPoalim.)

After refusing to grant Levinson the guarantees he demanded, Peres turned to Professor Chaim Ben-Shahar, president of Tel Aviv University, to serve as shadow finance minister. While Ben-Shahar is a respected economist, he lacked the political experience, backing, and stature within the party that Levinson had. To compensate for this, Peres announced that Ben-Shahar would head an economic "troika," which would include veteran Knesset member and Peres supporter Gad Yacobi as shadow deputy finance minister and Knesset Member Adi Amori. It is well known that a troika is a most difficult vehicle to drive, since the horses tend to pull in slightly different directions. Given the composition of Labor's economic troika and the extreme economic problems facing Israel, Peres' team did not inspire the public confidence that a powerful candidate like Levinson might have (had there been no rumor of scandal connected to the candidate). Ben-Shahar was not even given a realistic position on the Labor Party's Knesset list.

Meanwhile, Labor had lapsed into a state of lethargic overconfidence at the very time when public opinion polls showed that the party was losing its commanding lead over the Likud. Yigal Hurwitz had resigned as finance minister in January 1981 after slightly more than a year in office; this led to the scheduling of early elections in June 1981. Evidently precipitated by the Finance Minister Yoram Aridor's tactical reduction of taxes on luxury items (including color television sets and cars), the Likud began steadily to regain popularity. In addition to the mishandling of the drafting of Ya'acov Levinson, Peres was widely criticized for the publicity surrounding his meeting with the brother of King Hassan II of Morocco. In an editorial comment on March 31, 1981, the *Jerusalem Post* commented:

> While the polls flash their warning signals, the party bigwigs sit around, happily quarrelling over the division of the spoils of an imagined triumph. The wages of Labour's nonchalance and lethargy will be paid in full in June. For that is when the chickens come home to roost.

The results of the April election to the Histadrut were interpreted by both Labor and the Likud as victories. Although party optimists had predicted 70 percent of the vote, the Labor Alignment (which included Mapam) received 62.9 percent of the vote, compared with 57.1 percent in 1977. However, in 1977 Labor had had to contend with a promising new Democratic Movement for Change (DMC), which attracted many of its supporters. By 1981 the DMC was defunct and therefore was not a factor in the Histadrut election. Whereas support for the Likud declined from 28.1 percent in 1977 to 26.3 percent in the 1981 Histadrut election, after accounting for the votes for Rafi, which ran as part of the Likud list in 1977 and independently in 1981, the Likud held its own. Perhaps the most significant result of the Histadrut election was the fact that only slightly more than half of the eligible Histadrut members bothered to vote. The nonvoters reflected roughly the same proportion of the electorate that the public opinion polls indicated was undecided.

Rather than demonstrating party unity and the disciplined subordination of private and group interests to the public good, the Labor Party continued to display the opposite image. Although the fight for the top position was the most spectacular and well publicized of the divisive conflicts, the jockeying for position in the shadow Cabinet and on the Knesset list was no less intense. For example, the last-minute public reconciliation (three days before the election) between Peres and Rabin resulted in Rabin's being made shadow defense minister, a post that had been promised to Bar-Lev. There was even a major fight over the post of secretary-general of the party between Uzzi Baram (supported by the Jerusalem branch and the Beit Berl group) and Eliahu Speiser (head of the Yahdav group and a leader of the Tel Aviv branch). Although there had been a major decline in the relevance of the old factions based on the parties that merged in 1968 to form the Labor Party, there was no lack of factional competition based on a combination of traditional and newly emergent groups within the party.

Conclusion: Why Labor Failed to Return to Power

The failure of the leaders of the Labor Party to understand fully the reasons for their party's defeat in 1977, and their failure to undertake the necessary structural and ideological changes that an appreciation of these reasons would have required, constituted their most serious strategic mistake. They also made many costly tactical errors. I have already discussed many of them, such as Labor's overconfidence, the bitterly divisive contest between Rabin and Peres, the failure to co-opt Ya'acov Levinson as shadow finance minister, the power struggle between various groups within the party, the inability to reconcile serious ideological divisions and antagonisms between various groups in the party, and Shimon Peres' having become too involved in the minutia of these petty party squabbles. In addition, the Labor Party made many more mistakes on which the Likud successfully capitalized.

There were a number of serious problems with the way that the Labor election campaign was run. First of all, the constant feuding between the two party officials appointed to head the campaign staff, Aharon Harel and Michael Bar-Zohar, seriously impaired the effectiveness of the staff. Second, the election staff headquarters (unlike previous campaigns) was moved from the main party headquarters, a development that made communication between officials involved in the campaign more cumbersome. Third, there was no meaningful coordination between the official party campaign staff and the Citizens for Peres campaign staff. The latter was run by associates of Peres from his tenure as defense minister, who, as a nonpartisan group, were able to obtain funds that were not under the audit of the controller general as were the government-supplied election funds provided to the political parties. In short, the Labor campaign was poorly organized and run.

Prime Minister Begin's handling of the Syrian missile crisis in Lebanon and the Israeli bombing of the Iraqi nuclear reactor successfully shifted the focus of public opinion from domestic economic issues, which hurt the Likud, to security issues, which tended to rally public support around the incumbent government. Peres handled the last issue particularly poorly. Peres' and Labor's failure to keep public attention focused on the Likud's horrendous domestic record, particularly the unprecedented perilous state of the economy, was probably the most significant tactical failure of the campaign.

However, it is difficult to persuade an electorate, and particularly the less sophisticated sectors of it, that the economic situation is as bad as it really is when salaries are linked to a cost of living index and when a propitious cut in luxury taxes allowed the voters to buy such eagerly sought items as color television sets and automobiles at "bargain" prices shortly before the election. When everyday business and life go on as normal, and people adapt to living with an extreme inflationary spiral as well as they adapt to living with terrorism, the public tends to ignore the dangerous long-range consequences of present economic policy.

Labor conspicuously failed to counter the effects of long-term demographic trends, which deprived them of the support of many young native-born Israeli voters and a significant proportion of Oriental voters. The general decline of political commitment to political parties, expressed in the enormous floating vote, was particularly critical for Labor among these categories. Yosef Goell (1978) writes,

> Continuing public-opinion polls commissioned by Labour have shown that the major factor coloring the attitudes of large numbers of Sephardi [Oriental] voters toward the leading political parties is the religious and traditional symbolism their leaders project.

There are three analytically separate, but empirically related, aspects of these research findings: (1) the different appeal of the various parties to Oriental voters; (2) the appeal of religious and traditional symbolism to these voters; (3) the ability of party leaders to communicate successfully with the Oriental voters (and others) in an appropriate symbolic style to evoke their support.

No contemporary Israeli party leader, and certainly not Peres, can even begin to approach Prime Minister Begin's mastery of rhetorical style, which is rich in religious and traditional symbolism. Style, the relation between form and content in political rhetoric, has not been given serious treatment in the study of politics. Too frequently, concepts such as "charisma" are used inappropriately to account for the effectiveness of politicians in communicating with, and mobilizing the support of, various constituencies. More careful and systematic analysis of political rhetoric reveals that the successful mastery of such techniques as argument by *enthymeme*, in which propositions are left implicit or assumed, enable a politician to mobilize shared sentiments having a high emotional charge (Paine, 1981).

Although it would take systematic research on the subject to document such conclusions, my impression is that Begin was far more effective in appealing to the Oriental voters in their own code and in organizing their experiences through his symbolic appeals than was Peres. Begin, who is personally religiously observant, succeeded in projecting his image as a "proud Jew." In fact, he has frequently been called Israel's first Jewish prime minister, since none of the previous Labor premiers were religiously observant. In addition to respect for Jewish tradition and Oriental culture, another important aspect of Begin's public persona is that he appears to be a humble man without pretensions—a man of the common people. He managed to maintain his populist anti-establishment image even while he was prime minister.

The public image of Labor's leading figures among many Israelis, and particularly but not exclusively among Orientals, is that they form an elitist, arrogant, secular, Ashkenazi establishment, which appears to be condescending and paternalistic. Not only are none of the top Labor leaders personally religious, some give the impression that they are unsympathetic, if not actually hostile, toward Jewish religious tradition. Ever since Yitzchak Rabin broke the historic partnership between Labor and the National Religious Party by forcing the NRP out the Cabinet (which brought down his government), the gap between the two former allies has widened to an almost unbridgeable chasm.

To be sure, this is not entirely due to the actions of the Labor leaders alone. The shift in power in the NRP has brought the party under the control of the Young Guard led by Zevulun Hammer, the present minister of education and culture. The leaders of this group, many of whom are identified with the Gush Emunim (Bloc of the Faithful) and are more militant on religious issues and more adamant than most of the older party leaders about the need to retain territories, find Begin's Likud to be a much more desirable and accommodating coalition partner than Labor. Labor's support for the recognition of the conservative and reform movements in Israel and its co-optation of former Laborite Shulamit Aloni and her Citizens' Rights Movement into the Labor Alignment after the election, make Labor less attractive to the religious voters and less attractive as a potential coalition partner to the religious parties. Although Labor made appreciable gains over its performance in 1977 and received nearly as many Knesset mandates as did the Likud, the strong preference of the religious parties for a coalition with the Likud kept Labor in the opposition.

Prior to the election, Labor Party secretary-general Chaim Bar-Lev claimed that the central problem facing the party was, "to reach the sons of Salach Shabati" (Bar-Kedma, 1979). The reference is to Efraim Kishon's satirical film, which deals with the trials and tribulations (or to use the Israeli preferred term, the "absorption" problems) of a large family of new immigrants from Morocco in the early days of Israeli independence. Kishon aims his satirical barbs at the general cultural arrogance, intolerance, condescension, and paternalism displayed by the Ashkenazi veteran officials toward the new immigrants, most of whom were from Islamic countries. These officials representing the kibbutzim, public agencies such as the Jewish Agency and the Histadrut, the bureaucracy of the state, and the various political parties literally controlled the lives of the new immigrants in the early stages of their settlement. Since the Labor Party was the dominant party during this period, it was associated with the aforementioned characteristics of the veteran elite in their relationships with the dependent immigrants. Consequently, Labor continues to be the target of frustration and resentment, which have evolved and festered over the years in the face of the friction between development towns and neighboring kibbutzim, the negative image of unresponsive bureaucrats, the under-representation of Orientals in the higher echelons of power, and the correlation between class and ethnicity.

Kishon's film also highlighted the manner in which the political parties attempted to mobilize the votes of the new immigrants almost entirely through material inducements, which led to the development of party machines and patronage systems. In this system, new citizens who were unfamiliar with democratic party politics received a political education that emphasized (by implication) the importance of personal and/or particularistic familial/ethnic interests in a bargaining situation that traded political support for the largess of the highest bidder. The trend toward a decline both in the sense of more generally public or communal political obligation and in widespread commitment to political movements and parties can be traced to this period. Labor's relative failure to attract the support of the sons of Salach Shabati can be seen as the consequence of its earlier attitudes and policies and its failure to convince a significant portion of this constituency that it had turned over a new leaf.

Another example of the general erosion of wider units of political obligation and commitment in Israeli society can be found in the trade unions. Whereas the Histadrut formerly maintained a disciplined and solidly pro-Labor political constituency, the Likud had made considerable inroads in this last bastion of Labor supremacy. Both local union shops and major national trade union units—such as the electric corporation workers, transportation workers, sailors, El-Al maintenance workers—have exerted much greater independence in terms of collective bargaining agreements and political allegiance than ever before. This, of course, has adversely affected the Labor Party, but has implications far beyond the partisan interests of Labor.

I have attempted to demonstrate in this chapter that the behavior of the Labor Party in the opposition between 1977 and 1981, and the reason it has remained in opposition after the election in 1981, can best be explained by examining the causes for its being in the opposition in the first place. I contend that the leaders of the Labor Party failed to comprehend the fundamental cumulative factors that led to the party's decline and defeat. They therefore failed to initiate fundamental structural or ideological changes that would have been necessary to regain public confidence in the party and its leadership. The present coalition of the Likud and the religious parties is a shaky one and is not likely to last out its full term of office. However, rather than taking advantage of this situation by uniting its ranks, the Labor Party continues to fight its old fights. Rabin has indicated he may again challenge Peres, and Speiser is grooming his forces for a major bid for power. Labor may return to power by default—that is, through the failure of the present government. However, if it is to regain the leadership position it once enjoyed in Israeli society, it will have to undergo more fundamental reforms and changes than the present leadership has indicated willingness to initiate.

Notes

1. The two kibbutz movements affiliated with the Israel Labor Party were divided in their support of the two candidates for prime minister. Most of the Ichud tended to support Peres, whereas the majority of the Kibbutz HaMeuchad supported Rabin. Therefore, their merger, which formed the Tnua Kibbutzit HaMeuchedet (United Kibbutz Movement), was delayed until after the competition was resolved in the National Party Conference. Subsequently, the newly elected leaders of both movements, Zamir of Kibbutz HaMeuchad and Perlmuter of the Ichud, have been working to close the political gap between the two federations. If the newly emerging Tel Aviv–based urban alliance (with links to the moshav movement) succeeds it will be an even greater impetus for the newly united kibbutz movement to consolidate and strengthen itself through unity. Sharp criticism of the kibbutz movement by the prime minister, and from within the party by Eliahu Speiser, has provided additional incentives for the leaders of the kibbutz movement to forget their past differences and to unite to protect their common interests and ideology.

2. See Sammy Smooha, *Israel: Pluralism and Conflict* (Berkeley and Los Angeles: University of California Press, 1978). The Likud successfully exploited the resentment of the kibbutzim by many people in the development towns. In one case, local Likud leaders adapted a cartoon that originally had depicted Arab terrorists threatening Kiryat Shmona. The cartoon was relabeled, "The Kibbutz Mafia—quiet they are coming!" It depicted a subhuman, gorilla-like thug labeled "Kibbutz Movement-Alignment" and a pack of rapacious wolves bearing the names of neighboring kibbutzim descending on Kiryat Shmona. For more details see Helga Dudman, "Collective Resentment," *Jerusalem Post International Edition*, July 19–25, 1981, p. 14.

10

Democratization of Leadership Selection

Introduction

This chapter focuses primarily on the selection of the Labor Party candidates for the Twelfth Knesset (elected in 1988) as a case study of the opening up of the previously oligarchic process of leadership selection. There will be a briefer discussion of a more recent and far-reaching reform—the adoption of a party-wide primary system to select the candidates to the Thirteenth Knesset, including the top leader and candidate for the premiership. The analysis of the changes in the nominations process is the key to evaluating the extent to which Labor is undergoing internal democratization.

From its rise in the early twenties and the establishment of its hegemony in the Yishuv through almost three decades of its dominance of the political system of the sovereign state, oligarchic control of the nominations process was a key characteristic of Labor. As demonstrated in earlier chapters, this process hindered the responsiveness of the party, leading to a lack of genuine representation of important constituencies in party institutions and the party's Knesset faction. Eventually, the process contributed significantly to Labor's loss of power in 1977. Furthermore, Labor's failure to learn from the defeat, and its failure to make necessary reforms, contributed to the defeat of the party in the 1981 elections.

In 1981, half of the Labor candidates for the Knesset were chosen by a nominating committee of five members appointed by the Political Bureau, and half were elected by the district branches. The all-important ordering of the

This chapter is a revised version of the previously published chapter by Myron Aronoff entitled "Better Late Than Never: Democratization in the Labor Party," in *Israel after Begin*, by Gregory S. Mahler, Albany, NY: SUNY Press, 1990. Used with permission of SUNY Press.

names on the list (which determined who had a realistic chance of being elected) was done by an informal committee consisting of representatives from the kibbutz and moshav movements, and the three major urban districts (Jerusalem, Tel Aviv, and Haifa), with Uzzi Baram (Jerusalem) and Eliahu Speiser (Tel Aviv) playing leading roles. This process ensured the renomination of the main national party leaders, and their major protégés.[1]

The decision to abandon the rule adopted by the party's Second Conference (in 1977), which said that members who had served two terms in the Knesset were required to receive a vote of at least 60 percent of the Central Committee (a rule that had already been seriously compromised during the selection of the candidates for the Tenth Knesset in 1981) did not appear to be a good opening for democratic reform.

Baram Initiates Democratic Reforms

The major impetus for democratization began in 1984. Much credit for this must be given to Uzzi Baram. The election of the former secretary of the Jerusalem district to the position of secretary-general of the party by a very narrow margin (384 to 382) over Micha Harish (the candidate favored by party leader Shimon Peres) on October 30, 1984, paved the way for the reforms in Labor. Baram, son of the late former Minister of Labor Moshe Baram, based his campaign for party secretary-general on the platform of democratization. Although he met with considerable resistance along the way, and on at least one occasion actually resigned his post when it appeared that some of his demands for reform would not be accepted, he ultimately mobilized sufficient support to carry the day.

Major opposition came from the settlement (kibbutz and moshav) movements, which feared they would lose representation through the proposed reforms. Both ultimately agreed to accept change, but insisted that they choose their own candidates (which they were allowed to do as distinct units like the urban districts); they also demanded guaranteed positions on the list of Knesset candidates (which they did not receive). A key supporter of reform was the chairman of the Preparation Committee, which is responsible for setting the agenda of the National Party Conference. However, the subcommittee of the Standing Committee responsible for formulating the changes in the nominations process was chaired by a representative of a settlement movement and a member of the camp of Yitzchak Rabin, who opposed the reforms.[2]

In a meeting attended by five party leaders, Baram argued for far-reaching reform in order to give the members of the Central Committee (the party's largest decision-making forum) the feeling that they had real influence, and to overcome the party's stigma in the public mind of being a closed, unbreathing, elderly, Ashkenazi, oligarchic body. Shimon Peres proposed that he be allowed to choose two people (Rabin and Navon) for guaranteed positions beside himself. Another leader insisted that both the party and Histadrut secretaries-general

(Baram and Yisrael Kessar) also have secured positions on the list. A compromise between oligarchic appointment and democratic election of all Knesset candidates was accepted.

The National Party Conference held in April 1986—dubbed by Baram the "Democracy Conference"—accepted the proposed reform agreed upon by the top leaders and formulated by the subcommittee of the Preparation Committee that had passed it. The only change was the addition of the Speaker of the Knesset (Shlomo Hillel) to the list of top leaders with guaranteed positions on the Knesset list, apparently as a concession to party members of Middle Eastern background. In addition, Ezer Weizman had been promised a position toward the top of the list (along with two realistic positions for his supporters) when his Yahad party joined an alignment with Labor during the coalition negotiations after the 1984 election. The guarantee of the top seven places on the list to the top party leaders followed the Labor tradition of self-nomination by the elite, and was hardly a harbinger of significant democratic reform.

Selection of Candidates for the Twelfth Knesset

The 1986 Party Conference accepted the proposal of the party affairs committee that the Knesset candidates be evenly divided between those to be elected by the districts and those to be elected by the Central Committee in the first round. There were volatile debates in the Central Committee over how to implement the proposals passed by the Conference and still adhere to the party's constitutional requirement of guaranteed places for five women, two young members, a Moslem, a Druze, and a representative of the "neighborhoods" (i.e., a Jew of Middle Eastern background from an inner city area). It was felt that these relatively politically weak categories lacked the power to gain representation on their own. Baram's interpretation that these guaranteed places should be applied to the candidates for the central list in the first round of voting only was accepted. Therefore, twenty-three Knesset candidates were elected by the councils of the district branches, and twenty-nine were elected by the Central Committee.[3]

The twenty-three candidates elected by district councils conducted traditional campaigns among people with whom they were personally acquainted. Since the district secretaries have particularly strong influence in their districts, it is not surprising that the secretaries of the largest districts were among those elected. However, the eighty-five candidates for the twenty-nine places on the central list had to appeal for the votes of 1,267 Central Committee members, most of whom they either barely knew or did not know at all.[4] Whereas previously they had to persuade the party bosses of their personal loyalty to gain access to the Knesset list, this time they had to convince their peers that their presence on the party list would contribute to the party's victory at the polls. For the first time in the history of the Labor Party there was American-style personal campaigning for the votes of the Central Committee members.

Several deals (the English term was used with the Hebrew plural ending—"dealim") were made by various candidates representing different groups and branches that promised mutual support. The largest support deal was made between Tel Aviv, Jerusalem, Haifa, the United Kibbutz movement, the moshav movement, and the Shiluv, Kehila, and Mashov circles.[5] Among the 18 candidates who were part of the deal, all but 3 were elected to the central list of 29 that was elected on May 25, 1988. The purpose of such a deal was obviously to overcome the uncertainty resulting from free secret elections, and to guarantee the continued dominance of the traditional bastions of power in the party. Baram had campaigned actively against the deals and urged the members of the Central Committee to use their independent judgments.

The elections were held at the Tel Aviv exhibition and fairgrounds in a carnival atmosphere. The entrance to the grounds where the elections were held was lined for a mile with swarms of supporters of the candidates carrying banners and posters, many wearing T-shirts advertising their candidates, passing out brochures and leaflets, fruit, drinks, flowers, pens, badges, buttons, and various other gimmicks to boost their candidates. The festive atmosphere was not universally appreciated. One critic, former secretary-general of the Histadrut Yitzchak Ben-Aharon (who had always been one of the most effective spokesmen for democratic reforms in the party), considered the atmosphere "vulgar."[6]

A few candidates refrained from gimmickry. For example, Arie (Lyova) Eliav, former party secretary-general who had recently returned to the party fold, refused to allow his supporters to distribute the little sticker they had produced on his behalf since he felt it was undignified. Eliav, who was not part of any mutual support deal, received the second largest number of votes cast (nine less than Ora Namir, who was supported by the major mutual support deal). Ninety-eight percent of the Central Committee members voted. Namir received 962 of 1,247 votes cast. Each member was allowed to vote for up to twenty-nine candidates. The most striking result of the election was the large number of young, new candidates, many of whom were from Middle Eastern ethnic groups, who were elected on the central list. Some skepticism was expressed about how many of the fresh new faces would gain a realistic position when the Central Committee ranked the candidates.

Intensity marked the second phase of campaigning by the 52 candidates (23 elected by the districts and 29 by the Central Committee) for ranking of their positions on the list. The positions of the top 7 party leaders, the 3 representing Weizman's Yahad, the Muslim Arab, and the Druze representatives were determined in advance. Since Labor had received 44 seats in the previous election, it expected to receive approximately the same number in 1988.[7] A position beyond that was considered to be marginal to unrealistic depending how far down the position was on the list. The voting took place in 4 rounds, with 10 candidates elected in each round. Each candidate decided in which group of 10 she or he wished to compete. Obviously, the higher the group of tens, the greater the prestige and the greater the chance of entering the Knesset, but also the greater the competition. Candidates failing to gain election in earlier rounds were allowed to submit their candidacy in later rounds.[8]

The first group of 10 was contested by the younger generation of top party leaders aspiring to succeed those at the top whose positions had been guaranteed without election. Among the first 10 elected were the 6 ministers serving in the government at the time who had not been granted guaranteed places.[9] Five of those elected had been part of a mutual support deal,[10] but not everyone who had been part of the deal was elected (e.g., Micha Harish). The other half of the top 10 elected had not been party to any deals. Clearly, the deal, which had been relatively successful in the selection of the Central Committee's list of Knesset candidates, was less so in the first round of the ordering of the candidates. The Central Committee members rewarded the dedicated parliamentary work of Ora Namir (giving her the second highest vote), Chaim Ramon (the youngest Labor member of the Eleventh Knesset at thirty-eight—who was later elected as Labor's parliamentary whip), and law professor David Liba'i. Evidently this wider forum was more appreciative of dedicated and effective parliamentary performance than were the previous oligarchic nominations committees.[11]

If the deal was partially successful in the vote for the first 10, it completely broke down in the vote for the second. The second round was ironically termed by some the "Intifada ten" to dramatize its radical nature. (*Intifada* is the Arabic term for the civil uprising that had rocked the occupied territories since December 1987, discussed in the next chapter.) Five of the 10 were entirely new political faces and had never previously served in the Knesset.[12] This group also included 5 candidates of Moroccan origin, at least 5 who are under the age of 40, 3 mayors of development towns in the Negev, and 2 who were religiously observant. This group also included several prominent political doves (including the 2 religious candidates).[13]

The members of the Central Committee showed an obvious preference for those on the central list whom they had chosen over the candidates elected by the districts. In the first round of 10 not a single district candidate was elected. In the second round only 2 (Rafi Edri and Micha Harish) were chosen—more for their personal standings, parliamentary records, and the strong support given to them by Peres (with whom they are closely associated) than because they represented districts. Of the 6 district representatives elected in the third round, only Professor Shevah Weiss (who competed unsuccessfully in the previous rounds) was elected on the basis of his parliamentary record and the support given to him by Rabin.

The independence of the Central Committee voters showed most clearly in their preference for fresh new faces over the dictates of the deals made by the district leaders. The moshav movement and the strongmen of two of the three major city districts, traditional bastions of power in the party, did particularly poorly. This was in spite of the new deal they organized prior to the third round. No fewer than eight new faces were elected in this round. Responding to the pleas of Shimon Peres to support the moshav movement (which prior to the third round had failed to gain a single representative), they chose a newcomer, Gedalia Gal, over the veteran Ra'anan Naim, who had competed unsuccessfully in the first two rounds. They chose Haifa University professor Shevah Weiss over the Haifa district secretary (who ultimately ended up fifty-fourth—a completely unrealistic position). Michael Bar-Zohar was elected as a representative of Tel Aviv over the secretary of the Tel Aviv branch, Eliahu Speiser, who, in spite of being part of practically every deal going, withdrew after unsuccessfully competing in the first three rounds. Speiser had been a conspicuously inactive and unpopular parliamentarian.[14] His political ally Uri Amit, the mayor of Ramat Gan, also dropped out of the race after not being elected in rounds two and three.

The secretary of the Jerusalem district branch, Emanuel Zisman (also spelled Sussman in some sources), fared better and was elected fifth in the third round, giving him a safe place of thirty-third on the list. However, a relative newcomer from his district, Professor Shimon Shitreet (a young Moroccan academic), was ranked ten places higher. Another newcomer, Efraim Gur, a thirty-two-year-old deputy mayor of Ashkelon, became the first person from Soviet Georgia to gain a realistic position on the Knesset list; he gained the position after the Jerusalem secretary. Also, the kibbutz movement barely got its representative, Edna Solodar, elected to the last place in the third round after the active lobbying of Yitzchak Rabin (although Ya'acov Tzur and Avraham Katz-Oz, elected in the first round, also represent the kibbutz movement).[15]

Approximately half of the candidates in realistic positions were new faces. Approximately 30 percent represented Middle Eastern ethnic communities (half of them of Moroccan background), not including the Muslim Arab and Druze candidates. One-quarter of the candidates were forty years old or younger, two of whom were religious. Only four women gained realistic positions.[16]

In addition to being the most representative Knesset list in history in terms of age, ethnic, and geographical divisions, the Knesset list is also balanced between doves and hawks. Avraham Tirush (*Ma'ariv*, June 16, 1988:1) suggests that "approximately half of the first forty-one candidates are doves." Orli Azuli-Katz (*Yediot Achronot*, June 16, 1988:2) counts "twelve doves and twelve hawks and six 'yonetzim' "—a combination of the Hebrew terms *"yonim"* (doves) and *"netzim"* (hawks). She observes that the doves have received senior and visible placement. It is extremely difficult to determine whether the more democratic process of nominations had a direct influence on the ideologically balanced list that was produced.

Across the political spectrum the Israeli press praised Labor's achievement. *Ma'ariv* (June 16, 1988) led with a banner headline reading, "Revolution in Labor's List"; and the main editorial, entitled "New Epoch," praised the process of "internal democratization"(p. 14). Elan Schori, political correspondent of the liberal *Ha'aretz* (June 16, 1988:3), spoke of a dramatic revolution in Labor. He noted that "The members of the Labor Central Committee buried the system of arrangement committees." The Histadrut-owned *Davar* (June 16, 1988:7) highlighted the new faces, claiming that Labor had changed its face by turning to the development towns and the neighborhoods, and by making a covenant with the workers. Its main editorial claimed that the new system for electing the Knesset list had stood the test of democratization.

In the more conservative *Yediot Achronot* (June 16, 1988:2), Aviezer Golan said, "You don't have to be a Labor supporter to feel satisfaction with the demonstration of democracy in Labor's internal elections." In the same paper, Ronit Vardi wrote, "Amazing, simply amazing what the Labor Party did to itself last night. . . . Finally Labor looks like an organization of live people with autonomous desires and ability to influence" (p. 2). In the lead article in the *Jerusalem Post* (June 16, 1988:1), Michal Yudelman wrote, "The Labour Party yesterday elected a younger, more representative and more Sephardi list to lead it in the elections for the 12th Knesset. Some called it 'a revolution' and 'an earthquake.' " The main editorial observed,

> The party had just come out not only rejuvenated but intact from its first ordeal by internal democracy. That had not been preordained. . . . For the first time ever it was not a handful of party oligarchs who chose Labour's electoral list in the solitude of their smoke-filled rooms. That decision was now made by the nearly 1,300-strong Central Committee. And yet the sky did not fall. . . . The facelift undertaken by the Central Committee surgeons made Labour look younger, fresher, brighter, and more all-round Israeli than it had ever been before. (p. 24)

Yossi Wertner (*Hadashot,* May 27, 1988:16) seemed to express the consensus among Israeli political correspondents and pundits when he observed, "it is possible to officially declare the opening of an epoch of democracy in the Labor Party." Although there is little question that such a process has begun, it is not yet certain how far it will go and what the full ramifications of this process will be. Several changes have clearly taken place.

The most conspicuous change in Labor's nominations is the absence of a dominant national party machine controlling the process. Before, Shriege Netzer of the old Gush or Pinchas Sapir of the new Gush, directly and through their surrogates, could determine in many cases who would represent various internal party factions and interest groups, what the relative representation of many of the groups would be, and, most importantly, what would be the position of the candidates on the list. Traditionally, the Central Committee was a rubber stamp which approved the list after it was completed. Even after reforms were introduced enabling the district branches to elect a proportion of the Knesset candidates, the vital process of ordering the places of the candidates (both elected and appointed) was still performed by an oligarchically controlled committee. For the first time in the history of the party, what was previously determined in the proverbial smoke-filled room was now determined in the polling booths of the Central Committee.

The candidates elected through this more open process are more representative of the various constituencies that make up the pluralistic Labor Party in at least two different respects. First of all, as indicated earlier, the representation of various geographic areas (e.g., urban versus rural areas) and age and ethnic categories is proportionally closer to their distribution in the party and the nation than on any previous Knesset list. Categories and branches that were traditionally overly represented—veteran Eastern Europeans, Tel Aviv, Jerusalem, Haifa, and the kibbutz and moshav movements—have been somewhat weakened. Those who have traditionally been underrepresented, such as younger generations, those from Middle Eastern background, and the development towns (particularly in the Negev), have been strengthened. One very large category—women—has not yet made gains through this more open process.

The second sense in which the new list is more representative than previous ones is that the personnel chosen to represent the various constituencies was chosen by a more widely representative body. In the past, the bosses of the dominant national and district machines could easily assure their own nomination and that of their clients as the so-called representatives of various constituencies. This time the wider body frequently chose candidates to represent these constituencies who had qualifications other than being a party functionary or the client of a top party leader.

Still, many, if not most, of those elected to realistic positions were functionaries and clients of Peres and Rabin. In fact, this was the most important element of continuity of traditional Labor practices. In their enthusiastic reaction to Labor's new list, most observers failed to note that even among the freshest of the new faces, most had been closely associated with the party's organization for many years. Of the so-called "Intifada ten" elected in the second round, only one, Eli Dayan, the young religious, dovish, Moroccan mayor of Ashkelon, had not had a long association with the party establishment. He was formerly associated at different times with the religious-ethnic Tami and the Democratic Movement for Change. His counterpart, Amir Peretz, the thirty-five-year-old dovish Moroccan mayor of Sderot who came in first in the second round, worked for four years in the Organization Department of the central party headquarters and was chosen by the Municipalities Department of the party to lead the party's ticket in Sderot.

Among the other "new faces," there was a similar close association with the party organization and/or its top leaders. Avraham (Beige) Shochat served as mayor of Arad for twenty years and held many positions, including head of the organization of Labor's 1988 national elections. He was the leading candidate of the Rabin camp in the second round of voting. He is also the son-in-law of the late Levi Eshkol, former Labor prime minister. Avraham (Avrum) Burg, the dovish son of the former leader of the National Religious Party, served as adviser to Shimon Peres on Diaspora affairs. Prominent dove Dr. Yosef (Yossi) Beilin, who has held several important party and government posts, is the protégé and right-hand man of Shimon Peres. Similarly, the "new faces" in the third round were not new to party insiders. In fact, two could be considered professional party functionaries.[17]

What is most remarkable about the changes brought about by the Central Committee vote is that to a large extent the members who voted were themselves the products of the old oligarchic system. I repeatedly heard elderly European members of major city districts express in private conversations among themselves the need to elect young and Middle Eastern candidates representing the disadvantaged neighborhoods and the development towns.[18]

All of the members of the Central Committee with whom I spoke voted for candidates for a variety of different reasons. Significantly, none of the various deals attempted to determine an entire list of candidates for whom followers were instructed to vote. Being realistic, they left room for them to exercise their independent judgment.[19]

In sum, the result of this more open and competitive process was a more attractive and representative list of Knesset candidates than Labor has ever fielded. Many factors in addition to the list of candidates determine the outcome of national elections in Israel. Traditionally, most voters are unfamiliar with any of the candidates beyond the top few party personalities. However, in the past the Likud capitalized on having successfully projected the image of a young party more representative of and responsive to the Jews from Middle Eastern backgrounds. Given the positive publicity that accompanied the election of Labor's new list and the acrimonious conflicts that produced Herut's list, which contained only a few fresh new faces, Labor's list was an electoral asset in the 1988 campaign, although not sufficient to give it victory.[20]

Evaluation of the Consequences of Reform

The most crucial point is that the spurt of democratization that was expressed in the nomination of Labor's candidates to the Twelfth Knesset was a harbinger of wider reforms yet to come. It is important to recognize that there are many deeply entrenched vested interests perpetuating the status quo in Labor. These interests produced the state of entropy that prevented the democratization of the party since the first waves of demands for reform arose in the aftermath of the Yom Kippur War through Labor's fall from power in 1977 and thereafter. At every level of the party and the Histadrut (local through national) there are networks of functionaries whose livelihoods are dependent on the party and the Histadrut, and who have traditionally been the base of power of local, district, and national bosses.

Reforming the Labor Party and/or the Histadrut (the Labor-dominated General Federation of Labor) may be easier than reforming the constituent units of the former Soviet Union, but the analogy is not as farfetched as it may first appear. The founding fathers and mothers of Labor (and the Israeli political system and culture) were products of revolutionary Eastern Europe. They left a legacy of an Israeli variation of Eastern European democratic centralism wedded to a Western-style social democratic party. The melding of cultures in Israel is sometimes characterized as a combination of the shtetl and the Casbah, neither of which had particularly strong democratic traditions of the Western type.[21] Yet a dynamic, competitive, democratic political system emerged despite the absence of these democratic traditions among important sectors of the population. However, democracy was conspicuously absent in the internal affairs of the parties. In addition to the aforementioned influence of political culture, this can largely be attributed to the country-wide proportional list system of elections, which encourages oligarchic control of nominations of parliamentary candidates.[22]

In spite of these handicaps, the trend toward greater internal party democratization is definitely underway. It will be hard to turn the clock back to more oligarchic traditions of candidate selection in Labor. Although Labor did not fare so well in the 1988 election for success to be attributed to its attractive list, neither did it fare so poorly at the polls as to produce a backlash which would have resulted in regression to earlier oligarchic patterns. Clearly, other factors, such as the polarizing effect of the Palestinian uprising (Intifada), the political ramifications of King Hussein's dramatic abdication of responsibility for the Palestinians on the West Bank, and reactions to sensational acts of terrorism immediately prior to the election (among other events) all tended to work against Labor. I explore the impact of these events on Labor in the next chapter.

New Knesset members elected through the more open process are less dependent upon party leaders and district bosses. Many of the younger Knesset members were active in the attempt to prevent Labor from entering the coalition government under the Likud's leadership. The successful challenge by Chaim Ramon, who was elected Labor parliamentary whip, over the candidate backed by Shimon Peres was another tangible indicator of this new independence. While this produces certain problems by weakening discipline in the parliamentary faction, it has the salutary effect of creating freer and more open debates and more democratic decision making in the party. The fact that even the new faces are closely identified with top party leaders and the party apparatus is a strong check on excessive political independence. Another example of the new independence was Uzzi Baram's resignation as Labor's secretary-general in order to challenge the party leadership to leave the Likud-led government. He received support from a number of newly elected Knesset members.[23] They eventually succeeded in persuading Shimon Peres to leave the coalition government in March 1990.

A magical and instantaneous transformation of the party has not taken place. There have been attempts by individuals and groups detrimentally affected by the democratic innovations to return to the old system of nominations, and by some to manipulate the new system more effectively to their advantage, by ensuring that the "deals" are more binding. There continue to be many struggles over the pace and nature of change in the party. However, the direction of change has been established, and while there may certainly be setbacks in the process, there is a good probability of its spreading into other areas of party and national life.

The Selection of Candidates for the Thirteenth Knesset

The process that led to the selection of Labor's candidates to the Thirteenth Knesset began with the membership poll in December 1990 headed by Knesset member Binyamin Ben-Eliezer and was much less fraught with fraud and forgery than were previous ones. Labor's fifth Party Conference in 1991 was the most representative one in the party's history. At the first phase of this Conference, held November 19–21, the number of party members eligible to choose the Knesset candidates was dramatically expanded by the adoption of a system of primary elections. It was decided that all registered party members (approximately 162,000—a much more realistic figure than the fraudulent results of earlier membership drives, which were double this number) would vote in polling stations throughout the country. The first election would determine Labor's candidate for premier, and the second would select the party's slate of candidates for the Thirteenth Knesset.[24]

In the first national primary election held by the Labor Party on February 21, 1992, Yitzchak Rabin received 40.45 percent of the vote. Shimon Peres received 34.5 percent, Yisrael Kessar 19 percent, and Ora Namir 5.5 percent. Rabin barely managed to top the 40 percent which enabled him to avoid a second round run-off against Peres. He thereby became Labor's candidate for prime minister and led the party list to the Thirteenth Knesset. On March 31, 1992, 176 candidates vied for the first forty-five slots on the party's Knesset list. Approximately 110,000 party members—68 percent of the eligible voters—participated. The only guaranteed position was reserved for party secretary-general Micha Harish in the seventh spot on the ticket. In a rather complicated procedure, the entire party membership elected only the top 10 candidates (not counting Rabin and Harish). Positions 13 to 45 were chosen by regional districts—geographically based except for the kibbutz and moshav movements, which constituted separate voting constituencies.

The districts varied considerably in size. The largest, the Central District stretching from Bat Yam to Rehovot, had 19 candidates for two "safe" slots. These spots were considered safe because the candidates elected by the national constituency and those elected by districts were interspersed on the final list, and candidates from the larger constituencies were ranked higher than those from smaller ones.

There were a number of noteworthy consequences of this extension of reforms in the nominations process. The first was the dramatic turnover. Several leading Knesset members decided not to seek renomination; they included

Chaim Bar-Lev, Shlomo Hillel, Yitzchak Navon, Ezer Weizman, and Lyova Eliav—all of whom had held cabinet posts in the past. A number of other former cabinet members and veteran parliamentarians ran in the primaries but failed to gain realistic positions on the list. This group included Shoshana Arbelli-Almoslino, Avraham Katz-Oz, Ya'acov Tzur, and Michael Bar-Zohar. Gad Yacobi was elected to a marginal position on the list (forty-five), and Mordechai Gur was placed low on the list—the seventeenth slot in the national race which placed him thirty-four on the final list. This seriously set back his ambition to become premier.

Gur was not alone in having suffered a set-back for his political aspirations. The poor showing of the over-fifty-year-old generation will likely have significant ramifications for the issue of succession. These were the leaders who aspired to succeed Rabin and Peres for the top leadership. Mordechai Gur, Gad Yacobi, and Moshe Shahal had initially intended to challenge them in the primary. The results of the primaries strengthens the chances of the younger generation of party leaders presently in their forties, for example, Uzzi Baram, Yossi Beilin, Avraham Burg, Chaim Ramon, and Nissim Zvilli, to leap-frog over their generational elders to the top positions of party and national leadership.

The political set-back of what is sometimes called the "Continuing Generation" of party leaders also represented a significant weakening of the hawkish leadership of Labor. Katz-Oz, Bar-Zohar, and Arbeli-Almoslino were outspoken hawks (as was Hillel among the older generation of retirees). Gur attempted to assume leadership of the so-called centrists, but his stature has been considerably diminished. (A similar victory for younger leaders in the Likud resulted in a more hawkish Knesset delegation.)

Labor's Knesset delegation featured doves in prominent positions on the list—Avraham Burg (3), Chaim Ramon (6), Nissim Zvilli (10), and Uzzi Baram (12). They replaced Weizman and Eliav, who were prominent spokesmen for the doves. Among the other leading dovish Knesset members, Yossi Beilin (24), and newcomer Yael Dayan, daughter of the late Moshe Dayan (37), have national visibility. Most of the leading doves are closely associated with Peres.

Despite Rabin's personal victory, Peres emerged with at least ten of his close supporters as fellow Knesset members in the Labor delegation. Similarly, Histadrut Secretary-General Yisrael Kessar, who was elected to the eighth slot on the Labor list, heads a Histadrut faction in the Labor Knesset delegation of half a dozen members.[25] Ora Namir, whose popularity gained her the fifth spot on the ticket, was the only contender for the premiership who does not have a group of fellow Knesset members who personally support her. The gain for the Histadrut faction was offset by a significant loss by the kibbutz movement of its two former ministers, Tzur and Katz-Oz, which cut their Knesset representation in half, making it one of the major victims of the reform.

The Labor delegation in the Thirteenth Knesset has a young profile. Six Labor Knesset candidates are in their thirties and eighteen are in their forties. Fourteen of the top forty on the Labor list appeared for the first time and ten had served only one Knesset term previously. This unprecedented turnover indicates that the momentum for reform has succeeded beyond even the expectations of its most optimistic proponents.

Although the Likud played on Labor's dovish image, Labor's Knesset delegation contains "two former chiefs of staff [Rabin and Mordechai Gur], one Maj.-Gen. [Ori Orr], and three Brig.-Gens. [Binyamin Ben-Eliezer, Ephraim Sneh and Avigdor Kahalani]."[26] They collectively represent impressive experience and expertise in security affairs.

Labor took another step in overcoming its image as an Ashkenazi party. Among the top forty names on Labor's list seven were born in Morocco, three in Iraq, two in Yemen, one in Tunisia, and one in India. Two Israeli Arabs were elected on the Labor slate. The one important social group that remains woefully underrepresented is women. Although Ora Namir placed fifth on the list, she was accompanied by only three other women in realistic positions. (The Likud has only two women among the top forty candidates.)

The spirit of reform expressed in the adoption of the primary system is an expression of a long overdue revitalization of the Labor Party which may be a harbinger of its playing a more active and constructive role in restoring public confidence in a political system that has sunk to dangerous levels in the past decade and a half.

Notes

1. For a description of the nomination of Labor's Knesset list for the 1977 election see Giora Goldberg, "Democracy and Representation in Israeli Political Parties," *The Elections in Israel—1977*, ed. Asher Arian (New Brunswick, NJ: Transaction, 1980), 109–10; and for the 1981 election see Avraham Brichta, "The Selection of Candidates to the Tenth Knesset: The Impact of Centralization," in *Israel at the Polls, 1981: A Study of the Knesset Elections*, ed. Howard R. Penniman and Daniel J. Elazar (Bloomington: Indiana University Press, 1986), 22–24.

2. According to Mordechai (Motta) Gur (in an interview on July 27, 1988), Rabin called the proposed reform "idiocy and a disaster" (*timtume v'asone*). Gur claims that initially Peres was not much more enthusiastic about Baram's push for democratization, but that he is more careful with his words than is Rabin.

3. The Likud attacked this "undemocratic" aspect of Labor's nominations process. Whereas the dominant Herut component of the Likud virtually unanimously elected its leader Shamir to the top spot on the list (he was challenged by a little-known and uninfluential person), there was a bitter struggle among David Levy, Ariel Sharon, and Moshe Arens for the next three positions. It was suggested by a number of observers that Herut would have been better off emulating Labor than engaging in the public airing of internal party antagonisms. The Liberal Party, Herut's partner in the Likud, guaranteed the positions of its top three leaders. There was also considerable contention in Herut over the number and position of places on the Knesset list reserved for the Liberals as well as over the places Shamir had promised to Aharon Abuhatzira (Tami), and Yigal Hurwitz (Ometz) in return for their votes against the international peace conference proposed by Peres.

4. Candidates spent between $10,000 and $15,000. Whereas this may seem a relatively modest sum to the American reader, it is approximately a year's salary for most of the candidates. These expenses did not come from party coffers, but from the pockets of the candidates (with the help of family, friends, and close supporters).

5. See Yael Atzmon, "The Labor Party and Its Factions," *Jerusalem Quarterly* 31 (Spring 1984):118–29, for a discussion of the different types of internal groups and factions in Labor.

6. Yossi Wertner, "Namir First, Lyova Eliav Second," *Hadashot*, May 27, 1988, p. 3.

7. Mapam was granted six realistic places on the joint Alignment list with Labor based on the number it had prior to the electoral Alignment with Labor that took place in 1969. However, over the years Mapam had lost much of its electoral support, so it actually received more Knesset seats than its electoral strength warranted. During the negotiations over the formation of the National Unity Government, Mapam split from the Alignment with Labor and joined the opposition. Ezer Weizman's Yahad list (with three Knesset members) joined the Alignment with Labor thereby receiving the promise of three realistic places on the Labor list for the 1988 election. It was thought that Weizman was likely to bring Labor approximately the same amount of electoral support as had Mapam. Reports of scientific public opinion polls commissioned by Labor indicated that had the election taken place in July, Labor would have increased its representation in the Knesset. However, the results of the vote for the Alignment in the previous election were used as a guide for estimating realistic expectations for the 1988 election by most participants and observers of the internal party elections.

8. Ironically, the model for this panel system of candidate election was adapted from a system used for the first time by Herut (the dominant force in the Likud) in nominations of their candidates to the Ninth Knesset in 1977—the year they came to power for the first time.

9. Moshe Shahal, Shoshana Arbeli-Almoslino, Gad Yacobi, Ya'acov Tsur, Mordechai (Motta) Gur, and Chaim Bar-Lev.

10. Shahal, Namir, Arbeli-Almoslino, Tsur, Chaim Ramon, and Avraham Katz-Oz.

11. According to Avraham Brichta (in a personal conversation), Shriege Netzer, boss of the Gush, justified the oligarchic nominations process because (among other reasons) places could be assured for various interest groups and for excellent parliamentarians who might lack a power base in the party.

12. Avraham Shochat had recently entered the Knesset to replace a Labor M.K. who had resigned. This total did not count Arie Eliav who, although new to the Labor list after several years away from the party, had been a Knesset member previously.

13. Since the National Religious Party (NRP) became increasingly hawkish over the past few years, a group of former activists in the NRP joined Labor. It was hoped that the appearance of two dovish observant candidates on the Labor list (including Avraham Burg, the son of the former leader of the NRP, who some orthodox Jews consider to be insufficiently observant to qualify for the Hebrew term "dati," which is generally translated as "religious" or "orthodox" in English) would attract votes from moderate supporters of the NRP who are dissatisfied with the extremism of their party. In addition, as a reaction to the rightward swing of the NRP, a new religious party was established. The moderate Rabbi Yehuda Amital headed the Knesset list of this new Religious Center Party (Mamad). It failed to get the 1 percent of the vote necessary to receive a single Knesset seat.

14. On the bus carrying members of the Central Committee from the Haifa district to the elections, one of the members announced over the public address system that the rumor that the deal with Tel Aviv excluded Eliahu Speiser was not true, that he was part of the deal, and that this announcement was made in the name of the Haifa district secretary. The announcement was greeted by knowing smiles and laughter Later on,

while a video promoting the candidacy of Professor Shimon Shitreet (Jerusalem) was playing on the overhead television screen, someone again spoke over the public address system saying ironically, "Who is Speiser? Oh, he is part of the deal?" This provoked a certain amount of laughter. It appears likely that the exclusion of Speiser was deliberate and organized.

15. For a description of behind-the-scenes activities, see Shlomo Nakdimone, "It's All Politics," *Yediot Achronot*, July 7, 1988, p. 36.

16. Herut failed to elect a single woman (or Druze or Arab) to a realistic place on their Knesset list. Their Liberal partners on the Likud have only one woman in the lowest position that could be considered realistic. Although 65 percent of the 2,092 Herut Central Committee members are of Middle Eastern background, less than 20 percent of their Knesset candidates elected in July 1988 are Middle Eastern. See Michal Yudelman, "Male, Jewish and Mostly Ashkenazi," *Jerusalem Post*, July 8, 1988, p. 4.

17. Eli Ben-Menachem, the young Moroccan representative of the neighborhoods, and Ra'anan Cohen were both long-term party functionaries. I am grateful to Yehuda Hashai (former Knesset member and former head of the Municipalities Department of the party) for calling this to my attention. Baram (in an interview on July 27, 1988) readily agreed that to be elected by the Central Committee, a candidate had to have been actively involved in the party. However, he pointed out that few of the candidates were in a position to award patronage. Hashai disputes this, suggesting that many were indeed in such a position.

18. Since I traveled with the Haifa delegation (I was living in Haifa during this period of fieldwork), I heard more expressions of this kind from them. However, given the results of the voting, this attitude was obviously more widespread.

19. This is in sharp contrast with the published reports of the Herut Party internal elections, where the three major camps based around the personal leadership of Yitzchak Shamir and Moshe Arens, David Levy, and Ariel Sharon handed down instructions for voting for all candidates in every round of voting. According to reports, camp discipline was much stronger in Herut than in Labor. Also, tensions between the camps was much greater in Herut.

20. Although it has fewer fresh faces than Labor, the Likud gained a media star and serious claimant to future leadership in the form of former Israeli Ambassador to the United Nations Benjamin (Bibi) Nathanyahu (brother of Yonathan—a national hero who was killed leading the successful rescue of the kidnap victims at Entebbe airport in Uganda). He was a major electoral asset to the Likud in the campaign. None of the new Labor recruits to the Knesset list (or the veterans) revealed the television charisma of Nathanyahu.

21. The shtetl symbolizes the stereotyped way of life of the Eastern European Jews at the turn of the century, and the Casbah symbolizes the stereotyped traditions of North African Jews, who constituted the bulk of new immigrants in the early years of the state. Both stereotypes are gross oversimplifications.

22. Avraham Brichta, "The Selection of Candidates to the Tenth Knesset: The Impact of Centralization," in *Israel at the Polls, 1981: A Study of the Knesset Elections*, ed. Howard R. Penniman and Daniel J. Elazar (Bloomington: Indiana University Press, 1986), 20, cites Max Weber's observation (from *Politics as a Profession*) that such systems tend to produce either charismatic leaders backed by party machines or nominations systems based on manipulation and bargaining by party politicians and functionaries.

23. According to reports, Baram's group includes the following Labor Knesset members: Chaim Ramon, Lyova Eliav, Binyamin Ben-Eliezer, Emanuel Sussman, Ra'anan Cohen, Hagai Merom, Avraham Burg, Efraim Gur, Nava Arad, and Eli Ben-Menachem.

Independently of the group, Eliav demanded that Labor leave the government before the coalition broke up in 1990. He called for Labor to present the people and the world with an alternative peace plan. See Michal Yudelman, "Group of Labor Party MKs Attacks Leadership," *Jerusalem Post International Edition*, March 4, 1989, p. 5.

24. Both Uzzi Baram and Mordechai (Motta) Gur (in personal interviews on July 27, 1988) expressed their preference for primary elections in the districts as the system for nominations to the Thirteenth Knesset. On the other hand, Ora Namir (in an interview the same day) suggested that Labor would not go further with reforms, but would repeat the same system in the future. She said the wisdom of guaranteeing the top leaders' positions was proven by the divisive contest in the Likud.

25. Sarah Honig, "Shimon Peres, Avraham Burg and Ora Namir Are Big Winners in Primaries: Labor Chooses Young, Dovish Leadership," *Jerusalem Post International Edition*, April 11, 1992, p. 2.

26. Susan Hattis Rolef, "What Shamir Could Learn from Labor," *Jerusalem Post International Edition*, April 18, 1992, p. 6.

11

The Impact of the Intifada

Introduction

During the seven-year period in which it led the coalition government, the Likud failed to establish either political or ideological dominance. The end of the dominant party system was accompanied by the renewal of political polarization, as competition between the two major parties intensified during the 1981 election and the protest demonstrations against the controversial war in Lebanon.

The national election in 1984 resulted in a virtual tie between Labor and the Likud, with neither able to form a politically acceptable narrow coalition with the minor parties. They therefore formed a coalition government. The National Unity Government formed in 1984—in which the leaders of the two parties rotated the premiership and the Foreign Ministry—enabled Israel to withdraw its army from most of Lebanon following the debacle of the war (dubbed the Orwellian Peace for Galilee) waged by the Likud-led government. The new government also promoted significant steps toward economic reform.

As long as prospects for peace appeared to be remote, and there did not appear to be an acceptable partner willing to negotiate with Israel over the fate of the Palestinians and the status of the territories occupied by Israel as a result of the 1967 war, the Israeli government functioned relatively well. However, when Shimon Peres succeeded in negotiating an agreement with King Hussein of Jordan that involved a symbolic ceremonial international peace conference as a prerequisite for opening negotiations between Israel and a Jordanian/Palestinian delegation, Yitzchak Shamir went all out to mobilize the defeat of this initiative. This signaled the end of the honeymoon between Shamir and Peres, and opened

This chapter is a revised version of the previously published chapter by Myron Aronoff entitled "Labor Party and the Intifada," in *The Intifada*, ed. Robert O. Freedman, Miami: Florida International University Press, 1991. Used with permission of Florida International Press.

the campaign for the 1988 election. It was in this atmosphere of partial political paralysis that Israel confronted the beginning of the *Intifada* (literally "shaking," but in this context, "uprising").

The Sequence of Events

On December 8, 1987, an Israeli truck collided with two vans carrying Palestinian workers in the Gaza Strip, killing four Palestinians and injuring seven. Rumors spread that this was a deliberate reprisal for the murder of an Israeli businessman in Gaza two days previously. As the rumors spread, crowds of protesters, mostly youths, threw stones and Molotov cocktails at Israeli vehicles. The first victim of the Intifada was killed by Israel Defense Forces the next day while attempting to break up a demonstration. Roadblocks and burning tires were added to the stones and Molotov cocktails as the protests spread from the Gaza Strip throughout the West Bank.

On December 15, accompanied by much publicity, Ariel (Arik) Sharon moved into his apartment in the Muslim Quarter of the Jerusalem's walled Old City. Commercial strikes closed stores in East Jerusalem, Ramallah, Nablus, and throughout the West Bank. On January 3, 1988, nine Palestinians were deported for their role in what the government was then calling the "disturbances." On January 19, Defense Minister Rabin announced a new policy of using might, power, and beatings rather than live ammunition to quell the disturbances. Until then nineteen Palestinians had died since the outbreak of the uprising. On January 23, 1988, Abdel-Wahab Darawshe announced at a large demonstration of Israeli Arab/Palestinians that he was resigning from the Labor Party and establishing an independent Knesset faction in protest against Rabin's policy of beatings. (He eventually formed the Arab Democratic Party.)

During February, U.S. envoy Richard Murphy met separately with Prime Minister Shamir, who expressed reservations about new U.S. peace initiatives, and Foreign Minister Peres, who welcomed them. Peres continued to push for an international peace conference, and Shamir, threatening to force early elections, blocked an inner cabinet vote on a U.S. initiative presented by Secretary of State Shultz. Peace Now sponsored a rally of 50,000 demonstrators in support of the Shultz initiative, and Chief of Staff Shomron called on the government to reach an accord with Arab leaders in order to end the uprising. PLO leader Khalil al-Wazir (a.k.a. Abu Jihad) was gunned down in his home in Tunis, reportedly by an Israeli hit team. On April 21, 1988, Israel celebrated its fortieth year of independence.

On May 6, 1988, *Ma'ariv* reported a survey that indicated support for the Likud had risen from 33 percent in January to 39 percent in April, while support for Labor declined from 46 percent to 38 percent during the same period. Later that month in unprecedented democratic internal elections, the Labor Party selected its Knesset list, which included many fresh new faces of younger candidates. As discussed in the previous chapter, there were also large proportions of both Middle Eastern and dovish candidates.

Ramifications of the Intifada

King Hussein surrendered claims of Jordanian sovereignty over the West Bank and called on the PLO to take responsibility for it on July 31, 1988. On the fourth of August, as part of his severing of ties with the West Bank, he announced the termination and forced retirement of 21,000 civil servants. Since Shimon Peres and the Labor Party had emphasized the Jordanian option as their preferred scenario for solving the Palestinian problem for twenty-one years, this decision dramatically undercut the credibility of Peres and Labor.

At first, when Peres appointee Avraham Tamir, director-general of the Foreign Ministry, stated that the PLO was the national organization of the Palestinians (on September 1, 1988), it looked as if the Labor Party was signaling a major shift in its position. However, rather than declaring even conditional willingness to negotiate with the PLO under specific circumstances, Labor announced somewhat vaguely that, if elected in November, it would terminate Israeli rule over 1.5 million Palestinians. Four days later, Salah Khalaf announced that the PLO was ready to recognize Israel if Israel recognized the PLO and the right to Palestinian self-determination. Foreign Minister Peres claimed he would negotiate with any Palestinian who recognized Israel's right to exist and renounced terrorism, regardless of his biography (*New York Times*, September 25, 1988).

A poll published in the *Los Angeles Times* on October 14, 1988, indicated that among a representative sample of Israelis, 60 percent were willing to trade some land for peace, 46 percent favored trading all of the territories for peace, and yet 71 percent were convinced that the PLO did not want peace. The Intifada dominated public attention throughout the year, and dominated the November 1988 election, focusing attention on questions of peace, security, and relations with the Palestinians.[1]

I argued in my recent book, *Israeli Visions and Divisions* (which was in print prior to the 1988 election), that one of the political ramifications of the Palestinian uprising was a stronger shift to the right toward more nationalistic positions. I also suggested that, "With the doves becoming more dovish and the hawks more hawkish, people who had previously managed to avoid taking a position are being forced to do so. The population is becoming more polarized and the situation is moving in the direction that characterized the 1981 election campaign and the period of protest against the war in Lebanon."[2] Don Peretz and Sammy Smooha (1989:392), analyzing the results of Israel's Twelfth Knesset election (November 1, 1988) concur that the Intifada polarized the electorate, and that "both ends of the political spectrum were radicalized."

Labor received 39 Knesset seats in 1988, having absorbed Ezer Weizman's

Yahad party (which received 3 seats in 1984). It had received 44 in 1984 when it was part of an electoral Alignment with Mapam. Mapam received 3 seats in 1988. The new Arab Democratic Party headed by Darawshe, who had been elected on the Labor list in 1984, received 1 seat in 1988. The Citizens' Rights and Peace Movement (RATZ) received 5 seats in 1988—two more than it received in 1984, but the same number it had after Yossi Sarid and Mordechai Wirshubsky defected from Labor and Shinui (Change), respectively, to join RATZ during the Eleventh Knesset. The renamed Center–Shinui received 2 Knesset seats in 1988—down 1 from 1984 before Wirshubsky's defection. Therefore, although Labor declined in strength, its dovish potential coalition partners gained what it lost and the total for the camp remained exactly the same (50 Knesset seats).

Whereas the Likud lost 1 seat going from 41 in 1984 to 40 in 1988, this loss was absorbed by its potential partners to the right. Similarly, Techiya declined from 5 seats to 3, but Rafael Eitan, who had been elected on the Techiya ticket in 1984, picked up 2 seats in 1988 for his revived Tzomet movement. Meir Kahane's Kach, which received 1 seat in 1984, was barred from running in 1988, but the new Moledet (a slightly politer version of Kach) received 2 seats in 1988. Therefore, in 1988 the combined nationalist camp remained with 47 Knesset seats as it had in 1984.

The surprisingly strong showing of the non-Zionist ultra-Orthodox Torah Guardians or Shas (6 members of the Knesset), Agudat Yisrael (5 M.K.'s), and Degel HaTorah (2 M.K.'s) had little to do with the Intifada.[3] Forty-two days of protracted negotiations with the aforementioned religious parties, with the National Religious Party (5 M.K.'s), and with the three ultranationalist parties convinced Shamir that a new unity government with Labor was the lesser evil among the available options. Having unsuccessfully attempted to entice religious parties into a narrow coalition government led by Labor, Shimon Peres, supported by Yitzchak Rabin, persuaded his colleagues, who were deeply divided on this issue, to join a new coalition with the Likud under much less favorable terms than previously. Led by Uzzi Baram, who resigned his position as party secretary-general in protest against joining the new unity government, at least 15 of Labor's 39 M.K.'s argued that the party should remain in the opposition to protect its identity and to strengthen Israeli parliamentary democracy.[4] Peres and Rabin successfully persuaded the majority to join the coalition in order to save the country from an ultranationalist government.

Governmental Gridlock

The greatest single consequence of the formation of the new unity government has been the perpetuation of the stalemate on the most pressing issue facing the nation. On the day after President Hertzog called upon Yitzchak Shamir to form a new government, the Palestine National Council proclaimed a Palestinian state with Jerusalem as its capital. At the historic meeting in Algiers on November 15, 1988, the Palestine National Council (PNC) accepted United Nations Resolution 242, and vaguely called for peaceful coexistence in a durable and lasting peace. Following Yasir Arafat's clarification of his speech in the United Nations, the United States announced that it would engage in direct (low-level) talks with the PLO. There is little doubt that the leadership of the Intifada played a major role in influencing the PNC to moderate its position.

Meanwhile Peres was still pushing for his international peace conference and pretending that King Hussein had not been serious about washing his hands of the West Bank. Shamir reiterated his rejection of both an international peace conference and talks with the PLO. An Israeli intelligence report was leaked which suggested the need to talk with the PLO in order to end the Intifada. On April 6, 1989, Prime Minister Shamir proposed elections in the territories to choose leaders to negotiate with Israel the terms of self-government. The plan had been worked out with Defense Minister Rabin, which prevented Peres from presenting the plan on which he had reportedly been working.[5]

Peres had taken the Finance Ministry in order to save the kibbutz movement and Chevrat Ovdim of the Histadrut from bankruptcy, which is why both had pressured assiduously for Labor to join the unity government in the first place. He felt compelled to safeguard these last bastions of Labor support, but the price was significant. Not only was he no longer in a major foreign policy position, he was also burdened with responsibility for Israel's deteriorating economic situation.[6] On April 19, 1989, a poll of Israeli Jews was published indicating that Defense Minister Rabin was the most popular Cabinet member. On May 14, 1989, the Israeli Cabinet endorsed the Shamir/Rabin election proposal in a 20 to 6 vote.

The PLO had made further gestures of moderating their position. On May 2, 1989, Yasir Arafat said the PLO charter statements on Israel were null and void. On June 18 Mohammed Milhelm stated that the PLO would accept Israel's election proposals so long as the elections would be conducted with superpower guarantees. On June 26, 1989, Shamir told the Knesset Foreign Affairs and Defense Committee that the election proposal was more important for public relations than for practical purposes.

Rather than face a test of power in the Likud Central Committee with Arik Sharon, David Levy, and Yitzchak Moda'i, Shamir bowed to their demands that he pledge that the Likud would never return territories to foreign sovereignty, that Palestinians in East Jerusalem would not be allowed to participate in the elections in the territories, and that the elections would not be held until the uprising ended. Whereas Shamir personally agreed with these conditions, it was embarrassing to have to make them public and thereby to risk both alienating American support and losing Labor's participation in the government.

In fact, U.S. officials criticized these new strict conditions. Secretary of State Baker stated that the United States might support an international conference if

Israel made its election plan impossible for the Palestinians to accept. Labor threatened to withdraw from the government. However, on July 23, 1989, after tense negotiations, the Cabinet reaffirmed the original election proposal without mention of the Likud hard-line conditions, thereby averting the collapse of the unity government.

Three days later the PLO issued its own conditions for approving elections in the territories. Residents of East Jerusalem must be allowed to participate, freedom of speech and immunity from prosecution must be ensured, the army must be withdrawn from population centers on election day, the Israeli government must accept the principle of land for peace, and the United States and Egypt should provide monitors for the election.

The Labor Party Central Committee met in August and adopted a compromise solution that would enable Arabs of East Jerusalem who are Jordanian citizens to participate in the elections, but not in East Jerusalem. Although this compromise satisfied the contending factions within the party, it was not acceptable to the Likud.[7] During this period a group of Labor Knesset members established a Centrist Forum to repair what they viewed as the false dovish image given by an influential minority within the Knesset's ranks. Mordechai (Motta) Gur, who announced his ambition to become prime minister when he joined the party upon retirement as the chief of the general staff of the Israel Defense Forces (IDF), is one of the leading spokesman of the Forum. The lead editorial in the September 4, 1989, international edition of the *Jerusalem Post* concluded:

> Labour's message to the voters, in its essence, is that Israel's survival as a democratic Jewish state is incompatible with the permanent retention of all the occupied territories. If that "leftist" message is muffled, let alone erased, out of "electoral" considerations, Labour will no longer be an actor in Israeli politics but, at best, a spectator watching it from a supposedly good seat in the centre.

Deliberate delaying tactics by Prime Minister Shamir created considerable doubts in Labor about the viability of the election proposal, and there was talk of examining alternatives to it.[8] Shimon Peres and Yitzchak Shamir engaged in open disputes, which many observers viewed as connected with the former's fighting to retain leadership of the party in light of the rising popularity of Yitzchak Rabin.[9] Egyptian President Mubarak called Shamir's bluff by proposing a ten-point plan to break the deadlock in the stalled peace process. Both Peres and Rabin, who was sent to Cairo to represent the government in talks with Mubarak, responded favorably to the Egyptian president's initiative. A disgruntled Likud politician was reported as having said of Mubarak's proposal, "it's more like the ten plagues, only the Labour party treat it like the ten commandments."[10]

The tensions between Labor and the Likud over the Mubarak proposals are reflected in the banner headlines of the *Jerusalem Post International Edition* during the period: "Cabinet Rift Over Mubarak Plan Averted, Likud and Labour Leaders Agree to Put Off Response" (September 23, 1989); and "Shamir Ready to Go to Polls, Unity Cabinet May Break Up over Egypt Plan" (September 30, 1989). The latter lead article reported threats by Shamir to go to elections rather than compromise his initiative, and consensus among Labor ministers that they should leave the government if the Likud dealt a death blow to the Mubarak proposals. The prime minister's office charged Labor with "disloyalty" to the government's own proposals.

There was speculation that a split in the government would likely lead to a challenge to Peres' leadership of the party by Rabin whose popularity was steadily rising. Rabin has been called Labor's "teflon man." It was thought that he would be drafted to lead the party if it had to face elections at the time.[11] Several polls conducted during the year indicated that Rabin was the most popular minister in the Cabinet. Even some doves in Labor turned to Rabin as representing the best hope of dislodging Labor from the unity government and leading Labor to electoral victory. Some argue that Rabin could use his "hawkishness" to Labor's political advantage.[12]

Peres was therefore reluctant to hold new elections since he risked losing his position and the polls were not optimistic about Labor's chances. He assiduously courted the religious parties in the hope of forming a narrow coalition with them. Failing this he backed down from the coalition crisis as he had done in July when Rabin had pressed to remain in the government. In a lengthy interview published prior to his visit to the United States, Peres discussed his view of the peace process. The key tone was captured by the headline "The Americans Are The Critical Link." He stated: "A new opportunity has now been created. And much depends on the Americans."[13] In an analysis entitled "Why Bush Is in No Hurry to Take the Plunge," Wolf Blitzer correctly predicted, "the administration has no real stomach for undertaking the tough kind of decisions, the dogged hard work, and the political risks necessary to achieve progress."[14]

Frustrated in his attempt to get the United States to "save Israel from itself," Peres showed his irritation with his American allies in an interview published in *Ha'aretz*. One observer commented that the interview was "marked by a tone of petulance which clearly reflects the Labour leader's frustration at his inability either to influence official policy or to extricate his party from a government where it seems doomed to play second fiddle."[15] Peres courted the religious parties more fervently, still hoping to establish a coalition with them. Labor's threats to leave the government lost credibility. Shamir claimed that he would welcome new elections and reminded Labor that the coalition agreement stipulated that if one of the partners bolted the government, both parties must join in submitting a bill for early elections. Peres hoped that when Shamir returned from his trip to the United States. (conveniently, after the Histadrut election on November 13), Peres would be able to prove to the religious parties that the diplomatic initiative had been killed by Shamir.[16]

Secretary of State James Baker's proposed five-point framework for achieving Israeli-Palestinian talks, which was designed to get a dialogue started, became the next stumbling block over which Labor, the Likud, the PLO, and Washington argued. A letter from Foreign Minister Moshe Arens accepting Baker's proposals "in principle" but with "minor" reservations that essentially amounted to their rejection, was seen by the Americans as a ploy.[17] In spite of increased pressure from Washington, Arye Naor suggested that "Those who are waiting for heavy American pressure, as if we were still in 1956, 'to save Israel from itself' will probably be disappointed. . . . Scaling-down and disengagement, as indicated by Baker, are much more likely."[18]

Since the United States appeared to be disinclined to force the Israeli government to do what the Labor ministers wanted it to do, Labor was once again forced to face its perennial dilemma—to stay in or get out of the coalition. Only seven of the thirty-nine Labor M.K.'s complied with the request by Shimon Peres that they support the government in a no-confidence motion; the others abstained.[19] Yossi Sarid challenged his former colleagues in Labor: "Be honest with yourselves, withdraw from this government and tell the public what you know to be the truth—that there can be no peace without the PLO and without a withdrawal from the territories. Believe it or not, if you do you may even have a chance of winning." Dan Petreanu quotes Labor's faction leader Chaim Ramon as saying, "If our ministers thought it was electorally attractive they would immediately announce that they favour negotiations with the PLO."[20] Having been maneuvered by Shamir into squabbling over marginal details, Labor feared breaking up the government or facing the voters after having done so for what may appear to have been trivial issues.

According to one M.K., a major factor that prevented Agudat Yisrael from leaving the government at the time (although they did so later—at least temporarily) was:

> They [Labor] just can't be trusted to bolt the government. Rabin constantly indicates he doesn't want a narrow government—and he certainly doesn't want Peres to be prime minister. . . . Peres can't deliver the party by himself. This being the case, we have to look out for our own interests as best we can.[21]

On November 5, 1989, the "forum of four" (Prime Minister Shamir, Foreign Minister Arens, Finance Minister Peres, and Defense Minister Rabin) arrived at a compromise formula in which the government accepted Secretary Baker's five-point plan for Israeli-Palestinian dialogue, but sought assurances from the United States that Israel would not be obliged to talk with the PLO. The Likud wanted Israel's agreement to be subject to the assurances, while Labor felt the United States would not agree such a conditional acceptance. The decision exacerbated tension between the Shamir–Arens camp and the hard-line ministers led by Sharon, who threatened to convene the Likud Central Committee to oppose the decision. Shamir attacked his opponents, warning that this could lead to the breakup of the coalition. He warned that "Labour might conceivably be able to form a narrow government which, he charged, would begin negotiations with the PLO."[22]

When Labor threatened to leave the government previously Shamir taunted them knowing that they feared facing new elections. However, this was before Agudat Yisrael withdrew from the coalition, forcing the Likud to honor prior commitments that included freezing legislative efforts for electoral reform and a civil rights law. Peres claimed there was now a Knesset majority favoring territorial compromise, citing Halachic rulings of the spiritual leaders of the Orthodox Shas and Degel HaTorah. He claimed that Labor's increased coordination with the Orthodox parties could lead to a "coalition for peace."[23] Shamir was beginning to take seriously the possibility that Labor's wooing of the religious might pay off.

Labor had hoped the U.S. government would pressure Prime Minister Shamir to soften his qualified acceptance of Baker's five points, which Shamir euphemistically called "assumptions." However, Shamir was fortunate to arrive in Washington while Egypt and the PLO were still officially undecided about the Baker proposals. Predictions in the media of an imminent collision between the Bush administration and Shamir did not materialize.[24] In the meantime, the ultra-Orthodox parties, enraged by a Knesset vote in favor of a human rights bill and progress in preparing legislation for electoral reform, threatened to break their alliance with the Likud.[25]

The Likud had steadily encroached on traditional strongholds of Labor control. For example, in the local elections in February 1989 the Likud captured Beer Sheba, Holon, Ashdod, and other municipalities that Labor had previously controlled. For the first time in history the Likud succeeded in getting one of their mayors elected to the chairmanship of the Local Authorities Center, a voluntary association of all the mayors and local authority chairpersons in the country. Maxim Levy, mayor of Ramle and brother of Deputy Prime Minister David Levy, was elected to the office on June 20, 1989.

Given this trend and the tendency of the public to hold Finance Minister Peres and Histadrut Secretary-General Yisrael Kessar responsible for Israel's economic recession and high unemployment, the party faced the Histadrut election with some trepidation.[26] Therefore Labor's morale received a much needed boost with the results of the Histadrut election. Labor won 55 percent to the Likud's 27 percent. Mapam received 9 percent, and a Jewish–Arab list and the Citizens' Rights and Peace Movement received 4 percent each. Labor and Mapam ran on the joint Maarach list in 1985 and received 66 percent to the Likud's 22 percent. "The Labour Party's joy . . . was not so much because of the victory, but because of the absence of defeat."[27] The results were strongly influenced by deals made by Secretary-General Yisrael Kessar with the religious parties. This is another indication of a political rapprochement between Labor and the religious parties.

Further Consequences

The most significant consequence of the Intifada is that it convinced almost everyone that the status quo is no longer a viable solution. For example, a June 1989 survey conducted by the Israel Institute of Applied Social Research indicated that "Only 13 percent of the population (16 percent of the Jews, 4 percent of the Arabs) consider the status quo a solution."[28] "Israel's occupation was once dubbed benign. Today, with some 12,000 Palestinians under detention without trial, it would seem to merit a somewhat different epithet."[29] The very notion of a "benign occupation" has begun to be perceived for what it is—an oxymoron.[30] As Amos Oz has said of the Intifada, "What was will never be again, and what will be, is not what was."[31] The Palestinian uprising has successfully challenged many assumptions that had previously been taken for granted by many, if not most, Israelis, and many Palestinians as well. Among other things, it has renewed or redrawn the Green Line, which had disappeared from many Israeli maps and minds.

Asher Arian reports a hardening of attitudes on issues with short-term implications, but on areas of policy of more long-term importance, such as territorial compromise, he reports a slight rise in dovish views.[32] The short-term effect gave the Likud a slight edge over Labor in the 1984 election. The long-term effect could work to Labor's advantage under certain circumstances: one condition is that it clearly articulate a plausible scenario for peace that is an alternative to the Likud's policy of perpetuation of the occupation.[33]

Two additional ramifications of the Intifada had a direct impact on Labor. First, the uprising influenced King Hussein to officially abdicate responsibility for the West Bank, putting paid to Labor's two-decade policy of relying on the Jordan option. Second, the Intifada forced the PLO to moderate its stance, moving it toward a compromise political solution. Due to a failure of political courage, the leadership of Labor continued to follow public opinion polls rather than leading the nation. It failed to adapt to the new realities. Instead, through participation in the government, it provided what *Tikkun* editor Michael Lerner described as a "fig leaf" for Shamir's policies. Perennial rivalry between Peres and Rabin, internal divisions such as those between doves and hawks, economic interests of the kibbutz movement and the Histadrut, and other factors led Labor to enter the government. Some of these same factors prevented it from leaving the coalition until March 1990, which resulted in a narrow Likud-dominated government.

The new Centrist Forum pushed Labor to emulate the Likud, partly in reaction to the dovish forces in the party, partly as an electoral ploy, and for Motta Gur as a personal vehicle to the premiership. The movement to return Rabin to the helm of the party, supported by even a leading dove like Ezer Weizman, provided a serious constraint on Shimon Peres, who correctly perceived that if Labor had to face the electorate he was not likely to head the ticket.

Peres followed a policy of wooing the religious parties. He counted on the

Americans to pressure Shamir into accepting terms agreeable to Labor, but not to the Likud, to advance the peace process. In the absence of successfully pressuring Shamir, Peres seems to have hoped that the failure to do so would precipitate a crisis with Israel, thus providing a legitimate pretext for Labor to leave the government. Ideally for Peres, such a crisis would provide a sufficient excuse to allow Labor to violate the coalition agreement it signed with the Likud to support new elections. Failing this, it would at least provide Labor with a legitimate excuse to bring down the government and give it an issue to use against the Likud in an election campaign. Unfortunately for Peres, the American administration was reluctant to play the role for which it has been cast in his scenario. Yitzchak Shamir skillfully outmaneuvered Peres and ended up heading a narrow government with Labor in the opposition. Peres was double-crossed by Shas, which reneged on a commitment to join a narrow coalition led by Labor. Whereas it was seriously doubtful that Menachem Begin ever intended to fully implement the autonomy plan to which he agreed at Camp David, it is even less likely that Shamir intends to implement the plan, which he opposed from the outset. Although he was eventually pressured by the United States to enter into negotiations with Palestinian surrogates for the PLO, Shamir succeeded in doing so on his own terms. If the talks between Israel, the Palestinians, and the Arab states, which were ceremonially launched in Madrid and continued in Washington, fail to lead to a mutually satisfactory agreement (as is likely as long as the Likud dominates the Israeli government and is dependent upon even more extreme nationalist parties to maintain the coalition), the historic window of opportunity will likely close. If this happens the situation will deteriorate and the more extreme forces on both sides will be the beneficiaries.

Conclusions

There is no military means of ending the Palestinian uprising without undermining the ethical foundation on which Israeli democracy is based. Ironically, the Intifada, which began without PLO initiative or direction, has proven that Israel cannot achieve a political resolution without negotiating with the PLO and meeting the legitimate demands of the Palestinians. The Shamir government reluctantly agreed to negotiate with leaders of the West Bank and Gaza who are in fact surrogates for the PLO leadership. Public meetings between these "surrogates" and Arafat and other ranking PLO leaders make a charade of the Likud government's pretense that they are not negotiating with the PLO.

One of the main reasons why Labor broke up its coalition government with the Likud was in order to avoid being a party to the tragic consequences of what appeared at the time to be the aborting of the peace initiative. Yet, having failed to form a government, Labor found itself once again watching from the sidelines of the opposition benches while the Likud sat at the negotiating table engaging in peace talks.

If Labor ever hopes to regain the confidence of a sufficient proportion of the Israeli public to once again lead the nation, it must risk the possibility of electoral defeat.[34] It must articulate a vision of the nation that explains the opportunities created by the new realities. It must convince the nation that these opportunities make the risks that must be taken worthwhile. What is required is nothing short of a new paradigm to give meaning to the new realities.[35] It must articulate policies that realistically relate to these new conditions even if they violate what had previously been taboo, like negotiating with the PLO. It cannot do this by emulating the Likud. The original will always be more convincing and authentic than a cheap copy. In Chapter 12, I evaluate the extent to which Labor succeeded in offering itself as a genuine alternative to the Likud in the 1992 election campaign.

Notes

1. Don Peretz and Sammy Smooha, "Israel's Twelfth Knesset Election: An All-Loser Game," *Middle East Journal* 43, 3 (Summer 1989). The authors cite an August 1988 poll in the Continuing Survey of the Institute of Applied Social Research and the Smart Family Communications Institute of the Hebrew University in which 60 percent of the respondents indicated issues of peace and security, and 11 percent chose the territories, as the most important issue of the election campaign.

2. Myron J. Aronoff, *Israeli Visions and Divisions: Cultural Change and Political Conflict* (New Brunswick, NJ: Transaction 1989), 153. Dan Horowitz and Moshe Lissak, *Trouble in Utopia: The Overburdened Polity of Israel* (Albany: State University of New York Press 1989), also discuss the process of polarization in Israel, but do not discuss the role of the Intifada in this process. Mordechai Bar-On, "Israeli Reactions to the Palestinian Uprising," *Journal of Palestine Studies* 17, 4 (Summer 1988):52, mentions a similar radicalization to the right and to the left as a reaction to the uprising.

3. For analyses of the role of the religious parties in the election see Robert O. Freedman, "Religion, Politics, and the Israeli Elections of 1988," *Middle East Journal* 43, 3 (Summer 1989):406–22; and Avishai Margalit, "Israel: The Rise of the Ultra-Orthodox," *New York Review of Books*, November 9, 1989, pp. 38–44.

4. Peretz and Smooha, "Israel's Twelfth Knesset Election," pp. 400–401. For an analysis of the position of Labor members of the Knesset on Israel/Palestine and on socio-economic issues see Haim Baram, "The Decline of the Labor Party," *Tikkun* 4, 5, pp. 55–58. Baram divides the Labor M.K.'s into Doves (7), Two Staters (9), and Pragmatic Expansionists (21), with one undecided on the Israel/Palestine issue. The opponents to joining the new unity government came from the Two Staters, who believe the Israeli government should negotiate directly with the PLO, and from among the Doves, who accept the inevitability of serious territorial concessions. See Efraim Inbar, *War and Peace in Israeli Politics* (Boulder, CO: Lynne Rienner, 1991), especially Chapter 2, for a more detailed and nuanced analysis of the multidimensional character of the distinction between doves and hawks.

5. Allan E. Shapiro, "A Paradoxical Optimism," *Jerusalem Post International Edition*, July 8, 1989.

6. Shlomo Maoz and Avi Temkin, "The Devaluation of Peres," *Jerusalem Post International Edition*, July 8, 1989, pp. 1, 4.

7. Allan E. Shapiro, "The Key Issue in the Peace Plan," *Jerusalem Post International Edition*, August 19, 1989.

8. Dan Petreanu and Michal Yudelman, "Doubts in Labour Party over Peace Initiative," *Jerusalem Post International Edition,* September 9, 1989.

9. Michal Yudelman, "Strains Appear in Government," *Jerusalem Post International Edition,* September 7, 1989, pp. 1–2.

10. Peretz Kidron, "The Thunderbolt from Cairo," *Middle East Insight* (hereinafter *MEI*), September 22, 1989, p. 3.

11. Dan Petreanu, "Labour's 'Man Who Can Do No Wrong,' " *Jerusalem Post International Edition,* September 30, 1989, p. 3.

12. Ezer Weizman, Labor's leading dove in the Cabinet, is reported to have switched his support from Peres to Rabin after Rabin came out firmly in support of the Mubarak proposals. See Peretz Kidron, "Israel's Leaders Pulling in Different Directions," *MEI,* October 6, 1989, p. 3, subtitled "Weizman's Bombshell."

13. Menachem Shalev and Jeff Black, "Spotlight; 'The Americans Are the Critical Link,' " *Jerusalem Post International Edition,* September 23, 1989, p. 7.

14. Wolf Blitzer, "Why Bush Is in No Hurry to Take the Plunge," *Jerusalem Post International Edition,* September 23, 1989, p. 3.

15. Peretz Kidron, "If the PLO Is In, Israel Is Out," *MEI,* October 20, 1989, p. 9.

16. Dan Petreanu, "Labour's Threat: Is It Real This Time?" *Jerusalem Post International Edition,* October 21, 1989, p. 2.

17. Wolf Blitzer and Menachem Shalev, "Peace Process: U.S. Steps Up the Pressure," *Jerusalem Post International Edition,* October 28, 1989, pp. 1–2; and Wolf Blitzer, "U.S.'s Not-So-Subtle Pressure on Israel," *Jerusalem Post International Edition,* November 4, 1989, pp. 1–2.

18. Arye Naor, "U.S. Edges to the Sidelines?" *Jerusalem Post International Edition,* November 4, 1989, p. 8.

19. Dan Petreanu, "Labour's Dilemma," *Jerusalem Post International Edition,* November 4, 1989, p. 3. This is an excellent example of the weakening of party discipline in the Knesset discussed in the previous chapter.

20. Petreanu, "Labour's Dilemma."

21. Ibid.

22. *Jerusalem Post* Staff, "Israel Accepts Baker's Five Points; Shamir Facing Rift with Rebel Likud Ministers—PLO May Block Israel–Palestinian Talks," *Jerusalem Post International Edition,* November 11, 1989, p. 1.

23. Dan Petreanu, "Agudat Yisrael Leaves Government; Shamir Confident He Can Overcome Rebel Likud Ministers' Challenge—Coalition Strains as Labour Woos Religious Parties," *Jerusalem Post International Edition,* p. 3.

24. Wolf Blitzer and Menachem Shalev, "Shamir Skirts the Brink," *Jerusalem Post International Edition,*" pp 1–2.

25. Asher Wallfish and Dan Petreanu, "New Threat to National Unity Coalition— Ultra Parties Enraged by Human Rights Bill," *Jerusalem Post International Edition,* November 25, 1989, p. 3.

26. Ehud Katz, "Hobson's Choice: Labor at a Crossroads," *Israel Scene,* August 1989, pp. 3–4.

27. Dan Petreanu and Jeff Black, "Labour Buoyed by Histadrut Poll," *Jerusalem Post International Edition,* November 25, 1989, p. 3.

28. "Polls Apart on Policy for the Territories," *Jerusalem Post International Edition,* September 2, 1989.

29. Editorial Comment, "Law of Occupation" *Jerusalem Post,* November 16, 1989, reprinted in *Jerusalem Post International Edition,* November 25, 1989.

30. Eyal Ben-Ari, "Masks and Soldiering: The Israeli Army and the Palestinian Uprising," *Cultural Anthropology* 4, 4 (November 1989):372–89.

31. Robert Rosenberg, " 'What Was Will Never Be Again, and What Will Be Is Not What Was,' Says Amos Oz," *Jerusalem Post*, February 19, 1988, p. 4.

32. Data cited from a Jaffee Center study entitled *Public Opinion in Israel and the Intifada: Changes in Security Attitudes, 1987–1988,* printed in "Polls Apart on Policy," *Jerusalem Post International Edition*, September 2, 1989.

33. Haim Baram, "The Decline of the Labor Party," p. 58.

34. It cannot establish the kind of political and ideological dominance it once had since the socio-political, cultural, and systemic changes that have taken place make this a virtual impossibility. The transition from a dominant party system to a competitive party system has become institutionalized. Therefore, Labor can regain leadership, but not dominance of the system.

35. Such a political cultural paradigm is analogous with the scientific paradigms discussed by Thomas S. Kuhn in *The Structure of Scientific Revolutions, International Encyclopedia of Unified Science,* vol. 2, no. 2 (Chicago: University of Chicago Press 1962; 2d enlarged ed., 1970).

12

Facing the Future

Introduction

In *Israeli Visions and Divisions* (Aronoff, 1989), I analyze the current crisis of legitimacy in the Israeli political system. It is not my purpose to recapitulate or even to elaborate on that theme here. However, I think it is essential to state briefly the main thesis, since it provides the point of departure as well as the context in which I discuss the most important dilemmas facing the Labor Party today.

Following Ricoeur (1986), I suggest that a credibility gap exists in all systems of legitimation when they exceed their authority. This is perhaps especially so in the relatively rare type of political system that Duverger (1963/1965) identified as a dominant party system.[1] When the public identifies a political party with an epoch, the party can achieve ideological as well as political preeminence. The endurance of dominant cultural forms depends on their effectiveness in providing models for dealing with various existential and societal problems. As they become less effective in coping with such problems, their immutability becomes undermined as challenging alternative visions are advanced.

Profound social and economic changes in Israel led to dramatic changes in both the political system and the political culture. Labor's loss of political and ideological dominance has resulted in Israel's shift from a dominant party to a competitive party system. At the same time, Likud's failure to establish the hegemony of its particular ideological interpretation of Zionism (among other factors) has resulted in a highly polarized system where the two major political blocs achieved relative parity resulting in electoral stalemate, and their conflicting ideological visions offer contradictory "solutions" to the most fateful issues facing the nation.

I will not even attempt to summarize the many incidents and events that illustrate the erosion of the authority of primary political institutions of the state and of the political parties. Unfortunately, the widespread breakdown of law and order, the increasing resort to nonparliamentary political protest demonstrations, the increase in violence on both sides of the Green Line, and the official use of violence by the state to suppress the aforementioned activities are well known and extensively documented.[2]

The two large parties compete with each other for the support of the floating voters who tend to be more moderate. This ought to make both parties moderate their positions in order to capture the center. However, they must also compete with the more ideologically pure splinter parties on their fringes for the support of the more ideologically motivated electorate. In so doing in certain contexts they tend to emulate the more extreme views of the latter in order to compete with them more successfully. When parties are thereby forced into more extreme positions a chain reaction of extremism can occur.[3] (This did not occur during the 1992 election.)

For example, the call for the "transfer" (a euphemism for expulsion) of Palestinians, when first made by the late Rabbi Meir Kahane, was universally condemned as racist, but was picked up in a more "polite" form by established party politicians and has since gained much wider acceptance. In fact, in early February 1991, retired general Rehavim Zeevi, leader of the ultranationalist Moledet (Homeland) Party, which endorses transfer in its platform, joined the government. Zeevi was also made a member of the key ministerial committee on defense and security.

The Palestinian uprising that ushered in the year of 1988 resulted in an even greater degree of polarization in Israel. As a consequence, the doves became more dovish and the hawks became more hawkish. The initial moderating of the PLO's position and the political initiatives of the Egyptian president and the American secretary of state ultimately led to the demise of the coalition between Labor and the Likud and the formation of a Likud-led government based on the support of ultranationalist and ultra-Orthodox (non-Zionist) parties. The increasing reliance by the main political parties on non-Zionist religious parties to form coalition governments (and the possible future reliance of Labor on non-Zionist Arab parties) is another indicator of the current crisis in Zionism, the dominant motif in Israeli political culture and the main agency of legitimation of the political system.

Labor has never really gotten over the fact that it is no longer the dominant party in Israel. It has yet to conduct a comprehensive soul-searching (*cheshbone nefesh*) in order to learn the lessons of why it lost power and why it has failed to regain sufficient public confidence to return to power.[4] Rather than having carried out major and sweeping reforms after initially losing the public's confidence, changes were sporadic and largely reactive. There was no immediate reformulation of ideology and policy, but rather a gradual movement in the direction of a more dovish orientation. Most visibly there has been no change of top leadership. Although it has made piecemeal policy changes, Labor has yet to articulate a clear vision that could set the national agenda for the nineties and lead Israel into the new millennium.[5]

Modest internal reforms (initiated by former party secretary-general Uzzi Baram) began the process of opening up the nominations process. This gesture toward democratization led to the introduction of some fresh faces in Labor's Knesset delegation as well as in local and national party institutions. However, these preliminary reforms were too modest to attract much public attention or appreciation. Implementation of the nationwide primary election of Knesset candidates (discussed in Chapter 10) has led to more dramatic and significant results. Another reform undertaken at the Conference was the decision to reduce the size of the Central Committee from 1,400 to 901. This is the first time since the founding of the Labor Party that the size of one of its institutions has been reduced.

Leadership: The Problem of Succession

More visible to the public is the fact that the same two leaders, Shimon Peres and Yitzchak Rabin, whose no-holds-barred competition in 1977 significantly contributed to Labor's historic first electoral defeat, vied for the number one spot once again in February 1992. The internecine feud between Peres and Rabin, which renewed in earnest after Labor failed to form a government following the breakup of its coalition with the Likud in March 1990, has been and continues to be extremely damaging to Labor.

Peres initially defeated another bid by Rabin to head the ticket, which was prompted by surveys indicating Rabin had the best chance of leading Labor to electoral success.[6] Rabin's proposal for a vote to determine the party leadership received a 60 percent majority in a secret ballot among the slightly more than 100 members of Labor's Political Bureau. Yet Peres received 54 percent against Rabin's 46 percent of the 1,400-member Central Committee (except for approximately eighty committee members who were abroad) to defeat Rabin's proposal for a vote in early August 1990 on who was to occupy the party's top post.[7] The decision was to postpone the election of the party leader.

So the first dilemma facing Labor was the question of leadership and succession. Neither Peres nor Rabin was inclined to step aside, and their party had neither the courage nor the heart to give either or both of them the boot. This is primarily because with the demise of the old factions based on previous party affiliation, the support groups based around the two leaders have provided primary networks for political favors and mobility. They are the last vestiges of patron–client ties that have dominated Labor throughout its entire history. As was indicated in Chapter 10, Rabin received the support of 40.45 percent of party members as against 34.5 percent for Peres. The remainder were divided among the other candidates.

These contenders are from the generation of party leaders who have loyally served as obedient party functionaries (*askanim*) for so long that few have been able to demonstrate conspicuous leadership ability or initiative, and none have demonstrated charismatic appeal. Among those who initially announced that they might contend for the top post, only Histadrut Secretary-General Yisrael Kessar and Knesset member Ora Namir remained in the race.[8]

The younger generation of Labor leaders, like Knesset members Avraham Burg, Chaim Ramon, and Yossi Beilin, have begun to show greater independence and initiative (discussed below) and may be ready for the challenge to the top spot on the ticket the next time around. The inability to replace the top leadership may overshadow the public's perception of the significant changes in the selection of leadership and representation that have taken place, and which have paved the way for possibly dramatic changes of the top strata of leadership in the relatively near future. The undermining of the patron–client system of leadership selection is likely to attract and encourage more independent and, perhaps, more innovative leaders in the future.

Ideology/Policy

Peace and Security

The issue that most sharply divides Labor from the Likud is Labor's greater willingness to enter into more meaningful negotiations with the Palestinians especially and its readiness to make territorial concessions in exchange for a political settlement. Labor lost its long-cherished Jordanian option when Yitzchak Shamir succeeded in defeating the initiative of Shimon Peres and King Hussein to hold a symbolic international peace conference as a prelude to bilateral talks between Israel and a combined Jordanian/Palestinian delegation. Subsequently, particularly after the outbreak of the Intifada, King Hussein abdicated all responsibility for representing the Palestinians on the West Bank.[9]

It took Peres some time to reconcile himself to the loss of his favored option and to recognize that there was no alternative to direct negotiations with the Palestinians, which meant, at the very least, indirect talks with the PLO. The moderation in the PLO's position and the initiatives of Mubarak and Baker made it appear as if a genuine opportunity for a political dialogue with the Palestinians might be possible. Given initial refusal to accept the terms, which meant talks with surrogates of the PLO, Peres led Labor out of the unity government in March 1990. Peres' failure to establish a Labor government produced a new Likud coalition with the ultranationalist and ultrareligious parties, thereby reducing the possibility for successful political dialogue and compromise.

Initially, the new Defense Minister Moshe Arens' policy of keeping a low profile for the IDF in the territories significantly reduced the casualty rate for the Intifada. However, a number of factors—including the despair of the Palestinians in hope of attaining their right to political self-expression and the support of the PLO for the Iraqi occupation of Kuwait—led to a progressively deteriorating situation. The Temple Mount (or Haram al Sharif) incident in October 1990 (in which scores of Palestinians were killed by Israeli police who opened fire on them as some of them hurled rocks at Jews praying at the Western Wall) was a catalyst for a new wave and chain reaction of violence. The Islamic fundamentalist movements in the territories have been particularly active in encouraging acts of violence against Israelis.

In conditions of insecurity, uncertainty, and fear (of being stabbed by Palestinians or gassed by Saddam Hussein), the Israeli public became more hawkish and less open to appeals for moderation and compromise. This presented Labor with another serious dilemma. It could either move toward a more hawkish position, or it could take the electoral risk of trying to educate the public and offer significant alternatives to the policies promoted by the Likud.

Mordechai Gur, among others, argued for moving the party toward a more hawkish position on this issue, which he hoped to use as a springboard for his bid to take over the helm of party leadership. The party's Values Circle (closely associated with Yitzchak Rabin) charged the Likud with sabotaging negotiations with the Palestinians.[10] Yet Rabin criticized Labor doves for giving the public impression that peace cannot be achieved without a dialogue with the PLO.[11] Peres has gradually been nudged toward more dovish positions by the young intellectuals who gathered around him over the years.

In typical Labor fashion, a compromise between two more extreme positions was worked out and accepted during the first phase of the Labor's National Party Conference held November 19–21, 1991. An effective plea for party unity by Shimon Peres persuaded the doves to withdraw their proposed amendments, and those of the hawks were defeated by the delegates who approved the platform as presented by the Preparation Committee. The compromise resulted in a more dovish policy designed to distinguish the party from the Likud without getting the party too far ahead of the electorate.

With typical ambiguity, the party "abandoned its longstanding objection to negotiations with the Palestine Liberation Organization," but Shimon Peres and Yitzchak Rabin "each said he was still dead set against talking peace with a group that their party, like the Likud, regards as a terrorist organization."[12] A similar compromise resulted in upholding "national rights" for Palestinians, but the rejection of the creation of an independent Palestinian state. While the party expanded the concept of territorial concessions to include the Golan Heights, it reiterated its previously stated refusal to return to the pre-1967 war borders. In the second phase of the Conference (December 26–27) the party, in a concession to Golan settlers and hawks, affirmed that the settlements on the Golan Heights represented Israel's "security border."

"All in all, there was enough in the platform to appease both party doves and hawks, who had seemed a few days ago to be on the verge of a crippling split."[13] The threat of splitting the party is a legacy of the factionalism remaining after the demise of the historic factions based on the pre-Labor parties that merged to form the Labor Party in 1968. Whereas in the earlier phase, discussed in Chapter 8, the threat of a split came from the right (the hawkish Rafi, led by Moshe Dayan), at the 1991 Party Conference the threat came from the dovish left (many of whom had rallied around Peres—Dayan's old partner in Rafi). The doves were particularly concerned about the likelihood that Rabin might be elected as the party's candidate for premier in the February primary, which they feared might undermine their positions in the party and the Knesset.

Threat to Party Unity: Regaining the Center

Before the Conference, a group of dovish members of the Knesset, led by Yossi Beilin and Chaim Ramon, had called for an alliance with Mapam, Shinui (The Movement for Change), and the Citizens' Rights Movement (RATZ) in a new Israeli Democratic Party. Such a union would have signaled a more dramatic move to the dovish left on the issue of the territories than the platform adopted at the November Labor Party Conference, and a move farther to the right on social and economic issues than the platform adopted by Labor in 1991. Predictably, these proposals caused a furor. They were most strongly rejected by leaders of the kibbutz movement and the Histadrut, one of whom, Ya'acov Tsur, accused the merger's proponents of selling socialist values for the votes of the Soviet immigrants.[14] Mapam, the Citizens' Rights Movement, and Shinui, formed a joint list called Meretz for the elections to the Thirteenth Knesset.

The proposal for the merger of the dovish parties could be profitably considered in the light of historical experience. Following its joint list with Achdut Haavoda and the split with Rafi in 1965, Mapai began to lose political and ideological centrality. The process was further accentuated by the 1969 Alignment with Mapam, which was further to the left. Whereas previously Mapai had occupied the center of the political spectrum with two noncommunist parties to its left, after 1969 it headed a single, noncommunist, left electoral bloc. This placed it further to the left than Mapai had been previously. (By way of contrast, on the right, Gahal—and later the Likud—moved closer to the center than Herut had been previously.)

As a result, the Alignment was deprived of Mapai's firm control of the center, which was now unoccupied and therefore available for capture by the right. Mapai lost its policy centrality, which had been based upon its capacity to determine policy preferences—to set the political agenda—that both distinguished it from its major rivals and enjoyed majority support. This was replaced by a new distribution of opinion and policy that produced major policy differences within the parties.[15]

The main issue internally dividing Labor was the result of Israel's victory in 1967—the issue of the territories and their inhabitants. The contestation both over the borders and character of the state continues to be a contentious one. Furthermore, this issue, and the course of events following from it, has tended to move the political center of Israeli politics to the right of where it had been prior to the 1967 war—at least until 1992. The combination of Rabin's successful centrist appeal to disaffected Likud supporters and new voters and the independent united Meretz list mobilizing the votes on the dovish left provided the successful basis for the new Israeli government. Had Labor and Meretz united in one list they would not likely have been so successful.

Social and Economic Issues

A second issue that divided Labor then and continues to do so today is over how far to carry Ben-Gurion's policy of *mamlachtiut* (statism) as opposed to holding the line against the erosion of Labor's socialist heritage. The chairman of Labor's Knesset caucus, Chaim Ramon, and Peres protégé Yossi Beilin have proposed a number of statist reforms. At the symbolic level they suggested abandoning major socialist symbols like the red flag, the celebration of May Day, and the singing of the *Internationale*, which they claim are an anathema to many people, including the masses of Soviet immigrants arriving daily. In this case Beilin and Ramon carry the standard of *mamlachtiut* against the rear-guard action of the defenders of the crumbling last bastions of socialism in Israel, the kibbutzim and the Histadrut. On this issue, too, Israelis have become more conservative.

Such reforms have been strongly opposed by Mapam and by those in Labor who have the strongest stake in protecting the kibbutz and Histadrut establishments, including the Kupat Cholim health care system. Significantly, a proposal by Ramon to separate the party from the Histadrut and to liberalize the labor federation was soundly defeated in the first phase of the Party Conference. There was considerable speculation in the party and the press about Ramon's future and whether he would remain in the party following what several observers called an intemperate speech in the Party Conference—one that Ramon himself compared to an operation without anesthetic.[16] Ramon was elected sixth place on the 1992 Labor Party Knesset list—a highly prestigious position. This seems to indicate that his views are more popular with the rank-and-file membership than with the top leaders.

Both issues were intertwined with the loosely organized personal camps of Peres and Rabin and various other internal party formations. Groups like the Central Stream, formed in 1984 to counteract the dovish trend in the party, and the Forum for the Promotion of Peace, a dovish umbrella group formed after the 1988 elections, are essentially ideological and single-issue-oriented. Others, while they may have ideological overtones, are primarily groups oriented to gain power for their members. Examples of the latter are the Mashov group headed by dovish Knesset members Yossi Beilin and Avraham Burg, and the Kfar Hayarok group led by dovish Knesset member Chaim Ramon and secretary-general of the moshav movement, Nissim Zvilli.[17]

Proposals by the four young leaders of these last two groups (among others) at the Party Conference stimulated long-overdue serious debates over ideology, policy, and the future identity and character of the party. These debates produced a party platform that called for minimizing government involvement in the economy, privatization of government corporations, and giving priority to the private sector. A more "revolutionary" plank called for the separation of the Histadrut's political and labor union establishment from its holding company and forming managements and public boards for corporations on a strictly professional and business basis.[18] The debates also helped divert the top leaders from the petty carping and mutual recriminations that had characterized much party discourse since Labor left the government.[19] One the other hand, they created new strains within the party (even between such close long-time allies as Ramon and Zvilli) and with potential coalition partners. For example, the most controversial proposal—which created heated debate in the Conference and captured the headlines of the Israeli press—was one by Avraham Burg (son of the grand old man of the National Religious Party) to separate religion and the state. Burg's resolution was proposed on Thursday afternoon after most of the 3,000 delegates had gone home and was passed by a vote of 390 to 302. Shimon Peres and other party leaders immediately announced their intent to repeal this resolution because of the fear that it would alienate traditional and religious voters and prevent future coalitions with religious parties, particularly the NRP.[20] The leadership bureau met after the first phase of the Conference and prepared a new resolution on state and religion acceptable to religious and secular members; it stressed their opposition to the separation of state and religion, but urged separation of religion from politics. This proposal was virtually unanimously passed at the second phase of the Conference on December 26. In the national primary Burg was elected to the number three position on the list following Rabin and Peres. It is not unreasonable to assume that his stand on this issue enhanced his popularity and contributed to his success.

The 1992 Knesset Election

Labor's democratic primaries proved themselves in the 1992 Knesset elections. The younger Labor leaders have begun to articulate policies that have struck responsive chords among the party rank and file, earning them strong support in the party primaries. The younger leadership elected through more democratic processes and the substantive debates of genuine policy alternatives in the Party Conference helped to give the party a new sense of direction, purpose, and hope. It also gave the party a more positive, rejuvenated public image. The election of Rabin to the top spot also proved to be popular among the public.

The spirit of reform manifest in Labor spread to the Twelfth Knesset, albeit belatedly and reluctantly on the part of many. After much delay, lengthy bargaining, and significant compromises, the Law for the Direct Election of the Prime Minister was passed. However, it will not go into effect until after the Thirteenth Knesset completes its tenure. The delay in the implementation of the law was a concession to the Likud, since Shamir was adamantly opposed to it (correctly figuring that he was unlikely to win in a personal contest against Rabin).[21]

Labor, in its electoral strategy, treated the 1992 election campaign as if the new law had already gone into effect and strongly emphasized Rabin's leadership—including identifying itself on the official electoral list as "Labor, headed by Rabin" (an unusual, but not unprecedented phenomenon). The election slogan "Israel is waiting for Rabin" was a play on a song popular at the time of the Six Day War—"Nasser is waiting for Rabin." Labor's focus on Rabin was a successful strategy which led it to victory. It elicited from the Likud sharp personal attacks on Rabin's character that turned out to be counter-productive. These attacks included charges that Rabin had a reputed "nervous breakdown" shortly before the 1967 war when he was chief of staff. Another unsubstantiated charge was that he was an alcoholic. The charges were a desperate attempt to diminish Rabin's appeal to the disenchanted Likud voters.

Rabin focused his approach primarily on these potential swing voters from the Likud, first-time voters, and new immigrants. He practically ignored Labor's traditional base of support. In fact he did not campaign in the kibbutzim at all. According to voter surveys of polling places, Labor fared much better than the Likud (47 percent to 18 percent) in the competition for votes of the approximately 400,000 Jews from the former Soviet Union who arrived in Israel over the past three years. Polls shortly before the election indicated that the new immigrants would vote Labor by a margin of four to one as an expression of protest against the Likud government's failure to supply them with adequate and appropriate housing and employment. Forty percent of them are unemployed.

Of the more than 500,000 first-time voters (out of a total of 3.5 million voters), approximately half were new immigrants and the other half were eighteen-year-olds. Young Labor Party activists distributed hundreds of condoms bearing the slogans: "Watch Out for the Little Guy" and "Youngsters, Get To Work [Labor]" in an apparent appeal for the support of young voters. One wag observed that "The shot-glass [reportedly passed out by Likud activists] and the condom are this election's political symbols."[22]

In spite of the serious problems and choices facing the nation at this crucial crossroads, the election campaign was, according to most reports, one of the most lackluster in recent history. The electorate seemed to be indifferent and apathetic. A generous interpretation might ascribe the relative calm of the 1992 election campaign to the political maturation of the Israeli electorate. However, a less magnanimous appraisal might attribute it to boredom. Discussions in depth of the dominant issues facing the nation were conspicuous by their absence. Neither of the major parties offered major position papers on significant policy issues. No broad new vision of national purpose was articulated.

The focus on leadership hardly made for an exciting political spectacle. As Clyde Haberman observed, "Both men [Rabin and Shamir], whose combined age is 146, are studies in gray, so lacking in magnetism that neither one would set off an airport security detector."[23] Although polls prior to the election predicted gains for Labor, they had done so prior to previous elections in which the vote failed to correspond to these predictions. Also, most pundits predicted the formation of a reconstituted National Unity Government pairing Labor and the Likud. The prognosis of this format for continued political stalemate was not exactly an exciting prospect for many voters.

The minimum percentage of the national vote required for a party to obtain the first Knesset mandate was raised from one to one-and-a-half. This half-hearted compromise encouraged three of the smaller ultra-Orthodox parties (Agudat Yisrael, Degel HaTorah, and Poelei Agudat Yisrael) to run on the joint United Torah Judaism list. The minimum would have to be raised much more to curtail effectively the proliferation of political parties and electoral lists. Twenty-five lists were approved and five lists were disqualified by the Central Elections Committee for the 1992 election. Ten parties gained representation in the Thirteenth Knesset compared with fifteen in the Twelfth Knesset.

Conclusions

To a large extent the election of 1992 represented more a vote against the Likud than a resounding vote for Labor. There was a strong anti-incumbent mood driven as much, if not more, by economic factors, such as 11.5 percent unemployment (40 percent among recent immigrants), as by security concerns. The two are not unrelated. Labor was finally able to convince many voters (including those who supported the Likud previously) that much of the huge sums spent by the Likud government on settlements in the West Bank fulfilled primarily ideological rather than security needs, and diverted precious resources from more important domestic priorities. Rabin conveyed this through his call to reorder national priorities. Also Rabin was more convincing than Peres had been previously in reassuring the public that there is a safe road to peace. He was obviously aided by his military record and his performance as defense minister.

Just as Labor had been racked by public scandals in the 1970s, so the Likud has been embarrassed by a number of serious charges by the comptroller general (among others) regarding the operation of several of the government's ministries—particularly the Ministry of Housing under Arik Sharon. Shamir seriously miscalculated the public reaction to the loss of the ten-billion-dollar loan guarantee from the United States and the deteriorating relationship between the American and Israeli governments which it represented. Rabin's record of close and cordial relations with previous and the present American administrations was an important electoral asset. Whereas the extreme nationalists may revel in their isolation as proof of the inherent anti-Semitism of the world, most Israelis realize how important it is to maintain cordial relations with the world community, and especially with Israel's closest and most important ally.

The most significant factor in the 1992 election was the loss of support by the

Likud and the fact that Labor was able to gain a sizable share of the swing vote (a good part of it having gone to parties to the right of the Likud, especially Rafael Eitan's Tsomet). Meretz succeeded in expanding beyond the ten mandates its constituent parties had in the Twelfth Knesset by attracting new voters and picking up disgruntled Laborites who were turned off by what they viewed as Rabin's pandering to the right. Labor, Meretz, and the Arab parties have a blocking majority which can prevent the Likud from forming a government.

Rabin announced that he will continue the tradition of excluding the non-Zionist Arab parties from the government. He served notice that he would work to form a centrist government and that he alone would determine the assignment of ministerial posts. Rabin will obviously attempt to balance the influence of the liberal and dovish Meretz who are ideologically close to the doves in Labor (most of whom are closely associated with Peres) to counterbalance their ideological influence and the political influence of Peres as well. To do so he will likely bring at least one of the religious parties (more likely one of the non-Zionist parties like Shas than the more nationalistic NRP) into the coalition. They would counter the militant secularism of Meretz as well as provide a counterbalance to their dovish views.

While Rabin's strategy is designed to maximize his freedom of action, it has the inherent danger of potentially paralyzing his government. If he wants to make genuine progress in peace talks with the Palestinians and the Arab nations, he cannot afford to have a party in his government firmly opposed to territorial concessions such as Tsomet, which otherwise might make a convenient coalition partner. In addition to maximizing his personal freedom of action as prime minister, Rabin wants his government to reflect a national consensus. Unfortunately there is no national consensus on such issues as territorial compromise, the future status of the Palestinians, and the proper role of religion in the state.

In such conditions, leadership is of critical importance. There is the historic opportunity to resolve the deep conflicts with the Palestinians and with its neighboring Arab states, to gather in and resettle large numbers of potential immigrants from the former Soviet Union and to more successfully integrate those who have already come as well as those who arrived from Ethiopia. Israel more than ever needs the kind of bold, visionary, yet pragmatic leadership that the Labor Party provided the nation in the past. The leaders of Labor have been given a chance to prove that they have learned from their past mistakes, and that they deserve the trust the voters have placed in them.

The spirit of reform expressed in the Labor Party's democratic primary selection of Knesset candidates, and in the Knesset legislation for the direct election of the prime minister and in support of human rights, must continue in both forums if they are to be responsive to the will of the people. Responsiveness and accountability will provide the surest way out of the current and ongoing crisis of political legitimacy. The past actions of Labor have contributed to this crisis, and its future actions could greatly contribute to its termination.

Notes

1. T.J. Pempel, ed., *Uncommon Democracies: The Politics of One-Party Dominance* (Ithaca, NY: Cornell University Press, 1990) contains an interesting collection of essays dealing with various aspects of democratic dominant party regimes.

2. Sam N. Lehman-Wilzig, *Stiff-Necked People, Bottle-Necked System* (Bloomington/Indianapolis: Indiana University Press, 1990); Ehud Sprinzak, *Every Man Whosoever Is Right in His Own Eyes: Illegalism in Israeli Society* (Tel Aviv: Sifriat Poalim, 1986 [Hebrew]); Ian Lustick, *For the Land and the Lord: Jewish Fundamentalism in Israel* (New York: Council on Foreign Relations, 1988); Haggai Segal, *Dear Brothers: The West Bank Jewish Underground* (Jerusalem: Beit-Shamai, 1988); Robert O. Freedman, ed., *The Intifada* (Miami: Florida International University Press, 1991).

3. I discuss this phenomenon in Myron Aronoff, "Comments on Ehud Sprinzak," *Fundamentalism, Terrorism, and Democracy: The Case of Gush Emunim Underground*, Woodrow Wilson Occasional Paper, 1987; and in the epilogue of *Israeli Visions and Divisions* (New Brunswick, NJ: Transaction, 1989).

4. A party-appointed committee placed the blame for the party's defeat in the 1988 election on Shimon Peres. Jessica Kreimerman, "Peres Takes Blame for '88 Election Failure," *Jerusalem Post International Edition*, June 9, 1990, p. 6.

5. Nor has the Likud, which continues to ride the coattails of Begin's civil-religious populism even after power passed to the uncharismatic Shamir. The Likud continues to benefit from the inherent conservatism of the Israeli electorate and the sense of personal and national insecurity of many of the voters. Future developments could change such perceptions significantly, as happened when Sadat made his historic trip to Jerusalem.

6. For example, in a public opinion survey conducted by the Smith Research Center based on a sample of 1,200 adult Jews, 50 percent of the sample indicated a preference for Rabin over Yitzchak Shamir, who was the choice of 33 percent. Shamir polled 44 percent when paired against Shimon Peres, who was the first choice of only 29 percent of the sample. Published in *Jerusalem Post International Edition*, July 21, 1990.

7. Michal Yudelman and Asher Wallfish, "Peres Scores Surprise Victory," *Jerusalem Post International Edition*, August 4, 1990, p. 3.

8. Kessar said Labor's leadership crisis was "having a disastrous effect on the entire party and on its chances in the elections." Michal Yudelman, "Kessar Will Run for Labor Leadership," *Jerusalem Post International Edition*, December 7, 1991, p. 3.

9. King Hussein later announced his preference for a joint PLO–Jordanian delegation to peace talks with Israel and renewed his "confederation" initiative initially floated in 1970. See David Makovsky and Michel Zlotowski, "King Hussein Calls for Direct Talks," *Jerusalem Post International Edition*, June 8, 1991, p. 1. Although formally participating in joint delegations with Jordan in Madrid and Washington, the Palestinian delegation has shown unprecedented autonomy and initiative. While coordinating with the "expatriate" PLO leadership, West Bank leaders like Faisal al-Husseini and Dr. Hanan Ashrawi have gained both local and international stature. They have accomplished a significant victory already by establishing that no political settlement is possible without dealing with them, or at least with comparable Palestinian leaders resident in the West Bank and Gaza.

10. Michal Yudelman, "Labor Group Calls for Release of Top Palestinians," *Jerusalem Post International Edition*, December 8, 1990, p. 6.

11. Asher Wallfish, "Rabin: 'No Shortcuts to Peace,' " *Jerusalem Post International Edition*, May 26, 1990, p. 8.

12. Clyde Haberman, "Israel's Labor Party Takes Dovish Line," *New York Times*, November 22, 1991, p. A3.

13. Ibid.

14. Ehud Katz, "Out on a Limb: The Labor Party Loses Ground," *Israel Scene*, December 1990, pp. 4–5.

15. Peter Y. Medding, *The Founding of Israeli Democracy, 1948–1967* (Oxford/New York: Oxford University Press, 1990), 227–28.

16. Menachem Rahat, "Kessar: What to Do with This Victory," *Ma'ariv*, November 22, 1991, sec. B, p. 3; Amnon Abramovitch, "Report: 'Labor' against Hostile Media," *Ma'ariv*, November 22, 1991, sec. B, p. 1.

17. Efraim Inbar, *War and Peace in Israeli Politics: Labor Party Positions on National Security* (Boulder, CO: Lynne Rienner, 1991). Chapter 2 contains a discription of these groups in the context of an analysis of the divisions between hawks, yonetzim (an intermediary category), and doves.

18. Sarah Honig and Michal Yudelman, "Labor's Destiny in the Balance," *Jerusalem Post International Edition*, November 23, 1991.

19. Michal Yudelman, "Peres Chides Party for Self-Slander," *Jerusalem Post International Edition*, December 1, 1990, p. 5.

20. Michal Yudelman, "Labor Votes to Separate State and Religion," *Jerusalem Post International Edition*, November 30, 1991, p. 1; Menachem Rahat, "Peres Shocked: The Majority Supported Avraham Burg's Proposal to Separate Religion from the State," *Ma'ariv*, November 22, 1991, section 4, p. 1. For an intelligent discussion and critique of the resolution by a religiously observant Labor leader see Menachem HaCohen, "State and Religion: Siamese Twins?" *Jerusalem Post International Edition*, December 7, 1991, p. 8.

21. In addition, the Human Rights Law was adopted guaranteeing the right of every person to life, protection of property, freedom to leave and enter the country, and the right to privacy. Like electoral reform, there was strong public support for this legislation, but it was delayed (and watered down) because of coalition politics—particularly due to the opposition of the religious parties.

22. Allan Shapiro, "The Purpose, the Politician, and the Prophet," *Jerusalem Post International Edition*, June 20, 1992, p. 6.

23. Clyde Haberman, "Israelis to Vote, Facing Challenges, Fearing Stalemate," *New York Times*, June 22, 1992, pp. 1 and A9.

13

Concluding Perspectives

It has been my purpose through this unconventional study of the Israel Labor Party to provide explanations for important aspects of the party and Israeli society in general, and to indicate some of the wider implications and possible applications of such an approach. Students of politics have long been interested in the structural forms that varieties of political behavior take on and in the dynamics of such processes as the competition for power and leadership; the recruitment, mobility, and succession of leadership; the modes of conflict resolution; the making of decisions; and the role of ideology. Political anthropology places particular emphasis on the cultural context in the analysis of these phenomena. I shall briefly review some of the major findings of this study and, by comparing them with the findings of an important study of Mapai using a different approach, shall attempt to suggest the special contribution of the anthropological approach and some of its wider applications for the study of contemporary society.

In Chapter 2 I introduced the historical background of some of the main institutional and cultural features of the Israeli political structural characteristics and dynamic processes by focusing on the analysis of factionalism. I suggested that the relative degree of corporateness of a faction, in addition to the extent to which it could successfully mobilize independent resources, had significant ramifications for the relative success of each faction in its competition with the others. Through the examination of the various phases of the historical fission and fusion of the Labor parties in Israel, it was shown that the relative importance of ideology was not so much related to the degree of corporateness of the factions as to the specific socio-cultural environment of the political system at specific points in time. It was argued that the relative balance of positive and negative influences of factional competition on the political system—e.g., regarding its contribution to the relative stability of the government and the process through which leadership is recruited—has shifted over time to the increasing detriment of its overall effects.

There are clear indications that whereas the old factional divisions in the Labor Party based on former party affiliation, which in recent years have tended to focus primarily on the competition for power, are breaking down, new ideologically oriented factions are developing in the party caucus of Knesset members. This is indicated in the formation of the dovish and the more activist groups reported in Chapter 8. Extreme caution must be exercised in attributing positive and negative effects to such recent developments since the short-term effects are likely to contribute to greater instability of the present government, but the long-range effects may very well contribute to the renewal and reformulation of ideological positions in party policy. Reformulation of positions could in turn contribute either to a more vigorous commitment of party leaders and members to new policies that they might perceive as being more realistically aimed at solving some of the major problems facing Israeli society, and/or to new splits in the party. Neither possibility is inconceivable. (In the period between the time this was originally written and December 1991, both ramifications were manifested, as was shown in the last four chapters.)

There is a reciprocal relationship between stages in the mobilization of power and political support, the institutionalization of these relationships, and the changing role of ideology. Societal changes influence both the meaning and importance of ideology for the various actors in the political process, and the actors' capacity to relate ideology meaningfully and effectively to the major problems confronting the polity. I shall develop this point further after dealing with several other important variables involved in the argument.

The process through which candidates for membership in major party institutions, the legislature, the Cabinet, and so forth are selected reveals much about the nature of the distribution of power and authority within political institutions. It was shown in Chapter 3 that the candidate selection process in the Labor Party, which is influenced by both structural and cultural features of the party and the political system generally, is a major factor perpetuating the centralization of power in the Labor Party. The oligarchic tendencies fostered by the system of candidate selection are reinforced by the dependence of the majority of the members of party institutions on party-dominated institutions like the Histadrut for their livelihoods. These two factors interact with and reinforce each other. As a result, the most efficient means of advancement for ambitious party activists is to attach themselves as clients of powerful leaders, and to serve loyally and unquestioningly.

This system has discouraged many of the younger and more able potential leaders from remaining active in the party, and it has led to the frustration and alienation of many of those who did remain active. For most of those who attached themselves as clients to important patrons, it has meant conformity to the wishes of the patron and in many cases eventual abandonment of former ideals and policy goals, particularly those oriented toward internal party reform. Thus, many of the succeeding generations of secondary-echelon party leaders were by and large men of limited vision and ideas, adept at the game of political infighting, but judged by the top leaders themselves as lacking the essential qualities of leadership to take over the helm of the party and nation. This is one of the main reasons why the top leaders have turned to the army to recruit candidates for political office, in many cases preferring army recruits to those clients who have loyally served them and by so doing indicated a lack of ability to produce original ideas and take independent decisions and actions. As one top leader said of Abba Eban's failure to gain the backing of the main party bosses to succeed Golda Meir, "If he had ever once said 'no' to Sapir, Sapir would have probably backed him for the premiership."

These important aspects of party structure and organization were related to a close examination of the decision-making process. It was shown in Chapters 4 and 5 that the issue area is carefully controlled by the top leaders, who decide which issues will be debated and, in most cases, how the issues will be decided. As was illustrated through extensive analysis of the proceedings of the Standing Committee, even in the relatively free forum of the trusted secondary leaders consensual formulations were predetermined and obligatory, issues that threatened the positions of the top leadership and/or the unity of the party were suppressed, and issues that could not be suppressed were carefully controlled. Under such circumstances all pretense of meaningful participation in party institutions was lost. As was demonstrated in Chapters 6 and 7, representation was more often than not illusory, and there was almost a total breakdown in the chain of responsiveness that, according to the constitutional arrangements, was supposed to link the various levels of rank-and-file party members, members of the party institutions, and the leadership.

I completely concur with Medding's (1972:302) statement that,

> It is through internal party organization that interests may be pressed, leaders selected, and representation gained, and the manner and pattern in which these occur are of fundamental importance. . . . Participation, representation, responsiveness, internal constitutional arrangements, patterns of institutional coordination, and internal processes of decision making . . . will to a large extent determine the success of the policies of incorporation and aggregation, and how the party organizes internally will, in general, greatly affect the way in which it performs all its other political functions.

This is why I have concentrated my analysis on these features of the party. I therefore must ask how it is that my conclusions differ so sharply from those of Medding. I think the importance of these differences goes beyond that of the respectful criticisms I have of another scholar's work. I am hopeful that this discussion will bring out important aspects of the contribution of an anthropological approach to the study of politics in contemporary society.

First of all, it is important to recognize that Medding was dealing with Mapai from 1948 until 1969, and I am dealing with the Israel Labor Party (of which

Mapai is the dominant internal party faction) from 1969 until 1976. Clearly, the fact we are examining different historical periods—in a sense even different political parties—has a bearing on the difference in our interpretations and conclusions. However, if I were convinced that this factor accounted for the greater part of our differing views, I would not be writing any further on the subject. In addition to the fact that Medding and I have employed significantly different methodologies and conceptual frameworks, I have had the very great advantage of having read Medding's pioneering work (see my review of it, Aronoff 1973d), and the historical perspective of having been able to witness developments I view as being at variance with what could have been expected from Medding's conclusions. Given these factors, I shall point out what I consider to be some of the more significant aspects of the variance in our interpretations and conclusions.

I have already explained at length (in Chapter 6) my disagreement with Medding's claim that the party's institutions "where highly representative in terms of the party's social diversity." I place much greater importance on the second half of his sentence, "even if there was a marked degree of control over the exact identity of personnel making up this representative group which may not have been a true reflection of membership views" (Medding, 1972:302). Clearly, any application of the concept of representativeness must include the important aspect of responsiveness, which was lacking in the majority of the so-called representatives in Labor Party institutions, so the use of the term "representative" is inappropriate.

Medding (ibid.) documents the repeated flagrant violation of the party constitution, especially regarding internal party elections, which (1) clearly undermined the legitimacy of the electoral processes and those elected through it, (2) excluded or impaired the participation of certain groups, and (3) "led to centralization of control in the hands of narrower executive bodies." It is therefore difficult to understand how Medding drew the conclusions he did. He argues that "such centralization also provided the party with a degree of flexibility and capacity for improvisation, and prevented decision making processes from becoming clogged up" and "facilitated the process of coordinating the various institutions which the party controlled, in so far as the narrow party bodies (however chosen) included in their membership the leading personnel in these institutions" (ibid.). There have been those who have carried such arguments to their logical extremes by claiming that dictatorship is the most efficient system of all. I have offered evidence to show that rather than having fostered flexibility and efficiency in decision making, this system prevented the Labor Party from being responsive to major changes taking place in Israeli society—the very feature to which Medding attributed Mapai's great success in the past (see Medding, 1972:300).

Medding (1972:302) clearly documented the rise of the informal top executive bodies that effectively ruled the party and the nation. He analyzed the growth of the party machine, "which developed to fill the void in the performance of key political functions where formal processes either did not exist or were not so well suited to the task." Following with this functional analysis, Medding (1972:303) attributed many positive functions to the machine, among which he says it "provided a degree of coherence and centralization which the leadership was able to use, thus enabling it to concentrate on important state matters . . . [and] providing symbolic and psychological gratification." Beside this impressive list of attributed positive benefits of the machine, Medding (ibid.) "balances" the scale with the following negative features:

> But precisely because it arose on the basis of procedures and conditions that lacked legitimacy, it became the focus of intensive internal conflict that threatened internal cohesion and engendered severe problems of organizational maintenance. Whatever its positive contributions, its undemocratic character and influence brought with it serious negative consequences which sowed marked internal disunity.

Yet Medding followed these remarks with the conclusion that:

> The internal decision making process as we have analyzed it provides impressive evidence against Michels' theory of political party organization. . . . It shows clearly that there were many centres of decision making within Mapai, that various groups exercised power, and that there were different publics interested in, participating in and affected by decisions in different spheres. Generally speaking the processes that we analysed were based upon consensual power relations: the views of many groups were put forward or taken into consideration, and bargaining and mutual compromise characterised the discussions. (*This of course excludes the area of personnel selection dealt with above.*) (Medding, 1972:303—italics added)

Here, as in a passage quoted in Chapter 6 (Medding, 1972:161), Medding separates the processes through which individuals are selected for party institutions from the modes and manner of participation. I shall elaborate on my previous argument that while such analytic distinctions may be helpful, the failure to reintegrate and analyze their mutual effects on each other has seriously weakened Medding's analysis. This failure to analyze the dynamic interaction between these variables led him to make assumptions and conclusions which, when such an analysis is made, are not supported by the evidence.

One of Medding's main themes is, "within a competitive system, the greater a party's social diversity, the greater its need to base decision making upon bargaining and discussion, and the greater the success of the various mechanisms of follower participation and influence over leaders" (Medding, 1972:6). This theme is repeated as one of the major conclusions, which I quoted above at length (Medding, 1972:303). The failure to analyze the dynamic interaction between these variables resulted in a portrayal of Mapai as being considerably more democratic than it was in fact from the point of view of representation, broad participation in the making of decisions, and the exaggeration of the success of mechanisms of follower participation and influence over leaders. Medding's analysis does not allow for an accurate understanding of the failure of the Labor Party to adapt to subsequent social changes, a failure that led to the internal party crises in the aftermath of the Yom Kippur War, summarized in Chapter 8.

Throughout this book I have documented in considerable detail examples of the ramifications of the interaction between the products of an oligarchic system of candidate selection and local-level institutions that were ostensibly involved in the making of decisions and yet were shown to have not been doing so in any meaningful sense of the term, except perhaps symbolically. I have presented considerable evidence to show that the degree of influence of followers over leaders was very far from being as successful as Medding postulated was the case in Mapai. If the situation was as Medding stated, how could one explain the major crisis of confidence in the credibility of the top party leadership that characterizes the most recent period in Israeli politics and has precipitated the current mood of change and reform? (Moreover, how could one account for Labor's defeat in 1977?)

To what, then, can we attribute this marked difference in evaluation of, and conclusions drawn from, very similar, and partly identical, data? Although, obviously, differences in personality and outlook might partly account for this disparity, it would seem to me that divergences in methodology and conceptual focus account for the greatest number of differences. Medding relied primarily on extensive analysis of the written records of meetings of party institutions, other documents, and interviews with leading members of the party. I relied primarily on the systematic recording of the events reported at which I was personally present. Clearly, certain kinds of information are not likely to be contained in the official minutes of meetings or in conversations with even articulate and sensitive informants, particularly if a significant time has passed between the events in which one is interested and the interview. For example, the control and manipulation of the agenda of meetings, the techniques through which debates can be guided and manipulated and through which issues are suppressed, are not likely to be divulged in any detail through the methods conventionally employed by the political scientist. Most certainly, the subtle manipulation of symbolic meanings in ritual proceedings can only be perceived through participant observation or the viewing of visual and sound recordings of such events.

However, most political scientists are not likely to be looking for the suppression of issues, and certainly not for political rituals. In his introductory chapter, Medding discusses the relevant literature in political science on the structures and functions of political parties. He singles out the internal organization of political parties as largely determining their external actions and asserts, "the central question for investigation is its *power relationships*, upon which the performance of both its internal and external functions hinge" (Medding, 1972:5—italics added). He defines power very narrowly as "participation in decision making," which I think even most political scientists would find an oversimplification of a complex concept. Medding (ibid.) defines the two main forms of power as, "power based on coercive relationships, and power based on the need for the leadership to gain the cooperation of the party followers, in short, power based upon consensus or agreement." Medding refers to an elaboration of this theme in a previous publication (Medding, 1970) in which he strongly criticizes Michels' theory of political party organization concerning the "iron rule of oligarchy" (cf. Michels, 1958) for Michels' exaggeration of the coercive basis of power and his neglect of consensually based power. One of my major criticisms of Medding's work is that he has gone to the other extreme in overemphasizing consensus and underemphasizing coercive aspects of power in Mapai. I have tried to show in my analysis that both coercive and consensual aspects of power operate in the Labor Party. It is not a case of having to make a choice between *either* a theory stressing coercion *or* one stressing consensus, but clearly identifying both aspects of relationships of power in any given specific context. It is my evaluation that the Israel Labor Party would have to be placed between the two ideal-type paradigms of Michels and Medding, but is much closer to Michels' than Medding seems willing to admit.

Medding's almost exclusive preoccupation with power relationships is not unusual in the discipline of political science in general, and his exaggeration of the role of consensus at the expense of coercive aspects of power is characteristic of the particular school in American political science known as "pluralism," which has been extensively criticized in recent years. I do not cite this literature for two reasons: I do not think it is essential to my point, and I do not identify myself with all of the criticism raised against the pluralists, some of which has highly ideological and polemic overtones. While definitely wanting to refrain from participation in the polemic debate, I do wish to point out that a commitment to a pluralist paradigm, whether or not any ideological commitment is involved, tends to channel selectively the researcher's perceptions of reality in the favor of consensus, just as a commitment to an elitist paradigm tends to select the evaluation of data in the direction of emphasis on coercion (cf. Walton, 1966). My point is that an anthropological conceptual focus on the dynamic relationships between power and culture—the interaction between the exercise of power and the cognition of values and ideology of the political actors—enables the researcher to evaluate more accurately the degree to which coercive and consensual aspects of power relationships are operative in any given social context without biasing perceptions by postulating an a priori greater importance of one or the other. I would argue that this has fairly broad theoretical significance.

For example, I refer to my analysis of the ritual aspect of the proceedings of the Standing Committee in Chapter 5. In this analysis I attempted to evaluate the meaning of consensus in specific social and symbolic contexts through different levels and modes of analysis. In one sense, consensus in the Standing Committee was guaranteed by the selection of participants who were dependent upon the top leaders for their positions and advancement (which involves coercive aspects of power), who were dependent upon the party for their livelihoods (also involving forms of subtle coercion), and who had strongly internalized party norms and demonstrated an acceptance of the rules of the game (consensus). The high risks and potential costs of not abiding by the rules of the game provided coercive constraints that were reinforced by effective political socialization. Even the elaboration of the manipulative techniques that were used to arrive at the consensual formulations does not do full justice to the complexity of the problems.

The diverse and conflicting interests, loyalties, and ideological points of view that had to be reconciled to preserve party unity and to prevent indeterminate outcomes and potential chaos in the Conference were analyzed at one level in terms of the universal human drive to make order from chaos and to give meaningful explanations of the world. The fact is that this humanly constructed aspect of all culture is constantly threatened by the possibility that its "made-up" character will be revealed. I offered an explanation of how the actors in this particular situation attempted to reconcile the contradiction between the explanations offered by their ideology and their perceptions of social reality. I suggested that their choice of alternatives was limited by institutional and cultural constraints that were both coercive and normative in nature. I stressed the temporary and reactionary aspects of such ritualized "solutions" to issues involving major and urgent problems in Israeli society. I suggested that such critical problems that have emerged from a rapidly changing social reality can neither be denied, ignored, nor suppressed successfully for long. Whereas these assertions were predictive when written, recent developments have borne them out. (The evidence from the perspective of December 1991 is even more overwhelming.) I suggest that this is precisely the kind of contribution the unconventional approach I have employed can make to our understanding of contemporary society.

I boldly state that we cannot fully understand the nature of relationships of power without understanding how the people involved perceive these relationships and without understanding the meanings they attach to their values, norms, and other aspects of their culture. In short, the analysis of relationships of power is only meaningful within the context of the analysis of the manner in which the people involved understand and attach meanings to these relationships and to the socio-cultural environment in which they act. It is in this respect that I hope this unconventional study of the Israel Labor Party has offered both an additional important perspective on the party and Israeli society in general, and more general theoretical implications as well.

I now return to reformulate the postulated relationships among the stages in the mobilization of political power and support, the consolidation and institutionalization of these relationships, and the changing role of ideology. My focus has been on how meanings are ascribed by various categories of political actors. I have examined how effective ideology has been for them in attempting to solve major problems that confront the political party and the society in general. In the period preceding the independence of the state of Israel, Mapai succeeded in capturing the key positions in the institutions of the Yishuv and, most importantly, in the executive of the Jewish Agency. This success enabled Mapai to establish the dominant position of the party (and the dominant positions of the leadership within the party) by consolidating control of the distribution of the capital and human resources that flowed into the country from abroad. The leaders of Mapai succeeded to a great extent in gaining popular support. This legitimized the party's dominance as well as the leaders' own positions within the party) by building a broadly based party whose ideology projected it as being the vanguard that would (and did) lead to realization of the Zionist dream—the rebirth of the Jewish people as an independent state in their historic national homeland. Although there is strong evidence that there were oligarchic leadership elites who controlled the party internally from early stages of its development, there is also evidence to indicate that ideology played a significant role in internal power relationships and the formation of the party's policy.

With the consolidation and expansion of the party's dominant position through its control of the machinery of the independent state, and with the rapid expansion of its constituency through the immigration of a socially and culturally heterogeneous population of new citizens, Mapai attempted both to aggregate these new groups through incorporation into the party and to mobilize support by offering material inducements without basically altering its ideology. As one astute student of Israeli politics observed,

> The parties preferred the development of a gap between theory and practice to both ideological compromise with the new reality created as a result of the new immigration and, obviously, to foregoing from the start any attempt to enlist new immigrants who were unacquainted with the ideological legacy of the various parties into their ranks. (Lissak, 1974:17)

In addition, there is an inherent asymmetry of ideologies, particularly when they must be operationalized through their application to the issues that arise in the governing of a nation. As Seliger (1970:326) has perceptively observed,

> [W]hen ideology is made to function in the here and now it becomes subject to strains and stresses that endanger its relative consistency. In fulfilling its function of guiding political action, each political belief system is faced with the challenge of change. All such systems must deal with change, attempting either to perpetuate or to prevent it. In the process they are confronted with the challenge of changing themselves.

Seliger continues this argument, stating:

> For a party movement holding power or engaging in the contest about it, the need for a more or less frank restatement of the immediate goals inevitably

arises. In shaping specific policies in deference to prevailing circumstances, no party has ever been able to avoid committing itself to lines of action which are irreconcilable with, or are at least doubtfully related to the basic principles and goals in its ideology. A conflict results not simply between ideology and action but within ideology itself. (Ibid.)

For to outline possibilities of adaptation is one thing, the readiness of party leaders to undertake adaptation is another. While it is clear that it lies in the nature of the relation between thought and action that full correspondence between the two dimensions is never to be expected, the reluctance openly to subject ideology to revision, and particularly to do so constantly, is also a fairly general phenomenon. (Seliger, 1970:338)

The reluctance of the leaders of Mapai and later of the Israel Labor Party to adapt their ideology to changing social reality, which according to Seliger's findings is a general phenomenon, had particularly serious ramifications since changes in the social reality of Israeli society were taking place at a particularly fast rate. The cumulative changes in Israel resulted in a qualitatively different social reality by the end of the first twenty-seven years of its independent existence from what had existed when the ideology was originally formulated before Independence.

The leaders of Mapai were reluctant to adapt and change their ideology to the rapidly changing social realities of Israeli society. They increasingly relied on non-ideological inducements and incentives to mobilize support among the electorate and within the various ranks of party activists and leadership. This accompanied the internal party processes of deviation from constitutionalism and democratic procedures, and the development of an informal oligarchic power structure documented in the evidence presented by Medding. It is even possible that at a certain stage the positive benefits of these politically expedient developments outweighed the short-range negative influences as suggested by Medding. However, there is little doubt that these developments also directly influenced the significant decline in the importance of ideology within a wide spectrum of Israeli society, as documented by Arian (1968 and 1973), and among all levels of party activists and leadership, as shown in this book. I argue that these developments contributed to the undermining of the legitimacy and effectiveness of the party's elected representative institutions and the decisions ostensibly made by them, and directly contributed to the eventual undermining of the authority, confidence, and credibility of the top party leaders in the eyes of their followers and of the public at large.

I particularly stress the importance of the phases in the development of the political system and the element of time (short- and long-range perspectives) in the analysis of these developments and the relationships between them. It is entirely likely that at a particular stage in the development of the political system the need to make fateful decisions, particularly in a newly emerging nation that is taking form and is under constant threat of attempts to destroy it, may outweigh adherence to ideal democratic procedures in the selection of candidates for political office, in the making of decisions, and so forth. Indeed, when compared with the records of similar newly developing nations and with older established democracies in times of war and/or other national emergencies and crises, the extent to which the Labor Party and the political system of Israel as a whole have maintained crucial aspects of democratic freedom have been outstanding (cf. Klieman, 1976).

However, my concern here is to stress the long-term ramifications and consequences of sets of procedures as they affect the perceptions, attitudes, and values both of those most immediately involved in them and of members of the society who are more remote, but are nonetheless greatly affected by the outcomes of these procedures. In short, I contend that the ad hoc measures that were perhaps originally adopted for legitimate reasons, but deviated markedly from ideological principles without adapting the ideology to fit changing reality, cumulatively established a pattern of broad compromises made for political exigency. Pressing social and political problems were not debated in a way that allowed the presentation of a full range of possible solutions and their consideration for adoption and implementation. Individuals were co-opted as the ostensible representatives of groups without ensuring that they were responsive in any meaningful way to their constituencies. The eventual cumulative effects of these changes contributed to the undermining of basic values in the party and the society. They also contributed to the undermining of confidence in the credibility and authority of the leaders of the party and in the party as a whole.

Obviously, in considering the undermining of basic values in the society as a whole, which is beyond the scope of this study, many other groups, institutions—not the least of which would include the educational system—and social variables would have to be taken into consideration. However, it is clear that in a political system in which the dominant political party has had such a great role in the shaping of a society's development, the policies, procedures, and examples set by the dominant party and its leaders have been important factors in shaping and effecting, as well as reflecting and articulating, the values of the society as a whole. Surely, the recent revelations of financial corruption in the public economic sector, the government, and even the defense establishment (which until very recently was considered to have been untainted by such social ills that were recognized as almost commonplace in certain sectors of the society) are not unrelated to the negative aspects I have discussed in the dominant Labor Party of Israel.

The political arrogance exhibited by the leadership of Labor in the mid-1970s was considerably aided by an indifferent, apathetic, or at least acquiescent public. The aspects of Labor of which I have been most critical were precisely those that fostered and encouraged acquiescence at almost every level of party leadership below the elite, and among party activists and the membership at large. I am personally encouraged by the recent indications that the public appears to have become somewhat less acquiescent. I hope to have shown that the anthropological approach is uniquely suited to the revelation of these vital aspects of political relationships, which have far-reaching theoretical as well as practical implications.

Bibliography

Abramovitch, Amnon. 1991. "Report, 'Labor' against Hostile Media." *Ma'ariv*, November 22, sec. B, p. 1 (Hebrew).

Almond, Gabriel, and Sidney Verba. 1963. *The Civic Culture*. Princeton: Princeton University Press.

Arian, Alan. 1968. *Ideological Change in Israel*. Cleveland: Case Western Reserve University Press.

———. 1971. *Consensus in Israel*. New York: General Learning Press.

———, ed. 1972. *The Elections in Israel—1969*. Jerusalem: Jerusalem Academic Press.

———. 1973. *The Choosing People*. Cleveland: Case Western Reserve University Press.

———, ed. 1975. *The Elections in Israel—1973*. Jerusalem: Jerusalem Academic Press.

———, ed. 1980. *The Elections in Israel—1977*. New Brunswick, NJ: Transaction Publishers.

———. 1980. "The Electorate: Israel 1977." In *Israel at the Polls*, ed. Howard R. Penniman, pp. 59–89. Washington, D.C.: American Enterprise Institute.

Aronoff, Myron. 1972. "Party Center and Local Branch Relationships: The Israel Labor Party." In *The Elections in Israel—1969*, ed. Alan Arian, pp. 150–83. Jerusalem: Jerusalem Academic Press.

———. 1973a. (1979). "Ritual in Consensual Power Relationships: The Israel Labor Party." In *Political Anthropology and the State of the Art*, ed. H. Claessen and S. Lee Seaton, pp. 275–310. The Hague: Mouton (deGruyter).

———. 1973b. "Communal Cohesion through Political Strife in an Israeli New Town." *Jewish Journal of Sociology* 15, 1:79–105.

———. 1973c. "Development Towns in Israel." In *Israel: Social Structure and Change*, ed. Michael Curtis and Mordecai Chertoff, pp. 27–45. New Brunswick, NJ: Transaction Publishers.

———. 1973d. "Review of P.Y. Medding's *Mapai in Israel*." *Jewish Journal of Sociology* 15:248–52.

———. 1974a. *Frontiertown: The Politics of Community Building in Israel*. Manchester: Manchester University Press, and Jerusalem: Jerusalem Academic Press.

———. 1974b. "Political Change in Israel: The Case of a New Town." *Political Science Quarterly* 89, 3:613–25.

———. 1974c. "An Anthropological Approach to the Analysis of Nonissues." *New Sociology* 1, 4:100–117.

———. 1975. "The Power of Nominations in the Israel Labor Party." In *The Elections in Israel—1973*, ed. Alan Arian, pp. 21–40. Jerusalem: Jerusalem Academic Press.

————. 1976. "Freedom and Constraint: A Memorial Tribute to Max Gluckman," and "Ritual Rebellion and Assertion in the Israel Labor Party." *Political Anthropology* 1:1–6 and 132–64. Reprinted in *Freedom and Constraint: A Memorial Tribute to Max Gluckman*, ed. Myron J. Aronoff, pp. 1–6 and 132–64. Amsterdam and Assen: Van Gorcum.

————. 1978. "Fission and Fusion: The Politics of Factionalism in the Israeli Labor Parties." In *Faction Politics*, ed. Frank P. Belloni and Dennis C. Beller, pp. 109–39. Santa Barbara, CA: ABC-Clio Press.

————. 1982. "The Labor Party in Opposition." In *Israel in the Begin Era*, ed. Robert O. Freedman, pp. 76–101. New York: Praeger.

————. 1987. "Comments on Ehud Sprinzak, *Fundamentalism, Terrorism, and Democracy: The Case of Gush Emunim Underground*." Washington, D.C.: Woodrow Wilson Occasional Paper.

————. 1989. *Israeli Visions and Divisions: Cultural Change and Political Conflict.* New Brunswick, NJ: Transaction Publishers.

————. 1990. "Better Late Than Never: Democratization in the Labor Party." In *Israel after Begin*, ed. Gregory S. Mahler, pp. 257–71. Albany: State University of New York Press.

————. 1991a. "The Labor Party and the Intifada." In *The Intifada*, ed. Robert O. Freedman, pp. 325–42. Miami: Florida International University Press.

————. 1991b. "Myths, Symbols, and Rituals of the Emerging State." In *New Perspectives on Israeli History*, ed. Laurence J. Silberstein, pp. 175–92. New York: New York University Press.

Atzmon, Yael. 1984. "The Labor Party and Its Factions." *Jerusalem Quarterly* 31 (Spring): 118–29.

Bachrach, Peter, and Morton Baratz. 1962. "Two Faces of Power." *American Political Science Review* 56:947–52.

————. 1963. "Decisions and Non-decisions: An Analytical Framework." *American Political Science Review* 57:632–42.

————. 1970. *Power and Poverty: Theory and Practice.* New York: Oxford University Press.

————. 1975. "Comment" (on article by Geoffrey Debnam). *American Political Science Review* 69:905–7.

Bailey, Fred G. 1969. *Stratagems and Spoils: A Social Anthropology of Politics.* Oxford: Basil Blackwell.

————. 1972. "Conceptual Systems in the Study of Politics." In *Rural Politics and Social Change in the Middle East*, ed. Richard Antoun and Iliya Harik, pp. 21–44. Bloomington: Indiana University Press.

Balandier, Georges. 1967 (1972 ed.). *Political Anthropology.* Harmondsworth, U.K.: Penguin.

Baram, Haim. 1989. "The Decline of the Labor Party." *Tikkun* 4, 5:55–58.

Bar-Kedma, Emanuel (assisted by Danny Karman). 1979. "Labor: The Courage to Change after the Calamity?" *Yediot Achronot*, February 9 (Hebrew).

Barnes, John A. 1969. "Networks and Political Process." In *Local-level Politics*, ed. Marc Swartz, pp. 107–40. London: University of London Press, and Chicago: Aldine.

Bar-On, Mordechai. 1988. "Israeli Reactions to the Palestinian Uprising." *Journal of Palestine Studies* 17,4 (Summer).

Barth, Fredrik. 1959. *Political Leadership among Swat Pathans.* London: University of London Press.

Ben-Ari, Eyal. 1989. "Masks and Soldiering: The Israeli Army and the Palestinian Uprising." *Cultural Anthropology* 4, 4 (November):372–89.

Ben-Dor, Leah. 1972. "Parliamentary Report—Little Socialist Riding Hood." *Jerusalem Post*, August 18.
Benedict, Burton. 1957. "Factionalism in Mauritian Villages." *British Journal of Sociology* 7:328–42.
Bensman, J., and R.J.C. Preece. 1970. "The Concept of Negative Consensus." *Political Studies* 18, 1:142–47.
Berger, Peter L. 1969. *A Rumor of Angels*. Garden City, NY: Doubleday.
Berger, Peter L., and Thomas Luckmann. 1966. *The Social Construction of Reality*. Garden City, NY: Doubleday.
Bernstein, Marver. 1957. *The Politics of Israel*. Princeton: Princeton University Press.
Betzur, Yehoshua. 1975. "Party Loan Decided." *Ma'ariv*, March 20 (Hebrew).
Birnbaum, Ervin. 1970. *The Politics of Compromise*. Rutherford, NJ: Fairleigh Dickenson University Press.
Blitzer, Wolf. 1989a. "Why Bush Is in No Hurry to Take the Plunge." *Jerusalem Post International Edition*, September 23, p. 3.
———. 1989b. "U.S.'s Not-So-Subtle Pressure on Israel." *Jerusalem Post International Edition*, November 4, pp. 1–2.
Blitzer, Wolf, and Menachem Shalev. 1989a. "Peace Process: U.S. Steps Up the Pressure." *Jerusalem Post International Edition*, October 28, pp. 1–2.
———. 1989b. "Shamir Skirts the Brink," *Jerusalem Post International Edition*." November 25, pp. 1–2.
Blondel, J. 1963. *Voters, Parties and Leaders*. Harmondsworth, U.K.: Pelican Books.
Bocock, Robert. 1974. *Ritual in Industrial Society*. London: George Allen & Unwin.
Brezezinski, Zbigniew K. 1962. *Ideology and Power in Soviet Politics*. New York: Praeger.
Brichta, Avraham. 1972. "Social and Political Characteristics of Members of the Seventh Knesset." In *The Elections in Israel—1969*, ed. Alan Arian, pp. 109–31. Jerusalem: Jerusalem Academic Press.
———. 1986. "The Selection of Candidates to the Tenth Knesset: The Impact of Centralization." In *Israel at the Polls, 1981: A Study of the Knesset Elections*, ed. Howard R. Penniman and Daniel J. Elazar. Bloomington: Indiana University Press.
Burstein, Moshe. 1934. *Self-Government of the Jews in Palestine since 1900*. Tel Aviv: HaPoel HaZair.
Butler, David, and Donald E. Stokes. 1971. *Political Change in Britain*. Hardmondsworth, U.K.: Penguin Books.
Carmi, Sarah. 1973. "Power in a Local Branch of the Israel Labor Party." Unpublished report of field research (Hebrew).
Charsky, Meir. 1973. "Distribution of Power and Influence in a Labor Party Branch." Unpublished report of field research (Hebrew).
Claessen, H.J.M. 1974. *Politiek Antropologie*. Assen: Van Gorcum. (Dutch).
Claessen, H.J.M., and S. Lee Seaton, eds. 1979. *Political Anthropology and the State of Art*. The Hague: Mouton (deGruyter).
Cohen, Abner. 1969. "Political Anthropology: The Analysis of the Symbolism of Power Relations." *Man* 4:215–35.
———. 1974. *Two-Dimensional Man*. London: Routledge & Kegan Paul.
Cohen, Erik. 1970. "Development Towns—The Social Dynamics of 'Planted' Urban Communities in Israel." In *Integration and Development in Israel*, ed. Shmuel Eisenstadt, Rivka Bar-Yosef, and Chaim Adler, pp. 587–617. Jerusalem: Israel Universities Press.
Cohen, Ronald. 1965. "Political Anthropology: The Future of a Pioneer." *Anthropological Quarterly* 38:117–31.

————. 1967. "Anthropology and Political Science: Courtship or Marriage?" *American Behavioral Scientist* (November/December): 1–7.

————. 1969. "Research Directives in Political Anthropology." *Canadian Journal of African Studies* 3:23–30.

————. 1970. "The Political System." In *Handbook of Method in Cultural Anthropology*, ed. R. Naroll and R. Cohen, pp. 861–81. Garden City, NY: Natural History Press.

Colson, Elizabeth. 1968. "Political Anthropology: The Field." In *International Encyclopedia of the Social Sciences*, ed. David L. Sills, pp. 189–92. New York: Macmillan and The Free Press.

Coser, Lewis. 1956. *The Functions of Social Conflict*. London: Routledge & Kegan Paul.

Crenson, M.A. 1971. *The Un-politics of Air Pollution*. Baltimore, MD: Johns Hopkins University Press.

Czudnowski, Moshe. 1970. "Legislative Recruitment under Proportional Representation in Israel: A Model and a Case-Study." *Midwest Journal of Political Science* 14:216–48.

Da Matta, Roberto. 1977. "Constraint and Licence: A Preliminary Study of Two Brazilian National Rituals." In *Secular Ritual: Forms and Meanings*, ed. Sally F. Moore and Barbara Myerhoff, pp. 244–64. Assen: Van Gorcum.

Debnam, Geoffrey. 1975. "Nondecisions and Power: The Two Faces of Bachrach and Baratz," and "Rejoinder." *American Political Science Review* 69:889–99; 905–7.

Deshen, Shlomo. 1970. *Immigrant Voters in Israel*. Manchester: Manchester University Press.

Despres, Leo A. 1967. *Cultural Pluralism and Nationalist Politics in British Guiana*. Chicago: Rand McNally.

Don-Yehiya, Eliezer 1975. "Religion and Coalition: The National Religious Party and Coalition Formation in Israel." In *The Elections in Israel—1973*, ed. Alan Arian, pp. 255–84. Jerusalem: Jerusalem Academic Press.

Douglas, Mary. 1970. *Natural Symbols*. London: Barrie & Rockliff, and The Cresset Press.

Dudman, Helga. 1981. "Collective Resentment." *Jerusalem Post International Edition*, July 19–25, p. 14.

Duverger, Maurice. 1963. (1965 edition cited.) *Political Parties*. New York: Wiley.

Easton, David. 1959. "Political Anthropology." In *Biennial Review of Anthropology*, ed. B. Siegal, pp. 210–62. Stanford, CA: Stanford University Press.

Eban, Abba. 1977. *Abba Eban: An Autobiography*. New York: Random House.

Edelman, Murray. 1964. *The Symbolic Uses of Politics*. Urbana: University of Illinois Press.

————. 1971. *Politics as Symbolic Action: Mass Arousal and Quiescence*. Chicago: Markham.

Eijk, C. van der, and W.J.P. Kok. 1975. "Nondecisions Reconsidered." *Acta Politica* 10, 3:277–301.

Eisenstadt, Shmuel N. 1967. *Israeli Society*. London: Weidenfeld and Nicolson.

————. 1969. "Some Observations on the Dynamics of Traditions." *Comparative Studies in Society and History* 11:451–75.

Eisenstadt, Shmuel N., Rivka Bar-Yosef, and Chaim Adler, eds. 1970. *Integration and Developments in Israel*. Jerusalem: Israel Universities Press.

Eliav, Arie. 1972. *Eretz Ha Tzvi*. Tel Aviv: Am Oved (Hebrew).

————. 1974. *Land of the Hart*, trans. Judith Yalon. Philadelphia: The Jewish Publication Society of America.

Fein, Leonard. 1967. *Politics in Israel*. Boston: Little, Brown.

Firth, Raymond. 1957. "Introduction: Factions in Indian and Overseas Indian Societies." *British Journal of Sociology* 8:291–95.

Fortes, Meyer, and E.E. Evans-Pritchard, eds. 1940. *African Political Systems*. London: Oxford University Press.

Freedman, Robert O. 1989. "Religion, Politics, and the Israeli Elections of 1988." *Middle East Journal* 43, 3 (Summer): 406–22.

———, ed. 1991. *The Intifada*. Miami: Florida International University Press.

Frey, Frederick W. 1971. "Comment: On Issues and Nonissues in the Study of Power." *American Political Science Review* 65:1081–1101.

Geertz, Clifford. 1964. "Ideology as a Cultural System." In *Ideology and Discontent*, ed. David Apter, pp. 55–72. New York: The Free Press of Glencoe.

Gluckman, Max. 1954. *Rituals of Rebellion in South-East Africa* (Frazer Lecture, 1952). Manchester: Manchester University Press.

———. 1955. *Custom and Conflicts in Africa*. Oxford: Basil Blackwell.

———. 1962. "Les Rites De Passage." In *Essays on the Ritual of Social Relations*, ed. Max Gluckman, pp. 1–52. Manchester: Manchester University Press.

———. 1963. *Order and Rebellion in Tribal Africa*. New York: The Free Press of Glencoe.

———. 1965. *Politics, Law and Ritual in Tribal Society*. Oxford: Basil Blackwell.

Gluckman, Max, and Fred Eggan. 1966. "Introduction" to Association of Social Anthropologists (hereinafter A.S.A.) Monograph Series, ed. Michael Banton. London: Tavistock.

Goell, Yosef. 1978. "The Labours of Labour." *Jerusalem Post International Edition*, June 13.

———. 1981. "Commentary: The General Who Turned Labour Party Boss." *Jerusalem Post International Edition*, January 4–10, p. 12.

Goffman, Erving. 1961. *Encounters: Two Studies in the Sociology of Inter-Action*. Indianapolis, IN: Bobbs-Merril.

Goldberg, Giora. 1980. "Democracy and Representation in Israeli Political Parties." In *The Elections in Israel—1977*, ed. Asher Arian, pp. 101–17. New Brunswick, NJ: Transaction Publishers.

Goody, Jack. 1977. "Against 'Ritual': Loosely Structured Thoughts on a Loosely Defined Topic." In *Secular Ritual: Forms and Meanings*, ed. Sally F. Moore and Barbara Myerhoff, pp. 25–35. Assen: Van Gorcum.

Gorni, Yosef. 1973. *Achdut Haavoda 1919–1930: The Ideological Principles and the Political System*. Ramat-Gan: HaKibbutz HaMeuchad Publishing House (Hebrew).

Graham, B.D. 1969. "The Succession of Factional Systems in the Uttar Pradesh Congress Party, 1937–66." In *Local-level Politics*, ed. Marc Swartz, pp. 323–60. London: London University Press.

Gutmann, Emanuel. 1972. "Religion in Israeli Politics." In *Man, State, and Society in the Contemporary Middle East*, ed. Jacob Landau, pp. 122–34. New York: Praeger.

Haberman, Clyde. 1991. "Israel's Labor Party Takes Dovish Line." *New York Times*, November 22, p. A3.

———. 1992. "Israelis to Vote, Facing Challenges, Fearing Stalemate." *New York Times*, June 22, pp. 1, A9.

HaCohen, Menachem. 1991. "State and Religion: Siamese Twins?" *Jerusalem Post International Edition*. December 7, p. 8.

Halpern, Ben. 1961. *The Idea of the Jewish State*. Cambridge: Harvard University Press.

Hertzberg, Arthur. 1966. *The Zionist Idea*. New York: Harper Torchbooks.

Honig, Sarah. 1991a. "Strongman of Labour." *Jerusalem Post International Edition*, August 30–September 5, p. 10.

———. 1991b. "Grim, Party-Pooping Polls Rain on Labor Parade." *Jerusalem Post International Edition*, November 30, p. 2.

———. 1991c. "Likud Would Welcome Early Elections." *Jerusalem Post International Edition*, December 7, p. 2.

———. 1992. "Shimon Peres, Avraham Burg, and Ora Namir Are Big Winners in Primaries: Labor Chooses Young, Dovish Leadership." *Jerusalem Post International Edition*, April 11, p. 2.

Honig, Sarah, and Michal Yudelman. 1991. "Labor Party's Destiny in the Balance." *Jerusalem Post International Edition*. November 23, p. 2.

Horowitz, Dan, and Moshe Lissak. 1973. "Authority without Sovereignty: The Case of the National Center of the Jewish People in Palestine." *Government and Opposition* 8:48–71.

———. 1978. *Origins of the Israeli Polity*, trans. Charles Hoffman. Chicago: University of Chicago Press.

———. 1989. *Trouble in Utopia: The Overburdened Polity of Israel*. Albany: State University of New York Press.

Hymes, Dell. 1974. *Reinventing Anthropology*. New York: Vintage Books (Random House).

Inbar, Efraim. 1991. *War and Peace in Israeli Politics: Labor Party Positions on National Security*. Boulder, CO: Lynne Rienner.

Jerusalem Post. 1975. Editorials: January 10, February 25, and March 25.

———. *International Edition*, 1977. September 12.

———. 1978. Editorial, "Labour in Decay." January 18.

———. 1979. January 28–February 3.

———. 1989a. Staff, "Israel Accepts Baker's Five Points; Shamir Facing Rift with Rebel Likud Ministers—PLO May Block Israel–Palestinian Talks." November 11, p. 1.

———. 1989b. "Polls Apart on Policy for the Territories." September 2.

———. 1989c. Editorial Comment "Law of Occupation." November 25.

———. 1990. "Labor Party Poll." December 15.

———. 1991. Staff, "Polls: Likud Leads Labor by Record Margin." December 14, p. 2.

Katz, Ehud. 1989. "Hobson's Choice: Labor at a Crossroads." *Israel Scene*, August, pp. 3–4.

———. 1990. "Out on a Limb: The Labor Party Loses Ground." *Israel Scene*, December, pp. 4–5.

Katz, Jacob. 1961. *Tradition and Crisis*. New York: The Free Press.

Kidron, Peretz. 1989a. "The Thunderbolt from Cairo." *Middle East Insight* (hereinafter *MEI*) September 22, p. 3.

———. 1989b. "Israel's Leaders Pulling in Different Directions." *MEI*, October 6, p. 3.

———. 1989c. "If the PLO Is In, Israel Is Out." *MEI*, October 20, p. 9.

Klieman, Aaron. 1976. "Emergency Politics: The Growth of Crisis Government." *Conflict Studies* 70:1–19. London: Institute for the Study of Conflict.

Korpel, Yonathan. 1973. "Leadership in a Labor Party Branch." Unpublished research report (Hebrew).

Kraines, Oscar. 1961. *Government and Politics in Israel*. Boston: Houghton Mifflin.

Kreimerman, Jessica. 1990. "Peres Takes Blame for '88 Election Failure." *Jerusalem Post International Edition*, June 9, p. 6.

Krivine, David. 1981. "Dissonance in Labor." *Jerusalem Post International Edition*, April 26–May 2, p. 11.

Kuhn, Thomas S. 1962. *The Structure of Scientific Revolutions. International Encyclopedia of Unified Science*, vol. 2, no. 2. Chicago: University of Chicago Press, 2d enlarged ed., 1970.

Kurtz, Donald V. 1973. "Political Anthropology: Issues and Trends on the Frontier." Ninth International Congress of Anthropological and Ethnological Sciences, Chicago.

Langer, Susanne K. 1942. (1967). *Philosophy in a New Key*. Cambridge: Harvard University Press.

Laqueur, Walter. 1972. *A History of Zionism*. London: Weidenfield and Nicolson.

Lehman-Wilzig, Sam N. 1990. *Stiff-Necked People, Bottle-Necked System*. Bloomington and Indianapolis: Indiana University Press.

Levite, Ariel, and Sidney Tarrow. 1983. "The Legitimation of Excluded Parties in Dominant Party Systems: A Comparison of Israel and Italy." *Comparative Politics* 15:295–397.

Lijphart, Arend. 1967. (2d ed. 1975). *The Politics of Accommodation*. Berkeley/Los Angeles: University of California Press.

Lissak, Moshe. 1974. "The Political Absorption of Immigrants and The Preservation of Political Integration in Israel." A paper presented at the International Political Science Association Round Table on Political Integration held in Jerusalem, September 9–13.

Lustick, Ian. 1988. *For the Land and the Lord: Jewish Fundamentalism in Israel*. New York: Council on Foreign Relations.

Mackenzie, Robert T. 1955. (1963 edition cited.) *British Political Parties*. New York: Praeger.

Mair, Lucy. 1934. *An African People in the Twentieth Century (Baganda)*. London: Routledge.

Makovsky, David, and Michel Zlotowski. 1991. "King Hussein Calls for Direct Talks." *Jerusalem Post International Edition*, June 8, p. 1.

Maoz, Shlomo, and Avi Temkin. 1989. "The Devaluation of Peres." *Jerusalem Post International Edition*, July 8, pp. 1, 4.

Margalit, Avishai. 1989. "Israel: The Rise of the Ultra-Orthodox." *New York Review of Books*, November 9, pp. 38–44.

Marx, Emanuel. 1972. "Some Social Contexts of Personal Violence." In *Allocation of Responsibility*, ed. Max Gluckman, pp. 281–321. Manchester: Manchester University Press.

Mayer, Adrian. 1966. "The Significance of Quasi-Groups in the Study of Complex Societies." In *The Social Anthropology of Complex Societies*. A.S.A. Monograph no. 4, ed. Michael Banton, pp. 97–122. London: Tavistock.

Medding, Peter. 1970. "A Framework for the Analysis of Power in Political Parties." *Political Studies* 18:1–17.

————. 1972. *Mapai in Israel*. Cambridge, U.K.: Cambridge University Press.

————. 1990. *The Founding of Israeli Democracy, 1948–1967*. Oxford/New York: Oxford University Press.

Merelman, R.M. 1968. "On the Neo-elitist Critique of Community Power." *American Political Science Review* 62:451–60.

Michels, Roberto. 1958. (1962 ed.). *Political Parties*. New York: Collier.

Mitchell, J. Clyde. 1969. "The Concept of Social Networks." In *Social Networks in Urban Situations*, ed. J. Clyde Mitchell, pp. 1–50. Manchester: Manchester University Press.

Moore, Sally F., and Barbara Myerhoff. 1977. *Secular Ritual: Forms and Meanings*. Assen: Van Gorcum.

Nachmias, David. 1973. "A Note on Coalition Payoffs in a Dominant Party System." *Political Studies* 21:301–5.

————. 1975. "Coalition, Myth, and Reality." In *The Elections in Israel—1973*, ed. Alan Arian, pp. 241–54. Jerusalem: Jerusalem Academic Press.

Nader, Laura. 1974. "Up the Anthropologist—Perspectives Gained From Studying Up." In *Reinventing Anthropology*, ed. Dell Hymes, pp. 284–311. New York: Vintage Books (Random House).

Nakdimone, Shlomo. 1988. "It's All Politics." *Yediot Achronot*, July 7, p. 36 (Hebrew).

Naor, Arye. 1989. "U.S. Edges to the Sidelines?" *Jerusalem Post International Edition*, November 4, p. 8.

Nicholas, Ralph. 1965. "Factions: A Comparative Analysis." In *Political Systems and the Distribution of Power*. A.S.A. Monograph no. 2, ed. Michael Banton, pp. 21–61. London: Tavistock.

———. 1966. "Segmentary Factional Political Systems." In *Political Anthropology*, ed. Marc Swartz, Victor Turner, and Arthur Tuden, pp. 49–59. Chicago: Aldine.

———. 1969. "Rules, Resources, and Political Activity." In *Local-level Politics*, ed. Marc Swartz, pp. 295–321. London: University of London Press.

Ofek, Avraham. 1973. "Political Networks and Power in a Branch of the Labor Party." Unpublished research report (Hebrew).

Paine, Robert. 1981. "When Saying Is Doing." In *Politically Speaking: Cross-Cultural Studies of Rhetoric*, ed. Robert Paine, pp. 9–23. Philadelphia: Institute for the Study of Human Issues.

Pempel, T.J., ed. 1990. *Uncommon Democracies: The Politics of One Party Dominance*. Ithaca: Cornell University Press.

Peretz, Don, and Sammy Smooha. 1989. "Israel's Twelfth Knesset Election: An All-Loser Game." *Middle East Journal* 43, 3 (Summer).

Perlmutter, Amos. 1969. *Military and Politics in Israel*. New York: Praeger.

Petreanu, Dan. 1989a. "Labour's 'Man Who Can Do No Wrong.' " *Jerusalem Post International Edition*, September 30, p. 3.

———. 1989b. "Labour's Threat: Is It Real This Time?" *Jerusalem Post International Edition*, October 21, p. 2.

———. 1989c. "Labour's Dilemma." *Jerusalem Post International Edition*, November 4, p. 3.

———. 1989d. "Agudat Yisrael Leaves Government; Shamir Confident He Can Overcome Rebel Likud Ministers' Challenge—Coalition Strains as Labour Woos Religious Parties." *Jerusalem Post International Edition*, November 18, p. 3.

Petreanu, Dan, and Jeff Black. 1989. "Labour Buoyed by Histadrut Poll." *Jerusalem Post International Edition*, November 25, p. 3.

Petreanu, Dan, and Michal Yudelman. 1989. "Doubts in Labour Party over Peace Initiative." *Jerusalem Post International Edition*, September 9.

Pettigrew, Joyce. 1975. *Robber Noblemen*. London: Routledge & Kegan Paul.

Pinto-Duschinsky, Michael. 1972. "Central Office and 'Power' in the Conservative Party." *Political Studies* 20, 1:1–16.

Pitkin, Hanna Fenichel. 1967. *The Concept of Representation*. Berkeley/Los Angeles: University of California Press.

Pocock, David. 1957. "The Bases of Faction in Gujerat." *British Journal of Sociology* 8:295–306.

Pye, Lucian W. 1962. *Politics, Personality and Nation Building*. New Haven, CT: Yale University Press.

Quiller-Couch, Sir Arthur. 1961. *The Art of Writing*. London: Capricorn.

Rabin, Yitzhak. 1979. *The Rabin Memoirs*. Boston: Little, Brown.

Rahat, Menachem. 1991a. "Kessar: What to Do with This Victory." *Ma'ariv*, November 22, sec. B, p. 3 (Hebrew).

———. 1991b. "Peres Shocked: The Majority Supported Avraham Burg's Proposal to Separate Religion from the State." *Ma'ariv*, November 22, sec. 4, p. 1 (Hebrew).

Ranney, Austin. 1966. "Candidate Selection and Party Cohesion in Britain and the United States." In *Political Parties and Political Behavior*, ed. W. Crotty, D. Freeman, and D. Galin, pp. 248–77. Boston: Allyn and Bacon.

Ricoeur, Paul. 1986. *Lectures on Ideology and Utopia*, ed. George H. Taylor. New York: Columbia University Press.

Rolef, Susan Hatis. 1992. "What Shamir Could Learn from Labor." *Jerusalem Post International Edition*, April 18, p. 6.

Rosenberg, Robert. 1988. " 'What Was Will Never Be Again, and What Will Be Is Not What Was,' Says Amos Oz." *Jerusalem Post*, February 19, p.4.

Safran, Nadav. 1963. *The United States and Israel*. Cambridge, MA: Harvard University Press.

Schattschneider, E.E. 1942. *Party Government*. New York: Farrar and Rinehart.

————. 1960. *The Semisovereign People*. New York: Holt, Rinehart & Winston.

Schwartz, David C. 1974. "Toward a More Relevant and Rigorous Political Science." *Journal of Politics* 36:103–37.

Scott, James. 1972. "Patron–Client Politics and Political Change in Southeast Asia." *American Political Science Review* 66:91–113.

Segal, Haggai. 1988. *Dear Brothers: The West Bank Jewish Underground*. Jerusalem: Beit-Shamai Publications.

Segal, Mark. 1971. Untitled column. *Jerusalem Post*, May 4.

Seliger, Martin. 1970. "Fundamental and Operative Ideology: The Two Principal Dimensions of Political Argumentation." *Policy Science* 1:325–38.

Shalev, Menachem, and Jeff Black. 1989. "Spotlight: 'The Americans Are the Critical Link.' " *Jerusalem Post International Edition*, September 23, p. 7.

Shamai, Nissim. 1972. "The Nature of the Competition for the Election of Labor's Central Committee." Unpublished seminar paper (Hebrew).

Shapiro, Allan E. 1989a. "A Paradoxical Optimism." *Jerusalem Post International Edition*, July 8.

————. 1989b. "The Key Issue in the Peace Plan." *Jerusalem Post International Edition*, August 19.

————. 1992. "The Purpose, the Politician and the Prophet." *Jerusalem Post International Edition*, June 20, p. 6.

Shapiro, Yonathan. 1976. *The Formative Years of the Israeli Labor Party*. London/Beverly Hills: Sage Publications.

Shils, Edward. 1961. *The Logic of Personal Knowledge*. London: Routledge & Kegan Paul.

————. 1968. "Society and Societies: The Macro-sociological View." In *American Sociology*, ed. Talcott Parsons, pp. 287–303. New York/London: Basic Books.

Shokeid, Moshe. 1968. "Immigration and Factionalism: An Analysis of Factions in Rural Israeli Communities of Immigrants." *British Journal of Sociology* 19:385–406.

Simmel, George. (1908. *Soziologie*.) 1963. *Conflict and Web of Group Affiliations*, trans. Kurt Wolff and Reinhard Bendix. New York: The Free Press.

Sinai, Joshua. 1980. "Review of *The Rabin Memoirs*." *Jewish Frontier*, January, pp. 28–29.

Smith, Michael G. 1966. "A Structural Approach to Comparative Politics." In *Varieties of Political Theory*, ed. David Easton, pp. 113–28. Englewood Cliffs, NJ: Prentice Hall.

————. 1968. "Political Anthropology: Political Organization." In *International Encyclopedia of the Social Sciences*, ed. D.L. Sills, pp. 193–201. New York: Macmillan and The Free Press.

Smooha, Sammy. 1978. *Israel: Pluralism and Conflict*. Berkeley/Los Angeles: University of California Press.

Somer, David. 1976. "Religion and the State: The 'Status Quo' in Israel." Unpublished Ph.D. dissertation, The New School for Social Research.

Sprinzak, Ehud. 1986. *Every Man Whosoever Is Right in His Own Eyes: Illegalism in Israeli Society*. Tel Aviv: Sifriat Poalim (Hebrew).

Stolzman, James D. 1974. "Edward Shils On Consensus: An Appreciation." *British Journal of Sociology* 25, 1:3–15.

Swartz, Marc, ed. 1968. *Local-level Politics*. Chicago: Aldine, and London: University of London Press.

Swartz, Marc, Victor Turner, and Arthur Tuden, eds. 1966. *Political Anthropology*. Chicago: Aldine.

Talmon, Jacob L. 1965. *The Unique and the Universal*. London: Secker and Warburg.

Tokatli, Rachel. 1972. "Two Decisions Not to Decide in the Standing Committee of the Israel Labor Party Preceding the Party Conference." Unpublished seminar paper (Hebrew).

Torgovnik, Efraim. 1979. "A Movement for Change in a Stable System." In *Israel at the Polls*, ed. Howard R. Penniman, pp. 147–71. Washington, D.C.: American Enterprise Institute.

Tuden, Arthur. 1969. "Trends in Political Anthropology." *Proceedings of the American Philosophical Society* 113:336–40.

Turner, Terence. 1977. "Transformation, Hierarchy and Transcendence: A Reformulation of Van Gennep's Model of the Structure of Rites de Passage." In *Secular Ritual: Forms and Meanings*, ed. Sally F. Moore and Barbara Myerhoff, pp. 53–70. Assen: Van Gorcum.

Turner, Victor. 1968. "Mukanda: The Politics of Non-Political Ritual." In *Local-level Politics*, ed. Marc J. Swartz. pp. 135–50. Chicago: Aldine, and London: University of London Press.

———. 1969. *The Ritual Process*. Chicago: Aldine.

———. 1977. "Variations on a Theme of Liminality." In *Secular Ritual: Forms and Meanings*, ed. Sally F. Moore and Barbara G. Myerhoff, pp. 36–52. Assen: Van Gorcum.

Twersky, David. 1981. "Labor Prepares for Battle." *Jewish Frontier*, March, pp. 4–7.

Urwin, Derek W. 1966. "Scottish Conservatism: A Party Organization in Transition." *Political Studies* 14:145–62.

———. 1970. "Social Cleavages and Political Parties in Belgium: Problems of Institutionalization." *Political Studies* 18, 3:320–40.

Verba, Sidney. 1965. "Conclusion: Comparative Political Culture." In *Political Culture and Political Development*, ed. Lucian W. Pye and Sidney Verba, pp. 512–60. Princeton: Princeton University Press.

Wallfish, Asher. 1990. "Rabin: 'No Shortcuts to Peace.' " *Jerusalem Post International Edition*, May 26, p. 8.

Wallfish, Asher, and Dan Petreanu. 1989. "New Threat to National Unity Coalition— Ultra Parties Enraged by Human Rights Bill." *Jerusalem Post International Edition*, November 25, p. 3.

Walton, John. 1966a. "Discipline, Methods and Community Power. A Note on the Sociology of Knowledge." *American Sociological Review* 31:684–88.

———. 1966b. "Substance and Artifact: The Current Status of Research on Community Power Structure." *American Sociological Review* 71:43–48.

Weiss, Shevach. 1972. *Local Government in Israel*. Tel Aviv: Am Oved (Hebrew).

Welsford, Enid. 1935. *The Fool*. London: Faber and Faber.

Wertner, Yossi. 1988. "Namir First, Lyova Eliav Second." *Hadashot*, May 27, p. 3 (Hebrew).

Wilson, David J. 1972. "Party Bureaucracy in Britain: Regional and Area Organization." *British Journal of Political Science* 2:373–81.

———. 1973. "Constituency Party Autonomy and Central Control." *Political Studies* 21, 2:167–74.

Winkler, Edwin. 1970. "Political Anthropology." In *Biennial Review of Anthropology*, ed. B. Siegel, pp. 301–86. Stanford, CA: Stanford University Press.

Wolf, Eric R. 1966. "Kinship, Friendship, and Patron–Client Relations in Complex Societies." In *The Social Anthropology of Complex Societies*. A.S.A. Monograph no. 4, ed. Michael Banton, pp. 1–22. London: Tavistock.

———. 1969. (1974 ed.). "American Anthropologists and American Society." In *Reinventing Anthropology*, ed. Dell Hymes, pp. 251–63. New York: Vintage Books (Random House).

Wolfinger, Raymond E. 1971. "Nondecisions and the Study of Local Politics." *American Political Science Review* 65:1063–80.

Yudelman, Michal. 1988. "Male, Jewish and Mostly Ashkenazi." *Jerusalem Post*, July 8, p. 4.

———. 1989a. "Group of Labor Party MKs Attacks Leadership." *Jerusalem Post International Edition*, March 4, p. 5.

———. 1989b. "Strains Appear in Government." *Jerusalem Post International Edition*, September 7, pp. 1–2.

———. 1990a. "Peres Chides Party for Self-Slander." *Jerusalem Post International Edition*, December 1, p. 5.

———. 1990b. "Labor Group Calls for Release of Top Palestinians." *Jerusalem Post International Edition*, December 8, p. 6.

———. 1991a. "Labor Votes to Separate State and Religion." *Jerusalem Post International Edition*, November 30, p. 1.

———. 1991b. "Kessar Will Run for Labor Leadership." *Jerusalem Post International Edition*, December 7, p. 3.

Yudelman, Michal, and Asher Wallfish. 1990. "Peres Scores Surprise Victory." *Jerusalem Post International Edition*, August 4, p. 3.

Yudelman, Michal, and Sarah Honig. 1991. "Likud, Labor Pushing April '92 Elections." *Jerusalem Post International Edition*, June 15, p. 4.

Zashin, Elliot, and Philip C. Chapman. 1974. "The Uses of Metaphor and Analogy: Toward a Renewal of Political Language." *Journal of Politics* 36:290–326.

Index

Myron J. Aronoff is professor of political science and anthropology at Rutgers University. He received his Ph.D. in political science from the University of California, Los Angeles, and his Ph.D. in anthropology from Manchester University (U.K.). Dr. Aronoff was a research fellow at Manchester University, a fellow of the Netherlands Institute for Advanced Studies, a professor at Tel Aviv University, and a visiting professor at the University of Cape Town. Professor Aronoff has received grants from the Joint Committee on the Near and Middle East of the American Council of Learned Societies and the Social Science Research Council, the National Endowment for the Humanities, the Ford Foundation, the Social Science Research Council of the United Kingdom, and the Bernstein Israel Research Trust. He is the author of *Frontiertown: the Politics of Community Building in Israel* (1974), the earlier edition of *Power and Ritual in the Israel Labor Party* (1977), and *Israeli Visions and Divisions* (1989); and the editor of six volumes of scholarly essays. He is the past president of the Association for Political and Legal Anthropology and was the founding president of the Association for Israel Studies.